SCOTTISH URBAN HISTORY

edited by
GEORGE GORDON
and
BRIAN DICKS

ABERDEEN UNIVERSITY PRESS

First published 1983
Aberdeen University Press
A member of the Pergamon Group

© Contributors 1983

British Library Cataloguing in Publication Data
Scottish urban history
1. Cities and towns—Scotland—History—
Addresses, essays, lectures
I. Gordon, George   II. Dicks, Brian
307.7′6′09411   HT133

ISBN 0 08 025762 3

PRINTED IN GREAT BRITAIN
THE UNIVERSITY PRESS
ABERDEEN

CONTENTS

ACKNOWLEDGEMENTS

The editors wish to thank Mrs J Simpson and Mrs M Macleod for typing services, Mr B Reeves for photographic work and Miss R Spence and others who have served as cartographers in the Department of Geography, University of Strathclyde.

They are also indebted to the following publishers for their permission to reproduce illustrations: Leicester University Press (for the three maps from the *Urban History Yearbook*, 1979), BBC Publications (chapter 2, figure 1), University of St Andrews (chapter 2, figure 3), and Croom Helm (chapter 2, figure 4).

The editors also freely acknowledge their debt to many students, colleagues and teachers who, collectively, have stimulated and shaped their interests in the general field of Scottish urban history.

Not least their gratitude goes to the editorial staff of Aberdeen University Press who with great efficiency have guided this book through its various stages of production.

GEORGE GORDON
BRIAN DICKS

July 1982

LIST OF CONTRIBUTORS

John Butt
BA (London) PhD (Glasgow)
Is Dean of the School of Arts and Social Studies and Professor of Economic History in the University of Strathclyde. He has published widely in the general area of Modern British Economic and Social History and contributed papers on Glasgow's Housing to S D Chapman's volume on British Working Class Housing and to the *Festschrift* in honour of W H Marwick, edited by Ian McDougall. His recent books include *'A History of the S.C.W.S.'* (jointly with J A Kinloch) and *'Industrial Archaeology in the British Isles'* (with Ian Donnachie).

Thomas M Devine
BA, PhD (Strathclyde)
Senior Lecturer in History, University of Strathclyde. Joint Editor of the journal, *Scottish Economic and Social History*. Author of *The Tobacco Lords* and editor of *Lairds and Improvement in the Scotland of the Enlightenment* and co-editor of *Ireland and Scotland, 1600–1850: Parallels and Contrasts in Economic and Social Development*. Numerous articles on Scottish history.

Brian Dicks
BSc, PhD (Wales), FSA (Scot)
Is Senior Lecturer in Geography, University of Strathclyde. He has published on the historical and contemporary geography of the Eastern Mediterranean and contributed to *The Stirling Region*. Articles published in several journals including *National Library of Wales Journal, Town Planning Review, Tidjschrift voor Economische en Sociale Geographie, Area, Landscape Review*.

Roderick C Fox
BA, PhD (Strathclyde)
Lecturer in Geography, Kenyatta College. Formerly held research post at Sunderland Polytechnic. He has contributed to *An Historical Geography of Scotland* and to various journals including *Transactions of the Institute of British Geographers* and *Area*.

George Gordon
MA, PhD (Edinburgh)
Senior Lecturer in Geography, University of Strathclyde. Co-author of *Urban Geography* and contributed to *A Geography of Scotland, The Stirling Region* and *An Historical Geography of Scotland.* Articles published in several journals including *Transactions of the Institute of British Geographers, Area, Urban History Yearbook, Scottish Geographical Magazine* and *Scotia.*

John R Hume
BSc (Glasgow) ARCST
Lecturer in Economic History, University of Strathclyde. Co-author of several industrial histories including *The Making of Scotch Whisky* and author of Volumes 1 and 2 of *The Industrial Archaeology of Scotland.* Contributed to many books including *Robert Owen, Prince of Cotton Spinners, Scottish Themes* and *Thomas Telford: Engineer* and to the *Scottish Historical Review, Industrial Archaeology* and *Industrial Archaeology Review.* Editor of various industrial and railways journals.

A Allan MacLaren
MA, PhD (Aberdeen)
Appointed Lecturer in Economic History at Aberdeen in 1965. Since 1968 Lecturer, subsequently Senior Lecturer, in Sociology at the University of Strathclyde. His main publications are *Religion and Social Class* and *Social Class in Scotland, Past and Present.*

John G Robb
BA (Strathclyde) MSc (London) PhD (Strathclyde)
Lecturer in Geography, Richmond-upon-Thames College. Formerly Project Officer, World University Services and Lecturer in Geography, St David's College, Lampeter. He has contributed articles to *Scottish Geographical Magazine* and *New Edinburgh Review* and read papers at various conferences.

Richard G Rodger
MA, PhD (Edinburgh)
Lecturer in Economic and Social History, Leicester University. Previously Lecturer in Economic History at Liverpool University and Visiting Professor at Kansas University. Contributed to several books including *The Victorian City, The Pursuit of Urban History* and *The Growth and Transformation of the City* and to many journals including *Business History, Urban History Yearbook* and *The Journal of Historical Geography.*

1

PROLEGOMENA

G Gordon and B Dicks

To many an outsider the popular image of Scotland is one of a thinly peopled land of moors, lochs and mountains, yet over four-fifths of the country's inhabitants live in what is termed the 'Lowlands' and the vast majority of these are urban dwellers 'whose rural links', writes I H Adams,[1] 'have been severed for almost 200 years'. Of contemporary Scotland's 5.2 million (1979) inhabitants, 1.7 million belong to the Greater Glasgow or Central Clydeside conurbation and a further 850,000 collectively comprise the population of its other major urban centres—Edinburgh, Aberdeen and Dundee. Yet, traditionally, Scotland is a country of small- and medium-sized towns, the majority of which trace their foundations to seigneurial grants and charters dating from medieval times onwards. Germane to the reality of the country's contemporary scene is the fact that, individually, the urban populations of medium-sized centres such as Ayr, Perth and Dunfermline, exceed the combined rural totals for the Highland, Western Isles, Orkney and Shetland regions.

In view of the essentially urban character of Scottish society it is somewhat unwonted that until recently its towns and cities failed to incite the cupidity of academics. To argue that the 'romance of the wild' has been a prominent factor in urban undervaluation might be disclaimed as an over-exaggeration, yet few academics would fail to acknowledge the long-standing precedent in Scottish historical studies that has channelled a major proportion of research away from the urbanised Lowlands into the Highland and Island regions where a significant element of impressionable interest still remains. Without question, the 'Road to the Isles' has received considerably more academic attention than the 'Road to Dundee' or, for that matter, the roads to other Scottish towns and cities. This volume follows in the wake of some recent studies in Scottish urban history[2] and, like these predecessors, its major objective is to redress the persisting distortion that has arisen from this rural-urban academic imbalance.

Viewed historically, the problems, complexities and enigmas of Scotland's urban narrative, one that differs significantly from the record south of the border, makes its study a relevant and gainful exercise in interdisciplinary discussion and collaboration. This collection of essays, the product of specialists in the cognate disciplines of history, geography and sociology, brings together

[1] References are at ends of chapters.

1

nine critical and previously unpublished studies purposely commissioned to provide a range of historical themes and a discursive commentary on some of the major issues of Scottish urbanism. Selecting essays of key interest inevitably involves subjective decisions and the studies that follow form neither a random nor, critics might argue, a totally representative sample either topically or chronologically. While not claiming to impinge on every aspect of Scottish urban history an attempt has been made to cover those periods considered as being crucial in the development of the country's urban traditions. It is hoped, also, that a balance has been attained between those essays which emphasise the traditionally empirical approach to urban history and those that are illustrative of broader themes, the culmination of which is the formulation of theories and the testing of hypotheses. Any method of selection and subsequent organisation presents difficulties, yet such purely editorial shortcomings, if seen to exist, should not detract in any way from the intrinsic merits of the individual essays. Inevitably, this volume will identify those areas that warrant more detailed attention in the future and, hopefully, such research will form the body of a further collection of urban historical studies.

Despite the overwhelming contemporary importance of urban settlement, the origin of the Scottish town is vague and uncertain and no evidence conclusively suggests that it is an institution of considerable longevity. Many have claimed, in fact, that there are no towns of purely Scottish origin; urban living, they argue, was not a natural outcome of forces active in early Scottish society but one that was imposed from without as an extraneous development. Compared with England (the south and east in particular) where a complex hierarchical urban system was instituted by the Romans, the Scottish town as a recognisable and distinctive physical, social and economic entity, made a dilatory appearance. The veracity of such a statement is, of course, largely determined by terminology for difficulty attends any attempt to adequately define a town or urban settlement, especially in a way that enables operative comparisons between regions and, more significantly, over periods of time. Thus the question, 'What makes a town'? or more relevantly, 'Which were the first Scottish towns'? remain matters of academic debate and speculation.

In the opening essay Dicks assesses the different and often dissident evidence relating to Scottish urban genesis. Burghs are first heard of in the written documents (mostly charters from ecclesiastical archives) of the third decade of the twelfth century. Prior to this period records are virtually non-existent; consequently it has been a hotly disputed subject among academics as to whether urban life began then or whether some forms of urban institution were already in existence. Charters generally referred to commercial privileges and it was this that formed the basis of Ballard's[3] 'commercial theory' of Scottish town origins. Other historians, including Neilson,[4] Murray,[5] Mackenzie[6] and Pryde[7] have contributed rival theories, but such a confusing mass of detail serves only to stress that in view of the limited value of reliable documentary evidence the perception of urbanism in early medieval Scotland remains particularly vague. Reiterating the sentiments of earlier writers, however, Dicks argues that it is unlikely that Scottish urban growth took place on a clean non-urban board for, as elsewhere in Britain, the medieval town must have been the amalgam of a pre-urban nucleus and some form of trading activity whose worth was subsequently recognised in a charter. The search for such nuclei presents many problems and it is here that archaeological investigation linked to documentary research has great potential. Recent excavations, as part of current programmes of urban rescue archaeology, have provided significant information on Aberdeen,[8] St Andrews,[9] and Edinburgh[10] and at Glasgow work is currently being undertaken. Dicks concludes that, as in any long-settled area, continuity of site must be regarded as the pervading theme and academics must be prepared for major revolutions in the historical understanding of Scottish town origins as empirical urban archaeology gathers momentum.

The difficulties in integrating empirical and theoretical approaches have long taxed scholars, yet there seems little doubt that a full understanding of the historical role of Scotland's urban settlements rests on the careful incorporation of both methodologies. Empiricism has always been overwhelmingly present in Scottish history and historical geography, and though the production of deductive theory is precluded by this approach, the logical conclusion of empirical analysis is the inductive derivation of theoretical principles. As Baker, Hamshere and Langton[11] assert, 'empirical techniques . . . must reach out for a theoretical framework and the theoretical analysis . . . must in turn reach out to embrace the complexities of the real world'. Largely in reaction to the protracted and incisive debates that centred on the often exclusive theories of medieval town origins many scholars have argued that such generalisations are both prejudging and misleading. Edith Ennen[12] was a persuasive advocate of the distinctiveness of medieval towns and of the diverse, often unique factors that influenced their morphology and growth characteristics. To her, however, empiricism was not equated with antiquarianism and 'distinctiveness' and 'diversity' implied neither erratic nor random development.

In the second essay Fox analyses the morphological characteristics and the natural and human factors responsible for the visual and functional distinctiveness of Stirling, one of Scotland's most prestigious historic burghs. It is customary to classify Scottish burghs according to their seigneurial origins, that is, whether founded by the king or, through crown prerogative, by prelates and barons. Stirling was created a burgh in 1226 by the Royal Charter of Alexander I and its subsequent function and morphology provides a useful illustration and critical commentary on a number of well-established descriptive models and hypotheses relating to medieval town character. Henri Pirenne,[13] for example, concerned with distinguishing the singular identity of medieval towns, as compared with the countryside, emphasised their roles as economic, defensive and legal entities. The three essentials of a fully-fledged medieval town, he argued, were summed up by the market, the wall and the charter. Stirling fits neatly into this descriptive model. Its defensive wall constituted one of the fundamental elements in the structure of the pre-industrial town, protecting its population and at the same time, constraining their day to day movements (see below). It formed a major item of investment which required public taxation and collective arrangements for its manning, though it also facilitated the levying of tolls, the proceeds of which were partly devoted to the maintenance and repair of the wall. Stirling's markets were symbolic of its economic function and, in many ways, of the burgh's *raison d'être*, while the charter was indicative of the whole range of legal and institutional character-istics that guaranteed the burgh its autonomy. But to stress the separateness of these attributes would be obscurant. As commented above charters were inextricably tied to commercial privileges, in particular to the trading mono-polies of the royal burghs whose territorial rights up until 1672 were confirmed by a number of Acts of Parliament. The essays of Rodger and Devine provide further commentary on these practices.

For each individual burgh, however, the charter stood for a large degree of administrative autonomy. Throughout Western Europe the new merchant classes which had emerged by the twelfth century were unable to function smoothly under seigneurial jurisdiction and manorial rule. The charters recog-nised the burghs as distinct legal territories whose authorities, as Rodger and Devine make clear, were responsible for local government, for the execution of distinctive economic policies and for carrying out public works and services. In order to fulfil these local obligations burgh councils were empowered to levy taxes and market tolls. In short the burgh was its own decision-making authority, one which urban researchers now regard as a major factor in shaping the formal structure of the pre-industrial town and indeed all successive growth phases in town development. Decision-makers, including landowners, private developers, building contractors, individual house-owners and planning authorities at a national and local level, are collectively responsible for the distinctive material residues of a townscape. Carter[14] has suggested F S Chapin's conceptual framework of 'values-behaviour-consequences' as a meaningful approach whereby urban form is viewed within the context of a particular societal stage or system whose values may be translated into human action, that is, behaviour, reflected in their decision-making with the outcome manifesting itself in a particular physical pattern. Built into the decision-making are various control processes which Chapin[15] has distinguished as 'priming' and 'secondary'. The former are basically major in scope and concerned with large-scale layout of areas and their infrastructural details. 'Secondary decisions' on the other hand, though often triggered off by the priming group, are con-cerned with detailed matters such as plot purchase and building construction. Control over the decision making process is essentially bound up with organised central control which in the burghs, as both Rodger and Devine show, is an expression of power and influence within the hands of an individual, an elitist group or corporate body.

The controls and constraints operating with respect to the decision-making processes in pre-industrial Stirling were similar to those of other contemporary burghs. By the seventeenth century the pattern of its streets and tenement boundaries were the fossilised remains of earlier structures. In the growth and development process, certain limits are established which, by their significance, act as fixation lines which structure the plan. In Stirling's case the town defences and ports, together with the pattern of burgage holdings can be considered as constituting major and lesser fixation lines, respectively. In relation to its defences, two processes develop, repletion within (intramural) and accretion without (extramural), though the latter belongs basically to post-seventeenth century growth.

Conzen's[16] concern with process in urban growth and his meticulous and pioneering analysis of town plan established the important concept of urban growth being ordered and conditioned by underlying structures in town morphology. His use of town plan as an analytical tool has since been adopted by Whitehand and Alauddin[17] in a preliminary consideration of the basic plan structures of Scottish burghs and by Macleod[18] and Dodd[19] in their in-depth analyses of St Andrews and Ayr, respectively. Though a few plans of individual Scottish towns exist from the mid-sixteenth century, it is not until the mid-eighteenth that plans and maps can be relied upon for their detail and accuracy and these culminate in John Wood's plans of some 48 Scottish towns between 1818 and 1828 and in the first town plans of the Ordnance Survey. Brooks and Whittington,[20] however, have analysed a recently rediscovered panoramic sketch plan of St Andrews which shows in unique detail the buildings and layout of a pre-industrial Scottish burgh. This 'bird's-eye' view of the burgh pre-dates the plans of Scottish burghs drawn in the 1640s by Revd Gordon of Rothiemay.

A broader view of decision-making is taken by Rodger in the third essay which traces the evolution of Scottish town planning. According to Burke: 'Medieval towns in Britain and elsewhere can be placed in two broad categories: "planned" or "planted" settlements built virtually in one operation in accordance with a development plan; and "adaptive" or "organic" settlements that grew gradually and at times rapidly, over the centuries as the need arose.'[21] In accepting the view of Scottish burghs as newly established 'plantation' settlements Rodger describes them as '. . . the precise twelfth century equivalents of our twentieth century new towns . . .', agreeing with Fox that within the constraints imposed by natural site factors there is clear evidence of a coherent overview stamped upon their developments. No urban settlement grew without some measure of forethought in the addition of new buildings or the replacement of obsolete ones, yet in addition to this piecemeal process a strong measure of planning philosophy is apparent for a number of

Scottish burghs. The revised plan of St Andrews that followed the conferment of its burgh status is a case in point and for Ayr, Dumfries and Perth it can be demonstrated that they were the products of a centralised perception of town planning. It is debatable that planning in this context implied (as with the European *bastides* and *villeneuves*) the selection and acquisition of previously undeveloped 'green-field' sites though Adams[22] suggests that the general uniformity in Scottish burgh layout might in fact relate to such a proposition. But whatever the degree of planning Rodger's submission is of particular interest to the problem of Scottish urban origins for it indicates that prior to the new medieval foundations in England, Wales, and on the continent during the late thirteenth and early fourteenth centuries, Scotland was the precursor of towns that displayed many features of planned settlement.

Though, as Rodger claims, the agents responsible for initial town planning remain somewhat vague, subsequent control rested with the organised central authority of the guildry which monitored not only mercantile affairs but almost every other aspect of burgh life. Administered by the Dean of Guild its ultimate authority was responsible for regulations that governed all physical alterations and additions to the urban fabric while a complex system of rules and codes of practice maintained a strong control and uniformity of action on 'burghscape'. Environmental decisions, for example, those relating to refuse, and decisions regarding the width of streets, vennels and other access points were aspects of guild control also noted by Fox. The Dean of Guild Court performed the functions of municipal machinery over a wide range of issues and, argues Rodger, the control of 'neighbourhood' became increasingly important as trade expansion was reciprocated in burgh growth. By the seventeenth century the guildry had moved into areas of environmental improvement and resource management and in the early eighteenth century Edinburgh's Dean of Guild was exercising well-defined building regulations.

Rodger's essay also traces the subsequent history and varying effectiveness of the Dean of Guild Court which, significantly, survived until 1975. The eighteenth and nineteenth centuries, however, witnessed first its decline—'attributable to, and adversely related with the ascendancy of the Town Council', and then its renaissance when the mounting pressure of urbanisation was met by the rapid formulation of vigorous building codes. Of the Courts, the Glasgow Court became a notoriously strict model for the expanding burghs of west central Scotland, and its severe and restraining building activities have been blamed for the city's late Victorian housing problems. Among the important regulations overseered by the rejuvenated Courts were those relating to such environmental hazards as fire and the incidence of epidemics, particularly typhoid and cholera, waterborne diseases which were traced to bad sanitation. Attempts at controlling river and smoke pollution, at acquiring a safe urban water supply and at protecting parklands and similar open spaces from urban encroachment were other significant areas of municipal response.[23]

As Rodger argues such municipal objectives were not overtly directed towards town planning, though the proliferation of statutory and byelaw provisions played a major role in shaping the urban landscape. The backbone or underpinning of municipal involvement in the fabric of urban life was provided by the continuing and extended concern of the Dean of Guild Courts. In the field of building regulations, therefore, as Rodger concludes, the Courts were major shapers of Scottish townscape and the precursors of modern town planning.

Devine's contribution to this volume also deals with the activities of the merchant classes, not however in terms of their role as 'urban planners' but specifically in terms of their social and economic impact on Scotland's rapidly expanding and changing economy. The merchant classes tend to be synonymous with urban growth and progress, and their economic, social and political status has long been recognised by academics, particularly for the late sixteenth, the seventeenth and early eighteenth centuries, a period regarded by Patten as 'the run-up to the economic advance of the later eighteenth and nineteenth centuries'.[24] Yet, overshadowed by the momentous economic and environmental transformation that came with industrialisation, the role of pre-industrial urban institutions in these changes, especially in Scotland, has not been fully appreciated. With particular reference to Glasgow, Edinburgh, Aberdeen and Dundee, Devine re-interprets the role of Scotland's merchant classes in the late seventeenth and early eighteenth centuries, a formative period for the country as a whole. The Royal Burghs after 1672 had lost their long-held monopoly of foreign trade, a factor that had maintained, in many cases artificially, their commercial and financial supremacy amongst Scottish towns. Restrictionalism, however, had also labelled them conservative and lethargic, especially to the widening commercial opportunities that followed the Act of Union (1707). A view commonly held is that towns lacked the spirit of enterprise and, consequently, the roots of economic advance have been sought in the Scottish countryside and amongst the landed classes.

Devine contends that the contrasts suggested between country and town in Scotland between 1660 and 1740 have been over-stated, a view adopted by Butt who argues that 'if . . . agricultural progress was one pre-condition of industrialisation (especially in a capital-starved country like Scotland), the development of commerce was another'.[25] There is considerable evidence to suggest significant changes in the institutional framework of mercantile activity during this period. The erosion of legal impediments to free trade between towns, the relaxation of burgess and guild controls and changes in the apprenticeship system provided a more vigorous commercial activity, especially when the former rigidities of the domestic economy began to recede. The greater volume of inter-urban and rural-urban exchange led to a more sophisticated credit structure, an important indicator of an increasingly articulated commercial enclave.

'Basic to any understanding of the dynamics of towns', writes Patten,[26] 'must be a sure knowledge of what made up their economies, and also what people actually did in them. Any approach to the internal workings and external relations of pre-industrial towns would be wise to recognise the part played by the individual, first and foremost.' The Scottish merchant class, Devine argues, was far from homogeneous in its social composition for it was only a minority that had the necessary expertise and financial support to pursue foreign trade (in particular) on a consistent basis. This elite, or 'merchant adventurers' as they were dubbed, formed a distinct body from the ordinary merchants. For England, at least, a number of papers, some classic (Unwin,[27] Kramer[28]) and others recent (Charlton[29]) have discussed the groupings and divisions of pre-industrial trades and urban occupations. According to Devine, if barriers existed in the later seventeenth and early eighteenth centuries to prevent easy access into Scotland's merchant communities, these were in the nature of contemporary economic and social relationships rather than any legal restrictions. The prominence of established families was perpetuated through inheritance and for many generations commercial 'dynasties' tended to control significant sections of enterprise. Equally, however, there were financial failures which, together with the high mortality rates of the time, brought some family 'monopolies' to an end. Yet social movement within the merchant communities of Scotland's larger burghs depended on commercial ability as well as inherited rank and basic to Scotland's industrial achievement in the later eighteenth century, Devine concludes, was the existence of an equally vigorous mercantile class that had already demonstrated its investment skills in terms of new commercial opportunities. 'In all pre-industrial societies', writes Butt,[30] 'capital tends to accumulate for effective industrial investment only if there is an efficient merchant group capable of penetrating the social and economic structure with its standards and practices.'

Urbanisation and industrialisation were the twin macro-scale processes which, from around the middle of the eighteenth century, transformed the pattern of settlement, the economy and the nature of society. Population growth in the nineteenth century added nearly three million people to the figure of 1.6 million recorded in 1801, in the first national Census of Scotland. Progressively these forces favoured agglomeration, a fact crudely measured by the absolute and relative growth of the four cities. In 1801, the cities accounted for 11 per cent of the national population but by 1901 the proportion had increased to 35 per cent.[31] Thus the nineteenth century marked the transformation from a predominantly rural to an urban society and the emergence of the cities as major economic, social, political and spatial phenomena. The bald statistics simplify a complex web of changing relationships which affected every aspect of life and work in Scotland.

What was happening was really a collective act of supreme subtlety which involved a re-ordering of space and time, of authority and freedom, of custom and contract, of work and leisure.[32]

The essays by MacLaren, Robb, Gordon, Hume and Butt primarily focus upon the cities, using them as laboratories for the investigation of social and economic processes, akin to Weber's notion of the city as the spectroscope of society. Of course, the cities did not initiate every change or innovation. Thus Owen's pioneering socio-industrial project at New Lanark reflected attitudes towards urbanism, industrial organisation and the development of communities sparked by urbanisation and industrialisation rather than city growth *per se* or city-based policies and ideas. Indeed the general processes operating during the phase of transformation stemmed from urbanisation and the growth of urbanism but as the cities assumed dominance so these influences became specifically associated with that type of settlement and, in the Scottish context, particularly with Glasgow.

Many of the economic, spatial, social and policy aspects of urban growth related to all urban settlements, regardless of size, location, functional specialisation and geographical location. Nonetheless those variables significantly altered the timing and precise character of growth and change creating considerable inter-settlement variety at regional and local scales. Previously, most urban settlements performed marketing and administrative roles but gradually a wider array of specialisms developed as illustrated by the rash of mining settlements working the Ayrshire, Central, Fife and Lothian coalfields, the oil-shale settlements of West Lothian, the spa settlements such as Crieff and Moffat and the holiday resorts adjoining the Clyde and on the east coast of Scotland. The transformation from a mercantile to an industrial economy created new class fractions such as the industrial capitalists, a new elite in urban society, whilst the substantial growth in unskilled labour greatly enlarged the proletariat. Thus the transformation had spatial, economic and social implications at both the inter-urban and intra-urban scales.

Initially the problems of transport, limited sources of energy and poor energy transformation ratios placed a premium upon industrial development at waterside locations. Subsequently other resource endowed sites benefitted but improvements in the transportation of goods and the emergence of industrial linkages combined with the economic benefits stemming from mechanisation and economies of scale, cumulatively favoured urban and industrial agglomeration. During the nineteenth century, first textiles and then metal trades formed the leading industrial sector at the national scale, although greater diversity occurred at regional and local scales. The capitalist economy required a growth and diversification of professional services, notably in banking, insurance and legal services. It also fostered technological development and generated a demand for new industrial skills. Another facet of the transformation involved the gradual replacement of craft workshops and traditional markets by industrial premises and specialised marketing facilities, viz. shops and warehouses. Lythe[33] has suggested that the building industry was a major source of urban employment in pre-industrial Scotland. However, the

massive growth of the urban system and the profusion of unskilled construc-
tional tasks resulted in substantial relative and enormous absolute growth in
these activities in the industrial era. Moreover, the casual character of employment and irregularity of income which typified unskilled jobs affected other
dimensions of the urban situation, notably the standards of housing, health,
nutrition and the overall quality of life of the families of unskilled workers. The
size of this group in towns and cities meant that these problems frequently
became identified as important urban problems although some Victorian
analysts, most notably Marx, emphasised the structural causes rather than the
spatial manifestations of inequality and injustice.

The increased levels of production, consumption and exchange which characterised the Industrial Revolution encouraged an articulation of the urban
system with a general increase in the number of people in existing towns and
cities and the mushrooming of new urban places. In detail, the pattern
reflected specific circumstances and opportunities. For example, the steel town
of Motherwell grew rapidly in the second half of the nineteenth century.
Contemporaneously other places with substantial metal industries, such as
Falkirk and Coatbridge, also experienced a marked phase of urban growth. By
comparison, some established market towns, particularly in the Highlands and
Southern Uplands, suffered a relative decline in their importance in terms of
their ranking in the overall urban system.[34] Nonetheless, their local service role
was largely protected until the railways facilitated the extension of the service
areas of the cities in the second half of the nineteenth century.

Before the Industrial Revolution urban settlements were based on a
mercantile economy. The fact that these Scottish towns were small and compact
inevitably led to a close residential interdigitation of the social classes which
reached a particularly distinctive form in the vertical social zonation in
Edinburgh tenements in the eighteenth century. This complex geographical
pattern was based upon a clear social order in which the rights and privileges of
the elite separated them, economically, politically and socially, from the other
sections of pre-industrial urban society. Two differing models of the pre-
industrial city have been advanced. Sjoberg[35] envisaged the central core
occupied by a privileged elite with an encompassing crowded girdle of districts
housing the poor. A 'pre-occupation with money . . . ran counter to the
religious-philosophical value systems of the dominant group',[36] so merchants
tended to be excluded from the elite. MacLaren pursues the theme of a
changing elite and the emergence of class fractions in his essay on the Aberdeen
bourgeoisie 1830–50. He uses kirk eldership as an indicator of class
fractionalism and discusses the ability of the established religious-politico-
economic elite to respond to the transformation of urban society which was
taking place in the first half of the nineteenth century. Whilst particular conditions prevailed in Aberdeen during that period, notably in relation to the
geographical sources and religious beliefs of urban migrants, the emergence of

class fractions affected the bourgeoisie in all of the cities. There was a general trend challenging the institutional leadership of the dominant pre-industrial or early industrial fractions. Moreover, as the century progressed further fractions emerged to give a greater articulation to the status superstructure although widely differing contemporary political commentators recognised a simple dichotomised society. Interestingly, a spatial division was evident in the class fractions in Aberdeen suggesting that the social transformation had spatial dimensions, a feature investigated in greater detail in the essays by Robb and Gordon.

Vance[37] advocated a different model of the pre-industrial city which envisaged a many centred settlement based upon occupational clustering or craft districts. Apart from these districts, in which a form of vertical zonation was dominant, with masters living above their workshops and servants, apprentices and journeymen in cellars or attics, Vance agreed with Sjoberg that the elite would live centrally and the poor peripherally. Robb attempted to investigate transformation from the Vance model by using two addresses as a measure of increased separation of workplace and residence in the Gorbals district of Glasgow in the first half of the nineteenth century.

The urban transformation resulted in a replacement of the walking distance city by the modern dispersed urban form which is dependent upon the availability of mechanised transportation. Horizontal residential segregation based upon socio-economic status and family life cycle replaced occupational clustering and a social order reflecting traditional bases of power. Urbanism and industrialisation also nurtured the nuclear family and gradually eroded the role of the extended family. Increasingly, it also demanded societal solutions to problems relating to housing, health, employment conditions, environmental issues, human welfare and social justice. Rodger outlines some of the developments in planning controls whilst Butt discusses the multi-dimensional nature of the debate concerning the supply, price, amount, quality, location and funding of working-class housing in the period 1900 to 1950.

Knox has noted that 'although the transformation of urban social geography which paralleled the emergence of capitalism was radical and abrupt, it was a complex process . . . (with) several intermediate stages of urban development, . . . each contributing to both the morphological and the social inheritance of the capitalist city of today'.[38] He suggested three phases approximating to the years 1780 to 1830, 1830 to 1920 and 1920 to the present,[39] although it would be possible to argue further divisions. Additionally, the classfication would probably require some modification in detailed studies of individual cities. Knox may have exaggerated the abruptness of the transformation in that there was evidence of some precursors of economic, social and morphological change by the mid-eighteenth century in Glasgow and Edinburgh. The pre-existing order was not abolished at a stroke but persisted in dwindling residual form for many decades. Equally the transformation was a progressive process of articulation of new dimensions. For example, the role of clerk carried more status at the outset than at the close of the nineteenth century. By the latter period the massive growth of 'white collar' occupations had produced a finely developed hierarchy of managerial, supervisory and clerical occupations reflected in both pay and occupational status, although, within income limitations, most white-collar workers subscribed to middle class aspirations in terms of style of life and type of residential environment.[40]

On a variety of criteria a six stage model of the Scottish city can be advanced with the phases approximating to the years 1760 to 1830, 1830 to 1870, 1870 to 1918, 1918 to 1939, 1939 to 1970, and post 1970. Urban extension, notably in Edinburgh and Glasgow dates from the 1760s rather than 1780. Whilst the change from terraced town houses to suburban villas as the predominant middle-class residence was a gradual process it gathered momentum in the last three decades of the nineteenth century. Contemporaneously, as Hume illustrates, the development of suburban railways and tramways enabled the city to finally abandon the constraining friction of the residual influences of the walking city with the emergence of numerous new middle-class suburbs. Earlier more exotic components such as the 'marine' villas beside the lower Clyde capitalised upon the available means of transport but now the trend towards suburbanisation was feasible for a wide variety of middle-class and lower middle-class families. Gordon discusses the evolution and location of these new suburbs in Edinburgh and the part which they played in the changing mosaic of status areas in that city. The period between the World Wars marked the implementation of the 'Addison' Act of 1919 and subsequent Housing Acts which empowered local authorities to supply working-class housing in addition to closing or demolishing unsatisfactory properties. Again the process was evolutionary, the ground for the 1919 Act being gradually laid as Butt, Rodger and Gordon indicate, in earlier legislation related to insanitary and uninhabitable housing and concerned with the establishment of housing and sanitary standards in Scottish cities. The identification of a separate phase between 1939 and approximately 1970 can be justified on several counts. First, the motor car, buses and lorries, replaced the railways and tramways as the dominant means of inter-urban and intra-urban movement of goods and people. Second, a series of planning decisions in the immediate post-1945 period profoundly influenced contemporary urban history.[41] The building of New Towns, the decision to redevelop extensive tracts of the densely-populated inner city and to rehouse many families on peripheral estates and in other settlements and the intention to restrict urban sprawl and use planning legislation to direct urban growth were amongst the most influential policy decisions of that period in terms of impact upon the patterns of, and processes operating in, the cities and in the other settlements in their penumbra, notably in the Clydeside conurbation. Finally recent changes in policy such as the favouring of rehabilitation and improvement of existing residential areas rather than wholesale clearance or the greater emphasis upon the problems of inner city areas[42] rather than an over-emphasis of growth in the New Towns, suggest that a new stage has probably commenced.

The model outlined above appears to offer a potential analytical framework for the investigation of the economic, spatial, social and policy dimensions of Scottish cities since the middle of the eighteenth century. The essays by MacLaren, Robb, Gordon, Hume and Butt are not designed to illustrate the stages of the proposed model. Instead they take particular economic, spatial, social or policy dimensions and analyse them in a particular temporal and spatial setting using various sources of data and investigative approaches.

MacLaren measures changes in the class fractions of the bourgeoisie in Aberdeen by reference to membership of the kirk session, eldership in the Church of Scotland. Membership carried status and power, marking an individual's social and financial respectability. In Aberdeen at that time the elders were overwhelmingly middle-class in composition. MacLaren notes the business and residential propinquity of senior elders in the established residential districts in the east central area of the city. In the second quarter of the nineteenth century these elders became segregated, spatially and socially, from the newer members of the middle-class who occupied the new town houses in the westward extension of the high status area. The latter group included bitter critics of the prevailing order in the Church of Scotland, a fact of considerable significance in the progression towards the Disruption in 1843 when all fifteen ministers in Aberdeen seceded from the Church of Scotland. The established group of elders included many families with kinship or business connections into the rural aristocracy. More than half of the elders in 1830 were large merchants and manufacturers, professional men or retired gentlemen. Small shopkeepers contributed only one-eighth of the eldership.

A crucial point for MacLaren's analysis was the integration of middle-class roles at that time. The religious function of elder could not be separated from the business or civic roles of the same man. Additionally Aberdeen was unique amongst the cities in lacking a significant Catholic migration or indeed a substantial influx of migrants from furth of the North East and the Highlands and Islands. Thus the emerging differentiation of the middle-class in Aberdeen was primarily confined to occupation, residential location and membership of the moderates or evangelics in the widening schism within the kirk.

Statistical analysis of the social composition of the kirk session before and after the Disruption revealed a marked change in the eldership. Two strongly significant trends emerged, namely a reduction in the number of high status merchants and an increase in the numbers of small shopkeepers and tradesmen. MacLaren discusses the inability of the established elite to accommodate change and concludes that their position was initially challenged and then replaced by the new class fractions which gained support from the small shopkeepers and tradesmen.

Robb's study of social and residential change in nineteenth-century Gorbals uses directories and census enumerators' books as primary data sources to investigate the thesis that during that period the area declined from suburb to slum. The thesis of degradation advanced in other studies[43] proved to be an oversimplification of a complex picture principally due to the persistence of distinct sub-areas within Gorbals. Inevitably as the century progressed Gorbals, as a direct consequence of urban growth, was transformed spatially from suburb to inner city. There was evidence of increasing working-class proportions, particularly in North Hutchesontown, but not of universal abandonment by the middle class. In the second half of the century new middle-class properties were erected on the southern periphery of the area although tenements became the predominant house type rather than the Regency terraces of the initial suburban speculation by the Lauries or the villas of other suburban areas. Apart from middle- and working-class additions other physical changes included replacement of buildings with an increase in the density of development and the large scale remodelling in the 1870s of Gorbals Parish by the Improvement Trust. The Laurieston project faced stiff competition from middle-class speculation such as that around Blythswood Square. Nonetheless the planned suburb was within walking distance of the city centre and the existing *faubourg* of Gorbals village did not seriously detract from the potential attractiveness of Laurieston. Directory information for the first half of the nineteenth century revealed that, within Gorbals, two address households were primarily located in Laurieston, although bourgeois outliers had been established in parts of South Hutchesontown. As the shops and offices moved westward in the nineteenth-century migration of the Central Business District of Glasgow, the high status districts on the north side of the river also extended westward as the West End middle-class suburbs were developed.[44] Additionally in the mid- to late-Victorian era a substantial villa district was created at Pollokshaws and Pollokshields on the southern periphery. Apart from the competition presented by these new developments, the residential environments of Gorbals were also affected by adjoining industrial and railway projects. Nonetheless Robb found that Gorbals did not degenerate during the nineteenth century into one class slumdom. There was an overall trend towards a gradual lowering of social status but a complex, although changing, social mosaic continued to exist in Gorbals in the late nineteenth century. In part this was explained by the persistence of residual elements from earlier patterns but the construction of new properties where social heterogeneity was included suggested that the dominant process was not one of middle-class abandonment. If the late development of suburban railways was a contributory factor, then one should expect similar small-scale residential differentiation in early suburbs in other Scottish cities. Indeed Gordon[45] found a similar situation in mid-Victorian Edinburgh but the pattern resulted from a complex interplay of factors including the precise nature of the original development, the continued attractiveness of central locations, the perceptions of occupants, the composition of the housing stock, the prestige of particular districts and the accessibility of newer suburbs to the city centre. The pace of suburbanisation certainly accelerated after the development of suburban railways and urban tramways but the construction of the West End suburbs in Glasgow, some of which pre-dated those transport innovations, suggested that it would be dangerous to place too much emphasis upon the restrictive function of transportation on well-to-do middle-class suburban speculation in the early Victorian era. Housing tastes and comparative evaluations of possible residential environments were arguably more decisive factors for the leaders of the middle class.

Commenting on London's slums and suburbs, Dyos and Reeder observed that 'centrifugal forces drew the rich into the airy suburbs; centripetal ones held the poor in the airless slums. . . . The fact of the suburb influenced the development of the slum; the threat of the slum entered the consciousness of the suburb.'[46] Whilst these general tendencies operated during the nineteenth century in Scottish cities, the detailed pattern of status areas presented a complex picture. This is revealed by Gordon in the study of the status areas of Edinburgh, the most middle-class of the Scottish cities. The status areas of 1914 were defined from house valuation data which were significantly correlated with contemporaneous occupational and tenurial information. An evolutionary account of the pre-1914 development provided the background for a detailed analysis of the pattern of status areas and facilitated discussion of changes in the spatial structure during the period 1760–1914. The timespan embraced the transition from the pre-industrial to the pre-modern city, assuming the latter title is restricted to the situation where the local authorities are the principal supplier of working-class housing.

By 1914 the dominant high-status poles were located centrally in terraced mansion districts to the north and west of the original Georgian New Town. The principal middle-status zone occurred in the southern suburbs although there were clusters of middle-status flats in certain streets within, or adjacent to, the central high-status districts. The Old Town constituted the central portion of an arcuate zone of working-class housing which linked Gorgie to central Leith. By 1914 suburban growth had extended Stevenson's notion of two distinct cities based upon the Old Town and New Town districts into at least three, and possibly four, components. The finely-shaded middle-class suburbs were a distinctive new component. Additionally the emergence of a spatially discreet pattern of residential districts for the lower middle class and respectable working class, the aristocracy of labour,[47] possibly added a fourth dimension to the spatial structure. Apart from the complications created by new developments, the pattern of status areas was also affected by a variety of residual elements including the incorporation by urban expansion of previously independent settlements. Additionally functional change resulted from the expansion of the Central Business District and from institutional invasion of comparatively central sites such as those in the Lauriston district, which was situated between the Old Town and the green space of the Meadows.

Gordon discusses the relationship between the spatial pattern of status areas in Edinburgh and pre-industrial and ecological models[48] of urban growth and structure. Gordon concludes that the sector model offered the most persuasive representation of the pattern although the persistence of small-scale differentiation introduced greater complexity than the model anticipated. He notes that a satisfactory explanation of the pattern in Edinburgh required the inclusion of factors relating to the supply of housing and the location of developments in addition to an understanding of the persistence of remnants of earlier patterns. Mention is also made of the factors affecting urban morphology and urban growth, including discussion of the role of tramways and suburban railways in the process of suburbanisation of Victorian and Edwardian cities. Gordon concludes that the pattern of status areas in Edinburgh in 1914 was a particular resolution in time and space of a complex and dynamic set of relationships and processes.

Adams noted that 'transport systems have always exerted an influence upon the success or failure of towns'.[49] Indeed, from the middle of the eighteenth century, developments in transportation had profound effects upon the nature of the urban system and the size, shape and structure of urban settlements. Hume examines these themes in relation to the evolution of different modes of transportation. Both Kellett[50] and Dyos[51] attributed primary importance to the role of the railways in shaping the layout of Victorian cities. Kellett believed that the railways 'influenced the topography and character of its central inner districts, the disposition of its dilapidated and waste areas, and of its suburbs, the direction and character of its growth . . .'.[52] In some cases the construction of railways altered development proposals. For example, plans for an eastern middle-class extension of the New Town of Edinburgh were curtailed after the building of the railway to Leith.[53] Equally, railways specifically sought through subsidised fares to encourage development as in the case of the late nineteenth-century suburban villas at Lenzie.[54] However, many lacunae remain in our understanding of the detailed relationships between particular developments in transportation and alterations in the character and functioning of the urban system, specific phases of urban structure or precise processes and particular decisions related to the formation of, and alteration to, the pattern of urban land use. Land values and accessibility were major variables which influenced the development of particular sites but specific factors such as the decisions of landowners or speculators or site characteristics[55] relating to drainage or some other feature frequently determined the course and character of growth. Moreover other macro-scale processes operated. For example, Whitehand[56] correlated trade cycles with building cycles in the context of the residential development of Maryhill in the late nineteenth century. He also suggested that institutional invasion of the urban fringe occurred during a downturn in the building cycle when land prices were depressed and demand low.

Hume notes the influence which water transport had upon the location of a variety of industries, particularly during the first flush of industrialisation. Subsequently, the development of the railways introduced new locational forces. Additions and alterations to the structure of settlements included railway termini and workshops and commercial activity was stimulated in the immediate vicinity of stations, in a manner similar to that associated previously with the termini of the canals. The increasing centralist roles for the cities demanded improvements in transportation to ensure accessibility between parts of the city and to facilitate the growing intra- and inter-urban transfers of goods and people. The railways played a vital function in the evolving transport system. Hume also stresses the importance of the tramways in the context of intra-urban transportation, facilitating and encouraging urban growth and providing the essential flexibility demanded by the increasing spatial complexity of the late Victorian city.

Whilst the long distance carrier trade[57] declined after the development of the railways, local trade increased. The horse and cart remained the principal localised means of collection and distribution until it was replaced, in the twentieth century, by the lorry. Hume notes the limited economic range of carts which resulted in a comparatively close spacing between suburban mineral depots. Equally the scale of carting was reflected in the profusion of establishments, large and small, specialising in that activity and in the multiplicity of stables.

There were substantial intercensal fluctuations in employment in transport, with a marked decline in the mid 1890s but in aggregate the total number increased substantially between 1891 and 1911. Numerous family businesses were founded and the major transport companies developed extensive occupational hierarchies. New tasks were defined and incorporated into the prevailing system of socio-economic status. Some companies built housing for their employees. Gordon found evidence in Edinburgh of spatial association between workplace and residence for skilled, semi-skilled and unskilled railway employees, echoing the associational patterns displayed by many other industrial employees.

From the middle of the nineteenth century the various Reports of the Medical Officers of Health described living conditions in areas of urban deprivation and pointed to the causal associations between poverty, inadequate housing, overcrowding and high rates of morbidity and mortality. Although death rates, particularly infant mortality rates, did decline in the second half of the century, as the ravages of epidemics of infectious diseases were combated, the deprivation cycle remained unbroken. There was increasing levels of public concern and action, albeit often motivated by fear of infection, civil disorder or moral decline. Gordon[58] has described early attempts in Edinburgh aimed at supplying an improved standard of working-class housing but he concluded that these properties were beyond the means of most unskilled workers and others with irregular or low earnings. Allan[59] has described the workings of the various Improvement Acts in Glasgow and similar ventures took place in other cities. Whilst insanitary overcrowded housing was demolished the pre-occupation of the redevelopers with transport improvements and the erection of institutions produced a situation which Geddes aptly termed 'dehousing'.

Butt discusses the operational effectiveness of the working-class housing market in the late Victorian and Edwardian eras before turning to a sustained analysis of the various dimensions of the housing problem and the evolution of public policy on housing. The Housing, Town Planning, etc. Act of 1909 established much of the framework of later policies but failed to provide for the financial requirements of subsidised housing. Butt illustrates that much preparatory planning took place in advance of the Report of the Royal Commission in 1918 and the passing of the 1919 Housing Act. For some time local government officials had been aware of the need for direct participation in housing supply and management. The swelling tide of municipalisation also favoured intervention whilst the voices of planners and of proponents of the Garden City ideal added professional, practical and philosophical support. Given these facts it was not surprising that in January 1918 Parliament was informed that 297 out of 311 Scottish local authorities had prepared schemes for house-building. The Scottish Office had already circulated proposals to local authorities outlining a strategy for the development of local authority housing although details about the level of subsidy were only finalised with the passing of the Addison Housing Act. Thereafter levels of construction, standard and style of housing, and the purpose of projects were fundamentally influenced by the wording and subsidy policies of the various Housing Acts. To a considerable extent the alteration in emphasis in the various Acts reflected the political predispositions of the Government of the day. For example, whenever the Conservatives were in power, there was a reversion to faith in private enterprise. Another reason for change was that particular problems became so severe that new initiatives were deemed to be essential. By 1935 a report by a Scottish Departmental Committee found that overcrowding was a major facet of the housing problem in Scotland. The Housing (Scotland) Act 1930 made provision for slum clearance and rehousing, including a grant calculated on a *per capita* basis. The Housing (Scotland) Act 1935 sought to resolve the problem of overcrowding by fixing a minimum standard for overcrowding and supplying finance to provide consequential additional needs.

The virtual cessation of building during the Second World War further complicated the situation. Nonetheless, plans were made for post-war policies and two wartime reports, *Planning Our New Homes*[60] and *Distribution of New Houses*[61] proved to be very influential planning documents. Between 1945 and 1950 public enterprise virtually dominated the Scottish supply of new housing.

Despite the universality of the various Scottish Housing Acts, considerable differences existed between the housing experiences of the four cities in the first half of the twentieth century. Butt outlines the situation in each of the cities. The magnitude of the problem varied but the most intractable problems were found in Glasgow. Points of similarity also emerged such as the social stigma attached to new housing areas intended for families displaced by slum clearance legislation. Butt concludes that the market forces worked best in Edinburgh where the urban economy was most diversified. Whilst the various components of public housing policy improved the quality and quantity of working-class housing, overcrowding and deprivation were persistent problems awaiting social, political and economic initiatives.

The housing problem continued to dominate civic policies after 1950. There was a massive extension of the public sector. Vast new estates were constructed and extensive tracts of decaying tenements demolished in a process which generated powerful centrifugal forces upon the structure of cities. Part of the rehousing was only attainable with the development of the five New Towns. Glasgow also entered into overspill agreements with many settlements as a further means of relocating some of the families needing rehousing. The detailed housing policy varied temporally. Distinctive trends included the phase favouring multi-storey blocks and more recent legislation which intro-duced Housing Action Areas and General Improvement Areas. Policies of improvement and rehabilitation added greater variety to the policy and intro-duced new participants, the housing associations.

Despite these substantial efforts, significant problems remain unsolved. There are still substantial pockets of urban deprivation[62] and areas of over-crowded housing. In part, the problems have been redefined. For example, overcrowding is now officially defined as housing in which there are more than 1.5 persons per room. Nonetheless, the longevity of the housing problem indicates the multi-faceted nature of the topic. Although housing occupies a strategic position in a series of socio-economic relationships or cycles, the role may be associational rather than causative.

Another sustained source of concern and conflict was the physical expansion of urban areas and the consequential effects upon the adjoining countryside.[63] It is not possible, however, to investigate every aspect of the urban history of Scotland within the compass of one volume or do full justice to the various approaches to the topic. Hopefully, these essays provide a stimulating exposition of some of the principal facets of an important field of research in several disciplines.

REFERENCES

1   I H Adams, *The Making of Urban Scotland* (London, 1978), p. 9.
2   Adams (ibid.) and C McWilliam, *Scottish Townscape* (London and Glasgow, 1975).
3   A Ballard, 'The Theory of the Scottish Burgh', *Scottish History Review*, 13 (1915), 16–29.
4   G Neilson, 'On some Scottish Burghal Origins', *Juridical Review*, 14 (1902), 129–40.
5   D Murray, *Early Burgh Organisation in Scotland* (Glasgow, 1924).
6   W MacKay Mackenzie, *The Scottish Burgh* (Edinburgh, 1949).
7   G S Pryde, 'The Origin of the Burgh in Scotland', *Juridical Review*, 47, (1935).
8   G Simpson (ed.), *Aberdeen's Hidden History: a report on excavations in Broad Street* (Aberdeen Art Gallery and Museum, 1974).
9   See N P Brooks, 'Urban Archaeology in Scotland', in M W Barley, *European Towns, Their Archaeology and Early History* (London, 1977), pp. 27–30.
10 J Schofield, 'Excavations south of Edinburgh High Street, 1973–4' *Proc. Soc. Ant. Scot.* 107 (1975–6), 155–242.
11 A R H Baker, J D Hamshere and J Langton, *Geographical Interpretation of Historical Sources* (Newton Abbot, 1970), p. 14.
12 E Ennen, 'Les differents Types de formation des Villes Européennes', *Le Moyen Age*, II (1956), 399–411.
13 H Pirenne, *Medieval Cities* (Princeton, 1949).
14 H Carter, 'A Decision-Making Approach to Town-Plan Analysis: A Case Study of Llandudno', *Urban Essays: Studies in the Geography of Wales* (1970).
15 F S Chapin, *Urban Land Use Planning* (1965).
16 M R G Conzen, 'Alnwick: A Study in Town-Plan Analysis', *Trans. Inst. Br. Geogrs.* 27 (1960).
17 J W R Whitehand and K Alauddin, 'The Town Plans of Scotland: some preliminary considerations', *Scot. Geog. Mag.* 85 (1969), 109–21.
18 F J Macleod, *St Andrews: A Study in Urban Morphology.* Unpublished honours thesis, Dept. of Geography, Univ. of Strathclyde, 1974.
19 W Dodd, 'Ayr: a study in urban growth', *Ayrshire Archaeol. Nat. Hist. Collect.* (2nd series) (1972), 302–82.
20 N P Brooks and G Whittington, 'Planning and Growth in the medieval Scottish burgh: the example of St Andrews', *Trans. Inst. Br. Geogrs.* 2, no. 3 (1977), 278–95.
21 G Burke, *Towns in the Making* (London, 1971), p. 47.
22 I H Adams, op. cit. p. 31.
23 I H Adams, op. cit. 'Urban Reform', pp. 127–55.
24 J Patten, 'Urban Occupations in Pre-Industrial England', *Trans. Inst. Brit. Geogrs* (new series, 2 (1977), no. 3, 296–313, p. 296.
25 J Butt, *The Industrial Archaeology of Scotland* (Newton Abbot, 1967), p. 18.
26 J Patten, op. cit. p. 296.
27 G Unwin, *Industrial Organisation in the Sixteenth and Seventeenth Centuries* (first published Oxford 1904; reprinted London 1957).
28 S Kramer, *The English Craft Gilds* (New York, 1905).
29 K Charlton, 'The Professions of Sixteenth-Century England', *Univ. of Birmingham Hist. Jn.* (1969), 12, 20–41.

30 J Butt, op. cit. p. 18.
31 K J Lea, *A Geography of Scotland* (Newton Abbot, 1977), p. 58.
32 H J Dyos, *The Study of Urban History* (London, 1968), p. 19.
33 S G E Lythe and J Butt, *An Economic History of Scotland 1100–1939* (Glasgow).
34 G Gordon, 'Urban Scotland', in K J Lea, op. cit. pp. 199–210.
35 G Sjoberg, *The pre-industrial city, past and present* (Glencoe, Ill., 1960).
36 Ibid. p. 83.
37 J E Vance, 'Land assignment in pre-capitalist, capitalist and post-capitalist cities',
    Economic Geography, **47** (1971), 101–20.
38 P Knox, *Urban Social Geography* (Harlow, 1982), p. 7.
39 Ibid. p. 7.
40 See, for example, G L Anderson, 'The Social Economy of Late-Victorian Clerks', in
    G Crossick, *The Lower Middle Class in Britain* (London, 1977).
41 G Gordon, op. cit. pp. 211–25.
42 See, for example; Scottish Development Department, *Summary Report of an
    investigation to identify areas of multiple deprivation in Glasgow City.*
    C.P.R.U. Working Paper no. 7 (Edinburgh, 1973).
43 For example, S G Checkland, 'The British industrial city as history: The Glasgow
    case', *Urban Studies* **1** (1964), 5; J R Kellett, *Glasgow; a concise history*
    (London, 1967), p. 6.
44 M A Simpson, 'The West End of Glasgow 1830–1914', in M A Simpson and
    T H Lloyd, *Middle class housing in Britain* (Newton Abbot, 1977).
45 G Gordon, 'The status areas of early to mid-Victorian Edinburgh', *Trans. Inst.
    Brit. Geog.* n.s. **4**, (1979), 2, 168–91.
46 H J Dyos and D A Reeder, 'Slums and Suburbs', in H J Dyos and H Wolff, *The
    Victorian City* (London, 1973), p. 360.
47 R Q Gray, *The Labour Aristocracy in Victorian Edinburgh* (Oxford, 1976).
48 E W Burgess, 'The growth of the city: an introduction to a research project', *Pap.
    and Proc. Amer. Sociol. Soc.* **18** (1924), 85–97; H Hoyt, *The structure and
    growth of residential neighbourhoods in American cities* (Washington, 1939).
49 I H Adams, op. cit. p. 105.
50 J R Kellett, *The Impact of Railways on Victorian Cities* (London, 1969).
51 H J Dyos, 'Railways and Housing in Victorian London', *Journal of Transport
    History,* **2** *(1955),* 1, 11–21; **2** 2, 90–100.
52 J R Kellett, (1969), op. cit. p. xv.
53 A J Youngson, *The Making of Classical Edinburgh* (Edinburgh, 1966).
54 I H Adams, op. cit. p. 118.
55 P J Smith, 'Site selection in the Forth Basin'. PhD thesis, Univ. of Edinburgh
    (1964).
56 J W R Whitehand, 'Building cycles and the spatial pattern of urban growth',
    Trans. Inst. Brit. Geog. **56** (1972), 39–55.
57 A S Morris, 'The Nineteenth Century Scottish Carrier Trade: Patterns of Decline',
    Scottish Geographical Magazine **96** (1980), 2, 74–82.
58 G Gordon, 'Working-Class Housing in Edinburgh 1837–1974', in *Festschrift K.A.
    Sinnhuber,* vol. II (Vienna, 1979), pp. 72–8.
59 C M Allan, 'The genesis of British urban redevelopment with special reference to
    Glasgow', *Econ. Hist. Rev. (2nd series),* **18** (1965), 598–613.

60 *Planning Our New Homes* (Dept. of Health for Scotland, 1944).
61 *Distribution of New Houses in Scotland* (Cmd 6552) (1944).
62 Strathclyde Regional Council, *Urban Deprivation* (1976); Scottish Office, *A Study of Multiply Deprived Households in Scotland,* C.P.R.U. Paper (1980).
63 A B Cruickshank, *Where Town Meets Country* (Aberdeen, 1982).

2

THE SCOTTISH MEDIEVAL TOWN
A search for origins

Brian Dicks

While it is agreed that Western Europe during the late eleventh and twelfth centuries witnessed a remarkable growth, or regrowth, of urban institutions, instructed opinion is still far from accord as to the primary factors that provided the initial impetus for such pervading developments. From the nineteenth century onwards scholars from a number of cognate disciplines have propounded an exhaustive array of rival theories[1] reflecting not merely the historical complexity of medieval town origins but also the strength of which quickly became (and have remained) jealously defended academic differences. To abstract, least of all to name every relevant hypothesis would simply foment a tedious and confusing mass of detail, for even when compatible viewpoints are combined questions of emphasis and factorial priority remain contentious issues.

At the risk of over-simplifying a trenchant scholarly discourse, it is perhaps sufficient to state that the majority of these theories have centred about the relative importance of the various ingredients in urban functions—administrative, defensive, commercial, ecclesiastical, industrial and even agricultural—though, in general terms, arguments have tended to separate into two opposing camps, manned by the supporters of legal origins on the one hand and those of economic origins on the other. Deeply involved in questions of constitutional development many urban historians placed their primary emphasis on the acquisition of urban liberties stressing that it were these, embodied in town charters and burgh status, that favoured the growth of trade and commerce. In opposition and championed by Henri Pirenne (1862–1935), others heralded the new direction of historical involvement with economic explanations. One of the most productive and incisive of urban historians, Pirenne's Mercantile Settlement Theory, first published in 1893 and subjected to continuous refinement throughout his career,[2] became the most influential explanation of medieval town origins. Its basic premise related urban growth in Western Europe to the post-Carolingian revival of commerce when, under the stimuli of new political, economic and social conditions, merchant colonies set up permanent headquarters at suitable vantage points for the purposes of trade and manufacturing. In Pirenne's own words 'mercantile groups formed about the military burgs and established themselves along sea coasts, on river banks, at confluences and at junction points of the natural routes of communication'.[3] Though the emphasis was on change rather than continuity implicit in his arguments was the recognition of the significance of old-established sites as 'fixing-points' for the settlement of merchants and craftsmen, a process fully substantiated by Ganshof[4] who demonstrated the intimate relationship between medieval economic revival and certain pre-existing foci—the 'pre-urban cores' or 'nuclei' as they have been termed. Broadly speaking, therefore, what made the medieval town was a symbiosis between a pre-urban core and a trading settlement, which gave rise to a potentiality for growth. According to Lambert 'this potentiality for growth sprang more often than not from the function of the pre-urban core as a centre of administration, whether royal, manorial, ecclesiastical, or military, while the extent of the growth depended on the size of the market provided by the pre-urban core and its hinterland, the nodality of its siting, and the availability of raw materials and labour for the development of industry'.[5]

Prominent among these fixing-points were the old Roman settlements—the towns and also the forts and military camps—and an enduring problem in the urban history of Western Europe has concerned the degree of settlement continuity that existed from Roman to medieval times. Supporters of the so-called 'Romanist Theory', a rebuttal of Pirenne's insistence on change and discontinuity, advocated a direct link in urban traditions throughout the pre-Roman, Roman and post-Roman periods and in Southern Europe, at least, there can be little dispute that medieval urban life, institutionally as well as topographically, was derived in an unbroken, if remittent line from the later years of the Roman Empire. In many parts of Western Europe also the medieval centres that grew substantially, or were refounded, stood on or near to Roman sites with some of these in turn resting on even older foundations—the native *oppida* or tribal centres common to Western Europe. As C T Smith observes 'the antiquity and stability of town foundations is a striking paradox in the light of their role as the centres and even initiators of change in ideas, institutions, trade and industry'.[6] This continuity, however, seems to have been in terms of sequent occupance rather than in the direct inheritance of municipal and administrative functions though it should be stressed that throughout Western Europe the role of the Christian church, whose bishoprics often coincided with the old Roman *civitates*, was a decisive element in urban succession.

Beyond such statements 'Romanist' theory can be challenged on many grounds, the major and fundamental criticism relating to the fact that those areas of both Western and Northern Europe lying peripheral and well beyond the old Roman civil and economic frontier themselves shared, albeit in most areas belatedly, in the unprecedented upsurge in medieval urban expansion. Ever reproachful of misleading generalisations, and studiously avoiding the incitement to provide *the* theory for *the* medieval town, Edith Ennen[7] focused her attention on the underlying diversity of urban forms, stressing the discriminating conditions that fostered their birth or re-genesis. With the continuity question in mind she distinguished for twelfth-century Europe three differing, but by no means exclusive zones of urban development: (1) the southern, Mediterranean lands where both the institutional and physical form of the Roman urban community survived largely without disruption; (2) a confused intermediate zone where Roman municipal organisation disappeared but where enough of the urban fabric continued to provide the basis for sustained growth in post-Carolingian times, and (3) the north German area east of the Rhine, together with Scandinavian and other geographically or economically restricted environments in which the classical urban culture had little more than passing significance.

Though the boundaries between these zones were far from distinct and the processes at work within them often dissimilar, such a tri-partite regionalisation (to which an east European region of autonomous urban growth can be added)[8] constitutes a useful descriptive model against which the foundations and subsequent progress of medieval town life in singular areas may be viewed and tested. Conscious that any rigid application of embracing theory to more local situations is fraught with interpretive dangers, the remainder of this essay considers the origins of the Scottish medieval town against the broader European but, more specifically, the British background. Within Ennen's model, southern and eastern England fell within the intermediate zone of medieval urban growth, whereas much of the remainder of western and northern Britain belonged to those peripheral regions in which Roman traditions had less or, in the case of Scotland, debatable significance. Any attempts, therefore, to adjust the Scottish example to wider precedents proves from the outset to be both instructive and contentious.

THE NORTH BRITISH TRADITION

Hardly more than a generation ago it was fashionable for historians and archaeologists to relegate Scotland to a position in which its early peoples did little more than acquire, late and at second-hand, innovations—economic, social and technological—that had originated south of the border.[9] Though detailed re-assessment of the evidence has shown such a thesis to be largely untenable, it fails to obscure the significant truth that during the long centuries in which the Mediterranean was the vanguard of progress and cultural adaptation the peripheral position of Scotland, itself an integral part of Britain's conservative Highland Zone,[10] placed it far removed from the main stream of 'civilising' influences. Thus, states Mackie,[11] 'the great formative forces,—those of the Roman Empire, Christianity, and the Renaissance, for example— reached her relatively late and with diminished vigour. Moreover, and this is all-important, these forces had, in most cases, enriched the life of England before they reached Scotland. . . .'

Deterministic as this persuasion appears, there can be little contention that in terms of urban traditions Scotland was both a late and protracted developer,[12] for prior to the twelfth century there is little direct evidence, archaeological or documentary, to indicate any settlement that could qualify for the description 'urban'. It was during the reigns of David I (1124–53) and his successors of the House of Canmore that the curtain rises on what had been a 'Dark Age' of documentation to reveal an increasing number of settlements that were receiving crown privileges and the elevated status of burghs. In time these king's burghs (which collectively formed a major component in the Scottish policy of infeudation based on the Anglo-Norman model south of the border) acquired the epithet 'royal', though initially the relevant crown charters refer to them simply as 'my burghs'.

No original charters survive for David's reign but his burgh foundations are cited in later deeds and documents. Berwick, Edinburgh, Roxburgh, Aberdeen, Dunfermline, Crail, Elgin, Inverkeithing, Perth, Stirling, Linlithgow and Haddington[13] are each referred to as *burgo meo* and there are inferences that Peebles and Rutherglen[14] also had the status of burghs during David's reign. But, paradoxically, the earliest burghs on record—Berwick and Roxburgh—were subsequently lost to Scotland, the former ultimately destined to become an English border town and the latter failing to survive the warfare and destruction of later centuries. Royal authority also permitted churchmen and lay lords to found ecclesiastical and baronial burghs, both of which significantly contributed to Scotland's expanding urban mesh. Thus St Andrews, Glasgow, Brechin and Dunblane were early bishop's cities whilst Kelso,[15] Jedburgh, Paisley and the Canongate owned their superiority to monastic houses. Among the powerful and presitigious baronial foundations were Renfrew, belonging to the Steward family, and Lochmaben in Dumfriesshire whose superiors were the Lords of Annandale.[16]

On the death of King William the Lion in 1214 more than thirty burghs appear to have existed and both Alexander II (1214–49) and III (1249–85/6) added extensively to the list. Throughout the fourteenth century the practice of burgh erection was particularly fashionable and by 1500 the number had increased to about 150.[17] Such a multiplication inevitably had many social and economic repercussions, not least that the accompanying intensification of trade at all levels made them Scotland's doorways to foreign markets and the homes of small, but important commercially-orientated communities. The predominantly 'lowland' distribution of the burghs is not difficult to explain for the pattern reflects not only the strength of royal control in the southern and eastern sectors of the country, but also the fact that here were concentrated the main avenues of medieval local and regional trade.[18] It is significant that no burghs were founded in the Highland region or up the west coast between the

Clyde and the Pentland Firth. Not only did the restrictive environment of this general area preclude urban settlements, it was also judged to fall outside the sphere of effective royal control.[19]

In view of the exiguous historical evidence relating to the eleventh century, it might be argued that in the space of a few potent reigns, beginning with that of David I, Scotland was changed from a predominantly self-supporting agricultural and non-urbanised land to one whose national life became increasingly geared to inter-regional trade and commerce conducted from its newly established burghs. While there is obviously a great deal of truth in this reasoning it has similarly been suggested, or at least inferred, that the genesis of Scottish urban life stems from the granting of burgh charters, the presumption being that urban centres developed suddenly as part of deliberately planned crown policy. This, however, has been hotly disputed among many historians, the conflicting opinion, while acknowledging the burghs as innovations in the institutional sense, subscribing to the view that some basis for urbanism, if only crude and partial, must have anteceded their royal recognition. Duncan, ingeminating the sentiments of Murray,[20] Mackenzie,[21] and Houston,[22] stresses this point most forcibly: 'It will not do to argue', he states, 'that because there is no written evidence of eleventh-century towns in Scotland, there were no such towns', and he further suggests that scattered references to tolls, rents, grants and various trading liberties, chiefly in ecclesiastical archives, 'illuminate urban development, albeit obliquely'.[23] Thus, the question of Scottish medieval town origins must be seen not merely in terms of the insubstantial historical evidence but also in terms of what can only be described as a confusion of definitions and nomenclatures. The 'burgh' was a privileged community, usually a place of strength, to which the crown awarded *corpus juris*. The title, therefore, is a noumenon in law whilst 'town' and 'trade' are concepts in social and economic life.[24] From this it might reasonably be argued that places gaining burgh status must already have been centres of some local or regional significance—those natural foci of communications (especially where land and water routes met) to which trade gravitated. In creating burghs at such vantage points royal authority saw a means both of bettering trading circumstances and of diverting, through a system of tolls, a proportion of burgh profits into the royal purse. 'The tolls', as Duncan again suggests, 'go far to explain the king's interest in urban development; even if paid in kind, in the town they could readily be turned into money. They were a means of providing him with a cash income such as was not forthcoming from his estates nor from other landward sources. The rents of burgesses were similarly important to him, and it is indeed from these sources that the whole of David I's known revenue in money is derived. It is not surprising, therefore, that so active a ruler, with many projects costly in capital on hand, should have actively promoted the growth of burghs.'[25]

The above lines of argument, while not dissenting from the earlier expressed viewpoint of Scotland's dilatory urban growth, nonetheless allude to the importance in such development of 'incipient towns', that is, the pre-urban nuclei referred to previously. The search for these precursors—settlements revealing quasi-urban institutions—must rest firmly with the archaeologists, for with the dearth of documentary archives it is excavation alone that can determine the character of Scotland's pre-burgh settlements and also the topographical form of its earliest burghs. Until recently urban archaeology was a much neglected field and, in the Scottish context, Brooks[26] has usefully summarised the major difficulties that continue to inhibit current progress. But as in Wales, Ireland and, more especially, in England, initial results indicate something of the opportunities and corpus of information liable to come from future fieldwork. Until such definitive evidence becomes available, however, either in support of, or refuting current theorizing, the question of Scottish urban origins must, of necessity, remain inferential and controversial.

The remainder of this essay examines the roles, as urban fixing points, of a number of elements in Scotland's pre-burgh settlement pattern and draws extensively on the model developed by Carter[27] in his analysis of Welsh town origins and on Adams'[28] critical appraisal relating directly to Scottish urban beginnings. Carter recognised three elements in the early settlement pattern of Wales that could have acted as pre-urban nuclei: the forts of the Roman military occupation, the monastic and other ecclesiastical sites of Celtic chris-tianity and the native centres of tribal, secular power. As he affirms: 'It will be apparent . . . that here in the attenuated form usually associated with the Highland Zone, are exactly the same elements identified by Ganshof on the continent.'[29] In Scotland, however, as Adams alludes, even stronger differences in the status and historical prominence of these elements compared to European regions, including those south of the border, are factors of obvious influence in such comparisons. Nonetheless, the basic similarities remain and the contribution of these and related types of nuclei to the medieval urban pattern, as well as to its apparently delayed appearance, warrants further consi-deration. Also relevant to the Scottish example are the studies on Ireland by Butlin[30] and Aalock[31] which recognise the roles of royal centres, monastic houses and, singularly in the Irish context, Viking trading bases in the country's pre-medieval settlement mesh.

THE ROMAN LEGACY

It is customary in studies searching for urban origins to begin with the Romans who throughout their empire saw the town as an instrument to further the acceptance of conquest and colonisation. In Scotland's case, however, Roman urban influence signally contrasts with that of lowland England which fully experienced the innovative influence of urban life based on a modified contin-ental model. Whether from the economic and social points of view this, as some scholars have suggested, was little more than a luxury which sprang from a strong political-military function, the fact remains that much of the Roman fabric survived in the south and east to provide the essential re-growth points following what traditionally has been regarded as a period of urban decay. Some of the academic issues relating to the question of continuity between Roman and medieval towns have already been referred to and in no part of Europe has the debate been more contentious and intractable than in England. To a certain extent recent studies have now redressed the picture of universal urban decline and destruction following the Roman withdrawal from Britain, with current opinion emphasising at least some measure of continuity rather than total eclipse. In the words of Frere, 'towns might have been re-occupied after a period of emptiness because of the inevitability of the choice of the original site, and the compulsion of communications or other economic factors, but it is perhaps more likely that they never ceased to be occupied'.[32] Partly in support, Wacher[33] implies that it is probably safe to predict that a degree of physical occupation existed in almost every former Romano-British town but questions their survival as urban institutions, accepting instead that 'town life had been reduced to life in towns'. Hill employs the term 're-settlement' arguing that 'for continuity to be proved, town life must be shown to have survived the sixth century, and only at York, Canterbury and London is this suggested'.[34] Yet it can be no coincidence that when the impetus for a fresh start came the first places mentioned as centres of Anglo-Saxon trade are the tested foci of the old Roman towns, so sited that they automatically remained principal centres throughout the middle ages and down to modern times. Also significant is the concurrence between Christian bishoprics and Roman urban foundations, a characteristic that finds its counterpart throughout Western Europe.

Contrary to conditions in lowland England, the Roman occupation of Britain's Highland Zone failed, for the most part, to generate urban institutions, a fact related as much to its peripheral location as to its economically restrictive environments. For the Romans this was one of the fringes of Empire, a northwest region to be pacified, fortified and policed rather than colonised, especially when forays and invasions from unconquered Ireland could disturb this ultimate edge of their *pax romana*. Following the initial phases of conquest and expansion, therefore, a period of gradual territorial consolidation led to a basic division of Roman Britain (in the classic Fox tradition) into a 'lowland' civil and economic zone and a 'highland' military zone which in Wales and the southwest also provided important mineral resources. Yet boundaries and functions were far from exclusive: Wales, for example, remaining controlled by a network of forts and military roads, took advantage of such security by developing a modest urban and villa life in some of its more environmentally favoured areas. Two small Roman towns were laid out at Caerwent and Carmathen though the former, by far the more opulent, had no medieval successor.[35]

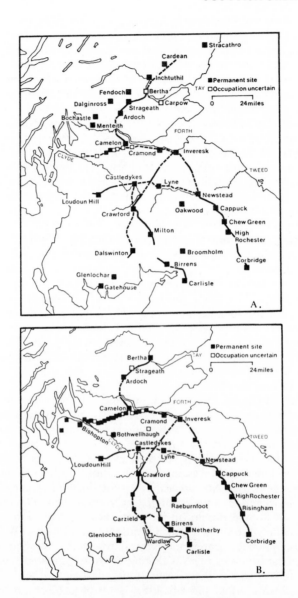

FIGURE 1   The Roman Frontier in Scotland: (A) North Britain in the Flavian Period
(B) North Britain in the Antonine Period. (Reproduced from *Who are the Scots* (ed. G
Menzies), BBC Publications 1972)

Scotland failed to fully excite the cupidity of the Romans and the country was never completely explored by a system of communications and, in that sense, never adequately colonised (Figure 1). Four decades after the invasion of southern Britain, in what is termed the Flavian period, the legions of Julius Agricola (appointed governor of Britannia AD 78–84) advanced as far north as Strathmore in their search for a suitable frontier. But the untidy conditions of this isolated northern flank and the impracticality of manning the legionary fortress of Inchtuthill on the Tay near Dunkeld led to the Roman retiral and the subsequent construction c. AD 122 of Hadrian's Wall as the British province's northern lines. Twenty years later, however, the Romans again pressed northwards to establish the new frontier at the Antonine Wall across the Forth–Clyde isthmus. This was precariously maintained until its abandonment towards the end of the second century—though some opinion supports a later date—in favour of the more strongly defended Tyne–Solway frontier. The whole of intramural Scotland, therefore, was a military zone never completely pacified and acting as a marchland between the indigenous northern tribes and the more settled communities south of Hadrian's Wall. In this southern portion of Scotland four major Iron Age tribal groups can be distinguished—the Novantae covered the area of Galloway and Dumfriesshire, the Damnonii to the north occupied the west coast to the Clyde, including its northern banks, the Selgovae held the central borders and the territory of the Votadini extended along the east coast zone between the Tyne and the Forth. Of these groupings the Selgovae and Votadini appear to have been the most powerful with their tribal centres or native *oppida* at Eildon Hill North, two kilometres south of Melrose, and Traprain Law, a detached outlier of the Lammermuir Hills, respectively. North of the Forth–Clyde line the names of some twelve tribes are recorded but they are not easy to differentiate historically or archaeologically. In general terms, however, the highland massif, the homeland of the Caledonians, divided the area between the tribes of the east coastal regions and those of the north and west coasts and islands—the Atlantic province.

In view of the erratic northern frontier and the problem of establishing tribal boundaries, the impact of Roman influence on Scotland is difficult to assess, but the conventional argument that such military advances did little to alter the general way of life and economy of North Britain[36] should now be accepted with far less enthusiasm, especially when European research has indicated the extension of Rome's influence far beyond the mere physical defended limits of the Empire. Evidence suggests that Scotland received a steady stream of coins,[37] pottery and manufactured articles from southern Britain in exchange for raw materials, particularly wool and hides. At Housesteads[38] the most impressive of the excavated forts in the very centre of Hadrian's Wall, archaeologists have indicated the presence of a major regional market where Roman pottery, glass and metal-wares were traded for the products of a predominantly pastoral society. Corbridge, Chesters and other mural forts had similar servicing

functions and the scatter of archaeological material outside the Scottish equivalents in Strathmore, along the Antonine Wall and in the intramural zone
might well indicate the presence of nascent civil settlements or *vici*. As yet,
however, only at Carriden (Roman Credigone), where the Antonine defences
reached the Forth estuary is there any sound evidence of a native settlement
attached to a fort,[39] but whether it acquired some form of self-government,
following the Housesteads model, remains unknown. It is interesting, however,
that its name appears to incorporate the *cair* element which, equated with
chester and *civitas*, was found in all the *civitates* names of Britain. Thus Kair
Eden—Carriden—gained some mark of recognition though it is highly
probable that in post-Roman times the *cair* prefix referred to nothing more
than the presence of Roman ruins.

    Without doubt the weakest aspect of current theorising about Scottish urban
origins relates to the inadequacy of the archaeological record which means that
the existence of other settlements attached to forts remains speculative. In
addition is the similarly dissident evidence relating to the apparent lack of concurrence between Roman sites and later settlements, though exceptions include
some of the forts along the Antonine Wall—Kirkintilloch for example—and
the harbour forts of Cramond and Inveresk (Musselburgh). In the case of the
latter two, a variety of archaeological and documentary evidence[40] substantiates
some continuity of function, particularly the recurrent use of the river Esk as
the estuarine port serving Musselburgh. Yet it would require little sustained
argument to demonstrate that 'continuity' in these examples is more apparent
than real and attempts to trace the ancestry of any Scottish burgh to a Roman
foundation can be nothing other than an unrewarded exercise.

    But to dismiss the influence of the Roman fort and road network as being
entirely negative would be both prejudiced and misleading for a reasonable
case can be made in support of some elements or levels of continuity, if not
specifically in terms of actual sites, then at least in terms of geographical situation and locality. The construction of Roman forts on the sites of native centres
is rare in Scotland and only at Cappuck in Roxburghshire, where an earlier
palisaded structure was deliberately obliterated by the Roman defences, does
this seem to have been the sequence. A more typical connection was that as
illustrated in the relationship between the Selgovian centre of Eildon Hill
North and the Roman fort at Newstead which confronts it a few kilometres east
of Melrose. Evidently the Selgovae were troublesome subjects and their capital
appears to have been dismantled and deserted during the Roman period, and
never to have been resettled. Newstead, named Trimontium (after the triple-
summited Eildon Hill), was built close to their centre of power and its nodal
position within the borders made it one of the most vital Agricolan forts in
Scotland. At the risk of overstating the argument for locational continuity, it is
noteworthy that Old Melrose was one of southern Scotland's earliest ecclesiastical sites. Initially episcopal in organisation and then monastic (see below), it

subsequently became an important Cistercian foundation among David I's border abbeys, though prior to its late elevation to burgh status there are only passing indications in the sources as to its urban character.

Such an illustration of the way in which successive settlements gravitated to well-tested locations reflects the influence of important geographical constraints in which accessibility and strategic position played major roles. Thus a kind of situational determinism can be said to have operated which is well reflected in the disposition of the Clyde Valley forts of Crawford, Castledykes and Bothwellhaugh whose carefully selected sites mark but one phase in a repeated pattern of settlement up to the Middle Ages and beyond. Lying 400 metres north of the modern village on the right bank of the Clyde the fort at Crawford was of great strategic importance at a point where the Roman roads from Annandale and Nithsdale met, the latter probably crossing the river south-west of the fort. But its siting must also have been influenced as much by the presence in the area of a considerable native population which in conjunction with the existence of important land routes, principally the main river valleys, formed a major controlling factor in the Roman settlement of Scotland. It can never be claimed that Crawford was a flourishing centre yet it may be noted that the importance of the site was still recognised in medieval times when Crawford Castle, originally a seat of the Lindsays, but later ceded to the Douglas family was built close to the Roman fort. Significantly, too, Crawford was the site of an early Christian foundation, appearing as an ecclesiastical burgh in 1242–9 and as a burgh of barony in 1510. As with many burgh foundations, however, the granting of a charter was not in itself any guarantee of urban success and Crawford's status reflected more the aspirations of its local lords than the economic stimulus provided by the area it was designed to serve.

Lanark, in contrast, close to the site of Castledykes, was well positioned to exploit the agricultural potential of Clydesdale and, according to Duncan, must have been a centre of considerable importance prior to its erection as a burgh. Lanark, in fact, was an early royal burgh and as Duncan affirms, 'one of the many centres of infra-local trade to which inter-regional traders could be attracted . . . by special measures such as an annual fair'.[41] Bothwell on the other hand—the centre of a baronial fief granted by Malcolm IV—was late in gaining burgh recognition (1602). Yet here again the element of continuity cannot be dismissed and its great stone castle, begun in the thirteenth century, must be seen as the medieval attempt to re-define what the Roman legions at nearby Bothwellhaugh had fully appreciated, the necessity for a strong military presence at the entry to Clydesdale.

North of the Antonine Wall the exemplar of locational continuity has long been recognised as the area around Perth where nodal advantages, including the navigable Tay and the meeting of important land routes, collectively functioned as the 'fixing-points' for a sequence of occupations. Medieval Perth was important not only because it was close to an early royal centre at Scone, but also because it was a flourishing seaport, but whether or not the Romans created a beach-head on its site in support of Agricola's operations remains debatable and inconclusive. Certainly the lower Tay was the scene of considerable Roman activity as is well attested by the forts at Bertha, north of Perth, and at Carpow on the Tay estuary. Contrary to earlier opinion the latter is no longer accepted as the site of Agricola's *Horrea Classis*[42]—the fortress and sea base for his northern campaigns—and it is wildly tempting to suggest, therefore, that Perth holds this honour. But controversy regarding the town's origins is interminable and the theory that it began as a Roman fort, an argument that has sought support in the plan and dimensions of its medieval defences, must, in the absence of sound evidence, be renegated to the realms of antiquarian enthusiasm.

THE NATIVE CENTRES

In view of the state of current knowledge relating to Roman Scotland it is somewhat paradoxical that the most convincing example of a settlement with incipient urban functions should be a native foundation. The excavations at Traprain Law have indicated an exceedingly large and prestigious tribal centre with a virtually continuous occupation beginning in the middle of the first millenium BC and spanning a period of about 1000 years.[43] The Votadini were fortunate in coming to some kind of diplomatic terms with the Romans and the philo-Roman character of their state is evident from the fact that at Traprain they were permitted to retain substantial ramparts, while the whole of their territory, stretching from the Tyne to the Forth, is conspicuous in the absence of Roman forts, the exception being Alavna (Learchild). Such peaceable relations encouraged trade and manufacturing and the number and variety of Roman objects, including numerous luxury items,[44] discovered at Traprain signify its role as an exceptional centre of exchange. This, then, was an *oppidum* in the classic sense, one which Feachem describes as 'a veritable *town* containing numerous inhabitants employed upon industries such as metal-working as well as on agriculture, stock-breeding and trading with the South . . . its degree of sophistication when compared to the bucolic settlements all round . . . make it by far the most important place in the late prehistory and early proto-history of Scotland, and of a wider area including north-eastern England'.[45]

With a centre like Traprain providing such strong evidence of nascent urban features it is difficult to reconcile the traditionally-held views of Scottish native society's inability to generate urban growth. Seen in context, however, it was undoubtedly Traprain's special status and artificially promoted role as a 'free' British centre or Roman protectorate that sponsored such a precedence. When, in sub-Roman times, this protection came to an end and with the Anglian advance along the east coast, Traprain's decline and desertion became inevitable. By the fifth century, however, the tribes of southern Scotland had evolved into primitive states and Celtic genealogies refer to the former Votadinian territory as Gododdin soon to be annexed by the Anglian kingdom of Bernicia.[46] Edinburgh and Stirling were the main British strongholds of the eastern lowland region but it is the excavations at the fortress-palace complex of Yeavering in Northumberland and Doon Hill[47] near Dunbar that are particularly relevant for shedding light on British-Anglian relations in the sixth and seventh centuries. Elsewhere in southern Scotland the picture after the fifth century is again one of native kingdoms emerging from the early Iron Age tribal structure that had prevailed during the Roman period. The kingdom of Strathclyde may be regarded as the geographical descendent of the former tribal area of the Damnonii. Its dynastic capital was at Dumbarton Rock—Alt Clut—and other impressive forts of undoubted local and regional importance included Dundonald in Ayrshire and Duncarnock in Renfrewshire. Rheged, occupying Dumfriesshire and Galloway, appears to have emerged from parts of Novantian and Segovian territories and throughout its area many older settlements were re-utilised, including the forts of Trusty's Hill near Gatehouse-of-Fleet, Tynron Doon in Dumfriesshire and the Mote of Mark in Kirkcudbrightshire.

North of the Forth–Clyde axis territorial conflicts between indigenous Pictish groupings and the incoming Scots—themselves initially torn by family and dynastic rivalries—led to both the re-occupation of earlier defences and the construction of important new strongholds. Although neither exclusive to, nor universal within the area, Scotland's Dark Age settlement north of the Forth and Clyde featured a number of large 'nuclear' forts, so-called from their structural arrangement consisting of a central 'citadel' and a series of outworks forming subsidiary enclosures.[48] They share a preference for rocky sites where natural outcrops can be incorporated into the defensive scheme as is well illustrated at Dundurn and Moncrieff in Perthshire and Dumyat in Stirlingshire. Though usually associated with the Picts[49] similar 'nuclear' structures, occupying equivalent defensible positions, are found in Dalriada, the kingdom centred on Argyll and its islands and founded by fifth-century colonists of *Scotti* from northeastern Ireland. The rock fortress of Dunadd in the Crinan Moss, together with Dunollie above Oban, Dunaverty on the Mull of Kintyre and Tairpert Boitter, presumably near Tarbert (Loch Fyne) are identified as the stronghold capitals of Dalriada's ruling families, as named in the *Senchus Fer nAlban*. Other classic 'nuclear' structures include the forts of Dalmahoy and Kaimes,[50] fourteen kilometres southwest of Edinburgh, and Ruberslaw in Roxburghshire.

Collectively, these and other centres of secular Dark Age power, relating to the period when Picts, Scots, Britons, Angles and, later, Scandinavians, strove for the mastery of central and southern Scotland, must be seen as potential pre-urban nuclei, similar to those native 'capitals' found in other Celtic areas. In

Wales 'royal' villages known as *maerdrefi* are accepted as having been important centres of court officialdom and provincial administration and, as Carter affirms, 'if any development were to take place by which a native nucleation achieved subsequent urban status, then these would be the nucleations concerned'.[51] This view, presented earlier by Lewis[52] in his work on the medieval boroughs of Snowdonia, also received support from Jones Pierce who argued that the charters of such towns as Pwllheli and Nevin 'mark a climax of natural growth involving the enfranchisement of fully-developed urban communities with roots firmly embedded in the pre-conquest history of Gwynedd'.[53] Ireland similarly had its royal centres but their roles as urban generating forces seem to have been subordinated by the significance of the chain of Norse or Viking strongholds established in coastal locations at Dublin, Wicklow, Arklow, Wexford, Waterford and Limerick (with other bases probably at Cork, Kinsale and Youghal). The active emphasis on trade and commerce indicates these early settlements as having many urban functions and by about 955 Dublin, at least, was minting its own coinage.[54]

Scotland also felt the military disruption and subsequent colonising impact of the Scandinavians whose intensity of settlement (as evidenced by the concentration of Norse place-names) was particularly marked in the Northern and Western Isles. But whereas in Ireland the transformation from raiding to trading can be fully demonstrated, there is little to suggest that Scottish Viking settlement produced anything other than agrarian-orientated communities of self-supporting farmsteads, though the scale of enterprise at some—Jarlshof,[55] not least—was impressive. Towns like Wick, Stornoway, Lerwick and Kirkwall all claim a large measure of Scandinavian antecedence but no information exists on the extent to which their early precursors were rooted in trade or had acquired incipient 'burghal rights'. As one of the main centres of the Norwegian kingdom, Gourlay and Turner[56] have argued that Kirkwall, first mentioned in the *Orkneyinga Saga*, must have possessed some urban privileges and the erection of the Earl's castle, together with the transference there from Birsay of the new cathedral shrine of St Magnus has to be interpreted as a measure of its regional influence. But the suggestion of a sustained evolution from Norse hamlet, through the early Norse town, to a full-scale Scottish medieval burgh presents many unanswered questions, for prior to Kirkwall's erection as a royal burgh by James II in 1486 (following the Scottish crown's acquisition of the Northern Isles), little hard fact exists on its early development. Furthermore, it is significant that prior to the twelfth century Scotland as a whole offers no indication of the existence of a regional, much less a national, coinage and numismatic finds from other countries dating from the fifth to the eleventh centuries are extremely rare and random in their geographical distribution. The implication, therefore, is of only desultory trading links with England and the continent, Scotland being, according to Duncan, 'a society whose commerce cannot deserve any other name than primitive'.[57]

Despite the vague, insubstantial and unresolved evidence relating to Dark Age Scotland the country's history, paradoxically, is rich (in comparison with other areas of Britain) in references to native centres. These are described in the sources either in the Latin as *urbs* or *civitas* (the former showing a wide range of application) or in the vernacular as *dun*—a term commonly used of forts and fortified places of all ranks.[58] *Dun* was also equated with *munitio* and *oppidum* and the use, in the *Pictish Chronicle*, of *Oppidum Fother* for Dunnottar and of *Oppidum Eden* for Edinburgh (i.e. *Dun Eideann*) suggests the interchangeability of these terms. Though certain names have defied any reasonable attempt to locate them geographically, Alcock has provided a tentative list of some sixteen sites 'intended', he states, 'partly as a basis for criticism and discussion by historians, partly as a problem of archaeological fieldwork'. Most are included because of some military action which referred to them 'in the sources as *obsessio, combustio,* or *vastatio* of Dun X . . . though mention of a battle, *bellum*, in the same phrase as a *dun* is no guarantee that the fort itself was involved in the action'.[59] Rather, as Graham earlier argued, 'allusions to battles taking place at or near forts . . . only imply that the defending force gave battle near a convenient fortified base, and that such potential bases were natural objectives for the attacker'.[60]

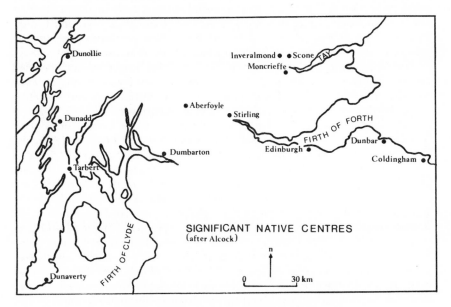

FIGURE 2   Significant Native Centres in Central Scotland

Figure 2 indicates the location of Alcock's native centres in southern Scotland though some have proved the subject of considerable debate, not least *urbs Guidi* controversially identified with Stirling's Castle Rock and one of the suggested strongholds of the Gododdin kingdom. From earliest times the rugged security of this site as a place of refuge and point of vantage must have attracted settlers, but there are no traces of early fortifications and Stirling fails to enter written history until the early twelfth century. But the description in *Historia Ecclesiastica* of *Guidi's* site and location along with that of Alt Clut, is strongly suggestive that Bede is comparing Stirling and Dumbarton Rocks, thus identifying principal strategic places—both natural fortresses—on southern Scotland's two great firths. Graham argues Stirling's early defensible advantages most forcibly: 'The Castle Rock is ideally suited to primitive methods of defence, and its command of the point where the north-going Roman road crossed the Forth must already, in the post-Roman centuries, have given it . . . strategic advantage.'[61] It also overlooked the head of navigation of the Forth and to this M E Root adds other salient site factors: 'Peat-bogs succeeding the forest lands surrounded the rock and accentuated its isolation', while in later centuries 'when the mosses were transformed into fertile plains, upon the impregnable crag was set a structure which became a residence and refuge for kings, a prison for recalcitrant subjects, and a storehouse of munitions'.[62] On all these grounds some record of a Dark Age Stirling must be inferred prior to its identification as a king's burgh in several charters early in David I's reign and to its inclusion, along with Roxburgh, Berwick and Edinburgh, in the prestigious Court of Four Burghs, a confederation that recognised the trading achievements of what were initially Scotland's most important burghs.

Among Scotland's other Dark Age 'capitals' Dumbarton has also provided concerted interest and optimistic theorising in the quest for urban origins. Here historical references, albeit fragmentary, span several centuries and comment on its battles, defences and general strategic importance.[63] In the words of Alcock: 'If there is one fortified place where we can be certain both of its identification on the ground and of its military role it is Alt Clut, Ail Cluaide, Petra Cluit, Clyde Rock; in modern terms Castle Rock, Dumbarton.'[64] Situated only eight kilometres from the western end of the Antonine Wall the rock has often been regarded as an obvious choice for a Roman fortified outpost, especially in view of the apparent military weakness of the Wall's left flank and the strategic need for some control of the Vale of Leven. To date, however, no Roman remains have been identified amongst the rock's medieval and later structures and the claim, attractive as it is, that a Roman settlement called *Theodosia* grew up around its rock is another example of the antiquarian imagination that has fancifully coloured Scotland's Dark Age. What *is* known is the troubled times that followed Strathclyde's separation from kinsmen in Wales in 613—the date attributed to the Anglian conquest of Chester—and British, Irish and English sources, though contentious and often contradictory, speak of a succession of native rulers battling first against the Picts, then against the Scots, the Norsemen and the Angles. Bede's reference to Alt Clut as *civitas* and *urbs* indicates its importance as a political centre of the Brythonic Britons and this accords with its Gaelic name *Dun Breatann*—'Fort of the Britons'. Surely the great defensive character of Dumbarton (as indeed Stirling and Edinburgh) possessed all the makings not merely of a pre-burgh nucleus but, more positively, those of a quasi-urban settlement; it is known that this native fort became a royal castle, the centre of a sherrifdom and, by 1222, a king's burgh, while its early charters granted it special privileges in respect to shipping. But again, in keeping with other native centres, the intervening centuries remain obstinately elusive and though Alcock has indicated the complimentary nature of Alt Clut's documentary and archaeological evidence— which is further supported by radio carbon dating—the broader chronologies and, equally importantly, its economic and topographical character remains unknown. If, as many have assumed, a collection of rude huts occupied the base of the fort, evidence for these has yet to be found. The rock's historicity, however, makes it an obvious choice for further excavation and multi-disciplinary study and a longer-term campaign of research on similarly documented forts might hopefully lead to a better understanding of the role of major native centres in the urbanising process.

Of the sites identified on Figure 2 many, it should be stressed, failed to generate subsequent urban traditions, a fact related as much to the poverty of their general surroundings as to their isolation from what became the main areas of medieval trade and royal control. Consequently, some of these sites, particularly Dunadd, best preserve their Dark Age structures and are of major archaeological significance; elsewhere later occupation, itself an indication of the 'fixing' roles of some native centres, has tended to obscure any earlier record of settlement either wholly or to such a degree that renders any remains of limited historical value. Stirling, Dumbarton and Edinburgh Castles are all cases in point and at Dunbar also—the British *Din-bar* ('summit fort')—there is little tangible evidence to bridge the important period between its first mention in early chronicles and its full recognition as a burgh.

Equally obscure are the archaeological and documentary chronologies for the native centres of the lower Tay, though Alcock's inclusion of Inveralmond, Scone and Moncrieff (probably Monab Croib mentioned in 729 as the scene of a battle) further supports the general thesis of significant settlement continuity throughout the area. The test case must again be Perth yet, in spite of a number of fugitive documents that speak of its early 12th century success as a port,[65] the town's pre-burgh status and, importantly, its relationship to neighbouring native centres, chiefly Scone, remains largely conjecture. Possibly the *Castellum Credi* referred to in the *Annals of Ulster*, Scone had been a place of major political influence from early Pictish times and in 728 its Mote Hill, a substantial nuclear fort, was the scene of another important Tay battle; here too

Kenneth MacAlpin, following his victory over the Picts in 843, brought about their union with the Scots to form a single kingdom of Alba north of the Forth–Clyde line. As Scotland's dynastic 'capital', therefore, Scone acquired the status for attracting a sizeable community and by 1124 it had also become the site of an influential Augustinian priory, responsible amongst other things for the colonisation of the new cathedral-priory of St Andrews. Thus, it is somewhat anomalous that despite its prestigious political and ecclesiastical functions, Scone never became a burgh, a situation that must seek explanation in the commercial competition of neighbouring Perth. One indication of this is illustrated in the fact that when Malcolm IV allowed the canons of Scone the services of a smith, skinner and tailor, these craftsmen enjoyed the privileges of the burgesses of Perth, in other words the priory was allowed to share the labour and specialised crafts of the neighbouring town.[66] There is no question, therefore, that the medieval settlements of the Perth area offer major and interesting fields for further historical and archaeological investigation, not least that involving the relationship between church and secular centres and their respective roles in burgh development.

ECCLESIASTICAL NUCLEI

In Europe the important role of religious organisation, episcopal and monastic, in urban revival has been well attested with the church, according to Pounds,[67] proving to be the principal bearer of the urban traditions of the vanished Roman Empire. The urban significance of Christianity's spread into Gaul was stressed by East[68] and similarly throughout England the old Roman towns were selected by bishops as the seats of their sees, a process that either revived or, at places like Canterbury, London, York and Lincoln, sustained something of their former administrative and economic functions. But in Scotland the role played by the church in the urbanising process is as uncertain as that played by the early centres of secular power though, possibly, the 'fixing' potentialities of some of the latter were eventually exceeded by those of the more prestigious religious sites, a tendency analogous to developments in sixth and seventh century Ireland. Ecclesiastical theory postulates the growth of towns around and under the protection of a church and though a case for continuity can be demonstrated in which a number of early shrines subsequently gained urban status—St Andrews, Glasgow, Canongate, Brechin, Dunfermline and Peebles being prominent examples—the extent to which Christian foundations acted as quasi-urban forms still awaits archaeological clarification.

In terms of its ecclesiastical organisation Scotland again fell peripheral to developments south of the border. As Smout affirms: 'Nothing shows the isolation of Scotland from England and from Europe as forcibly as the position of the church immediately before Malcolm (Canmore) came to the throne.'[69] Yet at least six centuries earlier—though as Cruden comments, 'The origins of

Christianity in Scotland are so obscure as to be beyond conjecture'[70]—the new faith had become established in the southwest. Here at Whithorn excavations have brought to light a modest and early Christian cell, possibly Ninian's *Candida Casa* referred to by Bede. From similar primitive enclaves Christianity penetrated southern Scotland with a rudimentary episcopal rather than a monastic structure firmly based on the existing framework of the native kingdoms. A fifth-century diocese centred on Carlisle[71] appears to have extended westwards into Galloway to serve Rheged. Memorial stones of the fifth and sixth centuries suggest that, together with Whithorn, Hoddom and Kirkmadrine were important sub-Roman ecclesiastical sites. By the sixth century three other dioceses can be recognised, one centred on the Tweed valley and serving northern Bryneich or Bernicia from sites such as Old Melrose, Stobo and Peebles, a second located around the Forth and serving Gododdin from Abercorn, Abernethy and possibly Kirkliston near Edinburgh, and a third corresponding with Strathclyde though whether its main religious house was situated at the traditional site of Glasgow or at Govan further west on the Clyde remains uncertain.

This early episcopal structure was fundamentally altered by organisational changes that stemmed from the arrival in the sixth century of monks from Ireland. The most renowned was Columba founder in 565 of the monastic community at Iona on the western fringes of Dalriada. In the years that followed Columban-type sanctuaries were established on islands, promontories and high ground throughout Scotland and the territorial expansion of what was essentially a missionary church meant that the older episcopal centres also adopted the monastic structure. In the Borders and Northumbria Columban Christianity came into conflict with the Roman-style religion, the Synod of Whitby in 663 being a determined bid to settle doctrinal differences and bring the Scottish Church in line with more catholic precepts. But the former never assented entirely to the Roman way and the Scandinavian period served only to promote its singularity and strengthen its separateness from England and Western Christendom.

When the saintly Margaret (queen of Malcolm III) came north she found many ritualistic and organisational irregularities in the Scottish Church, including the influential presence of eremitical communities of Culdees—the latter-day Celtic monks—whose name derived from *celí De*—'vassals of God'. The early nature of their life is not entirely certain, but whatever their origin in Ireland (where they initially constituted a conservative élite of monks) it is clear that in Scotland many Culdee communities had become lay or secular clerics and administrators. Such communities were found at Dunkeld, St Andrews and Brechin and by simple change of name the Culdees became the influential canonry of Scotland's medieval dioceses. Their liberty of action, which characterised diocesan organisation as a whole, must be postulated as a significant factor in urban growth.

From what was basically a series of infusions of Christianity, Scotland, on both sides of the Forth–Clyde axis, became the inheritor of numerous early ecclesiastical sites of which the majority—relating principally to the sixth to eleventh century period—have been recorded and briefly described by Macdonald and Laing.[72] Collectively these must again be regarded as potential pre-urban nuclei though their early eremitic character and the tendency for many to be sited away from the general ground plan of Dark Age tribal settlement were obviously precluding factors to their roles as fixing points for settlement. By virtue of such isolation Bowen, writing of Wales, claimed that 'Celtic churches . . . lacked great nucleating powers in settlement patterns',[73] though Carter[74] and others agree that they must have played some part in the urbanising process, especially those sites that became centres of cloistered communities, consisting initially of little more than a few primitive cells grouped about a small oratory. In Scotland a similar situation to that in Wales can be assumed in which some monastic 'retreats', particularly those associated with important saints and martyrs, attracted not only the devout and curious but also the enterprising. By the ninth century it was recorded that 'the little places where hermits settled . . . are now the resorts of pilgrims where thousands assemble'.[75] Provided they were conveniently located these communities afforded many of the conditions attractive to subsequent urban growth, yet there were others, including Iona, whose environmental situation pre-empted such developments. Ecclesiastical theory speaks of religious complexes maintaining administrators, craftsmen and traders and it was commonplace that a small attendant market supplied the clergy's daily needs. According to Pryde[76] the church in Glasgow (in all probability erected on the site of the earlier Celtic cell) needed the services of farmers, fishermen and sundry craftsmen—secular pursuits that provided the bases for its dual medieval role as both city and burgh. Yet not until the twelfth century does Glasgow emerge into the full light of historical record, the relevant period preceding its foundation as an ecclesiastical burgh (1175–78) remaining archaeologically and historically evasive.

Similar conditions regarding the paucity of early evidence are shared by most of the ecclesiastical settlements that became medieval burghs; even at St Andrews, the prime Scottish witness to the functional variety of a medieval town as an ecclesiastical, educational and commercial centre, written sources appear late and despite some exciting recent rescue archaeology, excavation has (so far) proved unable to fill the gaps in its chronological record. What would prove of immense value, not only to St Andrews but to the study of Scottish medieval urbanism as a whole, would be evidence proving the precise location of the pre-burgh settlement, the community associated with the early monastic enclosure of Kinrimund. That such a settlement existed is verified in Bishop Robert's foundation charter of the mid-twelfth century which refers to David I granting him the former *vill* as well as permission for establishing a burgh at what by this time was known as St Andrews. Affirming the academic value of co-ordinating a variety of topographical, documentary, archaeological and, in St Andrews case unique cartographic material, Brooks and Whittington[77] have furnished convincing inferential evidence for the site of the pre-burgh nucleus but conclude that its precise location and, more especially, its functional characteristics remain the problems of the urban archaeologist.

Charters and documents refer to *vills* belonging to other early ecclesiastical centres. Brechin, for example, an ecclesiastical and royal burgh in 1165–71, is known to have had a sizeable pre-burgh settlement, but whether this was additional to the large Culdee monastic community, which earned it the title of *magna civitas* ('the great city'), remains uncertain. Gourlay and Turner[78] suggest that the answer might lie in the town's topography for the existence of a pre-burgh secular settlement would account for the awkward axis of the town's High Street along a steep and difficult slope. Had the layout of the burgh been completely planned from its inception, it seems likely, they argue, that 'a more practical route would have been chosen'.

Another topographical problem of principal interest in the search for town origins concerns the relationship of the so-called Old Town of Peebles to that of the later burgh. As already stated, Peebles was an early Christian site and is known to have been a royal burgh in 1152–3 when rent from the *firma burgi* was assigned to the chapel of its castle,[79] yet it is not at all clear what sort of pre-burgh settlement existed west of Eddleston Water or what influence it had on the development of the burgh. Jeburgh's antecedents are equally confusing though its selection by David I as the site of an Augustinian monastery must relate to the two settlements established on the river Jed around 854 by Ecgred, Bishop of Lindisfarne. Both were referred to as Gedwearde,[80] a duplication which re-appears in David's charter to the abbey between 1147 and 1156. By 1165 Jedburgh had become a burgh and further reference to an earlier *villa* on its site suggests that its new status was the result of adult baptism rather than the creation of an entirely new foundation. Its pre-burgh importance, in fact, is supported by the discovery there of tenth- and eleventh-century coin hoards which suggest its role as a centre of exchange on the route from Northumbria to the Forth valley. At Kelso[81] also, though its development was greatly over-shadowed by the significance of Roxburgh, there are a number of inferences to what was probably an active settlement prior to the Tironensian house established there by David I in 1128. Malcolm IV's charter to the abbey uses the term *burgus* for Kelso but *vill* would seem to be more appropriate to describe the settlement that became an ecclesiastical burgh in 1237.

Certain church nuclei, therefore, appear to have played active roles in the processes of both urban siting and growth. Scotland's medieval cathedrals, for example, not least Glasgow and St Andrews, occupied the sites of earlier Christian cells and as episcopal organisation became more sophisticated the corresponding needs for increased services by the mother churches provided a firm basis for urban growth. Similarly the early Christian sites of the Borders (as well as elsewhere in Scotland) were instrumental in attracting monastic foundations around which a town could develop. But this process could not have been quite so simplistic and the extent to which such founding was also influenced by the presence of an Anglo-Norman motte or castle is another issue that seeks consideration.

THE CONTINUITY QUESTION

Such is the state of Scotland's early documentation that the preceding discussions on urban origins have been forced to rely heavily on inferential arguments and, wherever possible, have sought the support of comparisons and conclusions from other parts of Britain. In view of this many might argue that the conventional idea of Scotland's medieval burghs as being the products of 'imported' Anglo-Norman urbanism has not been significantly challenged. Yet in the face of evidence from other regions of Dark Age Europe suggesting early forms of urban life or urban nuclei, it is becoming increasingly difficult to exempt Scotland from these processes of change that led towards fixed urban forms of settlement. Some order of incipient urbanism prior to the eleventh century must have provided the basis for the more dramatic and sweeping changes that accompanied the feudal age.

The pervading theme of the foregoing discussions has been settlement continuity and it is worth stressing again that on both sides of the Forth–Clyde line territorial boundaries and settlement locations have shown a remarkable degree of historical persistence. The growth of Pictland, for example, can be traced from the late Bronze Age through to early Christian times and beyond, while it has already been shown that the tribal structure of the Roman Iron Age formed the basis of the early British kingdoms as well as the diocesan divisions of the church in southern Scotland, later to be adapted for feudal purposes. In view of this continuity it seems reasonable to suppose that native centres, secular and ecclesiastical, correspondingly grew in influence and stature, but the question to be asked is the extent and level to which continuity can be projected into the post-1100 period. Did the feudal age bring changes in settlement sites in addition to those changes that affected Scotland's society and economy in general, or was the clearly identified urbanisation of the Anglo-Norman period a reflection of a process already under way?

The beginnings of Anglicisation in Scotland can be traced to the foundation of the House of Canmore by Malcolm III whose marriage to Margaret, a devout Saxon princess, led (as intimated below) to a phase of church building in the English manner. The Benedictine house at Dunfermline, the foundations of which remain under the nave of the later abbey, was founded by Margaret *c.* 1074 and it is significant that it was a daughter-house of Christ Church, Canterbury, the mother-church of Christianity in Britain. Though a period of anti-foreign national resistance followed the deaths of Malcolm and Margaret the pro-English policy of the Canmore dynasty developed into pro-Norman under Malcolm's youngest son David I whose reign might be said to mark the beginnings of feudal Scotland. Having been raised in an English court David brought many Normans to Scotland giving them grants of land together with important lay and church offices. Most of these settlers, French and Flemish as well as English, were established in small fiefs but extensive estates were also created in areas not ruled directly by the king. Regular monasticism, as already seen, also flourished as a result of David's patronage. Thus, both landed estate and a powerful church established Anglo-Norman feudalism as the basis of government, a factor that had a radical effect, in lowland Scotland at least, on the character of settlement. Above all it led to the growth of towns on the English model and with them an economy dependent on the burgh as the territorial focus of trade.

The spread of Anglo-Norman influence is readily represented by the distribution of mottes (Figure 3), a pattern which also provides a useful commentary on the question of continuity between feudal and earlier times. These earthen mounds, crowned by and sometimes incorporating a timber tower, were the strongholds of the new feudal lords and, consequently, they too must be regarded as potential urban fixing points. Though widespread, their distribution is noticeably uneven; they are most numerous in southwest Scotland, in Ayrshire, the Clyde Valley and Mentieth, with a fair spread in Fife, Angus and the northeast lowlands, all areas where the crown was initially dependent for much of its authority on the allegiance and local control of landed magnates. For obvious reasons mottes are scarce within the Highland region and, significantly, also in the southeast—the Lothians and the Borders—an area of intensive feudal settlement securely held by the crown. The question arises, therefore, as to what part mottes played as pre-urban nuclei, to which Adams has no hesitation in replying 'in the early stages it appears to have been very little'.[82] Surviving mottes in centres like Lanark, Peebles and Elgin probably represent the early remains of castles associated with the establishment of royal burghs, but elsewhere in lowland Scotland they were initally inactive in sponsoring urban growth. This is well illustrated in Galloway where, in spite of their large number, urban life was poorly developed. 'Only later', as Adams again affirms, 'does one find burghs of Barony being erected in the lee of these by then derelict structures.'

In contrast, the Scottish medieval castle was a very different matter. Some, as instanced above, had their origins in earlier mottes, but a convincing number, rather than being erected *de novo* sought out the old native centres whose sites guaranteed the Scottish kings a tested method of control. The distributions of selected Anglo-Norman foundations are shown in Figure 4 and collectively they summarise the predominant areas of feudal influence. The burghs refer to those established by 1214 and it takes no expert eye to appreciate the close areal

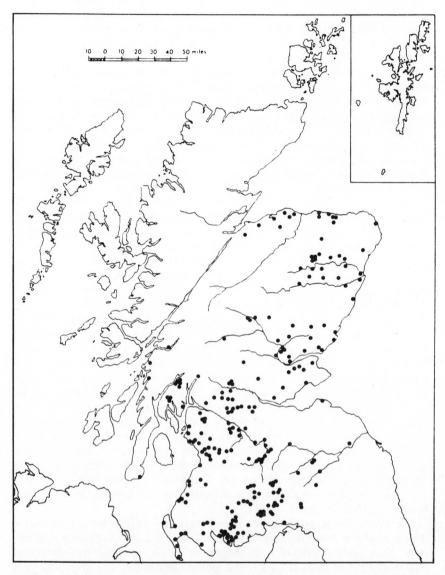

FIGURE 3   The distribution of Anglo-Norman mottes or castle mounds. (Reproduced from P McNeill and R Nicholson, *An Historical Atlas of Scotland, c400–c1600.* University of St Andrews, 1975)

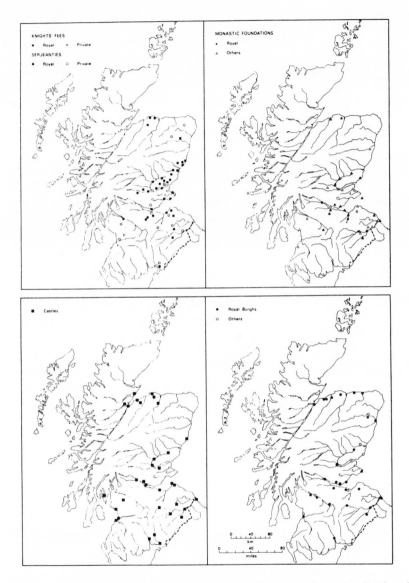

FIGURE 4   Early Norman foundations recorded by 1214 (castles by 1249) showing the main areas of Norman influence and later of strong burgh evolution (after Simpson and Webster and Adams). (Reproduced from *The Making of Urban Scotland*, I A Adams, Croom Helm, 1978)

correlation between their location and other feudal institutions. In addition, and basic to the tenets of this study, these burghs, with few exceptions, occupy either the sites or relate to the general localities of one or more of the pre-urban nuclei suggested below as being central to the urban fixing process. But as well as defence and territorial control, the economic motive was equally strong in early burgh siting. As stressed earlier the king's revenue came from his burghs and though the scale of local and regional trade was undoubtedly modest, it is clear that the king favoured what must already have been established centres. Perth, the most rapidly developed of David I's burghs, is the clearest example of this for the growth it shows by the middle of the century, stresses Duncan, 'could not be the consequence of only fifty years of development no matter how active the king's encouragement.'[83] At Perth, therefore, there is strong indication that its urban roots pre-date its growth as a burgh and on this example alone the simple picture of the Anglo-Norman introduction of town life into Scotland has to be questioned.

REFERENCES

(Abbreviation, *PSAS—Proceedings of the Society of Antiquaries, Scotland*)

1 For a useful summary of the leading theories, together with critical papers on medieval town origins, see J F Benton (ed.), *Town Origins: The Evidence from Medieval England* (Boston, 1968).
2 H Pirenne, *Medieval Cities* (Princeton, 1949).
3 Ibid. p. 105.
4 F L Ganshof *Etude sur le Développement des Villes entre Loire et Rhin au Moyen Age* (Paris-Bruxelles, 1943).
5 A M Lambert, *The Making of the Dutch Landscape* (London and New York, 1971), pp. 137–8.
6 C T Smith, *An Historical Geography of Western Europe before 1800* (London, 1967), p. 297.
7 E Ennen, 'Les différents Types de formation des Villes Européennes', *Le Moyen Age*, II (1956), 399–411; see also ibid., *Frühgeschichte de europäischen Stadt*, (Bonn, 1953).
8 N J G Pounds, *An Historical Geography of Europe, 450 BC–AD 1330* (Cambridge, 1973), p. 263.
9 S Piggott and W D Simpson, *Illustrated Guide to Ancient Monuments. Vol. VI: Scotland* (Edinburgh, 1970), p. 10.
10 For the basis of this type of analysis see C Fox, *The Personality of Britain* (4th edn) (Cardiff, 1947), pp. 15–24.
11 J D Mackie, *A History of Scotland* (London, 1964), p. 11.
12 Many have argued that Scottish 'medieval' conditions, which were reflected in urban form and function, ended only with the Treaty of Union in 1707.
13 See G S Pryde, *The Burghs of Scotland: A Critical List* (Oxford, 1965).

14 T Thomson and C Innes (*et al.*), *The Acts of the Parliaments of Scotland*, vol. I, p. 76.

15 The term *burgus* is early applied to Kelso in the charter of Malcolm IV which confers a number of previous grants on the abbey.

16 C Innes, *Ancient Laws and Customs of the Burghs of Scotland*, xliii.

17 For distribution maps of medieval burghs and accompanying texts see P McNeill and R Nicholson, *An Historical Atlas of Scotland* c.400–c.1600 (St Andrews, 1975).

18 R C Fox, The Burghs of Scotland 1327, 1601, 1670. *Area* 13, no. 2 (1981), pp. 161–7.

19 T C Smout, *A History of the Scottish People 1560–1830* (London, 1973), p. 28.

20 D Murray, *Early Burgh Organisation in Scotland* (Glasgow, 1924).

21 W M MacKenzie, *The Scottish Burghs* (Edinburgh, 1949).

22 J M Houston, 'The Scottish Burgh', *Town Planning Review* 25 (1954–5), 114–27.

23 A A M Duncan, *The Edinburgh History of Scotland Volume I: The Making of the Kingdom* (Edinburgh, 1978), p. 465. See also: 'Perth: the first century of the burgh', *Trans. Proc. Perthshire Soc. Nat. Sci.* 11 (1974), 30–50.

24 McNeill and Nicholson (1975), p. 20.

25 A A M Duncan (1978), p. 475.

26 N P Brooks, 'Urban Archaeology in Scotland' in M W Barley (ed.), *The Archaeology and History of the European Town*, Council for British Archaeology (London, 1977).

27 H Carter, *The Towns of Wales* (Cardiff, 1966).

28 I H Adams, *The Making of Urban Scotland* (London, 1978).

29 H Carter (1966), pp. 3–4.

30 R A Butlin (ed.), *The Development of the Irish Town* (London, 1977).

31 F H Aalock, *Man and the Landscape in Ireland* (London, 1978).

32 S S Frere, 'The end of towns in Roman Britain', in J S Wacher, *The Civitas Capitals of Roman Britain* (Leicester, 1966), p. 87.

33 J Wacher, *The Towns of Roman Britain* (London, 1974), p. 411.

34 D Hill, 'The Burghal Hidage: the establishment of a text', *Medieval Archaeol*, 13 (1969), 84–92.

35 V E Nash-Williams, *The Roman Frontier in Wales* (Cardiff, 1969).

36 A Piggott, 'Native Economies and the Roman Occupation of North Britain', in I Richmond (ed.), *Roman and Native in North Britain* (London, 1958).

37 D C A Shotter, 'Coin evidence and the northern frontier in the second century AD, *PSAS*, 107 (1975–6), 81–92.

38 See R C Bosanquet, 'The Roman Camp at Housesteads', *Archaeologia Aeliana* (2nd series), 25 (1904), 193–300. For the civil settlement see *Archaeologia Seliana* (4th series), 1932 onwards.

39 P Salway, *The Frontier People of Roman Britain* (Cambridge, 1965).

40 A Graham, 'Archaeological notes on some harbours in eastern Scotland', *PSAS*, 101 (1968–9), 200–85.

41 Duncan (1978), pp. 471–2.

42 R E Birley, 'Excavations of the Roman fortress at Carpow, Perthshire, 1961–2', *PSAS* 96 (1962–3), 184–208.

43 R W Feachem, 'The fortifications on Traprain Law', *PSAS*, 89 (1955–6), 282–9.

44   See A O Curle, *The Treasure of Traprain* (Glasgow, 1923).
45   R W Feachem, *A Guide to Prehistoric Scotland* (London, 1963), p. 121.
46   For the Anglian advance into southeast Scotland based on place-name interpreta-
     tion, see McNeill and Nicholson (1975).
47   See note in *Medieval Antiquity,* **10** (1966), 176–7.
48   L Laing, *The Archaeology of Late Celtic Britain and Ireland* c.400–1200 AD
     (London, 1975), p. 69.
49   R W Feachem, 'Fortifications', in F Wainwright (ed.), *Problem of the Picts*
     (London, 1955), pp. 66–86.
50   A Graham, 'The nuclear fort of Dalmahoy, Midlothian, and other Dark Age
     capitals', *PSAS* **83** (1948–9).
51   H Carter, (1966), p. 10.
52   E A Lewis, *The Medieval Boroughs of Snowdonia* (London, 1912).
53   T Jones Pierce, 'A Caernarvonshire manorial borough', *Trans. Caernarvon Hist.
     Soc.* **3** (1941), 9.
54   P H Sawyer, 'The Vikings and the Irish Sea', in Moore, D (ed.), *The Irish Sea
     Province in Archaeology and History* (1971), p. 91.
55   J R C Hamilton, *Excavations at Jarlshof, Shetland* (Edinburgh, 1956).
56   R Gourlay and A Turner, *Scottish Burgh Survey: Kirkwall* (Dept. of Arch., Univ. of
     Glasgow (1977), 2).
57   A A M Duncan (1978), p. 463.
58   See A Graham, 'Archaeological gleanings from Dark Age Scotland', *PSAS,* **85**
     (1950–1), 64–91.
59   L Alcock, 'A multi-disciplinary chronology for Alt Clut, Castle Rock, Dumbarton',
     PSAS, **107** (1975–6), 103.
60   A Graham (1950–1), p. 74.
61   A Graham, 'Guidi', in Notes and News, *Antiquity* **33** (1959), 63–5.
62   M E Root, *Stirling Castle: History* (Edinburgh, 1948), p. 13.
63   I MacIvor, *Dumbarton Castle* (Edinburgh, 1958).
64   L Alcock, (1975–6), pp. 104–5.
65   A Graham, 'Archaeological notes on some harbours in eastern Scotland' (Perth),
     op. cit.
66   Duncan (1978), p. 470.
67   N J G Pounds (1973), p. 190.
68   W G East, *An Historical Geography of Europe* (London, 1967), p. 113.
69   T C Smout, (1969), p. 20.
70   S Cruden, *Scottish Abbeys* (Edinburgh, 1960), p. 10.
71   L Laing (1975), p. 42f.
72   A D S Macdonald and R L Laing 'Early Ecclesiastical sites in Scotland: a field survey,
     parts 1 and 2', *PSAS* (1967–8), pp. 123–44 and (1969–70), pp. 129–45.
73   E G Bowen, *The Settlements of the Celtic Saints in Wales* (Cardiff, 1956).
74   H Carter (1966).
75   As quoted by S Cruden (1960), p. 13.
76   G S Pryde, 'The city and burgh of Glasgow 1100–1750', in R Miller and J Tivy
     (eds.). *The Glasgow Region,* (British Association, 1958).
77   N P Brooks and G Whittington, 'Planning and growth in the medieval Scottish
     burgh: an example of St Andrews', *Trans. Inst. Brit. Geogrs.* **2**, no. 3 (1977),
     278–95.

78 R Gourlay and A Turner, *Scottish Burgh Survey: Brechin* (Dept. of Archaeology, Univ. of Glasgow, 1977).

79 *Royal Commission on the Ancient and Historical Monuments of Scotland: Peeble-shire* (Edinburgh, 1967).

80 Ibid. *The County of Roxburgh.*

81 A T Simpson and S Stevenson, *Scottish Burgh Survey: Kelso* (Dept. of Archaeology, Univ. of Glasgow, 1980).

82 Adams (1978), p. 16.

83 Duncan (1978), p. 470.

3

STIRLING 1550–1700
The morphology and functions of a pre-industrial Scottish burgh

R C Fox

This study of Stirling is divided into two main sections; the first examines the various components of the burgh's distinctive pre-industrial morphology, relating medieval appearance to functional necessity, and the second assesses the role of the local decision-makers who, constrained by both natural factors and by the social and institutional frameworks of the time, were collectively responsible for the burgh's townscape and functional organisation. Primarily the study presents a static 'period picture' of the burgh and draws its evidence from a variety of sources including Council Records and those of guild and trade incorporations, the Register of Sasines (which recorded the legal possession of feudal property) and Royal Charters. Thus, most of the study relies on a synthesis of dissimilar material to give an overall picture of the pre-industrial burgh. For the period under discussion only the Hearth Tax provides a systematic and comprehensive data source and its evidence is briefly discussed at the conclusion of this study.

SITE FACTORS AND DEFENCES

Local geographical factors in the guise of site and situational advantages were the dominant influences on the groundplan and general layout of Scotland's early burghs. Between them they usually dictated the location of the castle, often provided the natural amenity of a harbour and invariably influenced the alignment of traffic routes into and through the settlement which in turn were commonly related to the nodal advantage of a river crossing. On all these counts Stirling might be regarded as a classic example of the close relationship between local topography and burgh form. Its Castle Rock, in geological terms a volcanic sill remarkably similar to Castle Rock, Edinburgh, rises abruptly above the carselands to the east, west and north.[1] From earliest times it provided a natural defensible site, while the narrow ridge sloping eastwards from the fortalice provided the basis (again as in Edinburgh) for the burgh's civil settlement. Yet Stirling's position can also be compared with that of Perth[2] for both burghs came to occupy the foci of converging routeways at what, in pre-industrial times, were the lowest bridging points of the rivers Forth and

52

Tay, respectively. It is no coincidence, therefore, that Stirling, Edinburgh and Perth were traditionally regarded as Scotland's three main strongpoints; by the middle of the fifteenth century both Stirling and Edinburgh had acquired substantial stone fortifications, while Perth's defences consisted first of a palisaded clay and turf wall and a ditch which was followed by a stone enceinte. Elsewhere in Scotland burgh defences had a more limited visual impact though individual centres took every advantage of natural features for protection and defence. Both Inverness and Aberdeen were enclosed by ditches and earthworks,[3] Dunbar was partially protected by an early seaward wall and at St Andrews the extant half mile of towered wall on the burgh's southeast side (rebuilt in the early sixteenth century) protected the priory rather than the town proper.

Stirling's burgh wall, one of the fundamental elements in the town's pre-industrial structure, had the dual function of securing its population and of constraining their day-to-day activities. No mural remains are extant on the burgh's northern side, but here the river Forth, though somewhat distant across the Burgh Roads, Shiphaugh and Burgh Muirs (Figure 1), provided a useful outer defensive line while the inner defences, probably linked the tails of the burgages and followed the sharp break of slope of the Little Gowan Hills. Stone from the Easter Crags quarry (adjacent to the Burgh Gate in the southeast) was used for the construction of defences and the Council Records of 26 October 1547, stress the need for both labour and money

> to be expendit upone the strengthing
> and bigging of the Wallis of the toun,
> at this peralys tyme of neid, for
> resisting of our auld innimeis of Ingland.[4]

The castle played a major role in the burgh's defence. At the time of Edward I's invasion it was reckoned to be the strongest in Scotland but by Stuart times, though its role as a vital strategic fortress was maintained, the castle had become a permanent royal residence. Long before the sixteenth century it had acquired its commanding architectural dignity, its Great Hall functioning as both parliamentary chamber and the venue for state ceremonies. But it was the Palace, commissioned by James V that greatly enhanced the image and fashionability of both castle and burgh throughout Scotland. In many historic burghs it is sometimes difficult to appreciate the significance of the castle as an element in burgh planning, but at Stirling, as at Edinburgh, its contemporary national and local prestige was matched by its visual prominence and topographical position. As if to underline the dual urban functions of crown and church, Stirling's Holy Rude, 'the most dramatically sited of all medieval burgh kirks'[5] further enhanced the dramatic skyline.

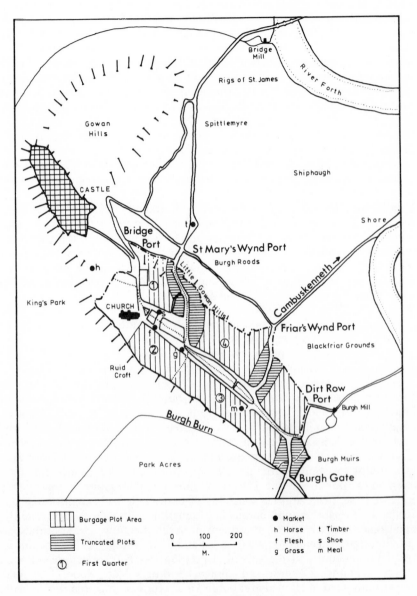

FIGURE 1   Medieval Stirling

BURGH GATES AND ACCESS

In peacetime the predominant function of the burgh defence was that of a toll, and customs barrier. As Houston has commented: 'In view of the trading privileges within each free burgh, the exact delimitation of the burgh was essential whether the town had a defensive site or not'.[6] Access was restricted to the ports or gates which were closed at night and could be closed in times of danger, not least epidemics. Stirling's traffic was funnelled through five ports—the Burgh Gate or Barres Yett, Dirt Row Port which led to the Burgh Mill, Friar's Wynd Port to Cambuskenneth Abbey, and St Mary's Wynd Port and Bridge Port, both leading to the old bridge. Built in 1591, the Burgh Gate, as the only entry from the south, formed the principal means of access. In keeping with its important function it comprised of a monumental arched structure from which hung a large iron gate and portcullis. Yet all the ports were wide enough to admit a horse-drawn cart, a regulation that served the burgh's commercial needs. Within its defences Stirling's pre-industrial street pattern took its basic form from a single through street, a structural characteristic which Whitehand and Alauddin[7] have shown to be present in the majority of early Scottish burghs. In Stirling this main artery was the old *Hie Gait* which by the sixteenth century had assumed a number of street nomenclatures, yet it maintained its original alignment and in the southeast section its original name. Figures 1 and 2 illustrate its original lozenge shape—wide in the middle but tapering at both ends. On entering the town through the Burgh Gate this southeast to northwest axis, after first forming High Street, progressed along Baxter Wynd to the Belgebrig* (Figure 2) where it turned north at Bow Street, skirting the lower end of High Street before descending St Mary's Wynd to the latter's port and then the bridge. In places steep, narrow and otherwise congested, a mark of its importance was reflected in the fact that throughout its length it was paved, a characteristic shared only with High Street and Castle Wynd. The latter, descending steeply from the castle forecourt, forked to form the broad wedge of High Street and the Back Row or Flesh Market which provided a more direct downhill link with the southeastern part of the burgh. Mears' highly diagrammatic sketch of Stirling's early morphology indicates a large open market area (Figure 3) in which subsequent building encroachment led to its subdivision into High Street (modern Broad Street) and Back Row—contemporary St John Street with Baker Street, Spittal Street and King Street forming its extensions.

THE BURGAGES

The confining influence of Stirling's defences, together with the internal arrangement of its streets and wynds, governed the pattern and linear orienta-

---

* The Belgebrig was an arched bridge over a small stream that ran through the middle of the burgh.

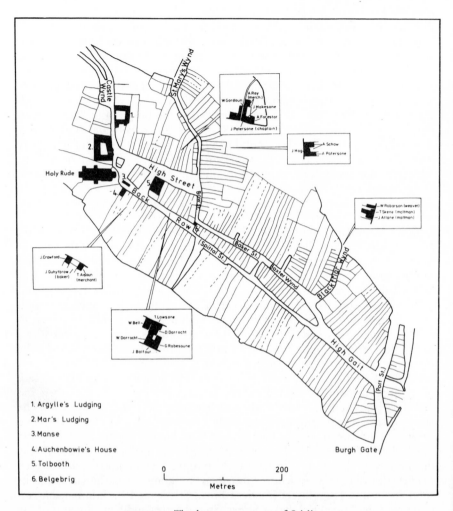

1. Argylle's Ludging
2. Mar's Ludging
3. Manse
4. Auchenbowie's House
5. Tolbooth
6. Belgebrig

0   200
Metres

FIGURE 2   The burgage pattern of Stirling

tion of the burgh lands. This influence, of course, was reciprocal for the arrangement of the burgh's original arable rigs, abutting at right angles to the built-up access-ways was a major determinant in the alignment and dimension of wynds and closes. Burgh lands were divided amongst the burgesses and property ownership was a pre-requisite for admission to their enfranchised community. The normal unit was the house lot or tenement burgage consisting of a narrow-fronted dwelling house behind which a strip of land extended often to the burgh boundaries. Toft was a term originally applied to the dwelling only, though subsequently it came to refer to the house site rather than to the actual building. The dimensions of these strip-shaped plots were initially conditioned by the former arable rigs and, consequently, many were still the original rood size, a feature that was also significant in the pre-industrial plan of Edinburgh.[8] Such were the physical pressures on space in all Scottish towns, however, that the width of street frontages was subsequently set by the Laws of the Four Burghs at one burgh perch (said to have been three metres),[9] though in practice burgage widths and lengths varied considerably on account of local site factors and as a result of internal amalgamation, exchange and general reorganisation of the burgh's lands. By the sixteenth century Stirling's burgages and associated property units can be distinguished into four broad types (Figures 2 and 3) which, in effect, formed the basic planning framework of the pre-industrial burgh.

Most conspicuous on Figure 2 are the series of lengthy burgages extending back from the central street axis to form a uniform, especially to the south of High Gait etc., herring-bone pattern. Some illustrate the process of burgage infill of what were initially agricultural allotments. Much of the pressure on burgage sites came from craftsmen needing workshops or storage areas and the use of closes and pends became the most convenient way of linking their outbuildings and yards with the burgh's streets. Wynds, closes and pends were (and still are) a common feature to other Scottish burghs. In a plan of Edinburgh in 1742[10] there were 186 wynds and closes which represented the built-up area enclosing the rigs and access paths. In Stirling the process of infill, or what Conzen[11] terms burgage repletion, is best illustrated in the plots running between High Street and St Mary's Wynd. Thus the truncated plots in this part of the burgh, together with those on either side of Blackfriar's Wynd and adjacent to the Burgh Gate formed the second morphological type of burgage structure. But though related to infill their truncated linear form was primarily a function of street and wynd alignments which precluded the development of 'standard' burgage dimensions. Restrictions on space, therefore, and the above-mentioned land requirements for enfranchisement were the factors responsible for this second, albeit unevenly developed pattern.

With intra-mural space at a premium in the majority of pre-industrial towns the burgess traders were often forced to encroach on what were the only areas of available land—those originally set aside for markets where the all-important exchange of goods and services generated within the local hinterland took place. A comparison of Figures 1 and 2 reveals this process of 'market colonisation' which can be regarded as Stirling's third type of property element. By the sixteenth century merchants and craftsmen in the High Street–Back Row area had replaced their temporary trading booths by more permanent structures, a repletion process which seems to have received full burgh condonement when

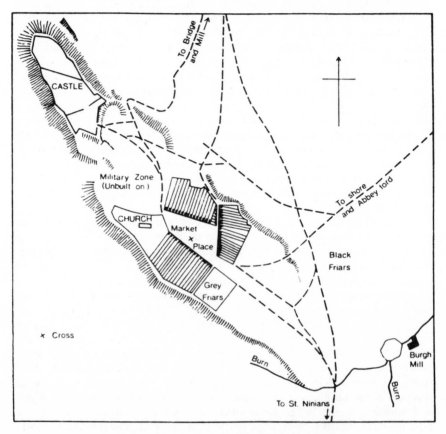

FIGURE 3   The morphology of Stirling (after Mears)

the Tolbooth, whose present structure dates from 1704, was built to face High Street and its mercat cross. Market colonisation was also a significant feature to the east of the Belgebrig where the formerly wide Hie Gait, as far as Blackfriar's Wynd, was divided into two streets whose alignments today are preserved as Baker Street and Spittal Street. In Hie Gait the shape and alignment of these market colonies were obviously governed by those of the properties surrounding them and their fragmentation, still represented in Stirling's contemporary street plan, reflected both piecemeal development and the need for transverse access between Baxter Wynd and Spittal Street. These colonies reflected the burgh's expanding commercial activities. Workshops and a strong presence of breweries (common to all early burghs where water supplies were unsafe) characterised Middle Row, while forebooths specialising in a variety of produce fronted many dwellings.

In comparison with Stirling's range of burgage holdings the fourth type of property element was markedly different and indicative of the town's status as an eminent Royal Burgh whose castle was both a stronghold and royal residence, a functional duality that ended only with the 'Forty-five'. Thus the burgh lands adjacent to the castle in the northwest were occupied by large and separate property units whose structural differences from the 'standard' burgages were further emphasised in building architecture. Such properties included the church and burial ground of the famous Holy Rude, one of the few medieval kirks remaining in Scotland, Cowane's Hospital (built in 1639—49 on the wish John Cowane for the support of 'tuelf decayed gilbrother'[12]), the Valley lands that formed an open area and pleasance and a number of noblemen's town houses or lodgings. According to Nimmo[13] the latter belonged to the Earls of Morton, Glencairn, Cassilis, Eglinton, Lennox, Montrose, Linlithgow, Buchan, Argylle and Mar, and to Lords Semphill, Cathcart, Ochiltree, Glammis, Ruthven and Methven.

Yet there was another side to pre-industrial Stirling's 'quality of life'. A pervasive element was the amount of filth and rubbish that accumulated its streets. The Council Records of 16 December, 1616, graphically describe the conditions of its byeways and ordered that

> . . . all the nichtbouris of this burgh to remove their fuilyie aff the hie streittis, and noch to lay the same thair upoun heirinafter nor suffer the same to ly longer than 24 houris efter the same is brucht out of thair houssis and cloissis; and ordanes all the present middingis to be tane off the streittis betwix this and the first day of Januar nixt.[14]

High building densities, together with the congested mixture of housing, workshops, byres and other agricultural properties were collectively responsible for insanitary accumulations of waste, as were the street markets whose locations were determined by the burgh council.

THE MARKETS

As in all medieval and post-medieval towns, access to and within the town was a crucial factor. Stirling's markets were sited in relation to the burgh's through route though they were not on it. High Street, Back Row and Middle Row were the main commercial venues and housed the important flesh, grass and shoe markets, while the meal market functioned where High Gait adjoined Back Row, a location known as 'Archie's Nuick'. Here grain was sold to the burgh bakers and seed to the crofters of the surrounding region. Stirling's timber and horse markets, both requiring more space and manoeuvrability, occupied locations beyond the burgh defences to the northeast and northwest respectively.

All streets that acted as market venues needed sufficient breadth to facilitate the delivery of goods, the passage of pedestrians and animals and the setting up of stalls or forebooths from which traders and craftsmen plied their produce and wares. These were usually leased separately from the properties they fronted and in High Street the Sasines refer to the forebooths that faced onto the mercat cross and Tolbooth, both of which symbolised the trading functions of the burgh. Here, as in Middle Row, street congestion was intense, a condition that was somewhat eased in Back Row with the central alignment of the fleshers' forebooths downhill from the manse. Its steepness facilitated drainage and some graphic accounts describe the mixture of blood and offal that crept downslope, a prime cause no doubt of the Council's continued pleas for cleanliness.

In order to facilitate movement and ease congestion both burgh and royal decrees endeavoured to keep the through route free from all manner of obstruction, even to the extent of clearing away forestairs that led from street level up to property entrances. The Council, it seems, was ever vigilant against encroachment and on 7 November 1547, was forced to consider

> . . . the narrowness of the passage at the nuke and poine passade to the touin burne (*near the Burgh Gate*) qunair William Malice usis Schoing hors, the rouim is nocht convenient tharto becaws of stopping of passage, that nother horsmen, futmen nor leid men, may gudlie pass by but cummir, and therfoir has dischargit the said William of all schoing of hors in the saide passage frathis our furth undir the pane of ane unlaw.[15]

The Burgh Council's other main concern was that of maintaining the monopolistic trading privileges of the burgesses which meant the levying of various dues that collectively went to the upkeep of burgh ports, market places, the bridge, the shore and the Tolbooth, where market produce was weighed. Bridge, port and market dues provide interesting information not only of the finances accruing to the burgh but also of the local produce exchanged and exported. Table 1 refers to the market custom dues levied in 1641, though the amounts were doubled for the periods covered by Stirling's four annual fairs. With one exception all burgesses and freemen were exempt from market dues, a significant financial advantage of burgess and guild membership. However, they were liable to bridge duties though, as Table 2 indicates, these were substantially lower than for non-burgesses and unfreemen. Port Custom dues were also selective and varying rates applied to freemen of the burgh, freemen from

Table 1   *Market custom dues 1641*

	Pence
One load of merchandise: skins and hides	8
wool	8
lint and hemp	8
One burden of merchandise, hemp, skins, wool, etc.	4
One horse-load of flesh, fishes, grain, other provisions	4
One burden of flesh, other provisions, etc.	2
One load of ploughgraith, carts, wains, harrows, barrows, etc.	4
One load of lime, earthen pots and pitchers (imported/exported)	4
One burden of lime, earthen pots and pitchers (imported/exported)	2
One horse, mare, staig, ox or cow	8
One sheep fit for slaughter	2
One lamb	1
One score of geese	12
One stone of wool, butter, cheese, tallow, Scots lint, weighed and sold in the Burgh: by Freemen	2
by others	4
Stand room and hall mail for each load of victual imported	12
For the measuring of each load of victuals sold and measured	12

Table 2   *Bridge duties 1641*

	Pence Burgesses and Freemen	Non-burgesses and Unfreemen
One sack of wool, cloth, skins, lint, hemp and plaidings	2	24
One load* of butter, cheese, tallow, iron	6	12
One load* of victuals, flesh, fish and other provisions	4	8
One load* of salt, plants, leek or fruit	2	4
One horse load of hides	4	16
One horse, mare (to be sold)	6	12
One ox or cow	4	8
One sheep	1	2
One swine	4	8
One tun of wine	?	24
One tun of beer	?	16
One load of ale	?	8
One load of coal	?	1

* One burden charged half duty

other burghs and unfreemen. For a number of items Stirling's burgesses were charged substantially lighter duties, especially on hides and skins which formed an important source of local revenue and a major article of export, particularly to the Low Countries. The burgh's skinners and tanners were concentrated at the 'skinners mailing', a cluster of tanpits sited adjacent to the Burgh Burn, east of the Burgh Gate. But it was weaving that formed Stirling's staple craft industry. Demanding little more in terms of facilities than a room or a shed attached to a property, the weaving trade was scattered throughout the town. Its significance can be gauged from the frequency with which the activities and competition of the weavers of the surrounding villages of Castlehill, Bannockburn, Cambusbarron and Torbrex are mentioned in the Council Records.[16] Other significant trades included the pottery within Dirt Row Port and the maltings in Blackfriars Wynd.

THE DECISION-MAKERS AND URBAN ZONES

A wide literature now exists on the relevance of the behaviour approach to an understanding of urban form and the second part of this essay attempts to explain the morphological and functional characteristics of pre-industrial Stirling with reference to the burgh's main decision-making bodies. 'Urban development', according to Webber,[17] 'has been guided, directed, stimulated at some points, redirected or perhaps blocked at other points, through a complex and never ending stream of decisions, some of them public and many of them private'. A similar argument is voiced by Carter who stresses that 'the idea of control over the decision-making process is essentially bound up with organised central control which is an expression of power and influence within the hands of an individual or corporate body'.[18] From the time of its first Charter both Scottish Crown and Burgh Council formed Stirling's paramount decision-making authorities. The influence of the latter on such major functional aspects as the location of burgh markets and the width of streets and wynds has already been indicated; yet in other ways, and due mainly to its effective control of burgage land, the Burgh Council was instrumental in both initiating and maintaining functional and morphological zones based on commercial, manufacturing and, in particular, residential locational preferences.

The rights and privileges of the burgess community were concomitant with the holding of burgage lands, an apportionment system introduced at the time of burgh foundation as a means both of acquiring revenue and of encouraging urban development. Though by 1600 land ownership was no longer a prerequisite, the traditionally entrenched system, as indicated above, imposed major restraints on burgh layout and on urban expansion and structural compromise. As trade grew and Stirling's population increased, new burgages were laid out within the confines of the burgh defences and by 1550 the evidence indicates that this was accomplished through such processes as repletion, burgage truncation and market colonisation. Burgage revenue (originally granted to Dunfermline Abbey) had long passed to the Burgh Council which together with the trading dues discussed above went into the community's 'common good'. Thus within the defences the Council controlled the major part of urban land and was responsible for the promulgation of a range of regulations and restrictions that collectively governed development. An edict, dated 5 March 1598, reads:

> It is status and ordanit be the saidis bailleis and counsall that na person or persons presum to tak on hand to build, edifie or big, any hous or work within this burght or territorie thairof, in any tym cuming, without the adwyse and consent of the counsall of the said burgh haid thairto, undir pan of tuenty poundis money to be payit be any person or personis contravend the samyn, toties quoties, to the common guid of the said burgh.[19]

The Council also owned land outwith the burgh defences, acquired by purchase from various landowners whose readiness or reluctance to sell or exchange was a major controlling influence on the subsequent expansion of the burgh. Such transactions, transfers and annexations are detailed in the records; in 1506, for example, the Crown obtained from the Council the Gowan Hills to the northeast of the castle in exchange for the Valley and the Park Acres south of the Burgh Burn. The Church was another important land-owning authority and in 1567 Queen Mary granted the Council

> the manor places, orchards, lands, annual rents, emoluments and duties whatever which formerly belonged to the Dominican or teaching friars and Minorities or Fransciscans of our said burgh of Stirling.[20]

A number of properties were also owned by the trustees of Cowane's Hospital, known as the Over Hospital, and the other major philanthropic institution, Robert Spitall's Hospital, the Nether Hospital. Both held lands whose revenues financed almshouses, but in 1637 the Burgh Council was granted

> the advocation, donation and right of patronage of the said hospital called Spitallis Hospital and Cowanes Hospital, and with all the sundry lands, rents, tenements, and possessions whatsover belonging to the same. . . .[21]

Within the controls imposed by the land-owning bodies locational preferences, particularly in terms of residential priorities led to marked townscape contrasts and the formation of a number of distinctive urban zones. Reflecting at one end of the scale wealth and influence, and at the other basic necessity, burgh housing ranged in social status from the grand residences of the aforementioned nobility to the mean dwellings of crofters and craftsmen who had neither the funds nor (possibly) the predilection for affectation. The castle and its immediate environs proved a major pole of attraction for those residents

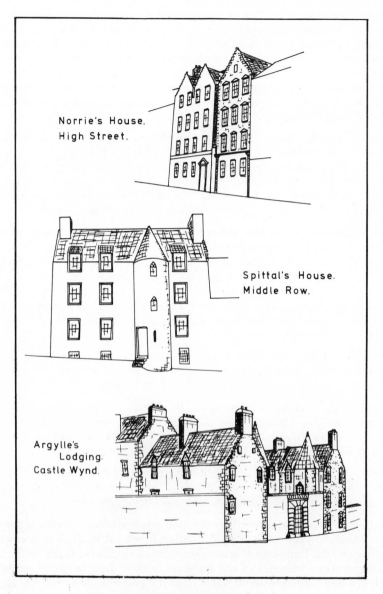

Norrie's House.
High Street.

Spittal's House.
Middle Row.

Argylle's
    Lodging.
Castle Wynd.

FIGURE 4   House types of medieval Stirling

with personal wealth and, concomitantly, social influence. The large and architecturally embellished courtyard houses of the Duke of Argylle (Figure 4) and the Earl of Mar were little less than scaled down versions of country mansions transferred to an urban setting where they aped the prestige of the royal palace. Both were protected by defensive screen walls and strong gates, necessary structural additions, especially for Mar's Ludging which in the sixteenth century housed one of Scotland's most influential families and a major power behind the Scottish throne. Built in 1570-2, yet never completed, all that survives today is the battlemented but ornate gateway—*Mar's Wark*—which stands at the head of Broad Street, the old High Street. Argylle's Ludging, in contrast, built in 1630 by William Alexander, First Earl of Stirling, and extended by Archibald Campbell, First Marquis of Argylle, remains one of the finest extant examples of seventeenth-century Scottish domestic architecture. This upper part of the burgh also contained other buildings deliberately sited for visual impact. As befitting the place where royalty was crowned and John Knox preached the Holy Rude remains a dominating building adjacent to which is Cowane's Hospital,

> . . . a commodious place within the burghe for the sustenying thairintill the nomber of tuelf decayed gilbrothers, burgessis and induellers. [22]

Completed at the cost of 'the soume of fourtie merkis usuall money of this realme', its beneficiary John Cowane was a prominent member of the burgh's guildry and the hospital (really an almshouse and subsequently the Guildhall) is recorded as being a mark of 'his zeal to the glorie of God . . . and of the love he had to this burgh'. The Tolbooth was another prominent building. Originally a duty and tax-office, by the reign of James IV it also functioned as council chamber, court house and prison—an architectural embodiment of the collective powers of the burgess community. The surviving three-storey building, complete with tower, is the design of Sir William Bruce and dates from the early years of the eighteenth century.

Unrestrained by the burgage plot structure, Stirling's northwestern sector constituted a distinctive upper-class enclave, a fashionable concentration of the nobility and affluent. The departure of the Court to England inevitably removed some of the *raison d'être* for this quarter though the High Street and Castle Wynd continued to attract influential merchants whose relative wealth was reflected in properties which occupied enlarged burgage sites. Bruce of Achenbowie's house, for example, was built adjacent to the burgh kirk on three amalgamated burgages and similar extended sites were sought after. Yet the determinant influence of the burgage is illustrated by the High Street properties of other merchants, clerks, notaries and provosts whose narrow stone-built tenements, up to three-storeys high, had their gable ends abutting · the street. By the sixteenth century French Renaissance influences, together with other building designs from the Low Countries, were reflected in such

architectural embellishments as window pediments, sometimes initialled as on
Norrie's House (Figure 4), crop-stepped gables, dressed-stone quoins and
circular stair wells (e.g. Spitall's property in Middle Row), the latter providing
access to upper floors. Roofing materials were predominantly of local origin and
chiefly slate, though pan-tiles shipped from the Low Countries as ballast were
common alternatives.

In broadest terms the affluence and social standing of Stirling's pre-
industrial inhabitants declined in a southeasterly direction away from Castle
Wynd. At the burgh's opposite end, geographically and socially, the Burgh
Burn formed the significant locating factor for the town's tanners and other
industries. Here the rough timber and thatch dwellings of the poorer classes
were associated with what undoubtedly was an untidy attendance of barns,
malt and pottery kilns and tan pits. Convenient and cheap to build, such
properties proved major fire hazards and on 9 October 1649, the Council discharged

> . . . all candlemakers and utheris of meltings of any tauche, tallow, or
> crakkingis, within the bodye of the toun fra this furthe, bot in uther roums
> of the toun, under a great pane, and the drum to go throw the toun for that
> effect. [23]

Further commentary on such zonal gradation in Stirling's pre-industrial
townscape and urban functions can be gleaned from the sources. As previously
stated, no comprehensive evidence, with the exception of the Hearth Tax
returns for 1694, is available to reveal in detail spatial patterns and variations.
Yet from the extant evidence it is possible to reconstruct, if only in the most
general way, social and occupational differences, particularly between the
burgh's northwest and southeast sections where the prime locational poles, as
noted, were the castle and the Burgh Gate and Burn, respectively. The Council
Records for 1544–50 usefully sub-divide the burgh into four almost equally
populated quarters (Figure 1) and list the property-owners in each. In the First
Quarter 105 property-owners lived in St Mary's Wynd, Castle Wynd and on the
north side of High Street. The 98 property-owners of the Second Quarter
occupied Back Row, the south part of High Street and the north side of Middle
Row. Ninety-nine owners lived to the southeast of the Belgebrig in the Third
Quarter and 103 owners occupied the Fourth Quarter which extended north of
the Belgebrig from St Mary's Wynd to Port Street. In total, however, the burgh
had 440 property-owners, 35 being landward burgesses living outside the town
defences.

Incorporated with the Council Records and the Protocol Books of the notaries
are the Register of Sasines which record the legal possession of feudal property.
Any land charter, and all buying, selling and leasing of property in Scotland
was accompanied by a precept in which the grantor authorised his ballie or representative to give 'actual, real and corporal' possession of the subject of

transfer to the grantee or his agent. This was symbolically done by handing over earth and stone or some other token of agreement, and written evidence of the transfer—the giving of Sasine—was registered by a notary public in the Protocol Books. For the 1550–1650 period, 89 Sasines are preserved in the Burgh Records; they name the buyers and sellers, describe the property concerned in the transaction and, what is of considerable interest, occasionally refer to the occupations of the transactors. Frequently, too, an accurate location of the property is given, though references such as 'the kingis hie way' are of little value since technically every street belonged to the king. In 1556 the transference of property is recorded between Walter Cowsland (burgess) and James Makesome and his wife. It concerned a tenement and its yard (Figure 2) on the north side (no street is named) opposite the mercat cross between the tenement of Sir John Patersone (chaplain) on the west, A Forester of Garden on the east, the common way (High Street) on the south and A Roy's yard on the north. The transaction also included life rental of the forebooth which fronted the tenement. Other 'neighbourhood' reconstructions are possible from the Sasines and these are also located on Figure 2.

With reference to Sjoberg's[24] class model of the pre-industrial town it is possible, albeit crudely, to relate the information recorded in the Sasines to Stirling's four quarters outlined above. An elite class, consisting of king, nobles, court officials, military and religious leaders occupied the top of Sjoberg's pre-industrial social and occupational hierarchy. The lower class, which Langton[25] further subdivides, was primarily composed of the merchant burgesses and included such influential personages equivalent to Stirling's burgh provost and deacon of the merchant guild, other burgh officials and some craftsmen. The third division of pre-industrial urban society consisted of the so-termed 'outcasts', a varied group including night-soil carriers, leather workers, midwives, prostitutes and lepers—all trades, occupations and human conditions, in fact, regarded as 'unpleasant'.

Though dominated by the burgesses, Stirling's First Quarter included a substantial number belonging to the elitist group including, as already seen, the Earl of Mar and the Duke of Argylle. Also in Castle Wynd was the house of George Buchanan (1506–82), the son of a Stirlingshire laird and the greatest latinist of his day. He is regarded as the epitome of the cosmopolitan Renaissance *savant*, attaining the influential post of tutor to James VI over whom he exercised a compelling influence.[26] In addition, Crags Close housed the properties of two earls, a knight, a minister of religion and a chaplain. The upper echelons of the lower class were represented by a lawyer or notary and six important merchants, while towards the quarter's southeastern boundary along St Mary's Wynd there is further mention of four bakers, a butcher and a maltman. The west side of St Mary's Wynd also housed a tailor, a flesher and two former servants, of the king and Duke of Argylle, respectively, then reduced to society 'outcasts'.

Adjoining the burgh's First Quarter along St Mary's Wynd, Stirling's Fourth Quarter, due to the paucity of Sasine references is difficult to characterise. Only craftsmen are mentioned, including a weaver and two maltmen in Blackfriars Wynd, a mealmaker in Dirt Row and a weaver and potter in Hie Gait. Yet, as the Hearth Tax evidence makes clear, this quarter's northeastern section shared some of the First Quarter's social prestige, though away from St Mary's Wynd its social standing rapidly declined towards Blackfriars Wynd and the Dirt Row Port which, as its name suggests, was a zone of 'unpleasant' occupations.

The Sasines also fail to provide sufficient locational information to adequately characterise the burgh's Second and Third Quarters though again, away from the church and the manse, a similar decline in social and occupational standing appears to have taken place. No members of the elite class are recorded as living in Middle Row though a commissary or bishop's representative and three merchants are mentioned, together with four weavers, two bakers, a gunsmith and a cutler. In Back Row the social and occupational mix was similar with a notary, four bakers, a weaver and a flesher. Both Back Row and Middle Row had representatives of the 'undesirable' professions in the form of skinners and Middle Row housed another of the king's former servants who had fallen on bad times. The concentration of tanners around the Burgh Burn has already been noted, but the lowest in the burgh's social grouping were the lepers who inhabited the Leperman's Croft outside the Burgh Gate.

By way of conclusion to this period study of pre-industrial Stirling it is of interest to briefly consider the information contained in the 1694 Hearth Tax which provides the first systematic survey of the burgh's housing stock. This tax, an idea borrowed from France, was one of Parliament's ways of raising additional revenue and was based, at least in the government's opinion, on the equitable principle that the affluent bore the heaviest financial burdens, the individual sums demanded being roughly proportional to the individual taxpayer's ability to pay. The argument ran that, since richer men lived in bigger houses than poorer men, and since the size of a house could be approximately assessed by the number of fireplaces it possessed, counting hearths was a quick, cheap and fair way of levying the new tax.[27]

Based on Stirling's four quarters, Table 3 indicates the important information contained in the Hearth Tax which lists the number of house-owners and tenants, and the all-important number of hearths, from which useful ratios can be obtained. The poor and destitute were exempt of tax and comparison of their figures with those liable to tax is of great interest, especially in terms of occupation densities. In addition to domestic hearths, those of kilns, smithies and maltings etc., were also taxed, the majority in Stirling's case being located in the burgh's Second Quarter.

The returns indicate that Stirling's First Quarter had both the highest number of hearth owners and the highest number of hearths, the high ratio of hearth to owner being indicative of its affluence and large average size of dwelling. The Fourth Quarter, with 4.8 hearths per owner and other relatively high ratios appears equally conspicuous. Being adjacent to the First Quarter, the St Mary's Wynd area in particular, shared with it similar property and social characteristics, though further down the ridge its nature changed to resemble that of the Second and Third Quarters, the former housing a substantial

Table 3   *Hearth Tax 1694*

Liable for Hearth Tax	Quarters				
	First	Second	Third	Fourth	Total
Hearth owners	84	48	53	57	242
Hearths	393	92	167	276	928
Tenants*	139	83	73	99	394
Hearths/Tenant	2.7	2.0	2.3	2.5	2.4
Hearths/Owner	4.7	3.7	3.2	4.8	3.8
Tenants/Dwelling	1.7	1.7	1.4	1.7	1.6
Poor					
Dwellings	15	36	17	16	84
Hearths	46	92	47	33	218
Tenants	41	65	41	24	171
Hearths/Tenant	1.1	1.4	1.1	1.4	1.3
Hearths/Dwelling	3.1	2.6	2.8	2.0	2.6
Tenants/Dwelling	2.7	1.8	2.4	1.5	2.0
Other hearths					
Waste	15	7	—	27	49
Kiln	3	4	—	1	8
Malt Kiln	—	3	—	—	3
Barn	1	—	2	—	3
Malt Barn	—	—	—	1	1
Smithy	1	—	—	—	1
Workhouse	—	—	1	—	1
Oven	—	—	—	1	1

* This includes owner-occupants.

segment of the burgh's poor. Both First and Fourth Quarters also had a significant number of 'waste' or vacant properties, the reason for which remains obscure. Were they awaiting new tenants or owners, thus indicating a rapid turnover in property transaction? Or were they an indication of some element of decline, a concomitant of the fact, perhaps, that by the end of the seventeenth century the burgh's northwestern section was suffering socially from the withdrawal of the court and many of its attendants to England? Certainly throughout the eighteenth century the physical expansion of Stirling was slow though the original core was now intensively urbanised. Even as late as John Wood's survey in 1820 the burgh still focused on the old town which preserved in its streets and wynds an essentially 'medieval' appearance, the product of many centuries of growth, adaptation and change.

REFERENCES

1   J S Richardson and M E Root, *Stirling Castle (Edinburgh, 1963), p. 3.*
2   G Gordon, 'Urban Settlement', in D W G Timms, *The Stirling Region* (Stirling, 1974), p. 191.
3   C McWilliam, *Scottish Townscape* (London, 1975), p. 36.
4   R Renwick (ed.), *Extracts from the Records of the Royal Burgh of Stirling, I. AD 1519–1666* (Glasgow), p. 53.
5   C McWilliam, op. cit. p. 43.
6   J M Houston, 'The Scottish Burgh', *Town Planning Review* **25** (1954), 115–18.
7   J W R Whitehand and K Alauddin, 'The Town Plans of Scotland: some preliminary considerations', *Scot. Geog. Mag.* **85** (1969), 109–21.
8   W Cowan and H R G Inglis, 'Early Views of Edinburgh', *Scot. Geog. Mag.* **35** (1919), 315–27.
9   See I H Adams, *The Making of Urban Scotland* (London, 1978), p. 33. Also M Bateson 'The Laws of Breteuil', *English Historical Review* **16** (1901), 110.
10 Cowan and Inglis, op cit.
11 M R G Conzen, 'The Use of Town Plans', *Study of Urban History* (1968), pp. 113–30 (ed. H J Dyos).
12 Renwick, op cit. p. 173 (n. 1).
13 W Nimmo, *History of Stirlingshire* (1877), vol. I.
14 Renwick, op cit. p. 145 (n. 1).
15 Renwick, op. cit. p. 50 (n. 1).
16 D B Morris, *The Trade Incorporations of Stirling* (Stirling, 1929), no. 5.
17 M M Webber, 'The Roles of Intelligence Systems in Urban Systems Planning', *Jn. Am. Inst. Planning* **31** (1956), 293.
18 H Carter, 'A Decision-Making Approach to Town Plan Analysis: A Case Study of Llandudno', in H Carter and W K D Davies (eds.), *Urban Essays, Studies in the Geography of Wales* (1970), p. 68.
19 Renwick, op. cit. p. 197 (n. 1).
20 Renwick, op. cit. p. 133 (n. 10).
21 Renwick, op. cit. p. 143 (n. 10).
22 Renwick, op. cit. p. 173 (n. 1).
23 Renwick, op. cit. p. 59 (n. 1).
24 G Sjoberg, The Pre-industrial City (Toronto, 1965).
25 J Langton, 'Residential Patterns in Pre-industrial Cities; Some Case Studies from Seventeenth Century Britain', *Trans. Inst. Brit. Geogr.* **65** (1975), 1–27.
26 T C Smout, *A History of the Scottish People 1560–1830*, (London, 1973), p. 171.
27 J J Bagley, *Historical Interpretation: Sources of English History, 1540 to Present Day* (London, 1971), pp. 122–32.

4

THE EVOLUTION OF SCOTTISH TOWN PLANNING

R G Rodger

There is a curious omission in the historiography of town planning. It is that examples of early town planning almost invariably overlook the Scottish dimension, or at most reduce it to a few cursory remarks about Craig's New Town plan for Georgian Edinburgh.[1] The rudiments of town planning and the search for an 'ideal city' have, of course, spanned centuries. This has spawned studies of pre-Christian cities in Greece and the Middle East, Peking, the fourth-century Maya settlement at Yucatan, Inca cities of South America, and the planned community of Angkor Thom in South East Asia. Medieval monastic towns, twelfth- and thirteenth-century *bastides* of southwest France, renaissance tracts by Alberti, Scamozzi and Filarete, and the New World settlements at Pennsylvania and Savannah have continued the tradition of conscious urban design, of planned layouts. While Craig's plan for eighteenth-century Edinburgh is part of this ancient and distinguished lineage, Scottish town planning has two other, arguably more important, contributions to make.

The first is to place newly established or 'plantation' Scottish towns firmly within the wider framework of structured urban development, and the second contribution is to analyse how daily planning decisions may, *de facto*, just as effectively shape urban development, admittedly with varying degrees of cohesiveness, though they lack any formalised plan to achieve this. Less attention is devoted to the first aspect, for, if it has been neglected in the literature of town planning, its credentials have long been authenticated in Scottish urban history. Furthermore, that the formation of a new town was associated with an imposed plan is both more obvious and more readily established than in the grey area associated with the implementation of administrative procedures, which, though mundane and individually less than crucial, nonetheless imprinted a pattern on the physical fabric of the urban area. Scottish town planning, therefore, was conceived and executed not just in terms of an overall view of subsequent urban development but also evolved in the daily defence of the same principles upon which such urban development and town planning were founded. Such a level of minutiae was, in fact for most burghs, the cutting edge of controlled or planned development and after a brief consideration of Scottish towns in the medieval period, forms the major part of this essay.

I

That Scottish burghs were the newly founded creations of David I in the twelfth century is now clear. According to Pryde,[2] 'there is no authentic evidence of burghs before his time', and another authority has commented, 'The evidence does not show a gradual evolution from agricultural communities to towns; it shows the creation of towns as such.'[3] By the death of William thè Lion in 1214 more than thirty burghs[4] had been created and 'this period of urban revolution in the twelfth century'[5] had set Scotland's political and economic future on a different course.

This indeed was the motive. Military domination and strategic control formed a vital strand in the thinking behind the burghs created at Ayr, Lanark and Dumfries, from which points the containment of rebellious elements was possible, a strategy also relevant to the urban plantations of Inverness, Elgin and Forres following the uprisings in the northeast in 1160.[6] Here the military motive, which gave rise to the 'garrison theory'[7] of Scottish burgh origins has obvious validity, and forms a contemporary northern dimension, again on the very fringe of European civilisation, to a similar policy adopted by English kings along the unstable Welsh border. Regional political control, an omnipresent issue for medieval Scottish kings, witnessed a decisive change in strategy, therefore, under David I in the guise of numerous urban settlements. Premeditated urban plantations and their internally planned features became the instruments of this policy shift. Beforehand, regional subjugation had been attempted from the isolated military might of the castle and the regional jurisdiction associated with its sheriffdom. But from the early decades of the twelfth century a permanent settler presence, military, civil and judicial, was established by the conferment of burghal status. Identity of interests, safety in numbers and the lure of trading privileges were the attractions which persuaded potential residents and traders to congregate within the protective orbit of the newly created burgh and thereby collaborate in the strategic attempt to control the periphery of the Scottish kingdom.

Within their defined boundaries Scottish burghs enjoyed trading and certain manufacturing monopolies which, in conjunction with their assured access through specific ports, ensured the distinctive development of the medieval town in Scotland.[8] Such privileges, which of course existed within English and continental European urban boundaries were however both more fully developed and exclusive in Scotland.[9] For example, Perth had a monopoly of trade in the sheriffdom of Perth and Inverness, Haddington and Aberdeen in their own sheriffdoms, advantages which led one writer to comment that there were 'few analogous grants of trading rights to English or to French towns'.[10] As a consequence there was a concentration of economic activity within the burgh and subsequent growth points were substantially dependent upon the commercial success of established towns. Trading privileges were not in themselves sufficient reason for urban growth; Roxburgh, Fyvie and Falkland, for example, failed to exploit their status and monopoly position, or found the vigorous competition of an adjacent burgh overwhelming. But, perhaps more significantly, rural trade was limited and the evolution of a second rank in the urban hierarchy was successfully controlled for almost four centuries though the commercial advantages given to medieval burghs were not absolutely and immediately exclusive and other non-Royal burghs vied for trading access to the hinterland. [11]

This brief view of the origins of Scottish burghs serves to illustrate that the foundations of David I and his immediate descendants were '. . . the precise twelfth century equivalents of our twentieth century new towns . . .' [12] As such their lay-outs were governed by natural features, for example, the dominant position of the castle, and the main thoroughfare or 'hie gait' was usually determined by the principal transport link to the castle, abbey, bridge or harbour. [13] But within such constraints these new towns were also planned, for although the precise steps by which decisions were arrived at are ill-documented, there is clear evidence of a coherent overview stamped upon the initial developments. For example, at Dumfries and Perth the methodical procedures for laying out the burgh have been traced with respect to the considerable calculations involved in adapting a formal concept to the features and contours of the actual site. [14] In St Andrews the congestion of the original settlement led to a revised town plan. [15] Archaeological evidence to this effect has demonstrated that the former settlement was, with the conferment of burghal status, redesigned c.1150 with two parallel streets and a market place. [16] In both St Andrews and Dumfries it has been argued, subsequent extensions were also planned and the shape of the burgage plots, their size and relation to one another and to the newly created street pattern were carefully considered. In the development of Ayr during the early thirteenth century a new town was laid out slightly apart from the disadvantageous site of the existing Sandgate community, and here too 'the designer chose a line for the main street sufficiently far from the river to allow space for the plots and then laid out the boundaries of the sides of this civic space cum main street so that the space widened or narrowed to suit the proposed function'. [17] Furthermore, it has been shown that at a more detailed level an overall conception of town planning existed in medieval Ayr. Plot frontages of measured proportions were set at right angles to the street, the tails of the plots devised in such a way as to prevent illegal entry to the burgh, and vennel entrances to the main street were staggered to avoid traffic congestion. In these subtle details a coherent framework is evident. As the author of the Ayr study concluded, 'As Letchworth, Stevenage and Cumbernauld unmistakably show the planning philosophy and techniques of their own times, Ayr shows the aims and methods of comprehensive planning of its day.' [18]

This theme of formalised layout is a recurrent one amongst several authors. If the town plan sometimes assumed an irregular form or was based on a linear pattern this proved not so much that the town had evolved in some organic or unstructured manner, but that the scale of medieval urban settlements was of very modest proportions and that the planners could incorporate the social and economic requirements of the burgh within a simple single-street design. Occasionally 'T' or 'Y' shapes were utilised and the parallel and rectangular street systems also emerged, though mostly confined to the burghs of Fife and other busy east coast ports where Flemish exiles and mercantile contacts with continental towns were influential factors in this pattern of development. Crail and St Andrews are two such examples of rectilineal development and Perth 'was laid out with exceptional formality within its town wall',[19] though in a number of burghs the parallel-street plan 'resulted from the subsequent additions to an original street plan'.[20] In such cases the path or lane which connected the tails of the burgage plots was often elevated to the status of a secondary street once urban expansion had extended the original linear development to the limits of practicality. Beyond a certain point ease of contact, traffic flows and savings in time could be realised by rectangular developments superimposed upon the initial linear structure, and in this respect the medieval town plan represented a continuing influence on subsequent urban morphology.

Little is known about the planners themselves. There is a suggestion that the king appointed a surveyor to draw up proposals, as at Dumfries.[21] Almost certainly where strategic considerations were at issue, such as the location of civil buildings in relation to the castle—and this was applicable to thirty one of the initial thirty three burgh foundations—then the king's advisers would have expressed an interest in the configuration of the new town. Indeed in view of the fact that so many of these twelfth and thirteenth century burghs were entirely new settlements based on a castle, it is difficult to see who other than the king's nominees would have initiated the original demarcation of burgages. Economically, too, the royal interest was at issue, for the conferment of burghal status and the associated trading privileges was linked to regal revenues from the burgh.[22] The burgesses' obligations and self-interest, therefore, dictated that an unstructured, uncoordinated town development might prove prejudicial, and to avoid this the merchant community delegated powers of spatial control to their representatives. The head of this merchant guild body, the Dean of Guild, it would appear, not only monitored additions and alterations but was also instrumental in deciding where vennels, closes and other access points and facilities should be located. Indeed in the 1970s the Glasgow, Milngavie and other Dean of Guild Courts still granted a 'lining', sanctioning building work, a modern version of the medieval 'lynour' or 'lynaris' which signified the surveyor's division, allocation and purpose of land usage.[23]

The agents responsible for bringing town planning features to medieval Scottish 'plantations' remain somewhat vague. A mixture of the king's surveyors, the head or Dean of the merchant guild, and, in the ecclesiastical burghs, the scholarly draughtsmanship which existed within their cloisters, were variously responsible. What is clear is that at or before the time of new medieval foundations in England and Wales, in south-west France and central Europe, new towns were created in Scotland and that these displayed many features of planned settlements. Although irregularities existed, and inevitably a degree of unstructured development emerged, building alignments, street patterns and widths, land use and environmental considerations possessed a coherence consistent with a centralised perception of town development from the outset. Indeed these are precisely the criteria adopted as evidence of the existence of modern town planning.[24]

II

Once founded the burghs quickly adopted a code of Burgh Laws and Edinburgh, Stirling, Roxburgh and Berwick appear to have been especially prompt to plagiarise the framework already established in Northumbria, at Newcastle. Elsewhere the new burghs appear to have taken over 'without much variation' the same burgh laws.[25] Mostly devised to protect mercantile privileges and the rights associated with their monopoly of trade within a defined area, those procedures fanned out to deal with activities which less directly affected the interests of the merchant guild. It was in this wider executive branch of burgh administration that the second contribution to town planning was made, and if less demonstrative of the formulation of an overall plan for a new town, this continuous involvement at the particular level of the built environment was as decisive in establishing a framework for urban development. This, then is the second contribution of town planning to Scottish urban development, to which the essay now turns.

The agency responsible for monitoring mercantile affairs, the guildry, was active at the very early stages of urban life in Scotland. The head of the burgesses, the Dean of Guild, held hearings and delivered judgments regarding the town's affairs, and if the merchant interest was a dominant influence on those affairs, it was not always paramount. The interests of the customer were also considered as, for example, in the open display of wares. Hence the law that 'wha that syl sell flesche . . . he sal sett his flesche opynly in his wyndow that it be sene commonly till al men that will tharof'.[26] Similarly, regulations governing the market place and commercial codes as well as environmental decisions regarding refuse, came within the legitimate purview of the laws of the burghs as administered by the Dean of Guild and his brethren. And it was precisely the adoption of such rules and codes of practice which introduced a degree of control and uniformity to the physical development.

Possible early references to the merchant guild and their burghal administration occur in royal charters to Aberdeen by William the Lion in 1179 and 1209, though with his successor Alexander II, the first certain reference occurs in 1222. Alexander II also confirmed the existence of burgh guilds in Elgin,

Perth and Stirling at the same time. Although formed earlier the guild was known to be active in Cupar (1369), Irvine (1373), Edinburgh (1403) and Ayr (1430).[27] In fact in the fourteenth and fifteenth centuries the majority of Scottish burghs had concentrated their municipal administration in the hands of the Merchant Guild, whose terms of reference though mainly concerned with the protection of burghal privileges in matters of trade, also extended to issues affecting the physical development of the town.[28]

The Dean of Guild Court, a sub-committee of the General Court of the Guild, performed the function of municipal arbitration machinery over a wide range of issues, one of which, the control of 'neighbourhood', became increasingly important as trade expansion encouraged growth and development in the early modern urban communities of Scotland.[29] Where the interests of one person impinged directly or indirectly on the property or amenity of others, representation could be made to the Dean of Guild for adjudication. The growth of this aspect of the Edinburgh Dean of Guild Court's function was eventually reflected in the necessity for the specific documentation of cases in a 'Nychtbourheid Buik' which recorded a proliferation of cases concerned with this type of infringement.[30]

Although active, therefore, from the medieval origins of the burgh, the ongoing administration through the guild produced conflicting interests as the town developed. The protracted feuding of burgesses and craftsmen, Guildry and Town Council over qualifications for guild entry and burghal administration culminated in the clarification of functions, duties and electoral procedures in the Decree Arbitral of 1583,[31] one of three crucial decisions in the last two decades of the sixteenth century which affected the controlled physical shape of the early modern Scottish burgh.

The political in-fighting of sixteenth-century guilds and town councils is worthy of further research,[32] but for present purposes it is sufficient to note that irrespective of the assault by the Council on its wider responsibilities, the Dean of Guild Court exerted absolute power both before and after the Decreet in matters relating to building control. The confirmation of neighbourhood jurisdiction in 1583 which gave the 'dene of gild and his counsall . . . the haill burding in decyding all questiouns of nichtbourheid'[33] reaffirmed the medieval powers and penalties of the Dean of Guild Court. Typical Edinburgh decisions such as requiring the demolition of the 'ruynous and decayit' gallery of 'Jhonne Lawsoun of Hieriggis',[34] or demanding 'Jhonne Rubertsoun, saidler, to remove and tak down'[35] his shop were reinforced by fines where 'the pairty being fund to haif done the wrang'[36] by infringing neighbourhood would be required to pay up to twenty shillings. The nature and importance of the matters coming before the Court was highly variable, therefore, but the seriousness of the responsibilities in deciding upon the issues was indicated by the power to fine even the bailies and councillors for absence from the Court sittings.[37] Thus although mainly involved with the settlement of private disputes the late sixteenth-century Dean of Guild Courts reasserted some guiding principles relating to town development and the welfare of inhabitants.[38] Certainly from the available sixteenth-century documentary evidence, the Dean of Guild Courts continued their medieval obligations to monitor private developments, defend the public interest insofar as the safety of buildings, access to streets and public highways was concerned, and, in a rather negative manner, discourage, through their scrutiny and power to fine, such building activities as they perceived to be contrary to the interests of their inhabitants.

The second development towards the end of the sixteenth century related to this perception of community interests. Representation on the guild council was, until 1584, skewed towards the merchants and burgesses of the burghs. However, from 1584, when the constitution of the Edinburgh Dean of Guild was remodelled, and with merchants and craftsmen almost equally represented, the nature of Dean of Guild business began to alter as mercantile interests were partially counter-balanced by non-mercantile subjects such as building control.[39] Though continuing to be involved with minutiae—resolving whether James Arbuckell's water pipes could discharge on to the roof of Arthur Temple's Edinburgh property[40]—and also occupied with a diverse range of matters, including the upkeep of old wells, the bell in Greyfriar's kirk and the loft in the Tron church, admission of apprentices and the mustering of a guard,[41] the Dean of Guild Courts were increasingly disposed to protect a more broadly defined public interest and to shape and control town development generally.

That the Dean of Guild Courts were desirable instruments for controlled town developments may be judged by the third decision of the late sixteenth century. The extensive activities of the Edinburgh Dean of Guild Court were, as has been mentioned, paralleled in other burghs where similar institutions acted as planning watchdogs. But where Dean of Guild functions had not been employed an act of 1593 encouraged other towns to emulate the Edinburgh example.[42] The efficacy of such an exhortation is difficult to judge, but it is at least suggestive of a successful functioning of the Edinburgh Dean of Guild Court's screening of building developments.

Charged with these expanded horizons the seventeenth century dawned with more vigorous efforts to control both the environmental and building development. Measures to prevent fire, the provision of a code of building regulations, a register of land use, and opposition to the encroachment of private landowners upon public land were the explicit forms which this attempt assumed.

Under the stimulus of an extensive fire in Edinburgh in 1674, and no doubt with an eye to the security of their own properties, the Dean of Guild Court, acting under a general instruction from the Town Council,[43] framed a number of clauses, later integrated into a more comprehensive set of building rules, to minimise fire risks. The prevalence of timber building provided 'a reddie fewall to the fyre', which, with the 'venalls and closes being so narrow and houses so thick and joyned togither', threatened the entire town.[44] The predominantly high-rise type of tenement building in Scotland, particularly in Edinburgh, introduced a strong incentive to control fire, and the fact that the fire of 1674 had been halted by buildings constructed with 'stone and lyme' was not over-looked by the Dean of Guild Court. Henceforth, the Court vetoed building plans which employed timber construction in stairs or adjacent to the exits from houses, and opposed the future use of timber-framed housebuilding. Further-more, in recognition of one element of human motivation, they provided tax exemption for seventeen years for those house owners who demolished and rebuilt property using stone materials.[45] Although sometimes circumvented, the Dean of Guild ruling was a stimulus to a more lasting and substantial mode of construction, and in conjunction with controls on shops selling combustible products, did provide a greater level of protection for the population as a whole whilst simultaneously imposing a restricted measure of urban planning and control.[46]

Planned environmental improvements, admittedly prompted as a response to a crisis, were extended increasingly to other fields during the seventeenth century. Allied to the problem of fire hazards, but also motivated by concern for the environment, the Dean of Guild Court laid down directives to raise chimney heights and thus diminish the smoke nuisance in 'Auld Reekie'.[47] This type of regulation regarding existing buildings became incorporated in the building code for new properties which was gradually evolving, and by the end of the seventeenth century covered, in addition, such aspects as the type of materials, the uses of timber, and the height and certain design features of buildings.[48] Indeed the absolute jurisdiction and power to veto over projected building operations were powerful forces in the emergence of acceptable codes of building practice. Any construction required the approval of 'the dean of guild and his counsell' from whom the applicants, if successful, obtained a 'jedge and warrant to proceid',[49] and thus based largely on the precedents of case law and a limited number of formal rules, a minimum standard of con-struction emerged. Certainly in Edinburgh by 1698 a coherent body of building regulations existed,[50] and as one authority commented:

> The greater part of the work of the old Dean of Guild Court resembled the modern functions. It dealt with the amenity of the town, the supervision of buildings according to regulations, and decisions regarding complaints between neighbours.[51]

Decisions of the Dean of Guild Court, for example those relating to 'the benefit of the sune' which certain residents were deprived of due to the height of neighbouring buildings,[52] or the access and light to a shop and cellar,[53] were individually insignificant, yet cumulatively they were demonstrative of a wider perception of urban development than that simply based on a narrow view of personal gain or on *ad hoc* solutions to administrative or judicial problems. No doubt the serious view that Court took of itself was partly the product of self-justification, but the practical outcome offered the elements of a coherent municipal approach to urban growth in the early modern period. Thus the expense of street cleansing, the removal of middens and other sanitary arrangements were vindicated in terms of 'keeping the town neat and clean in tyme coming'.[54] Even the context and the use of the future tense in the council minutes of 1677 and 1682 indicates a contemporary perception and degree of town planning in the field of environmental welfare.[55]

A stronger strand of planning infiltrated municipal thinking when the Dean of Guild was instructed '. . . to informe himself what waste grounds within the Town of Edinburgh were convenient to be build for the decoration of the Cittie and conveiniencie of the Inhabitants . . .'.[56] Some appreciation of land use and resource planning throughout the entire urban area, therefore, began to penetrate municipal thinking at the turn of the seventeenth century, for the council went on to indicate that if proprietors failed to develop the amenities of their properties, they would be disposed of to others 'to undertake so good a work'.[57]

The interest in this type of activity probably emanated from the persistent encroachment of private landowners on public land. Enclosing portions of common ground, obstructing highways and other infringements were, from time to time, observed in the late seventeenth century during the Riding of the Marches, an exercise undertaken by the town burgesses to ensure that the burghal boundaries were respected.[58] Ultimately, in Edinburgh in 1715, this function was devolved upon a specially created Committee on Public Works, which was also interested in such issues as planning changes in communications within the city by forming new streets and in planting trees in certain areas in an effort to improve the amenity and landscaping of the capital.[59] Again concern for the wider community benefits and an awareness that each piece of land within the urban area functioned as part of the whole was evident in these activities.

By the early decades of the eighteenth century Edinburgh exercised reasonably well-defined building regulations through the Dean of Guild, and in addition, by its own decisions and those of the Town Council, discharged a more general supervisory function over the development of the town. Elsewhere a similar, if not identical pattern emerged for at an early stage forty-one of the sixty-six medieval royal burghs had possessed Dean of Guild Court powers,[60] and the subsequent introduction of Dean of Guild Courts, as in Kirkcaldy in 1659[61] owed much to the Edinburgh model, while in towns other than royal burghs the magistrates acted in that capacity, though in a rather different constitutional position.[62] Although a continuing dialogue in respect of guild and town council powers saw an erosion of Dean of Guild jurisdiction by successive steps in 1681, 1729, the 1780s, 1824 and ultimately in the Municipal Corporations (Scotland) Act 1833,[63] the building regulations and town planning functions remained intact and inviolable due to the fact that, as one authority writing in 1752 emphatically stated:

> The jurisdiction of the dean of guild courts is distinct, and several from that of the provost and bailies, not subordinate to them . . ·. warrants and decrees are not liable to any review before the magistrates, who cannot in the least intermeddle therein; but they are subject to controul of the court of session.[64]

Despite the constitutional autonomy of the Dean of Guild Court in building, amenity and planning matters, the inroads into its other powers during the eighteenth and early nineteenth century were sufficient for this institution to fall into disuse. Arguably, in Edinburgh, preoccupation with the emerging New Town plan in the second half of the eighteenth century deflected the relevant building authorities from adequate scrutiny in the older parts of the burgh. Elsewhere the infrequency of building applications, the sole remaining responsibility of the Court in many burghs, reinforced the view that it was largely superfluous. Thus emasculated in its wider role, the vestigial Dean of Guild Court duties regarding building and land use also fell into disuse, and in Lerwick, Forfar and Stirling, for example, were ineffectively embraced by the town councils themselves.[65] Hence the available building and town planning powers which were widespread in the early modern period were gradually eroded in practice by the growth of municipal corporations who, in their efforts, to assert their own authority over burghal affairs, coincidentally dealt a death blow to precisely that agency which, in the rapidly industrialising environment of the early nineteenth century, had much to offer in terms of controlled urban development. From a potentially sound position regarding urban expansion at the beginning of the eighteenth century the political balance and the supremacy of the town council effectively neutered the Dean of Guild Court as a planning tool. The nadir of this planning agency was reached in 1868 when only twelve such institutions were still operative in Scottish burghs, albeit in the most important centres of population.[66]

Thus the decay of the Dean of Guild Court in many Scottish burghs was directly attributable to, and inversely related with, the ascendancy of the Town Council. Many abuses in land use and building development were only possible due to the demise of this medieval institution, and although its continuation did not ensure immunity from a range of urban problems of a sanitary and environmental nature, the mid-Victorian realisation as to the desirability of screening proposed building inclined many authorities to press for further powers. Some achieved their aims through private acts—Glasgow (1866), Edinburgh (1867), Dundee (1871) and Greenock (1877) were cases in point[67]—but other towns were provided for under the terms of the Lindsay or Burgh Police (Scotland) Act, 1862, which allowed them to institute Dean of Guild Courts or equivalent authorities with powers, duties and jurisdiction modelled on their existing counterparts. However the act, like many in the nineteenth century, was only adoptive, and it was thirty years before a subsequent act[68] compulsorily required the enforcement of building regulations and the rudiments of town planning. Only under the mounting pressures of urbanisation, and with the underlying threat of legal sanctions did the municipalities disinter their erstwhile competitor as a useful watchdog governing the physical development of the town. Even then, it was only in the last two decades of the century that the reincarnated Dean of Guild Courts mushroomed, from approximately 20 in 1880[69] to 106 by 1898, and to 189 by 1912.[70]

In the last third of the nineteenth century the hallmark of the renaissance of the Dean of Guild Courts was a tough code of building regulations of which the Glasgow Court was a noted and vigorous model for many rapidly expanding burghs in west-central Scotland.[71] Indeed so demanding were the Glasgow building byelaws that numerous experts directly attributed the late Victorian housing problems to the additional construction costs required to meet the letter of the law.[72] In Glasgow, for example, the additional material requirements compared to those of London were 25 per cent for a three storey and 45 per cent for a four-storey building.[73] Similar disparities applied to roofing costs, foundations and internal finishing, and inevitably these were reflected in rents which were substantially higher per cubic foot of space in Scottish burghs.[74]

With the passage of the Housing and Town Planning Act, 1909, and the construction of government housing schemes at Greenock, Rosyth and Gretna just before and during the First World War, Scottish town planning moved into a different era.[75] Not that these projects were particularly significant quantitatively, but they were the portents of post-war planning and, more ominously from the burghs' viewpoint, of central subsidised housebuilding— and arguably of poorly planned council estates. Such twentieth-century innovations did not destroy the Dean of Guild Court—it endured until 1975[76]—but it did mark the twilight of the Courts' function as the sole protector of community interests regarding the physical development of the built environment.

It cannot be claimed that this medieval institution was universally effective in championing a coherent, structured view of urban development. Lapses in administration, inconsistencies, the demise of the Dean of Guild Court in certain locations testify otherwise. But in its spheres of operations—building regulations, the control of space and light, environmental constraints on smoke and refuse—jurisdiction in these matters in effect stamped a code of practice on both the existing fabric of the town and subsequent additions to it. While lacking any formalised structure plan, the Dean of Guild Court did, nonetheless, predetermine the directions urban development would take and the characteristics it would adopt. Thus if the initial medieval settlements often possessed a positive outline which urban development would follow, the Dean of Guild Courts acted in a more negative manner determining what the minimum acceptable standards would be. Both approaches, the aggregate overview and the regulated local level, it is argued, were the legitimate forbears of modern Scottish town planning.

III

The eighteenth- and nineteenth-century city fathers did not rely exclusively on the Dean of Guild Court in their attempts to influence urban development. Indeed as part of their efforts to assert their independence and self-importance a number of alternative, and thus often uncoordinated, strategies emerged. As the sphere of operations for the Dean of Guild Courts tended to retract during the nineteenth century so that the administration of building regulations became virtually their sole remaining area of responsibility, so a vacuum in the more creative medium of town planning emerged and this was the void which local councils increasingly filled, sometimes rather reluctantly, as they provided facilities and amenities for their residents.

Only rarely, and then on a very modest scale, was this involvement in the style of a formalised layout in rectangular street plans. Clearly Georgian Edinburgh is exceptional in this regard, but such geometric street designs as there were owed more to the revenue maximising strategies of private developers of estates such as the Blythswoods, other west-end developments in Glasgow, and later of a meaner quality, central Clydebank.[77] Occasionally the modest local authority improvement or clearance schemes of the second half of the century had a similar effect. Mid-nineteenth-century Scotland, however, remained aloof from the more imaginative geometrical patterns of urban expansion evident in European capitals and in American cities.[78]

Strictly speaking there was an exception, at a level which initially could not really be described even on the most flexible definitions as urban. This was a widespread tendency to systematically plan and lay-out villages which was under way in eighteenth- and nineteenth-century Scotland.[79] This 'planned village movement' was a response to rising agricultural productivity and the accumulation of rural food surpluses, increasing population, the perceived vices of the lowland city, and a lingering, chieftain-like paternalism for the welfare and number of people attached to the landowners' estate. The strategy: to found a new nuclei of population in order to attract rurally based industry which offered both employment prospects and increasing demand for agricultural products. The influence of military settlements was marginal though in this attempt to pacify the highlands there is an interesting but faint echo of David I's policy. Fishing settlements were of greater importance and they, too, were the result of internal forces centrifugally separating highlanders from the land. These newly created villages of c.1730–1830 were numerous—more than 150 of them—and geographically widespread, though the greatest concentrations occurred along the Moray and Aberdeenshire coastlines and on the southern margins of the Grampians. They were planned by the landowner who commonly offered building plots at reduced feus, provided building materials, loans to manufacturers, and might offer to build a church, school or hall, and give common land for bleaching. The landowner, moreover, also determined the physical appearance of the new village by deciding the plot shapes, building line and height, and design features, and the supervisory role of the estate office was a powerful unifying force in this respect. Of these entirely new settlements many retained an economic toehold and survived, and some such as Ullapool, Inverary, and Pultneytown preserve a conspicuous parallelism in their modern street patterns. Others remain settlements of some consequence—Callander, Tobermory, Oban, Ballater, Helensburgh, Newton Stewart, Grantown, Penicuik, Helmsdale. Thus precisely at that stage when town planning controls were under greatest attack in the major centres of urban Scotland many minor foundations were emerging largely as a product of the personal initiative of the landowner. Most of the new creations foundered. Uncompetitiveness, high costs of production, and the intrusion of cheaper lowland and English products transported by the railway were sufficient influences to stifle the development of most of these proto-industrial initiatives.

In the major urban centres, however, it was the absence of such a clearly co-ordinated view of future urban development which produced several inconsistencies in the pragmatic decisions of the town councils. For example, in the latter years of the eighteenth century the Edinburgh council's proposals for the drainage and landscaping of the 'Meadows' and the common land known as the 'Boroughmuir' were only partially realised as the sale of certain portions of these areas proved irresistible to the council.[80] The inflated value resulting from improvements in the immediate vicinity also inclined early nineteenth-century Glasgow councils to relinquish parts of Kelvingrove for housebuilding purposes, a decision which, as protesting residents noted, ultimately sanctioned the construction of high-rise tenement dwellings on hill-top positions when the council was avowedly attempting to preserve amenities in central districts.[81]

Contradictions of a different variety arose in Edinburgh at the end of the eighteenth and in the early nineteenth century. Efforts to control the expansion of the city to the north were undertaken through powers derived from several Westminster statutes. Simultaneously, however, an opportunity to obtain 26 acres of land immediately to the south of the city boundary was passed over,[82] and thus for almost a century, until 1848 when the boundaries were extended, large tracts of the southern suburbs were beyond the controlling jurisdiction of the burgh council.[83] On another occasion the expression of an aesthetic appreciation of the capital prompted some notable civic architectural works in the early nineteenth century—Register House, the Royal Institution and the Royal Exchange, for example—and this sensitivity towards the physical appearance was extended to the prohibition of further building in the neighbourhood of the Castle, or to the south of Princes Street.[84] But about the same time, 1825, the council had to be goaded into action by public opinion, inflamed by an article in The Scotsman[85] which extolled the scenic beauty of Salisbury Crags and decried the desecration of an amenity, immortalised in Scott's *Heart of Midlothian*, due to extensive and uncontrolled quarrying. The eventual ban on this activity, imposed by the council for the preservation of the environment, was largely the product of pressure from 'persons with taste and with a sense of beauty (who) formed a solid phalanx and saved the rocks from destruction'.[86]

It was mounting nineteenth-century urban pressures, combined with increasing statutory responsibilities across a wide spectrum of activities which provided local authorities with a greater measure of control over land use. The purchase of sites for school buildings, cemeteries, gas and water works, and provisions for sanitoria, fever hospitals and Poor Law workhouses ensured that an increasing, though indirect, control of urban development was firmly lodged in municipal hands.[87]

In a more systematic approach, early Victorian officials took exception to environmental hazards and consciously planned their elimination, or at least their diminution. Intense population pressure on existing amenities required a positive, centrally directed campaign across a variety of environmental fronts, and it was in the context of impending urban crises that municipal action was at first reluctantly undertaken. The progressively more demanding building regulations were part of this campaign to prevent defective construction and planning in the future and other initiatives were pursued with a more immediate purpose. The threat of fire in the seventeenth century had galvanised municipalities into providing building controls, scrutinised by the Dean of Guild Court, and in the nineteenth century fear of contagious disease produced a like effect. Building regulations and sanitary controls were invoked in an effort to reduce the likelihood, and in the event of an outbreak, contain the extent of cholera and other epidemics.

Municipal objectives were not, therefore, overtly directed towards town planning in this respect. But the practical outcome of the proliferating statutory and byelaw provisions was to shape the urban landscape. Efforts to control river and smoke pollution fell into this category, and explicit attempts were made to control water and smoke effluents from industrial undertakings. Hence the councils of Edinburgh and Leith concerned themselves with measures for the purification of the Water of Leith, whilst in Glasgow, sixty miles of underground sewers were constructed between 1848 and 1860 to relieve the River Clyde of its daily inflow of untreated sewage.[88] Building regulations were extended so as to cover chimney height in an effort to ameliorate the effect of noxious industrial gases and domestic fires.[89] Moves to obtain a pure and quantitatively adequate water supply were also a response to this type of environmental stimulus, and the town councils of most burghs played an important role in the provision of these amenities. The Loch Katrine water supply of Glasgow is the most noted of these, and in towns such as Stirling, Dumfries and Aberdeen,[90] and even in remote, almost rural townships such as Lerwick and Campbeltown,[91] the planned provision of public water was a primary responsibility of the municipal authorities.

Another area of municipal response was in the realm of parkland. Throughout the early decades of the nineteenth century councils had been anxious, in the face of the encroachment by builders on vacant sites, to ensure that certain areas of the inner city remained sacrosanct. Leith Links, the Perth Inches, Glasgow Green and similar planned open spaces were early examples of a conscious policy towards community welfare which can be attributed to Town Councils and Dean of Guild Courts alike. In later Victorian years this loosely defined objective became a central pillar of municipal policy as the onslaught of population pressure, whether due to natural increase or rural emigration, dictated combative strategies to overcome 'the semi-asphyxiated city'.[92] In response, therefore, the city of Glasgow acquired 839 acres, costing £465,000 between 1867 and 1900, and Edinburgh corporation added 563 acres in six purchases between 1884 and 1900 at a cost of £151,000 to the ratepayers.[93] Similar council acquisitions in Perth, Dumbarton and Leith, amongst many burghs, were undertaken with the expressed intention of securing a measure of amenity for all social groups. This extended to local authority financial aid to the botanical gardens in both Edinburgh and Glasgow, where assurances were sought and obtained by the council regarding free admission to working class groups.[94]

Early Edinburgh Improvement Acts, those of 1753, 1767, 1785–7, 1806 and 1842 for example, whilst authorising some imposing public buildings, had, as a by-product, cleared areas of the city in order to make sites available for these prestige projects.[95] The beneficial effects of creating more space, light and air, and of reducing the number of inhabitants per acre were not pursued in any systematic attempt to extend such advantages to the populace as a whole, either in the capital or elsewhere. Again, however, the sanction of epidemic disease created a more favourable climate for such activities, and in the major cities of Scotland each local authority commenced the clearance of the most insanitary houses. Glasgow created the precedent in 1866, and in two distinct phases of demolition considerably affected the physical appearance of the central city zones.[96] Edinburgh followed suit, though on a diminished scale; some 2721 houses were cleared between 1867 and 1885 compared to 30,000 in Glasgow over the same years. Similar purges occurred in other Scottish towns.[97] Thus by levying a special assessment upon ratepayers the city authorities obtained sufficient capital to buy properties. Having done so, they announced their intention to close and demolish them. Although not wholly guiltless in creating further pressure on adjacent accommodation, several distinct advantages did accrue to these council initiatives, which, it has been argued, were a conscious attempt to plan city developments.[98] New transport access routes, wider streets with higher traffic bearing potential, improved urban amenities including parks and spaces and, by no means least, a qualitative improvement in the minimum standard of accommodation, with attendant implications for living conditions and mortality rates were directly linked to the activities of Improvement Trusts in many burghs during the last third of the nineteenth century.[99]

Although not as comprehensive as the town planning initiatives contemporaneously being developed in Letchworth or in another context in the company housing at Port Sunlight and Bournville,[100] within the framework of existing urban communities the various efforts of the Scottish Dean of Guild Courts and Town Councils during the second half of the nineteenth century provided an approximation to the idea of the planned town. Furthermore, within the confines of traditional Victorian values of laissez-faire, the town planning concept, predictably less co-ordinated than in its twentieth-century version, was one of the first areas in which Benthamite utilitarianism was adopted and tailored to provide an underlying philosophical rationalisation of what was urgently becoming a necessity for the continuation of civilised urban life.

IV

The backbone to municipal involvement in the fabric of urban life was provided by the continuing and extended concern of the Dean of Guild Courts in the field of building regulations. Allowed to lapse in the many eighteenth- and early-nineteenth-century burghs, the effectiveness of this institution was reasserted in the post-industrialisation period, and although largely confined to overseeing building standards, its old 'neighbourhood' functions were reintroduced in a different form by the town councils of most Scottish burghs. As in the pre-modern period, although often acting in a defensive manner, the Dean of Guild Courts sought to preserve amenity, instil aesthetic and architectural values, and supervise the internal arrangements and external appearance of buildings with a life expectancy sufficiently long as to influence the physical appearance of burghs for several generations. That their decisions were recorded in a 'Neighbourhood Book' may in itself be an indication of the Dean of Guild Courts' own assessment of their community function.

Long before the Housing and Town Planning Act, 1919, had reached the statute book town planning initiatives of various types had prospered in Scotland. In their very earliest stages medieval burghs were 'planted' in the surrounding countryside and many were consciously designed as a result. Later plantations, the modest though numerous planned villages of improving landowners, and the Victorian town councils' environmental endeavours—the parks, clearances, water supplies and buildings associated with their mounting responsibilities in the fields of health, education, and poverty—variously made significant contributions to partial and overall planning. Such positive proposals for structured urban development were simultaneously underpinned by the regular meetings of the Dean of Guild Courts whose items of business were almost invariably petty but whose decisions, usually based on a few guiding principles, were of importance in shaping Scottish townscapes. As such for centuries they represented in many Scottish burghs a last line of defence in respect of building developments and without which uncontrolled, unstructured urban development would have inevitably resulted. If their activities were indistinctly articulated in town planning jargon their decisions nonetheless had a similar effect, and judged on historical and even on twentieth-century criteria, the Scottish Dean of Guild Courts, early town plans and a spectrum of wider environmental initiatives were undeniably the precursors of modern town planning.

REFERENCES

1 The bibliography of early town planning is expansive, but see for example, H Rosenau, *The Ideal City in its Architectural Evolution* (London, 1959); E A Gutkind, *Urban Development in Western Europe*, vol. VI, The Netherlands and Great Britain (New York, 1971); G C Argan, *The Renaissance City* (London, 1969); M W Beresford, *New Towns of the Middle Ages* (London, 1967).

2 G S Pryde, 'The Origin of the Burgh in Scotland', *Juridical Review*, 47 (1935), 271.

3 J M Houston, 'The Scottish Burgh', *Town Planning Review*, 25 (1954), 114.

4 These included Aberdeen, Berwick, Edinburgh, Elgin, Forres, Haddington, Inverkeithing, Inverness, Jedburgh, Lanark, Linlithgow, Montrose, Peebles, Perth, Renfrew, Roxburgh, Rutherglen, Stirling, Canongate, St Andrews. For a full list of the dates of foundation of Scottish burghs see G S Pryde, *The Burghs of Scotland: A Critical List* (Oxford, 1965).

5 Society of Antiquaries of Scotland, *Scotland's Medieval Burghs: An Archaeolgical Heritage in Danger* (Edinburgh, 1972), p. 8.

6 J M Houston, op. cit.

7 G Neilson, 'On some Scottish burghal origins', *Juridical Review*, 14 (1902), 129–40.

8 A Ballard, 'Theory of the Scottish Burgh', *Scottish Historical Review*, 13 (1915), 16–29.

9 T Keith, 'The Trading Privileges of the Royal Burghs of Scotland', *English Historical Review*, 28 (1913), 454–71, 678–90.

10 Ibid. p. 455.

11 G S Pryde, 'The Origin of the Burgh in Scotland', op. cit. p. 274, argues that 'the distinctively Scottish system of clearly defined and rigidly graded economic privileges was slow in evolving' and that 'it did not reach full maturity until David II's general charter of 1364 . . .'.

12   Society of Antiquaries of Scotland, op. cit.
13   C McWilliam, *Scottish Townscape* (London, 1975), p. 33.
14   W A Dodd, 'The Medieval Town Plan at Dumfries', unpublished Edinburgh
     M Phil thesis, 1978, 214–23; A A M Duncan, 'Perth: the First Century of the
     Burgh', *Transactions of the Perthshire Society of Natural Science*, 2 (1974),
     30–50.
15   N P Brooks and G Whittington, 'Planning and Growth in the medieval Scottish
     burgh: the example of St Andrews', *Transactions of the Institute of British
     Geographers*, new series, 2 (3) (1977), 278–95.
16   G Whittington, 'Medieval Towns Built to Plan', *Geographical Magazine*, 51 (8)
     (1979), 541–7; R G Cant, 'The Development of the Burgh of St Andrews in
     the Middle Ages', *Annual Report of the St Andrews Preservation Trust, 1970*
     (St Andrews, 1971).
17   W A Dodd, 'Ayr: A Study of Urban Growth', *Ayrshire Archaeological and
     Natural History Collection*, 10 (1970–2), 223.
18   Ibid. p. 318.
19   C McWilliam, op. cit. p. 35.
20   J W R Whitehand and K Alauddin, 'The Town Plans of Scotland: Some Pre-
     liminary Considerations', *Scottish Geographical Magazine*, 84 (1968), 111.
21   W A Dodds, thesis, op. cit. p. 214.
22   D S Murray, *Early Burgh Organisation in Scotland* (Glasgow, 1924); T Keith,
     op. cit.
23   Glasgow Dean of Guild Court Linings, Office of Public Works, Petitions and
     Plans, Strathclyde Regional Archives; Milngavie Dean of Guild Court Minute
     Book 1/3/1–2, Milngavie and Bearsden Public Library.
24   A R Sutcliffe, *A History of Modern Town Planning: A Bibliographic Guide* (Univ.
     of Birmingham Centre for Urban and Regional Studies Research Memo-
     randum no. 57, 1977), p. 1.
25   C McWilliam, op. cit. p. 29.
26   Ibid. p. 30.
27   R Miller, *The Edinburgh Dean of Guild Court: A Manual of History and Proce-
     dure* (Edinburgh, 1896), pp. 6–8.
28   J Colston, *The Guildry of Edinburgh: Is it an Incorporation?* (Edinburgh, 1887),
     pp. 115–16, quoting an act of 1593 c.184.
29   R Miller, op. cit. p. 21.
30   MSS Acts and Decreets of the Court of the Dean of Guild 1529–1646, Edinburgh
     District Council Record Office (EDCRO). See also M Wood, 'The Neigh-
     bourhood Book', *Book of the Old Edinburgh Club*, 23 (1940), 82–100.
31   MSS Decreet Arbitral Pronounced by His Majesty King James VI. EDCRO.
32   P J Murray, 'The Excommunication of Edinburgh Town Council in 1558', *Innes
     Review*, 27 (1977), 24–34 has recently shed some interesting light on the
     potentially adverse effects on Edinburgh's trade of a papal excommunication
     of the town council over the issue of the theft of a statue of St Giles, and the
     possible threat of competition from Leith. Murray also notes that the
     composition of the council was the president, treasurer, four bailies, ten
     councillors and thirteen craftsmen. The high proportion of craftsmen is of
     considerable interest, though possibly atypical at this early stage.

33 Edinburgh Town Council Minutes (TCM), 3 Mar. 1584, EDCRO.
34 TCM 11 Oct. 1553.
35 TCM 30 Jan. 1582.
36 TCM 25 Nov. 1573. A number of typical Dean of Guild Court decisions are cited
     in R Miller, op. cit. pp. 22–6.
37 TCM 18 Oct. 1566.
38 J C Irons, *Manual of the Law and Practice of the Dean of Guild Court* (Edinburgh,
     1895), pp. 11–21.
39 TCM 3 Mar. 1584.
40 TCM 12 Feb. 1669.
41 H Armet (ed.), *Extracts from the Records of the Burgh of Edinburgh* vol. 8 (Edin-
     burgh, 1962), pp. 1689–701.
42 1593, c.38.
43 TCM 22 Apr. 1674.
44 TCM 1 May 1674.
45 Ibid. The tax exemption was withdrawn in 1732.
46 TCM 26 Nov. 1701.
47 TCM 15 Dec. 1654.
48 TCM 2 Apr. and 5 Dec. 1684.
49 TCM 2 May 1649.
50 R Miller, op. cit. pp. 28–9 cites Acts of Council in 1674 and 1698 to this effect.
     See also TCM 22 Mar. 1717.
51 D Robertson and M Wood, *Castle and Town: Chapters in the History of the
     Royal Burgh of Edinburgh* (Edinburgh, 1928), p. 217.
52 TCM 2 Apr. 1684.
53 TCM 16 Mar. 1687.
54 TCM 14 Nov. 1677.
55 Ibid. and TCM 27 Oct. 1682.
56 TCM 8 Nov. 1700.
57 Ibid.
58 TCM 7 May 1669; 8 Dec. 1675 and 16 May 1701.
59 TCM 17 Oct. 1715 and 18 Apr. 1718.
60 R Miller, op. cit. pp. 5, 20.
61 TCM 2 Dec. 1659.
62 J C Irons, op. cit. p. 44.
63 Control over maritime affairs was lost in 1681 and weights and measures in 1824.
     The more general reform of 1833 ceded further powers to the council (3 and 4
     Will. IV c.76).
64 A McDouall, *An Institute of the Laws of Scotland* (Edinburgh, 1752), p. 582.
65 Commissioners of Police of the Burgh of Lerwick, Minute Book, 1875–1914,
     Lerwick Burgh Records, SRO 1/1/3 and 1/2/3; Dean of Guild Court Register
     of Plans and Sections, Stirling 1892–1914, Central Regional Archives. See also
     R Miller, op. cit. p. 20, for comments on the decay of Dean of Guild Courts.
66 J C Irons, op. cit. p. 34.
67 *Royal Commission on the Housing of the Working Classes, 1884–1885*. Evidence
     of J B Russell, Q. 19364; J K Crawford, Q. 18700; J Gentle, Q. 20594 and A J
     Turnbull, Q. 20088.

68   *55 and 56 Vict.* c.55.
69   R G Rodger, 'Scottish Urban Housebuilding, 1870–1914', unpublished Edinburgh PhD thesis, 1976, ch. 3.
70   *Judicial Statistics*, PP 1900 CIII Table XXXIX and PP 1914 C, Table XXXVII.
71   *R.C. 1884–1885*, Evidence of J B Russell, Q. 19435.
72   *Glasgow Municipal Commission on the Housing of the Poor* (Edinburgh and Glasgow, 1904). See for example evidence of Binnie, Questions 6481, 6491, 6509, 6760.
73   Ibid. Evidence of T L Watson, Q. 11161.
74   *Report of the Board of Trade Enquiry into Working Class Rents and Retail Prices with the Rates of Wages in certain occupations in Industrial Towns of the United Kingdom in 1912*, Cd. 6955, 1913, XXXVI.
75   M Swenarton, *Homes Fit for Heroes* (London, 1981).
76   Local Government reorganisation in 1975 under *21 and 22 Eliz. II.* c.65 was responsible for their ultimate disappearance.
77   A J Youngson, *The Making of Classical Edinburgh, 1750–1840* (Edinburgh, 1966); J R Kellett, 'Property Speculators and the Building of Glasgow, 1780–1830', *Scottish Journal of Political Economy*, 8 (1961), 211–32; M A Simpson, 'Middle-Class Housing and the Growth of the Suburban Communities in the West-End of Glasgow, 1830–1914', Glasgow BLitt thesis, 1970; *Post Office Directories*, Clydebank.
78   J Reps, *Town Planning in Frontier America* (Princeton, 1969); A R Sutcliffe, 'Environmental Control and Planning in European Capitals 1850–1914: London, Paris and Berlin', in I Hammerstrom and T Hall (eds.), *The Growth and Transformation of the Modern City* (Stockholm, 1979).
79   For details of the planned villages of this period see particularly J M Houston, 'Village Planning in Scotland, 1745–1845', *The Advancement of Science*, 5 (1948), 129–32; T C Smout, 'The Landowner and the Planned Village', in N T Phillipson and R Mitchison (eds.), *Scotland in the Age of Improvement* (Edinburgh, 1970). Smout produces a list of 126 planned villages.
80   M Wood, 'Survey of the Development of Edinburgh', *Book of the Old Edinburgh Club, XXXIV, 1974*, pp. 23–56.
81   M A Simpson, op. cit. pp. 301–2.
82   M Wood, op. cit. p. 140.
83   Anon., *Remarks on the Lord Provost's Vindication of the Municipality Extension and Police and Sanitary Bills Proposed by the Town Council* (Edinburgh, 1848), p. 19.
84   M Wood, op. cit.
85   *The Scotsman*, 16 Apr. 1825.
86   W F Gray, 'The Quarrying of Salisbury Crags', *Book of the Old Edinburgh Club, XVIII, 1932*, p. 183.
87   T Ferguson, *The Dawn of Scottish Social Welfare* (Edinburgh, 1948).
88   *The Builder*, 27 Feb. 1864; 4 Jan. and 1 Feb. 1862.
89   *Report on the Air of Glasgow* (Glasgow, 1879).
90   *The Builder*, 24 Dec. 1864; 11 Nov. 1865 and 10, 17 Nov. 1866.
91   Lerwick, TCM Oct. 1867–Jan. 1868; Campbeltown Dean of Guild Court Minute Book, 1877–1914 DC1/8/1, Argyll and Bute District Record Office.

92 A K Chalmers (ed.), *Public Health Administration in Glasgow* (Glasgow, 1905), p. 142.
93 *Scottish Land Enquiry Committee* (London, 1914), Report, pp. 464–6.
94 M A Simpson, op. cit. p. 304.
95 M Wood, op. cit.
96 C M Allan, 'The Genesis of British Urban Redevelopment, with regard to Glasgow', *Economic History Review*, 18 (1965), 598–613.
97 *R.C. 1884–1885*, Evidence of J K Crawford, Q. 18781; J B Russell, Q. 19382; T B Laing, Q. 20285; W J R Simpson, Q. 19946 and A J Turnbull, Q. 20200.
98 P J Smith, 'Planning Concepts in the Improvement Schemes of Victorian Edinburgh', paper presented to the First International Conference on the History of Urban and Regional Planning, London, 1977, and 'Planning as environmental improvement; slum clearance in Victorian Edinburgh' in A R Sutcliffe (ed.), *The Rise of Modern Town Planning 1800–1914* (London, 1980), pp. 99–133.
99 S Chisholm, 'The History and the Results of the Operations of the Glasgow City Improvement Trust', *Proceedings of the Philosophical Society of Glasgow*, 27, 1895–6, 39–56; J B Russell, 'Further Information on the Immediate Results of the Operations of the Glasgow Improvement Trust . . .', *Glasgow Medical Journal* (1876), pp. 235–46.'
100 J N Tarn, *Five Per Cent Philanthropy* (Cambridge, 1973), and 'The Model Village at Bromborough Pool', *Town Planning Review*, 35 (1964–5), 329–36.

5

THE MERCHANT CLASS OF THE LARGER SCOTTISH TOWNS IN THE LATER SEVENTEENTH AND EARLY EIGHTEENTH CENTURIES

T M Devine

Recent work in Scottish agrarian history has prompted a new assessment of the pace and pattern of economic change in rural society before 1750. The period before the 'Agricultural Revolution' of the later eighteenth century has been shown to be one of continuous development which seems to have visibly accelerated in the decades before the Union of 1707 thus establishing a firm base for the more radical alterations of later times.[1] The new awareness that rural society was far from static has, however, partly helped to confirm the conventional view that the towns were the conservative sector in the early modern Scottish economy. A powerful case can be advanced to demonstrate that they were more concerned with privilege than progress and attached to an older world of guild restrictionism and monopoly increasingly irrelevant in the new age of widening commercial opportunity.[2] On the other hand, the roots of economic advance can be identified in the Scottish countryside where landowners were establishing salt and coal industries outside the control of reactionary town oligarchies and founding 'burghs of barony' where the spirit of free enterprise could flourish. Thus, one agrarian historian asserts in a recent volume of essays that the landed classes were the pioneers in Scottish economic and social development before 1760 and that 'the towns rarely threw up men of any real stature . . . for the most part the burghs were rather sad places whose leaders wallowed in their own corruption'.[3] The purpose of the present paper is to suggest that the contrast between country and town in Scotland between 1660 and 1740 has been overdrawn and that whatever the relative importance of landowners and townsmen the contribution of the latter cannot be ignored. Through a consideration of the merchant classes of the larger Scottish burghs it is hoped to demonstrate that they did not remain immune from the wider economic changes of the period and that their 'conservatism' has been exaggerated.

The focus of this study is restricted to the merchants of the larger burghs of Edinburgh, Glasgow, Aberdeen and Dundee. These were by far the most significant towns in Scotland, accounting in 1705 for about 64 per cent of total burghal taxation as measured by the stent rolls of the Convention of Royal

Burghs.[4] Edinburgh and Glasgow alone contributed 35 per cent and 20 per cent respectively. Moreover, the dominance of these two major towns in Scottish commerce was further enhanced by the control which some of their leading merchants had over the trade of smaller and superficially independent centres in the eastern and western lowlands. The differences between the four towns in size, geographical location, trade connection and historical tradition is also significant because the danger of generalising from unrepresentative experience is at least minimised. In this period, as is well known, Glasgow grew rapidly and forged important transatlantic links with the tobacco and sugar colonies. Dundee, on the other hand, took a long time to recover from the Civil War of the mid-seventeenth century and retained her old connections with Europe. Edinburgh, despite the pace of Glasgow's development, remained the premier seat of commerce in Scotland with the largest and most opulent merchant community, while Aberdeen was an important centre of regional significance.

THE INSTITUTIONAL FRAMEWORK OF MERCANTILE ACTIVITY

It is part of the conventional wisdom of Scottish economic history that town merchants in the seventeenth century functioned within an elaborate structure of protectionism.[5] Only royal burghs had the legal right to trade overseas. Commerce in the 'liberty' of the burghs was reserved for official burgesses of the town. Entry to this class and in particular to the merchant guild, the élite of the business community, was jealously guarded to favour the kinsmen of established families. Both admission fees to full burgess-ship and the mandatory period of apprenticeship were markedly less onerous for those of burgess stock. Moreover, since the burghs pursued a policy of establishing limitations on prices and controls on marketing it is possible to argue that their public face was set firmly against competition and free enterprise. Yet, it is unclear how far these restrictions were always effective in reality or, if effective, the extent to which they inhibited Scottish development. Protectionism can be regarded as a response to rather than a basic cause of economic difficulties. On this reckoning, controls on competition are to be seen more as symptoms of chronic economic insecurity rather than in themselves the basic influence on distress. Equally, if this view is correct, a reduction in the force of protectionist legislation might be anticipated when better times developed after the crisis of the middle decades of the seventeenth century. In the forty years between 1660 and 1770 harvest failure became uncommon, *pace* the 'Seven Lean Years', and trade recovered.

At first glance some of the evidence is against such an interpretation. The royal burghs did lose their monopoly of foreign trade in the famous act of the Scottish Parliament in 1672 but this can be interpreted as evidence that the landed classes imposed a more realistic régime on the conservative towns. Moreover, throughout the later seventeenth century, the records of the

Convention of Royal Burghs still abound with attempts to preserve the rights of 'free' burgesses, limit the pretensions of 'unfree' towns and maintain the exclusive nature of the merchant classes by supporting rigorous enforcement of apprenticeship regulations.[6] Yet the Convention records, on which so many generalisations about the burghs have been based, are only a partial guide to real practice within the Scottish merchant community and may simply reflect the vested interests of those royal burghs which were adversely affected by changing patterns of trade. Significantly, for example, the distinction between privileged royal burghs and 'unfree towns' which the Convention sought to preserve, had been effectively undermined by the merchants of the larger towns who were exploiting these smaller centres for their own benefit. In 1691 the Convention itself acknowledged that the traders of those towns who supposedly benefited from the old monopolies were in actuality contributing vigorously to their rapid decay: 'It is resolved no longer to suffer the rights of royal burghs to be abused and encroached upon by there owne burgesses, whoe be joining stocks with un-freemen inhabitants in the burghs of regalities and baronies and other unfree places bothe in point of trade and shipping.'[7] A year after this resolution was passed the royal burgh of Dundee admitted that it had trading links with at least fifteen 'unfree' towns and villages.[8] Moreover, Glasgow's commercial position was vitally dependent on her satellite towns of Greenock on the Clyde and Bo'ness on the Forth: 'as to trade with unfreemen or unfree burghs there is ordinarily bought of the herrings exported by the merchants of Glasgow, about two hundred lasts from Greenock men as also the far greater pairt of Hollands commodities brought to this towne from skippers, seamen and others living at Barrowstowness and other places upon that coast.'[9] These smaller centres were complementary to the larger towns and in some cases their development reflected the marketing policies of the merchant class of the bigger burghs who were the main organising force behind the changing currents of trade. The royal burghs which complained so vociferously in 1692 about competition from burghs of barony and the like were not Glasgow and Edinburgh but smaller towns such as Linlithgow and Haddington.[10]

The erosion of legal impediment to free trade between towns was paralleled by the relaxation of burgess and guild controls within the burghs. From 1681, non-burgesses of the inland town of Stirling were permitted to carry on business within the burgh without the need to gain formal admission as burgesses. Instead, they were permitted to conduct trade upon making a small annual payment to town funds.[11] Here was a clear acknowledgement of the futility of attempting to impose traditional monopolies in a period of more vigorous commercial activity. Similarly, the Dundee guildry in 1696 agreed to admit new members on payment of a fee of £12 Scots rather than £60 as formerly and after a three year rather than the traditional five to seven year apprenticeship. It is evident from the guildry minutes that this change in policy reflected the difficulties recently encountered in administering the more rigorous controls.[12] The same trend was apparent in Aberdeen and Glasgow because by the 1720s, in both towns, burgess-ship seems to have become regarded as a mark of social distinction rather than a necessary qualification for the prosecution of trade.[13] The extent of the breakdown of the burgess-ship system became clearly apparent in Glasgow several decades later. In 1784 the Merchants House estimated that there were at least 135 merchants trading in the city who were not burgesses and guild brothers of the burgh, and among them were members of such well-known mercantile dynasties as the Buchanans, Speirs, Alstons and Bogles.[14] The growing irrelevance of legal controls is further illustrated by the inadequacy of disciplinary procedures against those who broke the law. Between 1715 and 1740 Aberdeen failed to prosecute anyone for trading while not a member of the guild, while Dundee fined only one person, Thomas Webster, 'Shipmaster of North Ferry of Dundee', £1 sterling for this offence in 1737.[15] Yet this leniency should not be taken as evidence that an 'unofficial' sector of trade did not exist or was so insignificant as not to merit serious attention; on the contrary, it occurred in a period when 'unfree' commerce was almost certainly expanding.[16]

The apprenticeship system had been a traditional constraint on entry to the merchant class both because of the lengthy duration of apprenticeship, the burden of fees which it imposed and the power it bestowed on established merchants to select recruits to the next generation. However, two changes in apprenticeship can be identified in the later seventeenth and early eighteenth centuries. First, there seems to have been a decline in the length of apprenticeships from seven years, apparently the common period in the middle decades of the seventeenth century for aspiring overseas merchants, to between three and five years by the early eighteenth century. Indeed, by the 1720s, three-year apprenticeships had become the norm in both Dundee and Aberdeen.[17] Second, in some towns, the total number of apprenticeships declined both in absolute terms and as a proportion of the total of new merchant burgesses. Between 1666 and 1700, 910 boys were apprenticed to Edinburgh merchants but, from 1701 to 1740, this figure fell to 279 although there is no evidence of a similar dramatic reduction in the number of merchant burgesses entered in the city in this period.[18] An annual average of 29 merchant burgesses were registered at Glasgow between 1715 and 1740 but only 2 per annum did so as a consequence of completing a formal apprenticeship.[19] Nor is it likely that these merchants had actually undergone a formal apprenticeship and then been admitted as burgesses on a different basis. The evidence of burgess admissions for Glasgow can be checked against the Merchants House Register of Apprentices. This confirms that only a total of 35 merchant apprentices were 'book'd' between 1715 to 1740, a figure which is remarkably close to the figure derived from the burgess register above.[20] A real decline in the number of apprenticeships seems to have occurred from earlier times. Between 1680 and 1715 the average annual number of new Glasgow merchant burgesses was 18 while the number of those obtaining burgess-ship by apprenticeship was 4 per annum. Judged by both absolute and relative criteria more merchants seem to have undertaken formal apprenticeships in Glasgow in the later seventeenth century compared with the first few decades of the eighteenth.

In essence, mercantile training in this period seems to have become less burdened by the strict letter of burghal law. It is tempting, for example, to see a connection between the apparent decline of formal apprenticeship in some towns and the the rise of alternative modes of mercantile education. In the later seventeenth century Scots enrolled in mercantile 'schools' in the great Dutch commercial centres of Amsterdam, Rotterdam and Dort where the arts of cyphering, accounting and languages were taught. When William Dunlop of Glasgow was in Dort in 1681 there were five fellow Scots from Edinburgh in his class and a much larger number under instruction in Rotterdam.[21] In the same way as Scots lawyers and divines went to the continent for advanced education in universities so Scottish merchants sought to develop their expertise in these commercial schools. In addition, from the 1690s, similar institutions were established in Scotland.[22] Glasgow employed a teacher in 'the airt of navigation, book-keeping, arithmetic and wryting' from 1695. Edinburgh appointed its burghal accountant, once a merchant, 'Professor of Book-keeping' to the city in 1705. Ayr and Dunbar also provided teaching in navigation and book-keeping from 1721 and these subjects became integrated into the curricula of the grammar schools in the smaller burghs of Stirling in 1728 and Perth in 1729.

There does seem to be sufficient evidence to suggest significant changes in the institutional framework of mercantile activity in this period. The ethic of the guild was arguably less influential than before and legal constraint on competition was rapidly becoming redundant. This development was partly cause and effect of wider advances in the Scottish economy. From the middle decades of the seventeenth century the supply of food markedly improved and this was the crucial regulator of everything from demand for merchant goods to the balance of payments. The 'Seven Lean Years' can be regarded in the long perspective as an abnormal phase, the result of exceptionally severe but ephemeral climatic conditions. Increasingly the problem for many Scottish farmers and landlords between 1660 and 1730 became one of food surpluses rather than grain deficiency. Moreover, the old rigidities of the domestic economy began to recede from the later seventeenth century. The physical size of the larger towns grew. Burghs of barony, villages and fairs proliferated. Commodity exchange increased, as demonstrated by the conversion of rentals in kind to rentals in money in both highland and lowland Scotland. Similar trends are suggested in the evidence of decline in regional price differentials for grain and in the vigour of the coastal trade in meal, salt and coal, demonstrated, for instance, in the Dundee shipping registers for the early eighteenth century.[23]

The greater velocity of exchange demanded quicker and more effective methods of settling credits and debits and this led to a more sophisticated use of the bill of exchange. In the mid-seventeenth century Scottish merchants had already become familiar with the bill of exchange as a credit instrument. Its use, however, was still restricted because of a lingering prejudice in some branches of foreign trade in favour of specie and the preference of many domestic merchants for coin.[24] Yet, a survey of eleven sets of mercantile papers for the 1720s and 1730s shows that those concerned in overseas trade by the early eighteenth century always used bills in their transactions and that these instruments were also widely employed by a wide spectrum of smaller merchants, retailers, packmen and cattle drovers.[25] By the 1720s the bill of exchange had begun to serve the purpose of a cash medium, circulating for much longer periods than before and used to cover very small sums and transactions.

All this is indicative of an economy in which the commercial enclave was becoming stronger. In such a context, the old institutional structure which had governed mercantile practice in the Scottish towns was likely to become increasingly inappropriate. Greater economic maturity at once rendered protectionism less necessary and, at the same time, more difficult to enforce. Legal controls had developed to suit the requirements of a society with a small, vulnerable and insecure commercial sector. Manifestly, they were unsuited to the needs of a new era.

THE SOCIAL COMPOSITION OF THE MERCHANT CLASS

It is important to recognise at the beginning of this section that the Scottish merchant class was far from homogeneous. The point is immediately obvious if the meaning of the term 'merchant' in burghal tradition and practice is considered. As John Gibson, himself a merchant, noted in his *History of Glasgow* published in 1777, 'by merchants are to be understood all those who buy and sell'.[26] He implied therefore a most complex and diverse grouping which included at one extreme the petty shopkeeper and packman, at the other the opulent merchant prince and between a myriad army of men of varied social and material standing. Only by simplifying these complexities is it possible to carry the discussion beyond the level of description and impression. Three major categories within the merchant class can be identified. First, there were those involved in trade who were not registered burgesses of a Scottish town. As has been shown, this 'unofficial' sector of commerce had always existed and seems to have become active in the later seventeenth century to such an extent that some towns acknowledged its growth by adjusting existing legal restrictions on permission to trade. Unfortunately, however, members of this group are inevitably poorly documented in town records and it is impossible therefore to examine them in any systematic fashion. It is tolerably clear, nonetheless, from the scattered references to them, that they were mainly men and women of relatively low status in the urban hierarchy because even if burgess-ship was becoming less important in strictly economic terms it still retained its value as a mark of social distinction. Normally, they seem to have plied the trades of small shopkeeper, pedlar, hawker and packmen and were concerned with retail services in the towns or in the buying up of goods from greater wholesale merchants for distribution in the surrounding countryside.[27] A typical reference to their activities is to be found in the Edinburgh council minutes of 1692 where there was noted the existence of, '. . . several persons who have taken up the trade of ale-selling and stableing albeit they have no title which is an incroachment on the burgess-rights . . . and a great many women, servants and others who turning wearie of their services, have, out of a principle of avarice and laziness, taken up little shops which is evidently hurtful to the trading burgesses who bear the publick burdens of the place'.[28] The importance of this sector lay in the fact that it permitted people of humble background and modest means to become involved in buying and selling to some extent though it is doubtful if many of them managed to move up very far in the urban hierarchy during their own lifetimes.

The second and third groupings both consisted of registered burgesses of the four towns considered in this study. For analytical purposes, however, they are distinguished by the extent of their participation in either domestic or foreign trade. In practice, of course, this distinction is to some degree an artificial one. Individuals who imported wine, such as John Innes and William Caldwell of Edinburgh in the 1720s, were also involved in marketing it throughout Scotland.[29] Similarly, merchants such as John Steuart of Inverness and Walter Gibson of Glasgow had interests in the domestic fisheries, exported fish to Europe and the New World and imported foreign commodities in return.[30] Examples such as these could be multiplied but they ought not to obscure the crucial point that only a relatively small number of merchants were regularly involved in overseas trade. At Glasgow in the later seventeenth century there was a merchant community of 400–500 strong in a town of about 12,000 in total population. Yet only about 20 to 25 per cent of all merchants were committed to foreign trade and invariably they were among the wealthier elements of town society.[31] The position in Glasgow reflected the economy of a burgh with important and growing overseas connections. At Dundee, in the same period, where foreign trade was in the doldrums but coastal commerce very active, the proportion of overseas merchants was probably even less than at Glasgow.[32] Only a minority, then, had the finance, experience and contacts to pursue foreign trade on a consistent basis: a distinction therefore tended to develop and became recognised in contemporary parlance between ordinary merchants and those who traded abroad, the 'merchant adventurers' or 'sea adventurers' as they were described.[33] It was embodied also in burghal law and tradition by the old regulation that, while all burgesses had the right to trade, only members of the merchant guild, for which entry fees were higher and social obstacles to membership greater, had the legal right to trade abroad.

The possibility of the existence of an élite group of merchants within the general merchant class is confirmed when the poll tax records for the 1690s are examined. In Aberdeen a small group of 27 men can be identified among the larger community of 239 merchant burgesses. Members of this inner circle possessed stock valued at 10,000 merks Scots (or about £530 sterling) and above. Seven possessed country properties in the vicinity of the burgh though ownership of land outside the environs of the town was relatively uncommon among the merchant class as a whole. The provost, dean of guild and magistrates of Aberdeen were recruited exclusively from the ranks of this élite. At the other end of the social scale, 62 merchants were reckoned to have stock valued at less than £27 sterling while the remaining 150 of middling status were assessed at between £27 and £260 sterling.[34]

In the two inner parishes of Edinburgh a similar pyramid-type structure existed though in the capital the number of opulent merchants was much greater than in Aberdeen and their individual stock more substantial.[35] In Tolbooth parish, 25 merchants, or almost one-third of the total resident there, had assets valued at 10,000 merks, or about £530 sterling, and above. Five, however, were worth 30,000 merks, a figure which no Aberdonian merchant could approach. In the same parish only two were estimated to own stock of less than 500 merks while 38 of the total resident merchant population were men of middling rank assessed at between 1000 and 10,000 merks. In the adjacent Old Kirk parish there was an even greater concentration of well-to-do merchants. Twenty-six of a community of 51 were reckoned worth 10,000 merks or above with five individuals valued at three to four times that amount. It follows from this that a satisfactory assessment of the social composition of the merchant class depends on the completion of two different but complementary tasks. First, one has to determine how easy or difficult it was to attain merchant burgess status in this period and, second, to focus specifically on the business élites of the towns and discover whether they were closed oligarchies or refreshed themselves through the recruitment of newcomers drawn from outside their own ranks.

On superficial examination major barriers did exist to prevent easy entry into the official merchant community of the Scottish towns. Legal restrictions were in decline but the main obstacles were not rooted in law but in the nature of economic and social relationships at the time. Merchant fathers commonly laid aside cash sums to enable their sons to set up business on their own account on attainment of their majority. Substantial amounts were often involved as when James Dunlop of Garnkirk, merchant of Glasgow, wrote a bond of provision in 1716 in favour of his son, John, for £175 sterling 'on his taking up a lawful trade'.[36] Such inheritance practices were a way of perpetuating the commercial prominence of many established families into the next and succeeding generations. The character of business life in the period tended also to benefit those with existing ties and contacts. To a considerable extent, especially in foreign trade, commerce functioned through a network of kin and personal connections. This was an era of developing but still unreliable communications, high risks and unsophisticated commercial law. The business world was thus a tight nexus in which a merchant's reputation and that of his family was his most precious asset: to deal with kin and trusted acquaintances was not simply understandable but justifiable. Nepotism had a basic commercial rationale.

In the light of this it is hardly surprising that merchants' sons formed the largest single category of new merchant burgesses admitted during the period covered by this study. From 1710 to 1730, 46 per cent of Edinburgh merchants gained entry to burgess status by right of their fathers while at Dundee 48 per cent did so between 1705 and 1740 and 30 per cent at Aberdeen from 1707 to 1740.[37] But these data also reveal that the majority of new entrants in each of these towns was born outside established families and gained burgess rank by marriage, apprenticeship, purchase or by some other means. Nor was this pattern unique to the *later* seventeenth century for the Edinburgh burgess register, which has been analysed for the whole of the century, suggests that numbers admitted through marriage or apprenticeship were consistently greater than those enrolled by right of a father. Moreover, the data if anything, underestimate the proportion of new men. One can only speculate on the number of merchants' sons who were simply awarded burgess status in a formal sense—because the cost of entry fees for them was entirely nominal—but who never went on to practice as professional traders.

It is appropriate now to ask whether there is similar evidence of movement among the inner élite of the merchant class. Here the barriers to mobility were more formidable than those limiting access to the merchant community as a whole. The most obvious one was financial. Membership of the socially prestigious merchant guild was probably almost a prerequisite for membership of the élite but to be accepted into this body required good connections and considerable means. The Guildry Court at Aberdeen resolved in 1751 that, 'When any persons apply to the Court for admission they resolved that none be found qualified unless they depon that they are worth one hundred and fifty pounds sterling of free stock and that they produce a certificate signed by two creditable burgesses attesting that the petitioner is of good character. . . .'[38] At Glasgow, fifty years earlier, the property qualification for a guild brother was about 3½ times that for a mere burgess.[39] Again, the greater merchants, as will be shown in more detail later, tended to diversify their assets and so, by minimising the insecurities of trade, endeavoured to preserve the integrity of the family fortune for future generations.[40]

To determine whether these influences were sufficient to stabilise the composition of the dominant merchant families in the Scottish towns the names and social backgrounds of those who controlled the institutions of civic authority were scrutinised, because membership of town council, burgh offices and the guildry courts offers a rough guide to the membership of the business élite. A comparison of the leading families of late seventeenth century Glasgow with those of the mid eighteenth century reveals a remarkably fluid pattern. Several families did manage to maintain their position. The Bogles, Dunlops, Corbetts, Murdochs and Buchanans were all noted commercial dynasties in the 1670s and 1680s and still of considerable eminence a century later.[41] Others, however, had disappeared while the continuing distinction of some was not inconsistent with the emergence of new elements within the very highest echelons of the merchant class. The great figures of the golden era of Glasgow's Atlantic trades, Glassford, Speirs, Cunninghame, Oswald and McDowall, were not only born outside the established circle but outside Glasgow itself. John Glassford's father was a merchant burgess of the nearby town of Paisley;[42] Alexander Speirs was the son of an Edinburgh merchant;[43] William Cunninghame's father was a trader in Kilmarnock who belonged to a cadet branch of the Cunninghames of Caprington, lairds in Ayrshire.[44] The Oswalds were from clerical stock in Caithness[45] while, the McDowalls, major partners in the giant West India house of Alexander Houston and Co., were the offspring of a Scots soldier who had made good in the Caribbean but could trace his lineage back to landed stock in Wigtownshire.[46]

The evidence of a turnover in the Glasgow mercantile élite, though significant, must however be treated with caution. The town's rate of growth in the eighteenth century was exceptional and so also, it might be argued, was movement within the higher echelons of the business class. An examination of the ruling families in Dundee and Aberdeen, two burghs with a less dramatic economic history than that of Glasgow, might determine how representative the position in Glasgow was. In both cases a similar steady movement among the élite can be identified. In the 1690s, Aberdeen was ruled by the Mitchells, Skenes, Johnstones, Robertsons and Gordons but, by the 1750s, little trace remained of any of these names in council and guildry records. Instead, a new grouping built around the Youngs, Brebners, Auldjos, Mores and Leys, had emerged to dominate the political and economic life of the burgh.[47] It is true that a simple turnover in names may not necessarily reflect changes in *family* status and position which could have been perpetuated through the female rather than the male line. On the other hand, the evidence of new surnames is at least an indicator of the steady recruitment of new men to the élite. Such a pattern also existed in Dundee. Between 1683 and 1720, membership of the Guildry Court, the body concerned with the maintenance and defence of the privileges of the greater merchants, fluctuated between 15 and 18. In 1689, 7 of the families present in 1683 were still represented. By 1702 the number had dwindled to 4 and all of the individuals concerned were the sons of the leading figures of the early 1680s. In 1708 only 2 names survived of the original membership and by 1715 there was no trace of any of the families who had served on the court three decades before.[48] The Glasgow experience therefore does not appear to have been untypical. The personnel of the élites was not obviously more stable than that of the merchant class as a whole.

Some reasons can be advanced for this social movement within the merchant community. Occasionally some members of the élite were lost to commerce by moving into landownership. Such was the case with the Skenes of Rubislaw in Aberdeen in the later seventeenth century and the Campbells of Shawfield in Glasgow in the early eighteenth.[49] But the evidence suggests that this was not a central influence on the changing social composition of the merchant class. First, as will be discussed in more detail below, only a small minority of successful merchants bought estates in this period.[50] Second, when land was acquired it was not often secured in sufficient quantity to permit families to completely sever their links with commerce. If the investment strategies of Glasgow and Aberdeen merchants are typical most trading families who became landowners retained their commercial interests over several generations.[51] It might indeed be argued that the buying of land gave mercantile families more security and so enabled them to perpetuate their position rather than cede it to newcomers.

A much more powerful agency of change was the growth in internal and external commerce which characterised the period 1660 to 1750. Most obviously this tended to widen and deepen the opportunities for men of commerce particularly as legal controls and restrictions diminished. Equally, however, a period of growth was also a period of commercial risk especially in some of the new and more lucrative branches of international trade. The expansion of Scottish North American and Caribbean commerce was punctuated by a series of spectacular bankruptcies in Glasgow which helped to limit the possibility of a self-perpetuating monopoly among a handful of rich families. Such commercial dynasties as the Buchanans, Dunlops, Dunmores, McDowalls and Houstons were all affected by financial disaster.[52] In other towns the incidence of financial failure can best be studied in the records of the merchant guilds. These institutions had the responsibility of providing support for those members who had fallen on hard times and their minutes are often a poignant guide to the fragility of contemporary business fortunes. So in Aberdeen in 1736, the pressures on the guild's finances because of the misfortunes that had overtaken some of its members were such that '. . . the monies belonging to the Guild Box is not in a condition to support the poor decayed brethern of guild of this burgh and their widows and children'.[53] In 1730, the funds of the Dundee guildry were deemed insufficient to meet the needs of families of insolvent members with the result that entry fees were raised to provide for these unfortunates.[54]

Moreover, high mortality rates in the seventeenth and early eighteenth centuries together with the desire of some sons to opt for careers outside commerce doubtless brought some families to an end in the male line. This process, however, left daughters and widows to provide opportunities for social movement through marriage and re-marriage. In all the towns studied, entry to burgess-ship by right of marriage was second only to paternity as the most common means of registration. Thus, of the 110 new merchant burgesses admitted at Dundee between 1705 and 1740, 47 obtained entry by right of a father, 27 by marriage, 25 by purchase and 12 by apprenticeship.[55] At Edinburgh from 1710 to 1720, 59 achieved burgess-ship by right of their fathers, 40 by marriage, 31 by apprenticeship and 24 by purchase.[56]

It is more difficult to determine whether the turnover in the composition of the merchant class also implied substantial social mobility within the hierarchy of the towns because the evidence on the social origins of new merchants is too incomplete to permit a systematic analysis. Nevertheless, extant data on the social background of Aberdeen and Edinburgh merchant apprentices do allow some tentative conclusions to be made though, since only a proportion of all merchants undertook a formal apprenticeship in the period, this evidence is only a very partial guide to the origins of the merchant community as a whole. Both the Edinburgh and the Aberdeen material suggest that when merchant apprentices were not sons of merchants they invariably came from similar social backgrounds to those who were. Overwhelmingly they were recruited from the middle strata of Scottish society. Of 27 Aberdeen apprentices in the period 1709 to 1740, 8 were sons of tenant farmers, 4 of ministers of the Church, 2 were sons of small landowners, 2 of craftsmen, 2 of lawyers and 1 was the son of a schoolmaster. The occupations of the remaining 8 fathers was unknown.[57] 279 persons were admitted to merchant apprenticeship in Edinburgh between 1701 and 1730. Of these, 84 were the sons of lairds, 42 were recruited from professional families with backgrounds in the law, the ministry and education, 30 were the sons of merchants in other Scottish towns, 37 of craftsmen burgesses (mainly from Edinburgh) and the occupation of 48 fathers was unknown. Aberdeen and Edinburgh did, however, differ in two respects. Almost all Aberdeen apprentices were born in the burgh itself or in its rural hinterland whereas a substantial minority of Edinburgh apprentices came from outside the capital and the south eastern region. Secondly, the social status of Edinburgh apprentices tended to be somewhat higher than that of the Aberdeen men. The number of Edinburgh merchant apprentices recruited from landed and professional backgrounds is especially significant.

Entry to the more lucrative types of merchanting was probably restricted to men of middle rank and above not because of legal restriction but through the system of patronage. The world of eighteenth-century commerce was little different from that of politics and the professions in this respect. Places were obtained through an informal but powerful network of clientage, connection and recommendation. Success in overseas trade required not simply business acumen and skill but introduction to a world where personal contacts were vital in the establishment of trust between merchants. Commonly, therefore, established merchants were approached by close and distant kinsmen, friends and associates who sought to find an opening in trade for their offspring. Adam Montgomery, a Glasgow factor in Stockholm in the early eighteenth century, took on several young Scots as apprentices but his letterbook shows that they were invariably his own kinsman or sons of his personal friends.[59] Similarly, Alexander Shairp, an Edinburgh merchant resident in Amsterdam in 1717, supervised the education of a number of the sons of his Scottish friends in the arts of book-keeping, ciphering and foreign languages.[60] These connections, however, were not unique to the European commercial context. Young men who sought positions in Scottish-owned plantations in the Caribbean or in Glasgow stores in Virginia and Maryland were placed in exactly[61] the same manner. This meant that despite the decline of legal controls access to the lucrative branches of trade still depended to a very large extent on the influence and power of those with an existing stake in them.

PATTERNS OF INVESTMENT AMONG THE GREATER MERCHANTS

The distribution of profits earned by merchants in the course of trade is, of course, a key aspect of the more general issue of the impact of the merchant class on the Scottish economy. It is vital to determine whether they tended to invest in 'productive' assets, for instance, in further expansion of commercial ventures or industrial concerns or in 'non-productive' assets, for example, in household furnishings, personal clothing and land. Yet, clearly, no precise indication of the distribution of merchant profits can be given because of the great variety both between merchants and over time in investment practice. Here it is intended merely to provide a general and tentative evaluation of the investment patterns of those merchants engaged in foreign trade because they were invariably the ones with the surplus resources to deploy elsewhere.

Some contemporaries did argue that mercantile profits tended to be dissipated in the purchase of landed estates or in other forms of consipicuous consumption. So William Seton, writing in 1700, complained that, 'So soon as a Merchant hath scraped together a piece of money, perhaps to the value of 4000 or 5000 lib. sterling instead of employing it for promoting Trade or by projecting any new thing that may be serviceable to his country, and to the augmenting of his stock, nothing will satisfy him but the laying of it out upon a land Estate, for having the Honour to make his son a Laird, that is, an idle person, who can find out as many methods in spending his Father's Money, as he had of gaining it'.[62] That some merchants managed to buy their way into land is beyond question. Land was both a sound investment and a route to an enhanced and enduring social position for a merchant's family. There are therefore several examples of successful traders buying estates scattered throughout the secondary literature.[63] Yet, almost certainly, Seton both exaggerated the extent of this practice and the adverse economic effects which, in his view, it inevitably caused.

Two sources of data demonstrate that merchants had only a limited impact on the land market before 1740. Firstly, land transactions recorded in the Register of the Great Seal were analysed for the years 1660–8.[64] These reveal that merchants only accounted for 5.7 per cent of all transactions and that only rarely did merchant involvement in the land market imply the purchase of a landed estate. Those merchants who obtained land did so commonly in relatively small quantities of less than fifty acres not as a means of enhancing their social position but rather in satisfaction of debts for which land had been employed as security. Thus, of 984 transactions recorded in the Register of the Great Seal over the longer period 1593 to 1660 involving non-landed groups, 300 were carried out as 'apprisings' by which the heritable rights of the debtor were sold for payment of the debt due to the appriser. The largest number of apprisings, about 68 per cent, was carried out by merchants.[65] It would appear that ownership of land within the merchant community can be regarded as an integral feature of the commercial régime rather than a means of withdrawing from trade. Secondly, the Valuation Rolls for Lanark, Renfrew, Stirling, Berwick and Midlothian were scrutinised for the eighteenth century because it was assumed that landownership patterns in these central lowland counties might reflect the estate purchases of the merchants of the larger towns. No significant penetration, however, was detected until after c.1750. The main trend revealed in the earlier period was the steady increase in the size of the properties of the bigger landowners at the expense of the smaller lairds, although this development was notably less marked in the western counties than in the eastern lowlands. This would suggest that the pattern over the entire period 1660 to 1740 was relatively stable. Both the Great Seal data and the Valuation Rolls tend to indicate that the typical purchaser of land was the great aristocrat rather than the town merchant.

Merchants who did manage to acquire estates were very much in the minority. Landownership was the mark of the especially successful trader if only because few at this time had the resources to embark on substantial purchases of territory. Daniel Campbell, the well-known Glasgow merchant, had to pay out £4000 for the estate of Shawfield near Glasgow in the early eighteenth century but as the poll tax data for the 1690s revealed only a handful of members of the Scottish business community could have afforded such an outlay.[67] Only 7 of the 239 merchants listed in the Aberdeen poll tax records owned a country estate and all of them were among the two dozen wealthiest men in the burgh.[68] Not surprisingly the merchants of the most prosperous and largest towns were the most active in the land market. Edinburgh merchants were pre-eminent in the later seventeenth century. Between 1660 and 1668 they accounted for about 61 per cent of all transactions involving merchants recorded in the Register of the Great Seal with Glasgow and Aberdeen men together accounting for a further 20 per cent. Nevertheless, this evidence in itself does not necessarily imply a haemorrhage of capital from trade to land. Only two examples have been uncovered so far of trading families who built up their estates to such an extent that they were able to sever their links with commerce. These were the Skenes of Rubislaw from Aberdeen and the Campbells of Shawfield from Glasgow. Recent analyses of the eighteenth century merchant class of both towns have shown that it was more common for families to retain links with *both* commerce and land over successive generations.[70]

In fact, the specific pattern of mercantile investment in land merely reflected the general business strategy of the greater merchants. No one activity was necessarily favoured at the expense of others and surpluses were distributed widely both to provide security against misfortune and maximise returns. There is very little indication of rash dissipation in current consumption or in extensive land purchases but much evidence of careful investment in a range of activities intended to generate continued profit. When funds were not absorbed in trade itself they tended to be deployed in the building and leasing of urban property, in the provision of long-term credit and in industrial investment. Local registers of deeds and sasines reveal a most active market in the buying and selling of small plots of land and tenement properties in which the merchant class was much involved.[71] Again, virtually every will and testament of overseas merchants showed the popularity of lending out surplus funds on personal or heritable bond.[72] The creditor received an annual 'rent' or interest and a 'liquidate penalty' or additional sum levied if the loan was not liquidated within the period of time specified in the original bond. Such loans could be maintained over a number of years and were increased or reduced as circumstances warranted. Some merchants became involved in a major way in the provision of these primitive 'overdraft' facilities. The 1715 testament of Henry Eccles, merchant of Dundee, documents his bonded loans to 24 individuals, including the Earls of Strathmore and Haddington. A total of £700 sterling had been distributed in sums varying from £8 to £100. On one of his loans, moreover, Eccles had been drawing interest since 1691 and on most of the other loans for periods of five to ten years.[73] Some Glasgow merchants, such as Peter Murdoch, Andrew Cochrane and Robert Robertson, became so committed to lending on bond that they can be regarded as proto-bankers and when they helped to establish banking companies in the city in the 1750s they were simply formalising and extending a business in which they had long been engaged.[74]

The provision of finance for industry was an increasingly common feature of the investment strategies of the greater merchants in the later seventeenth century. Throughout the period of the present study 'industry' was more typical of the country than the towns because it was obviously in the rural areas that coal-mining, salt-burning and textile production was concentrated. Yet, after 1660, the number of processing plants in the larger burghs rose significantly in the wake of expansion in internal and external trade. The protectionist policy of the Scottish Parliament was also partly responsible for this development as a determined effort was made to reduce the importation of foreign manufactures and the export of Scottish raw materials through exempting Scottish native manufactories from custom duties and taxation. Between 1660 and 1710 about 52 industrial ventures were established in the towns and, according to the sources consulted, survived after their inception for a minimum period of three years.[75] They were concerned with the production of a range of different commodities: sugar, wool, glass, soap, paper, leather, lead, pins, rope, linen, sailcloth, gunpowder, salt, hardware and spirits. Equally they varied enormously in size and significance. In 1675 the Glasgow Easter Sugar House had a capital stock of £5555 and in 1680, the Leith Glassworks had a first issue of stock totalling almost £17,000 but these were exceptionally large by the standards of the majority. The majority attracted capital sums of less than £500.

What, however, is more pertinent to this analysis is not so much the nature of the manufactory movement as such as the extent of merchant participation in it both in terms of enterprise and finance. It is possible to identify the origins of capital in 49 of the 52 ventures. Thirty-eight manufactories attracted merchant investment in combination with landed and professional groups while merchants were the sole source of capital in 34 cases. Landowners were the next most significant group with interests in 10 firms. Merchant capital was, however, decisive and was usually contributed in the form of joint-stock enterprise involving 5 to 10 individual partners. As in landed investment most capital derived from the merchant communities of Edinburgh and Glasgow. Edinburgh men were responsible for the creation of 19 establishments and Glasgow merchants for 16. The merchant classes of the other Scottish towns had only a minor role: Aberdeen traders helped to organise and finance 4 ventures and Ayr burgesses 1. In the second half of the eighteenth century, merchant capital was a major factor in industrial expansion but this was a development which had significant, though much more modest origins, in earlier times.

CONCLUSION

The Scottish achievement of industrialisation in the later eighteenth century was based upon a vigorous national response to emerging markets and technical advance. Whether or not these possibilities were exploited depended in the final analysis on the quality of Scottish business talent and initiative. It was therefore of importance that before the period of substantial growth, a vigorous mercantile class had already evolved in lowland Scotland and had begun to demonstrate the skills of careful investment and willingness to take advantage of new commercial opportunity. The old institutional structure of mercantile controls which had developed to service the needs of a more stagnant economic system was rapidly being abandoned in the later seventeenth and early eighteenth centuries. The extent of social movement within the merchant communities of the larger towns implied the evaluation of a setting conducive to enterprise, of a milieu in which status depended on commercial ability as well as inherited rank. Above all, the investment patterns of the greater merchant class reveal a marked tendency to fund productive assets which were geared to further profit growth and diversification. All this helps to explain why, when markets expanded rapidly after 1750, the Scottish business class of that era, which had been formed in the urban world of the early eighteenth century, responded in an efficient and positive fashion.

REFERENCES

1 See *inter alia*, R A Dodgshon, 'The Removal of Runrig in Roxburghshire and Berwickshire 1680–1708', *Scottish Studies*, **16** (1972); M L Parry and T R Slater (eds.), *The Making of the Scottish Countryside* (London, 1980); I D Whyte, *Agriculture and Society in Seventeenth Century Scotland* (Edinburgh, 1979); John Di Folco, 'The Hopes of Craighall and Investment in Land in the Seventeenth Century', in T M Devine (ed.), *Lairds and Improvement in the Scotland of the Enlightenment* (Dundee, 1979), pp. 1–10.

2 T C Smout, *A History of the Scottish People, 1560–1830* (London, 1969), p. 161.

3 I H Adams, 'The Agents of Agricultural Change', in Parry and Slater, op. cit. p. 157.

4 J D Marwick (ed.), *Extracts from the Records of the Convention of the Royal Burghs of Scotland, 1677–1711* (Edinburgh, 1880). Hereafter referred to as *Convention Records*.

5 The standard descriptions of the institutional framework of merchant activity are: W M Mackenzie, *The Scottish Burghs* (Edinburgh, 1949); David Murray, *Early Burgh Organisation in Scotland* (Glasgow, 1924); A J Warden, *Burgh Laws of Dundee* (London, 1872).

6 *Convention Records*, pp. 24, 26, 44, 46, 133, 209.

7 Ibid. p. 133.

8 'Register containing the state and Condition of every burgh within the Kingdome of Scotland in the year 1692', *Miscellany of the Scottish Burgh Records Society* (Edinburgh, 1881), p. 75.

9 Ibid. p. 81.

10 Ibid.

11 David B Morris, *The Stirling Merchant Gild and the Life of John Cowane* (Stirling, 1919), p. 73.

12 Dundee City Archive and Record Centre (DCARC), Dundee Guildry Book, GD/GRW/G1/1, 1570–1696.

13 Strathclyde Regional Archives (SRA), T-MH/2, Minute Book of the Merchants House of Glasgow, vol. 2, 1711–54; T Donnelly, 'The Economic Activities of the Aberdeen Merchant Guild, 1750–1799', *Scottish Economic and Social History*, **1** (1981), 27.

14 SRA, T-MH 13, List of Persons carrying on or concerned in Trade in the city of Glasgow, 4 Oct. 1784, but whose names do not appear in the Register of Freemen kept by the Town Clerks.

15 Aberdeen Charter Room, Town House, Aberdeen (ACR), A25/1, Aberdeen Guildry Minute Books; DCARC, GD/GRW/G1/2, Sederunt Book of Dundee Guild Court; GD/GRW/G3/1, Guildry Incorporation Account Book, 1696–1751.

16 J D Marwick, *Edinburgh Guilds and Crafts* (Edinburgh, 1910), pp. 182, 192, 204–5, 207; Helen Armet (ed.), *Extracts from the Records of the Burgh of Edinburgh, 1689 to 1701* (Edinburgh, 1962), pp. 121–2; DCARC, GD/GRW/G1/2, Dundee Guild Court Sederunt Book, 6 July 1728; ACR, A25/1, Aberdeen Guildry Minute Book, 12 Mar. 1736.

17 DCARC, Guildry Incorporation Account Book, 1696–1751; ACR, Aberdeen Registered Deeds, A.32.

18 CBB Watson (ed.), *Register of Edinburgh Apprentices, 1660–1700* (Edinburgh, 1929); *Register of Edinburgh Apprentices, 1701–1755* (Edinburgh, 1929).

19 J R Anderson (ed.), *The Burgesses and Guild Brethren of Glasgow, 1573–1750* (Edinburgh, 1925).

20 SRA, T-MH/2, Minute Book of Merchants House of Glasgow, 1711–54, Register of Apprentices Book'd.

21 Mitchell Library, Glasgow (ML), Dunlop Papers, D24/2a, William Dunlop to James Dunlop, n.d., *c*.1681.

22 Donald J. Withrington, 'Education and Society in the Eighteenth Century', in N T Phillipson and R Mitchison (eds.), *Scotland in the Age of Improvement* (Edinburgh, 1970), p. 170.

23 These trends are outlined in the following: Whyte, op. cit. pp. 222–45; R Mitchison, 'The Movement of Scottish Corn Prices in the Seventeenth and Eighteenth Centuries', *Econ. Hist. Rev.* (2nd ser.), **18** (1965); C L Horricks, 'Economic and Social Change in the Isle of Harris, 1680–1754' (unpublished PhD thesis, Edinburgh University, 1974); DCARC, Register of Ships of Dundee, 1701–13.

24 T C Smout, *Scottish Trade on the Eve of Union, 1660–1707* (Edinburgh, 1963), pp. 116–30.

25 Scottish Record Office (SRO), RH15/147, Papers of John Innes, merchant in Edinburgh; RH15/139, Accounts and Papers of William Nicoll, merchant in Edinburgh; RH15/186, Papers of William Cleghorn; RH15/54, Accounts and Papers of Edward Burd; W Mackay (ed.), *The Letter-Book of Baillie John Steuart of Inverness, 1715–1752* (Edinburgh, 1915); SRO, CC/8/85, Testaments of Robert Young, William Blair, Uthred McDowall; ML, B.325799, Copy Book of Letters of Adam Montgomery, 1700–1702 and Campbell of Shawfield Papers; National Library of Scotland (NLS), MS 1884, Letterbook of Alexander Shairp, 1712–19.

26 John Gibson, *The History of Glasgow from the Earliest Accounts to the Present Time* (Glasgow, 1777), p. 113.

27 *Convention Records*, pp. 133, 209, 212; Marwick, op. cit. pp. 182, 192, 204–5, 207; *Miscellany of the Scottish Burgh Records Society* (Edinburgh, 1881), pp. 75, 81; DCARC, Dundee Guild Court Sederunt Book, 6 July 1728; ACR, A.25/1, Aberdeen Guildry Minute Book, 12 Mar. 1736.

28 Marwick, op. cit. pp. 204–5.

29 SRO, RH15/147, Papers of John Innes, merchant in Edinburgh; RH15/126/1, Letters and other papers pertaining to William Caldwell, merchant, Leith c. 1720–34.

30 W Mackay (ed.), *The Letterbook of Baillie John Steuart of Inverness, 1715–1752* (Edinburgh, 1915); John McCure, *A View of the City of Glasgow* (Glasgow, 1736), p. 169.

31 T C Smout, 'The Glasgow Merchant Community in the Seventeenth Century', *Scottish Historical Review*, 47 (1968), 53–68.

32 For the relatively sluggish condition of overseas commerce in the early eighteenth-century Dundee see DARC, TC/TS/3–4, Dundee Register of Ships, 1701–13.

33 McCure, op. cit. p. 170; Robert Chambers, *Edinburgh Merchants and Merchandise in Old Times* (Edinburgh, 1899), p. 5.

34 J Stuart (ed.), *List of Rollable Persons within the Shire of Aberdeen in 1694* (Aberdeen, 1844). Hereafter referred to as *Aberdeen Poll List, 1694*.

35 Marguerite Wood (ed.), *Edinburgh Poll Tax Returns for 1694* (Edinburgh, 1951).

36 ML, MS 120, Dunlop Papers, Bond of Provision for James Dunlop, 1 Sept. 1716.

37 C B B Watson (ed.), *Roll of Edinburgh Burgesses and Guild Brethren, 1701–1760* (Edinburgh, 1930). Hereafter referred to as *Edinburgh Burgess Roll*; DCARC, Lockit Book of Burgesses of Dundee, 1513–1973; ACR, Aberdeen Burgess Book, 1694–1760. These calculations exclude honorary and 'gratis' burgesses of which there were many.

38 ACR, A.25/1, Aberdeen Guildry Minute Book, 29 June 1751.

39 McCure, op. cit. pp. 166 ff.

40 See below, PATTERNS OF INVESTMENT . . . pp. 104–107.

41 Smout, loc. cit.; T M Devine, *The Tobacco Lords* (Edinburgh, 1975); 'An Eighteenth Century Business Élite: Glasgow West India Merchants, c. 1750–1815', *Scottish Historical Review*, 57 (1978), 40–67.

42 James Gourlay, *A Glasgow Miscellany* (privately printed, n.d.), p. 43.

43 SRA, Register of Deeds, B.10/15/8435, Settlement of Alexander Speirs.

44 SRO, GD 247/10, Answers for William Cunninghame . . . 1.

45 W St Robinson jun., 'Richard Oswald the Peacemaker', *Ayrshire Collections*, 1950–4 (2nd ser.) III (1955).

46 P A Ramsay, *Views in Renfrewshire with Historical and Descriptive Notices* (Edinburgh, 1839), 163; SRO, GD 237/139, Minutes of Agreement between W McDowall and J Gordon, St Kitts, 28 Dec. 1723. For the position of those families which had retained their position from the later seventeenth century see M L Bogle MSS, Geneology of the Bogle family; A Dunlop, *Memorabilia of the Family of Dunlop* (privately printed, n.d.); Anon, *Old Country Houses of the Old Glasgow Gentry* (Glasgow, 1870); R M Buchanan, *Notes on Members of the Buchanan Society, 1725–1829* (Glasgow, 1931).

47 *Aberdeen Poll List, 1694;* A Munro, *Memorials of the Aldermen, Provosts and Lord Provosts of Aberdeen* (Aberdeen, 1897), pp. 244–62; ACR, A. 5–6, Aberdeen Council Register, 1690–1750; Donnelly, loc. cit. pp. 25–41.

48 DCARC, GD/GRW/G1/1–2, Dundee Guildry Book, 1683–1720.

49 ML, Campbell of Shawfield Papers, 1/576, Robert Campbell to Daniel Campbell, 10 June 1712; W F Skene, *Memorials of the Family of Skene of Skene* (Aberdeen, 1881), p. 131.

50 See below, PATTERNS OF INVESTMENT . . . pp. 104–107.
51 For Glasgow see Devine, op. cit. pp. 25–7; for Aberdeen, Munro, op. cit. pp. 244–62.
52 Devine, op. cit., pp. 7–8.
53 ACR, A.25/1, Aberdeen Guildry Minute Book, 19 Feb. 1736.
54 DCARC, GD/GRW/G1/2, Sederunt Book of Dundee Guild Court, 30 Jan. 1730.
55 Ibid. Lockit Book of Burgesses of Dundee, 1513–1973.
56 *Edinburgh Burgess Roll,* 1710–20.
57 ACR, A.21, Aberdeen Register of Indentures, 1622–1798.
58 *Register of Edinburgh Apprentices,* 1701–55.
59 ML, B.325799, Adam Montgomery Letterbook, 1700–2.
60 NLS, MS 1884, Letterbook of Alexander Shairp, merchant in Edinburgh, 1712–19.
61 Devine, op. cit. pp. 9–10, 83–4; loc. cit. p. 51.
62 William Seton, *The Interest of Scotland* (1700), p. 75.
63 See, for example, Smout, op. cit. (1963), pp. 78–9.
64 J H Stevenson (ed.), *The Register of the Great Seal of Scotland, 1660–1668* (Edinburgh, 1914). Hereafter referred to as *Register of the Great Seal.*
65 See the calculations in J di Folco's essay in T M Devine (ed.), *Lairds and Improvement in the Scotland of the Enlightenment* (Dundee, 1979), pp. 1–10.
66 SRO, County Valuation Rolls E/106. See also L Timperley, 'The Pattern of Landholding in Eighteenth Century Scotland', in Parry and Slater, op.cit. pp. 137–54.
67 ML, Campbell of Shawfield Papers, 1/576, Robert Campbell to Daniel Campbell, 10 June 1712.
68 *Aberdeen Poll List, 1694.*
69 *Register of the Great Seal, 1660–1668.*
70 Devine, op. cit. pp. 18–33; Donnelly, loc. cit.
71 See, for example, Edinburgh City Archives (ECA), Inventory of Miscellaneous Papers called Moses' Bundles; ACR, Burgh Court Deeds Recorded, 1736–40.
72 Many of the generalisations which follow are based on an analysis of approximately sixty merchant testaments for the period 1680–1740 in the Edinburgh and Glasgow commissary court records. See SRO, CC8/8 (Edinburgh) and CC9/7 (Glasgow).
73 SRO, CC 8/8/86.
74 SRA, B.10/15/5402, Disposition and Assignation, Robert Robinson to his Creditors, 1740; S G Checkland, *Scottish Banking: a History, 1695–1973* (Glasgow, 1975), p. 69.
75 The assessment of the number and capital structure of the town manufactories which follows is based on: SRA, B.10/15, Glasgow Register of Deeds; ECA, Inventory of Moses Bundles; ACR, Aberdeen Registered Deeds, A31–32; *The Acts of the Parliament of Scotland; The Register of the Privy Council of Scotland;* W R Scott, *The Constitution and Finance of English, Scottish and Irish Joint-Stock Companies to 1720* (Cambridge, 1910–12); T C Smout, 'The Early Scottish Sugar Houses, 1660–1720', *Econ. Hist. Rev.* (2nd ser.), 1961; A G Thomson, *The Paper Industry in Scotland, 1590–1861* (Edinburgh, 1974).

6

CLASS FORMATION AND CLASS FRACTIONS
The Aberdeen bourgeoisie 1830—1850

A A MacLaren

In common with other Scottish cities Aberdeen underwent a remarkable expansion in the hundred years from 1750 to 1850 when the population increased six-fold from around 12,000 to 72,000[1] However these figures conceal specific internal patterns in population growth which are of particular concern to this study. Hamilton's general observation has some bearing on the shifting population: 'There were two stages in the Industrial Revolution in Scotland— the first from about 1780 to 1830, when the cotton industry sprang up rapidly . . . and the second commencing in the thirties . . . when the metal industries gained very quickly on the textiles and soon surpassed them.'[2] It was in line with the rapid growth in textile manufacturing that the major expansion in population took place and from around 26,000 at the turn of the century the decennial increase soared to 29.6, 25.7, and 29.5 per cent in the first three decades of the nineteenth century. The near total collapse of the Aberdeen textile industry in the 1840s sharply reduced the decennial figure to 5.5 per cent. On the other hand Dundee, which had lagged behind Aberdeen in the first three decades, overtook and surpassed the Aberdeen population in the second three decades, largely on the basis of the expanding prosperity of the jute industry.[3] Unlike either of these cities, Glasgow sharing in the expansion of the metal industries, maintained a uniformly high decennial increase throughout all six decades. Indeed as Campbell points out, Glasgow by the mid-century was the 'main area of reception' for emigrants from throughout Scotland.[4]

However, the pattern of migration into Aberdeen differed radically from Glasgow and Dundee, and indeed any other Scottish city, with regard to at least one other important aspect. No other Scottish urban centre of comparable size enjoyed such a remarkable homogeneity of population. The 1851 Census shows that fewer than 20,000 of the population were derived from outside the city or county and of that number just over a thousand were Irish.[5] Some of the long-term and contemporary consequences of this remarkably homogeneity have been noted by Carter[6] in his study of the northeast peasantry. Our immediate concern, however, is with the effects of the demographic and socio-structural changes on the existing social formation.

Unfortunately the first three decades comprising the most rapid expansion of population in the first half of the nineteenth century is least well documented. Considerable data has been gathered on the Aberdeen bourgeoisie from $c.$ 1830–70[7] and a recently published article by Donnelly assists in filling-in some details of what he describes as an 'urban elite' prior to 1800. However, what he appears to be describing are dominant fractions of the bourgeoisie because the author himself admits that the same families who comprised the economic 'elite' also dominated the 'political elite' and that membership was open to 'outsiders provided they had wealth'.[8] Whatever the confusion over definition, the article is useful in that it provides a measure of the continuity of those class fractions which continued to dominate the economic, political, and religious institutions of the city in 1830.[9] Nevertheless this is not to say that important structural changes had not got under way in the preceding decades and that these changes were to reproduce in the bourgeoisie a new distribution of power among the various class fractions. Indeed it is contended that the massive expansion in population as a result of the development of manufacturing industry created not just a proletariat but released forces which led to the reproduction of 'new' class fractions within the bourgeoisie.[10] The consequence of the reproduction of these new class fractions was an increasing realignment and challenge to the institutional leadership of the dominant fractions.

The purpose of this chapter is to examine these changing alignments and the analysis will focus specifically on the impact of such changes on the composition of kirk session elders within the Church of Scotland. The data utilised will be derived from an earlier study of the Aberdeen eldership.[11] The first section will provide an outline ecclesiastical background to the events of the period; thereafter the eldership will be analysed in terms of their position within the prevailing social formation. This section will be followed by consideration of the social integration of the eldership as an institutional body; and subsequent sections will examine the eldership as an institutional 'vanguard' of the bourgeoisie, and the extent to which the pattern of eldership recruitment reflected the changing class fractional alignments. Finally an attempt will be made to draw out factors specific to Aberdeen as well as those with a more general urban application.

ECCLESIASTICAL BACKGROUND

It is not the purpose of this paper to enter into any Disruption controversy, nor is it intended to offer any new interpretation of that event although some additional insight may be provided. However, as the Disruption provides the data source for the analysis, an outline history is necessary. The Disruption of the Church of Scotland in 1843 was the culmination of a period which has become known as 'The Ten Years' Conflict'. Although ostensibly fought over the issue of patronage (whether the appointment of the parish minister was the privilege of the patron or the right of the kirk session and congregation), the real divisions between the two ecclesiastical parties ran much deeper than this. The struggle over patronage provided an institutional demarcation for what was, in effect, 'a cleavage between two incompatible philosophies of life'.[12] The Moderates were altogether more tolerant and permissive in their attitudes towards society and were certainly less puritanical regarding their own behaviour. Socially and culturally they were more akin to the country lairds to whom many of them owed their appointment. From their pulpits they stressed simple morality and rejected the fervent 'enthusiasm' of the members of the Evangelical Party who preached predestination and warned of the dangers of hellfire and damnation. Strict Calvinists in their attitude towards Salvation, the Evangelicals sought the regulation of society on these same Calvinist principles and condemned the 'cold moonlight' of the Moderates who read polite and elegant sermons to their congregation.

From 1833 the issue of patronage was fought out in the General Assembly of the Church of Scotland. Attempts by the Evangelicals to restrict the privileges of patrons by various Acts carried in the General Assembly were frustrated by the Moderates who successfully appealed to the House of Lords. The issue of 'non-intrusion' of ministers thereupon became one of the State denying the right of the General Assembly to modify its constitution. Despite appeals, Parliament refused to intervene, and in May 1843 the Disruption took place. About a third of the ministers and about a half of the elders seceded and formed the Free Church. Support for the secession varied throughout Scotland but was particularly strong in the highlands and in the cities. Measured simply in terms of clerical secession the Free Church gained a majority in the urban parishes of Glasgow (25 out of 34), Edinburgh (24 from 35), Dundee (9 from 14), and Aberdeen where all 15 ministers seceded.[13] The clerical secession mirrored a struggle at grass-roots within the kirk sessions of each parish church where the balance between Moderate and Evangelical was crucial in determining the overall pattern of secession in 1843. However the importance of the eldership lay beyond the ecclesiastical powers vested in the kirk sessions and this is confirmed by an examination of the position they held within the overall class structure.

CLASS FORMATION AND THE ELDERSHIP

Elders were elected for life by cooption of the existing session. Although deposition was possible it was extremely rare and was usually confined to cases of fornication or business insolvency. It was the duty of existing members of the kirk sessions to ensure that those coopted were unlikely to be guilty of such offences and it followed that the kirk session members recruited men known to themselves whose morality and business integrity were highly regarded. The office carried considerable administrative and financial obligations. Elders were expected to perform various quasi-legal functions as well as to investigate the social and moral behaviour of individual members of the congregation and the inhabitants of the parish. They were also expected to make considerably greater financial contributions to the running of the church. Morality, by itself, therefore, was not a sufficient qualification for office—the need for men of suitable socio-economic standing was of equal importance to the successful running of church affairs. It followed that those 'set apart' as elders were usually men who had pursued a successful business or professional career—this in itself being regarded as a visible sign of worth in the eyes of God. Failures did not become elders. Membership of the kirk session carried considerable prestige. It not only reflected an individual's undoubted social respectability, it was both a recognition and warranty of his financial integrity. Kirk session elders therefore, were not simply an 'ecclesiastical elite' within the Church of Scotland. Certainly they were responsible for the government of the Church but in many respects their authority rested on the secular attributes which they undoubtedly possessed. As a body they were drawn from a cross-section of the most 'successful' elements in middle-class society and accordingly each member individually contributed to the collective power of the kirk session by bringing with him the authority he possessed in the wider society.

The relationship between the eldership and class formation is a complex one and requires closer examination. The kirk sessions were overwhelmingly middle class in composition, and the authority vested in the sessions was upheld by that class. Institutionally the eldership operated as instruments of social control on behalf of the middle class and were expected by their own individual behaviour to provide a social model for the wider society. Consequently they could be regarded as an institutional vanguard of the middle class in that they interpreted class interests and provided a 'moral' leadership. In a sense, therefore, although in no way divorced from the class formation in terms of power, their peculiar combination of divine and secular attributes allowed a degree of flexibility in interpreting its usage. On the other hand this flexibility would result from the internal operation of the kirk sessions albeit that each elder is a member of the wider bourgeois society.

However, given the social composition of the eldership and the method of recruitment by cooption, they would seem to fit loosely Gidden's definition of what he terms a 'uniform elite'—'one which shares the attributes of having a restricted pattern of recruitment and forming a tightly-knit unity'.[14] This is not to imply that the eldership were in any sense an independent elite and it is clear from the above discussion that they were rooted in the middle-class social formation. However, although ultimately dependent on class power it is of some importance to examine the internal cohesiveness of the eldership in order to gain some insight into the interaction between the institutional vanguard and the class formation. Accordingly Giddens's characteristics of a 'uniform elite' are used only to probe the internal workings of the kirk sessions.

Finally it is important to note that although the eldership may share certain characteristics of a 'uniform elite', as a body they cannot be defined as such; nor indeed can they be seen as a specific class fraction which was bound by the overall needs of the class but yet retained a measure of specificity on the basis of occupational similarities or segmented economic interests. It might be possible to argue however that the eldership derived their support from certain dominant class fractions and the data would appear to support such a proposition. This is not to say that the eldership themselves comprised such a class fraction. Indeed the 'Ten Years' Conflict' was to demonstrate a divergence of fractional interests within the eldership. This divergence also illustrates one of the fundamental weaknesses of Giddens's typology in that his definition of a 'uniform elite' is essentially static and cannot incorporate dynamic social change. It follows that, whilst the definition may 'fit' certain of the characteristics of the eldership in 1830 in that the kirk sessions did have a 'restricted pattern of recruitment' and by their nature possessed a 'tightly-knit unity', it rapidly ceased to 'fit' in the face of structural changes in the class formation which are reflected within the kirk sessions. Nonetheless Giddens's definition does provide a useful starting point.

In the following sections the relationship between the eldership—the institutional vanguard—and the class formation will be probed more deeply. The first section will deal with the integrative features of the eldership; this will be followed by an analysis of kirk session powers; the third section will return to the theme of the institutional vanguard and the class formation in terms of an examination of eldership recruitment.

INTEGRATION WITHIN THE ELDERSHIP

Given the nature of the spiritual and secular qualifications one would predict that the eldership would be characterised by a high degree of social integration. This integration would be assisted by selective recruitment, followed perhaps by coherent and effective socialisation. Giddens distinguishes between what he calls 'social' and 'moral' integration. The former is concerned with 'the frequency and nature of the social contacts and relationships', and the latter— 'moral' integration—refers to the sharing of 'common ideas and a common moral ethos', and to the recognition of an 'overall solidarity'.[15] A third factor assisting integration would be numerical size. The problem would increase in relation to the number of members. Therefore a small body would be better able to retain an overall solidarity.

Prior to the Disruption the kirk sessions were made up of about 120 elders. These elders controlled all six city parishes in Aberdeen and comprised 15 congregations. There are strong indicators of a high degree of social and moral integration amongst senior elders ordained before the issue of patronage assumed importance. A persistent feature of the core of senior elders was both their business and residential propinquity. Despite the continuous and accelerating expansion of the city westwards after 1830 these families continued to occupy houses and business premises in the older residential districts in the east central area of the city. Their refusal to be attracted to the new and superior west-end housing may have been related to practical considerations such as the need to maintain business and commercial concerns which might have been put at risk by such a move. At a more ideological level it is clear that resistance to moving westwards was stiffened by a dislike and disapproval of those social elements which were in the forefront of the residential expansion. Increasingly those occupying these new town houses included among their number some of the most bitter critics of the prevailing order in the Church of Scotland. The fact that the Evangelicals were in the forefront of this urban expansion may well have associated the physical phenomenon in some way with men who were regarded as insolent social upstarts; men who exhibited a total lack of concern for existing social order and the property rights of patrons. Indeed more than two generations after the Disruption certain neighbourhoods continued to be associated with support for 'Moderatism'.[16] This reluctance to participate in the westward expansion of the city was not the consequence of financial constraints. A significant number of these families possessed substantial county properties which they had inherited or purchased over the previous three generations. Others had close family ties with the landed gentry. Indeed many of the families living in the east central area of the city were part of a much wider social network extending by both kin and commercial association into the landed families of the rural hinterland. This association had paid handsome dividends in the immediate past for it was from this association that much of the capital had been found for the rapid industrialisation of the city in the late eighteenth and early nineteenth centuries.[17]

Not unexpectedly, by far the largest occupational group represented in the eldership were the large merchants and manufacturers.[18] This single group made up about 38 per cent of the total number. Lawyers, professionals, and retired gentlemen together comprised 22 per cent and of the remainder only the small shopkeepers (12 per cent) were of any numerical importance. The large merchants and manufacturers, and the professional families—particularly the lawyers, tended to be closely linked by partnership and marriage. It was customary for younger members of one family to be apprenticed to another family business in order to learn the trade. It followed that a host of interlocking partnerships bound the major families to one another and one suspects that an economic consequence of this situation was a fairly restrained level of competition. These families dominated every major economic and political institution in the city and even after the passing of the Burgh Reform

Act in 1833 they continued to occupy all the important municipal offices. In the interstices of the social network there existed a number of less prominent family connections sharing in its prosperity and contributing to its continuing stability.[19]

At the commencement of the decade which led to the Disruption the eldership exhibited a high degree of social and moral integration. This integration manifested itself in shared business enterprises and residential propinquity, as well as the domination of every major city institution. The relatively small number of elders assisted social integration as did the fact that they were derived from specific class fraction within the city. It should also be noted, however, that many of the elders were also part of a much wider social network extending into the landed families of the rural hinterland from whom in the past they had drawn considerable investment support.

POWER AND THE INSTITUTIONAL VANGUARD

If we view the eldership as an institutional vanguard of the middle the expectation would be that the power conferred on the kirk sessions would be constrained within dictates broadly determined by class interest. These dictates would apply less to the running of the church as an organisation and would be concerned particularly with the other main sphere of kirk session activity as an instrument of social control. Thus predictably the eldership sought to preserve and advance bourgeois values by enforcing a generally accepted code of 'respectable' behaviour. It followed that the full weight of this power was brought to bear on the working class concerning a fairly wide range of social activities although particular attention was given to sexual immorality and alcoholic intemperance.[20] Apart from the most overt and scandalous cases the middle class escaped the scrutiny of the kirk sessions regarding this area of conduct. However, it would be mistaken to regard the power of the kirk sessions simply in terms of the authority vested in them as guardians of individual morality. Power was not only the capacity of the kirk session to impose its will; it was also related to the capacity of the eldership to prevent individuals doing what otherwise they might have done. Thus it could be argued that fear of exposure conditioned behaviour as much as kirk session activity. This fear itself was not derived solely from the capacity of the kirk session to warn of the possible hellfire consequences of deviant behaviour. As we shall see the more practical possibilities could not be ignored.

In terms of the analysis of social integration in the previous sections clearly it would be a mistake to attempt an assessment of the power base of the eldership in terms of spiritual characteristics alone. Whilst it might be argued that a man acting his role of elder was not effectively the same man acting as a cotton manufacturer, or as a city magistrate, such a concept—if useful in the contemporary situation—had no place in nineteenth-century society. Indeed to attempt to do so would be to misconstrue the nature of the office of elder and would run counter to the very basis of election to eldership. Calvinistic presbyterianism did not concede the possibility of separate roles. Anyone who failed to meet his debts in the business world had to cease forthwith from practising as an elder and a church member would be denied communion until he had satisfied those to whom he was indebted. Even a hint of financial insolvency could lead to investigation by the session and the practical consequences of an unconfirmed 'scandal' could be serious.

The power of the kirk sessions therefore, rested not simply on the spiritual aspects of eldership. The secular prerequisites were of equal importance in ensuring compliance. For the businessman, fallen by the economic wayside, appearance before the session amounted to investigation by one's peers. For all others it meant trial by a body of employers claiming the right to do so on the basis of the spiritual characteristics of their office. Moreover whilst it would be mistaken to see the office of elder as somehow independent from that of employer, it would be mistaken equally to attempt to view the other functions performed by the eldership as being divorced from the overall basis of kirk session power. The eldership had complete control over the distribution of poor relief and even after the passing of a new Scottish Poor Law in 1845 much of the power continued to lie in their hands. The kirk sessions also performed numerous quasi-legal functions such as issuing certificates of poverty in order that legal aid might be obtained, and supplying references as to the morality of individual parishioners seeking admission to infirmaries for medical treatment. The kirk session appointed the parish schoolmaster, tested his scriptural knowledge, and had the power to raise or lower his salary. As custodians of parish morality the elders undertook the 'purging' from the communion roll of all those whose spiritual condition or social behaviour were thought to be wanting.

Elders also attended meetings of the presbytery. Although this body dealt with the more scandalous offences referred from the sessions, its scope was wider and it could act on what were regarded as threats to public morality. Thus considerable pressure could be brought to bear on local magistrates—generally elders themselves and certainly always church members. In this way the presbytery would act to ensure the removal of nuisances such as low theatres, sabbath drinking-shops, brothels, and other distractions.

To conclude the eldership possessed a high degree of social integration and were deeply entrenched in a wide-ranging power base. This power extended from the institutional and quasi-legal functions carried out by the sessions, to the coercive powers of the magistracy, and the economic powers shared by a network of prominent families whose presence on the kirk sessions was regarded as an indicator of the social respectability and financial integrity of the eldership at large. Finally their position was further strengthened by the power vested in the eldership to coopt new members to the kirk sessions.

THE ELDERSHIP AND RECRUITMENT

When one turns to examine the pattern of recruitment to the eldership certain shortcomings become apparent in the above analysis of kirk session power. Firstly, the underlying assumption was that the eldership—the institutional vanguard of the class—existed in a fixed constant relationship with the class. It assumes a relative equilibrium between the institution and the class. A number of factors, however, could radically alter this relationship. The most obvious of these would be socio-structural change to the extent of altering the existing distribution of power among the various middle class fractions. In terms of the eldership this might mean an undermining of the legitimacy of the authority of the existing kirk sessions to act as 'moral' leaders of the class. The continuance of this authority would depend to some extent on the ability of the existing eldership to accommodate the new fractional alignments. Whilst this accommodation would be likely to take the form of an ideological adaptation the most easily measured example might be found in the changing pattern of recruitment to the eldership. As the distribution of power among the various class fractions altered this conceivably would manifest itself in expanding the numbers of those who considered themselves as possessing the necessary spiritual and economic requisites of office. In this sense there would be an expansion in the 'reservoir' of potential office-holders. Given the emergence of religious revivalism in the 1830s one would suspect this to be the case. However, before assessing the response of the eldership to changing circumstances it is necessary to examine and assess the nature of this 'reservoir' itself.

In terms simply of raw numbers the evidence suggests an expansion of the 'reservoir' particularly in the three decades preceding the 'Ten Years' Conflict'. It has already been noted that the decennial population increase in Aberdeen was never less than 25 per cent in these decades and from a population of around 26,000 in 1801 the city grew to close on 72,000 in 1851. Most of this increase was the consequence of migration from the rural northeast which in the same period underwent a relative decline. Obviously only a small proportion of this increase could be considered as possessing the necessary qualities of potential elders and measurement is hindered, as we shall see, by perceptual differences in defining the qualifications. However, one would predict a proportionate increase in the middle class size in line with the general growth in population.

In fact closer examination reveals a relative decline in the class fractions from which the eldership were customarily recruited, and a substantial increase in the numbers of men whose social origins were notably different from that of the existing eldership. As we have seen these men although evidently prosperous derived their wealth from an entrepreneurship which the long established business and professional families regarded as being of questionable respectability. Their enterprise exhibited a near-fearsome aggression which contrasted vividly with the staid respectability of the older families. The tendency of these new men to make and unmake any number of business partnerships, and to occupy and relinquish business premises, and (as has already been noted) to demonstrate a residential restlessness which drove them ever further westwards moving from house to house—all these factors brought them into contact with younger members of the legal profession who were not slow to realise the importance of this new flood of business. Beneath these merchants and lawyers, however, there lay a much expanded petty bourgeoisie which had grown in line with the city population. These men served the needs of the new urban population as shopkeepers, grocers, bakers, butchers, meal-sellers, clothiers, ironmongers, and as tradesmen provided the essential services of builders, blacksmiths, carpenters, plumbers, painters, nurserymen and so on. There had been similar increases in doctors, teachers, and a variety of clerks.

Table 1   *Social composition of kirk sessions before and after 1843*

(i)	(ii)		(iii)		(iv)	(v)
Status	Before		After		E	x^2
A	13		33		27	N.S.
B	4(– 1)		12		8	N.S.
High C	45(– 5)	75(– 7)	56	124	96	*
D	13(– 1)		23		27	N.S.
E	8(– 2)		16		17	N.S.
F	5(– 1)		13		10	N.S.
Low G	15(– 1)	42(– 7)	61	126	34	*
O	12(– 3)		25		26	N.S.
X	2		11		5	†

Total 117(– 14)   Total 250

Columns

(i)   See Appendix: Status Classification, p. 128-9.
(ii) Minus figures in parentheses indicate those dead, resigned, or uncommitted.
(v) x^2 N.S. = no statistical significance
      * = significant at 0.1 per cent level
      † = significant at 1 per cent level

Given that there would appear to be substantial structural changes taking place the question arises as to the extent to which these social changes were reflected in the social composition of the eldership. The starting point for a simple quantitative measurement of the social pressures making themselves felt on the pre-Disruption kirk sessions can be seen in Table 1 below.

Table 2 *Eldership recruitment, 1832–1842*

(i)	(ii)		(iii)		(iv)		(v)		(vi)	
	Crude estimate		Measure of						Effectiveness	
Status	of 'reservoir'		support		Wastage		Recruited		Loyalists	Seceders
High A	24		9		1		4		0	4
B	10	88	5	32	1	16	1	32	0	1
C	39		9		10		23		5	18
D	15		9		4		4		2	2
E	12		8		0		2		1	1
F	12		2		0		3		1	2
Low G	59	117	11	25	14	25	12	26	1	11
O	23		4		10		7		1	6
X	11		0		1		2		0	2

Columns

(i) See Appendix: Status Classification, p. 128-9.
(ii) Reckoned by sum of those recruited before and after Disruption and therefore presumed available.
(iii) Reckoned by sum of those recruited by Church of Scotland before and after Disruption.
(iv) Loss by death or resignation.
(v) Coopted. (vi) Loyalty or otherwise of those coopted.

What is immediately apparent from the above table is that there has been a remarkable numerical expansion of the eldership as a result of the Disruption. This is not surprising. Following the Disruption the seceders set about creating their own Free Church sessions. What is significant is whether or not this process led to any radical alteration in the social composition of the eldership. If one starts with a null hypothesis that the Disruption did not lead to any radical alteration in the social composition of the eldership and applies a simple chi-square test to the data it is immediately apparent that this hypothesis cannot be substantiated. There is a marked dilution in the socio-economic status of the eldership as a result of the Disruption. The most notable feature of this dilution is a very highly significant decline in the numbers of high status merchants serving as elders and an equally highly significant increase in the numbers of small shopkeepers and tradesmen. None of the other occupational groupings were subjected to an alteration in their representation at a level of any statistical significance. It seems reasonable to assume therefore, that one of the main areas of pressure on the existing eldership from the 'reservoir' came from this shopkeeper-tradesman group. Clearly this petty bourgeois group regarded themselves as suitable eldership material. It follows that a potential source of structural strain might result if the instructional vanguard stood in the way of the realisation of such ambitions. It is of some importance, therefore, to examine more closely the existing eldership's recruitment strategy in the decade preceding the Disruption.

Table 2 attempts a crude estimation of the size of the 'reservoir' simply by adding together all those recruited before and after the Disruption. This method is likely to underestimate the actual size of the 'reservoir' as it does not take into account those not called upon to serve who might well have been eldership material. However by these same means one can arrive at a crude measure of support for the prevailing 'institutional vanguard' within the 'reservoir' by adding together those recruited before and after 1843 who remained 'loyal'. It is obvious that these figures offer only crude approximations as they apply more accurately to the situation at the time of the Disruption itself. As the conflict developed over the preceding decade considerable re-alignments must have taken place within the 'reservoir' and indeed within the 'vanguard' itself. However, despite its shortcomings this method does reveal a remarkably low level of support for the 'vanguard' within the 'reservoir'. Out of a total of 205 potential recruits only 57 in the event were to remain 'loyal', and this factor in itself may have constrained the process of selection. On the other hand this tends to assume that the Disruption was inevitable and one has to look more closely at the strategy of recruitment in order to assess its effectiveness.

Between 1832 and 1842 41 elders ceased serving on the sessions through death and resignations brought on by ill-health. Fifty-eight were coopted to replace these men. There was a distinct shift in favour of high-status recruits notably merchants, and a decline in recruitment of low-status men who retained their numerical strength only. Thus 12 low-status merchants were recruited to replace 14 who left, and 23 large merchants were recruited to replace 10 who ceased serving. It would seem that the strategy adopted was to attempt to accommodate Evangelicalism without the social dilution of the existing eldership. The greater threat was seen as being the danger of being engulfed by the petty bourgeois. Even this compromise was regarded as regrettable by many members of the older family network. It was a regret confirmed by the intransigence of the newly recruited elders who steadfastly clung to their extremist ways and refused to be swayed by Moderate opinion. Indeed it soon became evident to the Moderate eldership that these men were no better than the petty bourgeois from whom many were in fact so recently derived. It was lamented that 'it would be well if the Assembly would enact a law against appointing servants, managers, and impudent boys to offices in the church'.[21] In the event of the Disruption the strategy of attempting to accommodate the Evangelicals was shown to have failed miserably. Of the 58 men coopted only 11 were to remain 'loyal'. As we have seen the measure of support in the 'reservoir' was certainly low by 1843 but this in itself does not explain the full force of the crisis confronting and now ultimately swamping the 'institutional vanguard'. Clearly there had been a serious misreading of the situation by the existing eldership and the nature of this misreading requires closer examination.

There is no reason to believe that the great expansion in the 'reservoir' need have presented a serious problem as long as it was accompanied by a continuing deference towards and a general acceptance of the leadership of the established network of dominant families. Given also the remarkable homogeneity of the city population it would seem all the more likely that these same families could retain an overall acceptance of their traditional role as community leaders. There is evidence to support such an outcome. An examination of the town council elections in the various city wards in the 1830s shows that it is members of these established families who are being elected and without a really serious challenge. The city was ruled with a calmness which at times approached nonchalance. Even after the election of the first reformed council in 1833 opinions tended to be unanimous and it was not until December 1836 that an actual division took place and a decision was taken on the basis of a majority vote by the town council.[22] Through their network of family businesses they ran the major aspects of the economic life of the city. Perhaps above all, it seemed that their socio-economic links with the landed families of the northeast provided a continuity which insisted upon respect and deference towards their social position. From their own perspective there would appear no reason to believe that their leadership was under serious long-term challenge in the Church or the city at large. Literary sources tend to confirm this belief. It was recalled that 'Public work, such as a member of the Police Board, or a Town Councillor, was looked upon as a waste of time, a kind of service which should only be undertaken by idle or wealthy men'.[23] This feature has been noted at a national level in Britain. Guttsman maintains that deference towards local political leadership in the form of the landed classes and their appendages 'goes hand in hand with the representation of the economic, social or religious interests'.[24]

Clearly, however, this observation does not apply to mid-nineteenth century-Aberdeen and indeed it may be mistaken to assume that deference towards an existing political leadership should be taken to mean deference at all levels of social activity. Carter has indicated the danger of such an assumption with regard to the northeast peasantry in the nineteenth century[25] and simply on the basis of the high rate of migration into the city from the rural hinterland one might assume that deference towards the existing political leadership was also born out of necessity and little more. Nevertheless the Disruption crisis took a much more serious form in Aberdeen than it did in any other comparable Scottish city. This leads one to question whether or not there were certain features which were unique to the Aberdeen social structure and which may have contributed to the scale of the crisis.

Certain unique features concerning Aberdeen are fairly evident although the precise contribution of these to the crisis are difficult to evaluate in any precise manner. The most remarkable feature—the social homogeneity of the city population—has already been noted. Whilst in the long run such a situation could be seen as broadly contributing towards social stability in terms of a shared cultural and geographical origin, these same elements conceivably might unify opposition to the existing ruling class fractions. Given the absence of a substantial cultural minority such as Roman Catholics which might be used as a means of 'uniting' the presbyterian middle class against the dangers of 'papal aggression' the lines of conflict were ultimately clearer between the conflicting class fractions. It is also possible that the association between existing ruling class fractions and the north-east landed class exacerbated the conflict simply because of the migrants' dislike of a rural landlordism from which they had 'escaped' in the previous decades. Given the presence of the basic issues of conflict it is possible therefore to see the social homogeneity of the city population as a means of heightening rather than hindering the development of the conflict. On balance, nevertheless, one would expect social homogeneity of population to assist the incorporation of new class fractions into the existing order with less difficulty than in a city where 'newcomers' were derived from a much wider geographical source. Significantly this did not occur. As we have seen the old ruling families failed to incorporate the new bourgeois class fractions into the existing order in a manner which would ensure the continued acceptance of their authority and leadership. The legitimacy of the 'institutional vanguard' was at first challenged and then totally engulfed by these new class fractions which allied themselves to an aspiring petty bourgeoisie within the class 'reservoir'.

One might be tempted to believe that the structural crisis which occurred was inevitable in the sense that there was no conceivable manner in which the existing ruling fractions could successfully accommodate the challenge to their leadership. Certainly, viewing the eldership as an 'institutional vanguard', it is difficult from a hindsight perspective to see how a different strategy of recruitment could have markedly lessened the crisis. Without our benefit of hindsight it seems more than likely that the nature and scale of the change was not fully understood. The Disruption which marked the end of their leadership in matters of religion was only one event in a process which was leading to social disintegration of an order which had continued in power since the eighteenth century. Ironically the crisis was hurried along by the relatively narrow economic resource base from which the leading families drew their power. Just as a challenge to religious leadership developed later into an overall leadership confrontation so the collapse of one or two of the leading families adversely affected all the others. The virtual total collapse of the Aberdeen textile mills was accompanied by a whole series of financial crises and scandals associated with railway investment which in turn brought the banking institutions to their knees. The interlocking network of families, whose position had seemed so secure, disintegrated as the economy of the city staggered from one disaster to the next, each more serious than the last. Moreover, just when financial assistance was most needed the inherent contradiction in the long-term needs of the landed class and the urban merchants made itself felt. The investment monies which had formerly flowed into the city from the rural hinterland now began to find their main outlets in North America and Australia.[26] Had any of these families approached the scale of wealth enjoyed by their Glasgow counterparts[27] the crisis might have been contained but it seems clear that the main distinguishing features between the old class fractions and the new were determined by culture rather than material prosperity.

IN CONCLUSION

Several factors emerge from this study which may have a general relevance to the analysis of social class formations in other cities. Firstly, dominant class fractions possessing a high degree of social integration and controlling an 'institutional vanguard' such as the eldership which has a relatively low level of recruitment, are most secure in their power when the middle class 'reservoir' remains comparatively stable in numerical terms. This would be particularly true of dominant fractions whose power rested on a fairly narrow economic resource base in the sense of being closely interlocked.

On the other hand the numerical size of the 'reservoir' is not in itself the crucial element in determining the relationship with the dominant fractions. As important is the general level of deference and acceptance of their overall leadership. However, it is mistaken to assume that a continued acceptance of the political leadership of the dominant fractions implies that such recognition extends to all aspects of leadership. One must distinguish between levels of deference. It follows that challenges to leadership may be related only to specific functions. For example a refusal to defer towards leadership in matters of religion may nevertheless be accompanied by a continuing deference in terms of political leadership.

However, it is possible that dominant class fractions exhibiting a high degree of social integration may be less able to sustain an attack on one area of their leadership simply because the power possessed is also so closely-knit as to be indivisible. Thus a specific challenge to one area of leadership would tend to become generalised although this was not the initial intention of the challenging fractions. It is possible that this particular case study has over-estimated the scale of this problem given that control over the kirk sessions was determined by the close association between the socio-economic and spiritual characteristics of eldership. In such a case a challenge to religious leadership would almost inevitably spill over into other areas of activity. Nevertheless it seems likely that a high degree of social integration limits ability to resist general involvement.

Finally there is the factor concerned with the social homogeneity of the urban population. Whilst one suspects this to be important it is likely that its importance rests on the presence or absence of other variables. Thus where deference and general acceptance of the existing dominant fraction remains high, shared social and geographical origins would further contribute to the overall stability. On the other hand these same features would assist the under-mining of the authority of the dominant fractions where levels of deference were low or in decline. Certainly in the case of Aberdeen this peculiar aspect of the urban population would appear to have exacerbated the crisis.

REFERENCES

1   These figures and those immediately following are derived from B R Mitchell and P Deane, *Abstract of British Historical Statistics* (1962).

2   H Hamilton, *The Industrial Revolution in Scotland* (reprint 1966), p. 1.

3   W Watt, 'Fifty Years of Progress in Aberdeen', *Transactions of the Aberdeen Philosophical Society* (1903), pp. 18—19). See also E Gauldie (ed.), *The Dundee Textile Industry* 1790—1885 (Edinburgh 1969).

4   R Campbell, *Scotland since 1707* (Oxford 1965), p. 179.

5   Census of Population, 1851. See also J J Saunders, *Scottish Democracy, 1815—1840* (Edinburgh 1950), p. 130.

6   I Carter, *Farm Life in Northeast Scotland 1840—1914* (Edinburgh 1979). In un-ravelling the social complexity of northeast peasant culture Carter sheds consi-derable light on the consequences for the urban social structure.

7   See A A MacLaren, *Religion and Social Class* (1974).

8   T Donnelly, 'The economic activities of the members of the Aberdeen Merchant Guild, 1750—1799', *Scottish Economic and Social History*, 1, no. 1 (1981), p. 30.

9   See J A Ross, *Record of Municipal Affairs in Aberdeen* (Aberdeen 1889) where the same family names appear in the Lists of Councils, etc. See also MacLaren, op. cit. pp. 221—55.

10 See N Poulantzas, *Classes in Contemporary Capitalism* (1975) for a stimulating analysis of this process.

11 MacLaren, op. cit. pp. 218—55.

12 R Rait and G S Pryde, *Scotland* (1954), p. 262.

13 For further details concerning variations in clerical secession see J McCosh, *The Wheat and the Chaff gathered into Bundles* (Dundee 1843).

14   A Giddens, 'Elites in the British class structure', P. Stanworth and A Giddens
     (eds.), *Elites and Power in British Society* (Cambridge 1974), p. 5.
15   op. cit.
16   J Martin, *Eminent Divines in Aberdeen and the North* (Aberdeen 1888),
     pp. 194–5, fancied that in certain streets 'the very air is laden with the breath
     of old "moderate" times'.
17   A Keith, *The North of Scotland Bank Limited* (Aberdeen 1936), p. 6.
18   These figures and those following are derived from MacLaren, op. cit. pp. 216–55.
19   For example members of the Blaikie family held the office of Lord Provost for 11 of
     the 14 years between 1833–46. Ross, op. cit. See also the careers of the
     Cadenhead, Simpson, and Whyte families in MacLaren, op. cit. pp. 228, 248,
     255.
20   For details and case studies of this process see A A MacLaren, 'Presbyterianism and
     the working class in a mid-nineteenth century city', *Scottish Historical Review*,
     46, 2, no. 142 (October 1967).
21   J Bruce, *The Aberdeen Pulpit and Universities* (Aberdeen 1844), p. 12.
22   Ross, op. cit. p. 97. The division took place on the issue of installing gas lighting in
     the West Church.
23   A S Cook, *Old Time Traders and Their Ways* (Aberdeen 1902), p. 42.
24   W L Guttsman, 'The British political elite and the class structure', in P Stanworth
     and A Giddens, op. cit. p. 41. Guttsman cites Vincent's study of Rochdale—
     broadly similar to Aberdeen in that it was a textile town—where support for
     landed elements was still strong in 1857.
25   I Carter, 'Class and culture among farm servants in the north-east, 1840–1914', in
     A A MacLaren (ed.), *Social Class in Scotland, Past and Present* (Edinburgh,
     1976), pp. 105–27. See also Carter, op. cit.
26   A Keith, op. cit. pp. 49–55. D S Macmillan, *Scotland and Australia, 1788–1850*
     (Oxford 1967), pp. 326–63.
27   Donnelly, op. cit. p. 39.

APPENDIX: Status classification code*

A   *Professional group* (university graduates): 1 advocates, 2 professors, lecturers—
    generally also practising medicine, 3 principals, rectors, headmasters of
    important educational establishments.
B   *Commercial groups*: 1 bankers, bank managers and agents, 2 cashiers, principal
    clerks, accountants, insurance company managers, and brokers, company
    treasurers.
C   *Large merchant-manufacturer group*: 1 suppliers of capital goods, timber, etc.,
    construction companies, ironfounders, textile manufacturers, wholesalers and
    importers, tobacco manufacturers, 2 suppliers of consumer goods and services
    catering for middle class, silversmiths, silk mercers, 3 suppliers of food and
    wines, grocers, vintners, etc., 4 commission merchants, ship agents.
D   *Retired-rentier group*: 1, shipowners, 2 landlords, those retired and living on
    income from rented property, shares, or capital; including Members of
    Parliament.

*   For further details see MacLaren (1974), pp. 218–19.

E   *'Public servants'* (I): doctors, druggists, 2 local government officials, building
    inspectors, architects, 3 shipmasters, marine and civil engineers.

F   *'Public servants'* (II): 1 teachers, 'stickit ministers', 2 clerks, writers.

G   *Small merchant-tradesmen group*: 1 shopkeepers, 2 self-employed tradesmen,
    agents living in premises, 3 foremen, overseers, 4 retired tradesmen and shop-
    keepers.

H* *Artisans and others*: 1 employed artisans, 2 semi- and unskilled, fishermen, rope-
    makers, etc.

O   *Uncertain*: individual cannot positively be identified.

X   *Unknown*: name of individual known, but no trace of occupation or place of
    residence.

* Group H is the one group containing working-class occupations although it is possible
that these may be present in Group X. Only *two* men were found to belong to this
category—a ropemaker and a fisherman. As they are of no statistical significance to this
study they were re-assigned to Group G3.

7

SUBURB AND SLUM IN GORBALS
Social and residential change 1800–1900

J G Robb

INTRODUCTION

The socio-environmental decline of inner city districts into slums and the development of new suburbs beyond were two closely connected processes involved in nineteenth-century urbanisation.[1] Prominent amongst the factors at work were socio-residential segregation and the progressive separation of workplace from residence at least for the middle class.

This study investigates the nineteenth-century socio-spatial evolution of the Gorbals district of Glasgow in the light of theory on the growth in scale of residential differentiation and the existing literature on the development of Gorbals. By the middle decades of the present century, the district had become the most notorious British slum, partly because of the grimness of the high-density tenement fabric. This aspect of the Scottish Victorian inner city presents an area of socio-spatial investigation largely unexplored to date. This is doubly surprising as the high-density '3-dimensional' social geography may have experienced a rather different evolution to the terraces and courts of the English and Welsh towns commonly studied. Secondly, the implications for generalisation abroad have been largely ignored. Indeed, England and Wales were unusual in global terms for not having developed a multistorey residential tradition prior to 1900.[2]

The close perceptual link between tenement and slum in the present century has lead to the demolition of much that was of architectural and residential value, according to Worsdall[3] and Hamilton.[4] Certainly, the experience of tenement life was and is not confined to the working class.

Social segregation in the nineteenth century may have been linked with slum formation in a number of ways. Sjoberg[5] posited a model 'pre-industrial' order where social segregation was limited to the concentration of the most powerful urban group near to the urban 'ceremonial centre'. Elsewhere, rich and poor, masters and men lived and worked closely together. Sjoberg's model has been heavily criticised (e.g. Burke[6]) but the concept of social status mixing in the 'pre-industrial' epoch (before c. 1800) remained compelling.

Vance[7] proposed that the basic socio-residential (and economic) unit of medieval towns was the 'occupational household', where master, journeymen and servants or labourers occupied the same premises, or lived in close proximity. Subsequently, early eighteenth-century Edinburgh and nineteenth-century Paris encompassed wide social spectra within single, tall tenement blocks; a 'vertical' social segregation (e.g. Chambers[8] and Vance[9]). Some studies of social patterns during Victorian urban expansion (e.g. Dennis[10]) hinted at certain stages in a process of progressive socio-residential distancing with urban growth and industrial development. Nineteenth-century commentators generally bemoaned this separation; Chalmers[11] saw the residential and moral separation between industrial masters and men as counter to the national interest. He contrasted the new segregation with the harmonious and orderly social intercourse which then prevailed in the 'patrician' cities of Oxford, Bath and Edinburgh. Disraeli[12] inveighed against 'vulgar exclusiveness' and expressed a mid-century Tory ideology of social leadership through spatial integration.

In Scotland, employers' interest in the welfare of the new industrial proletariat seemed to decline in proportion to the increased scale of manufacturing. Gauldie[13] quoted the Baxter brothers of Dundee, who were finding by 1868 'the double relationship of master and landlord at times awkward. . . . It is against our principle as employers to build houses'.

By the close of the nineteenth-century, *bourgeois* reminiscences of earlier social integration were often deeply tinged by nostalgia. J D Mitchell[14] recounted the history of an old house in Anderston, Glasgow, thus;

When William Gillespie treated himself to a residence in keeping with his own fortunes, he planted it beside his printfield, dwelling amongst his own people. It was the old way and a good old way it was; it brought the work right under the master's eye and it favoured kindly, neighbourly feelings between master and man.

To Gauldie and MacLaren,[15] spatial separation was complemented by the psychological abandonment of the working class by the middle class.

Spatial separation, to early nineteenth-century writers such as Chalmers, lessened the potential for kindliness and informal social control through the example of genteel behaviour. As direct middle-class involvement in inner city communities lessened, the physical fabric declined through lack of maintenance. Vance[7] has traced the shift of interests in inner-city housing from middle-class owner-occupation to absentee ownership, tenancy and high-density house-farming.

Social segregation has also been linked to the growth in scale of manufacturing.[16] Larger workforces were concentrated in larger working-class districts near to shipyards and foundries as the nineteenth century progressed.

Closely related to the progressive distancing of socially contrasted households was the change in journey-to-work patterns. As the means of production grew noisier, dirtier and more ugly, owners and managers were less willing to live nearby. From city centres, merchants, shopkeepers and professionals removed their families and reduced their contact with the increasingly unhealthy and unsafe inner districts. The urban transport revolutions of horse-omnibus, commuter train and tramcar accelerated a process already begun by the most leisured professionals. [17]

THE CHARACTER OF GORBALS

As a separate nucleus to the ancient City of Glasgow, Gorbals provided an opportunity to study the social and physical characteristics of a suburb drawn into a greater urban area. [18] The more recent image of the place (see Robb, 1979), [19] infamous for 'grime and crime', has roots in a history of inferiority. There was a medieval leper hospital near the south end of 'Bishop Rae's brig', the first stone structure to span the Clyde, in the fourteenth century. The 'pre-industrial' village contained a variety of old tenements which often fronted plots containing later structures (see Figure 1). [20-22] The ancient Barony of Gorbals, of which the village and parish of 1771 was the central focus, was administered in medieval fashion until the amalgamation with the city in 1846. A peculiar local variant of the feuing system survived until then which militated against new building and repairs to old structures in the village-parish of Gorbals. [23]

In the last decade of the eighteenth century large tracts of agricultural land around the city were feued out for development. [24] Much of the land around the village-parish of Gorbals was disposed of at that time. To the west (see Figure 2) the Laurie brothers feued Laurieston, [25] and began ambitious plans for a Regency suburb, with Carlton Place (completed about 1810), as the riverside focus. Eastwards, the proprietor, Hutchesons' Hospital, feued out smaller parcels with little regard for overall design save a regular streetplan and the district name of Hutchesontown. By 1900, Gorbals Ward included that portion of the old Barony divided between Gorbals Parish and the more recently built-up districts of Laurieston and western Hutchesontown.

As Kellett, [24,26,27] Checkland [28] and Simpson [29] related, the development of Laurieston as a middle-class suburb was doubtful from the beginning. The Laurie brothers were unable to dispose of the large steading as rapidly as they had hoped. In neighbouring Tradeston and to the south, industrial interests threatened the amenity of the grand design, as David Laurie [30-32] was at pains to point out. Ord [33] , Kellett [24,26,27] and Checkland [28] considered that the decisive blow was struck by William Dixon, local coal master and proprietor of the ironworks known as Dixon's Blazes to the south (Figure 2). About 1800, Dixon built a waggonway across undeveloped Laurieston to supply coaling quays in Tradeston, after procuring a temporary recall on an injunction put up by James

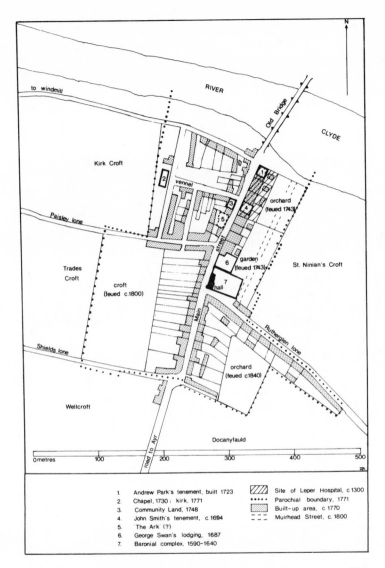

FIGURE 1   Gorbals parish: pre-1800 composite plan Sources: McDonald (1912):[20] McArthur (1778):[21] Kyle (undated):[22] O.S. (1860)

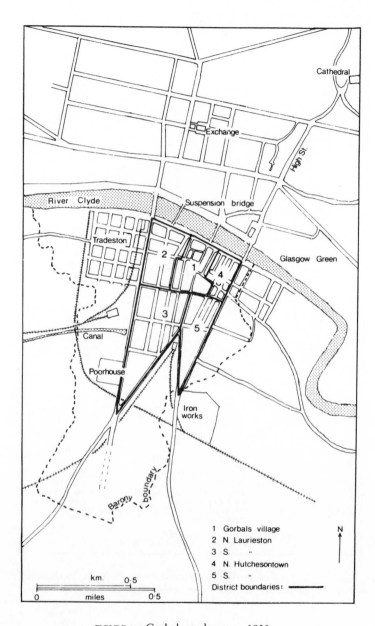

FIGURE 2   Gorbals study area *c.*1850

Laurie against such an event. Kellett and Checkland concurred on the social and environmental decline that the waggonway symbolised;

> . . . a project for the middle class dwelling on the south side was destroyed; the gains to the industrialist made him wholly without scruple (Checkland).[28]

The hoped-for arrival of the wealthy middle class people upon which the Laurie brothers had relied never occurred and those streets which had been laid out in spacious and expensive style remained as follies, tokens of the Lauries' ambitious intentions for the area (Kellett).[34]

Those genteel residents who had arrived soon decamped for the more guaranteed exclusiveness of the Blythswood estate and the growing outer West End, leaving Gorbals to be '. . . rapidly overrun by the working class'. (Simpson).[29] The housing already built in Laurieston was left '. . . to become warrens of one and two-roomed houses for casual labourers', (Kellett),[27] and a 'slum annexe to Gorbals [Parish]'. (Kellett).[26] So much so, according to Lindsay,[35] that Gorbals had become by the 1880s '. . . perhaps the worst and certainly the most notorious slum in Europe . . .'

Contemporary accounts indicated that the worst housing, sanitary and 'moral' conditions in early and mid-nineteenth century Glasgow were found north of the river. Symons[36] and 'Shadow'[37] revealed that the central 'wynds' around Trongate and High Street contained a population '. . . many degrees worse in terms of physical and social debasement . . .' than even the most inferior operatives, the impoverished hand-loom weavers. The 'wynds' of Edinburgh and Glasgow were the oldest 'pre-industrial' sections of those cities. By the 1860s, conditions in the central, 'pre-industrial' core of Gorbals elicited the concern of the Medical Officer of Health.[38]

> The whole parish, notwithstanding some improved localities in which the Corporation has already bought up a considerable amount of decayed property, may be described without much exaggeration as a swarming mass of pauperism, and too often hopeless indigence, in which the value of the property is depreciated to the last degree by exorbitant poor-rates, and by certain unfortunate peculiarities in the feudal tenure . . . it presents all the evils of the Bridgegate [north of the Clyde] in an exaggerated degree.

Pagan,[39] reporting on the deliberations of the city Dean of Guild Court in the 1840s, was at pains to identify the deterioration of Gorbals Parish with Irish immigration. He implored landlords to protect the interesting old buildings of the village (including the baronial mansion and a number of old tenements (Figure 3)).

> We are really grieved to part with some of these old landmarks of the city, and we cannot help urging the proprietors of such houses as still exist to pay

some little attention to them, and above all to prevent them falling prey to the hordes of Irish immigrants who have a fancy to burrow in these ancient spots. When once tenanted by these modern Huns the destruction of the fabric is not far distant.

Impressions of Hutchesontown in the first half of the nineteenth century were lacking in contemporary accounts, due in part to the absence of a single energetic and eloquent developer in the mould of David Laurie. Ord[33] confined his remarks on the development of the district to isolated milestones in growth. Early maps indicated that Hutchesontown was more quickly built up than Laurieston. Nuisance prevention was not rigorously pursued by the superior or the individual subject superiors. As early as 1818, the sisters Bryce of Thistle Street were complaining to the Gorbals Police Commissioners of smoke issuing from a neighbour's starch-house (G.P.E. minutes; 11 December 1818).[40]

FIGURE 3   Thomas Annan's view of Main Street, Gorbals Parish, in 1868. The turreted
building was the baronial mansion (centre right)

Worsdall[3] noted that;

Hutchesontown began as a middle-class development, but by mid-century, with the growth of a multiplicity of industries close by, it subtly changed to a working class area.

In similarity with Laurieston, the social change was not necessarily reflected in the physical fabric. Both districts retained elements of architectural finesse and unity. Indeed, some contemporary accounts suggested that social contrasts survived between the districts at least down to the 1850s. Pagan[39] described the continued building of middle-class tenements in Laurieston in the forties, and 'Shadow'[37] compared the *bourgeois* social character of the area with the degraded population on the opposite bank of the Clyde.

HYPOTHESES

Ward[41] has suggested that Victorian levels and kinds of residential differentiation were unlike modern large-scale patterns. Carter and Wheatley[42] have certainly demonstrated the close interdigitation of status groups in a single period-picture, that of the mid-nineteenth-century core of Merthyr Tydfil.

A general hypothesis, embraced within the span of the nineteenth century, might postulate that tenemented districts underwent a progressive change in the scale of residential differentiation, from tenement through street to neighbourhood or district, as 'modern' or 'industrial' levels became established. The tenement interposed an additional potential level of differentiation at a small scale, between the individual household and street. In Glasgow and elsewhere, the tenement has been identified as an important unit of community, centred on the close and common stair, back-green and wash-house.[3] Did the urban middle class tarry in their proximity to lower-status households, or did they rapidly emulate the decentralising aristocrats of eighteenth-century Edinburgh?[43]

Specifically, the literature suggested:

(a) the general social decline of tenements originally built for middle-class occupation;
(b) that fewer socially mixed tenements were evident at later dates than at earlier dates, social and physical distance becoming congruent, and that new tenements added to the stock progressively took on socially uniform profiles from the start;
(c) that erstwhile middle-class property was generally subdivided to meet the rent-paying abilities of lower-status occupants;
(d) that the middle class had virtually ceased to live in Gorbals by the 1890s or earlier.

These statements were used as working hypotheses in the analyses of social and residential data originating from the City Directories and census enumerators' books.

THE DIRECTORY EVIDENCE

In order to obtain indicators of the changing social topography of the component districts of Gorbals, total household information was processed from the census enumerators' books for the years 1851, 1871 and 1891. For the half century before dependable census returns were available, the City Directory volumes yielded some insight.

The directories presented a self-selecting sample of individual entries for analysis. The social bias of the directory entries in favour of the middle class is well known.[44-46] The entries for Gorbals at decennial intervals from 1802 to 1842 were classified according to a scheme which distinguished between professionals and merchants on the one hand, and tradesmen and craftsmen on the other. As the Glasgow directories contained second (business) addresses where relevant, these were used to express the relative sophistication of the work–home separation.

Table 1   *Directory entry classification*

Group
1   Professionals: one or two addresses.
2   Merchants and manufacturers with one or two addresses.
    All other occupations with two addresses.
3   Commercial: one address.
4   Trades and crafts: one address.
5   Other: manual, services: one address.
6   Unspecified: retired, independent means, etc.

Because of the innate bias against working-class inclusion in these listings of 'prominent' or 'useful' citizens (according to the criteria of the time), the classification is status rather than social class-sensitive. However, its application to those entries traceable to Gorbals evoked strong indications of emerging social contrast during the first half of the nineteenth century.

The population of Gorbals Parish stood at about 5000 during the first decade of the nineteenth century[47] compared to a handful of inhabitants in Hutchesontown and probably none at all in Laurieston until the first houses in Carlton Place were occupied, about 1805. Figure 4 shows the total number of directory entries located in the three districts at decennial junctures. This indicates the social 'take-off' of Laurieston in comparison with the fluctuating trend for Gorbals Parish and a much shallower increase for Hutchesontown.

   An analysis of the changing social composition of the district 'directory population' is presented in Figure 5. The percentage of entries in each directory falling within the three districts and the social groupings adopted in Table 1 is shown.

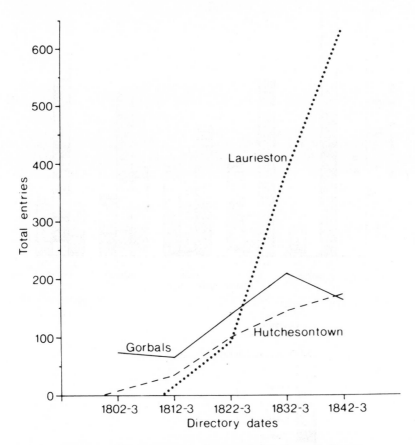

FIGURE 4   City Directory entries: population change indicators

   In 1802, the Parish district was characterised by a preponderance of trades and commercial entries, presumably working and living at the same address. Traditional urban occupations typified the Parish entries; shoemakers, tailors, spirit dealers and grocers. Throughout the period of study, there was little change, apart from a slight shift of emphasis from trades and crafts to shopkeeping. There was a small, variable high-status component.

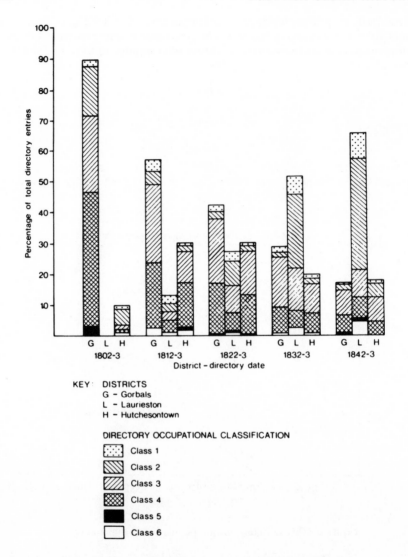

FIGURE 5   City Directory entries: social change indicators

Laurieston evidently became the residential choice for a growing concentration of entries allocated to groups 1 and 2 throughout the study period. The district's character as a suburb in the modern sense (where home and work are separated, rather than united as in the traditional *faubourg*) seemed to have been firmly established.

Cartographic evidence showed that by the 1840s the built up area of Laurieston and Hutchesontown had extended beyond the southern boundary of Gorbals Parish. For the purposes of this analysis, Laurieston and Hutchesontown were subdivided into northern and southern divisions, as shown in Figure 2.

Table 2 compares the five resultant districts in terms of their second-address directory entry compositions in 1842—3.

Table 2   *City directory 1842—1843: Address information by district*

District	Total entries	Percent of study area total	Total of 2-address entries	Percent of district totals with 2 addresses
Gorbals	162	16.9	18	11.1
N Laurieston	392	40.9	222	56.6
S Laurieston	233	24.3	159	68.2
N Hutchesontown	141	14.7	30	19.0
S Hutchesontown	30	3.1	14	46.7
Study area totals	958	99.9	443	—

There is evidence of a strong emergent distinction between 'new' and 'old' Hutchesontown, a contrast not so evident between S and N Laurieston.

In order to identify intra-district contrasts, Figure 6 was prepared, using the 1842 directory data on selected occupations. These were;

(a) *Professionals and mercantile*
    Ministers, doctors, surgeons, teachers, writers (lawyers), accountants and architects.
    Merchants (not wine or spirit).
    Manufacturers.

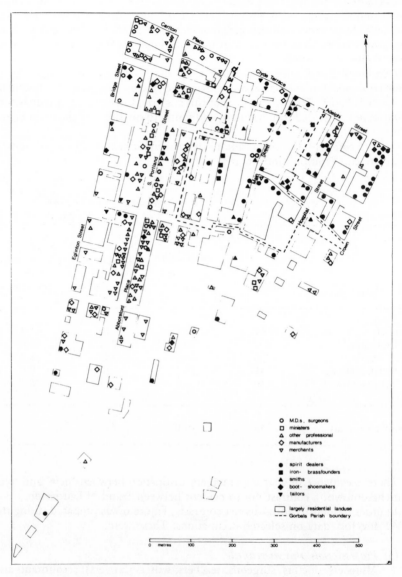

FIGURE 6   Gorbals 1842–3. Selected Directory entries: residential distribution

(b) *Trades and dealing*
Metal workers: ironfounders, brassfounders, smiths, blacksmiths, tin-smiths, coppersmiths, gunsmiths.
Boot and shoemakers.
Tailors.
Spirit dealers.

From the resulting distribution a clear pattern of high status residence emerged. The main concentration of merchants and professionals occurred not only along Carlton Place, but down the central spine of Laurieston, the S Portland Street–Abbotsford Place axis. Smaller outliers of this '*bourgeois* heartland' had been established on the fringes of development, particularly on Hospital and Crown Streets in S Hutchesontown.

By contrast, the Parish district and N Hutchesontown to the east contained the greatest clustering of the trades and crafts group, interspersed by small pockets of professionals and substantial capitalists (judging from the available evidence). Clearly, by the fifth decade of the century, Laurieston and other small enclaves had intensified rather than lost its middle-class suburban character. Middle-class tenements were being built (Figure 7) rather than Regency

FIGURE 7   Nos. 1–11 Abbotsford Place in 1968, immediately prior to demolition. Each house contained 6 or 7 rooms, each building accommodated 8 households

terraces, but they were obviously not being converted into solely working-class warrens.

The survival of pockets of trades and crafts entries in Laurieston and professionals in Gorbals Parish and certain streets of N Hutchesontown hinted at a certain degree of small-scale social segregation. In terms of the majority of the population excluded from the city directories, the extensive tracts of residential land use lacking symbols in Gorbals Parish and western Laurieston were notable. A complete survey of households in all sections of society necessitated analysis of the census enumerators' books for 1851 and subsequently.

THE CENSUS EVIDENCE

Household data from the censuses of 1851, 1871 and 1891 were linked to individual tenements or building-groups identified through address entries and the Ordnance Survey maps of 1860 and 1896. Thus the social composition of individual tenements or small groups of tenements were measured at the three census dates, using the household social classification suggested by Royle.[48] This system exploits information on occupational skills, servant-keeping and employees to define five social groups, as set out in Table 3. For convenience, the two manual groups (IV, V) were taken to approximately encompass working-class households. Groups I, II, III were taken to define a broad middle-class group, including *petit bourgeois* clerks and shopkeepers (III) and major industrialists, merchants and professionals (I).

The linking of census household information to individual steadings on the maps proved relatively straightforward in Laurieston and most of Hutchesontown. There, tenement addresses followed a rhythmic progression of grouped common-close households interspersed by single address households, those with their own street doors. In Gorbals Parish as many as sixty families laid claim to a single address; some of the long, narrow plots indicated in Figure 1 were replete with jumbles of other structures by 1851.

Every effort was made to distinguish between commensal lodger-households and those occupying separate premises. Anderson[49] warned that the imposition of the English census definition of 'house' on Scottish enumerators rendered house data before 1880 'quite meaningless' (p. 138). In practice, Gorbals enumerators consistently demarcated independent households (*including* lodgers) within each tenement address, though without recording storey or position on the building plan. Many did indicate 'backlands' where they occurred, or implied their presence with gaps in the lists of individuals' particulars. From 1861 in addition, enumerators were empowered to give each household's number of rooms, a source of information and a check on other details combined.

Ultimately, it was feasible to construct a distribution of 'residential units' at each census year. These units corresponded to building plots, and in most cases contained a single domestic structure. 'Residential units' represented the smallest fragments of residential fabric it was possible to consistently identify.

Table 3 *Social classification of Census EB household information* (after Royle, 1977[48])

Group	Qualifications
I	Heads whose households (1) employed more than 25 people (2) contained at least one servant per household member Heads of professional occupation whose households contained at least one servant per three members
II	Heads whose households (1) employed between 1 and 24 people (2) contained at least one servant per three household members Heads of professional occupation who kept no servants
III	Heads keeping servant(s) not included above Heads of nonmanual occupation, including commerce
IV	Heads of skilled manual occupation
V	Heads of unskilled manual occupation
VI	Residual (undeclared occupation)

The physical development of the five Gorbals districts from 1851 was subject to three major types of change.

(1) Additions to the built-up area in the south. The last parcels of unoccupied land were not developed until the 1880s.

(2) The replacement of certain low-density properties by tenements. Cottages in the Laurieston back-streets and lanes, and villas with large gardens near the development fringe in the 1850s were subsequently demolished and replaced piecemeal. Cartographic evidence from the OS 1860 and 1896 maps confirmed this.

(3) The large-scale remodelling of the Parish district from 1870 to 1890 by the City of Glasgow Improvement Trust.[50]

The latter redevelopment phase has attracted attention as a force which possibly spread inner-city physical and social *malaise* into the surrounding inner suburbs such as Laurieston.[45,51] It has been assumed that this occurred through the displacement of the central slum population by clearance; the return of the dispossessed poor to the reduced volume of new housing was effectively barred by higher rents. In Gorbals, as north of the river, both census and maps demonstrated that street-widening and the siting of new, large-scale institutions in the Parish drastically reduced the space available for tenement construction.

These physical changes are reflected in the five district population totals at each of the chosen censuses, given in Table 4.

Table 4 *Population totals*

| | 1851 | | 1871 | | 1891 | |
	Number	Percentage study area total	Number	Percentage study area total	Number	Percentage study area total
Gorbals Parish	11,181	30.9	10,162	23.1	5,709	14.3
N Laurieston	8,257	22.8	8,724	19.8	7,925	19.9
S Laurieston	6,490	18.1	11,764	26.7	12,309	30.9
N Hutchesontown	6,591	18.2	5,996	13.6	5,279	13.3
S Hutchesonton	3,628	10.0	7,396	16.8	8,584	21.6
Study area totals	36,147	100.0	44,042	100.0	39,806	100.0

Source: Census enumerators' books.

The population of the five districts in the mid-nineteenth century was already large and dense. Comparisons of similarly-sized urban areas composed of terraces and courts proved valuable. The inhabited area of Gorbals in 1851 roughly equalled that of Aberystwyth at that time, which accommodated 14 per cent of the Gorbals total. Similarly-sized Cardiff housed half the population of Gorbals at that date.

The demographic contrast between the northern and southern districts is clear from Table 4. Whilst the three northern divisions fluctuated or declined in population between 1851 and 1891, the southern districts grew apace. The most radical district change occurred between 1871 and 1891 in Gorbals Parish where the population fell by half due to the destruction of most of the 'pre-industrial' housing, and the subsequent construction of an entirely new townscape in massive red-sandstone four-storey tenements (see Figure 8).

To monitor aspects of changing social segregation at different scales, the social composition of every 'residential unit' at the three chosen dates was calculated. The residential balance within each unit was expressed in terms of the percentage of households displaying a particular attribute. There are disadvantages in employing percentages where the total number of households in any unit varied only between 1 and 60. As an expression of the exclusive presence or absence of an attribute amongst the households of a unit, percentages were judged valid. A measure of 75 per cent for a variable in a unit of 4 households may be considered in a different light to a similar proportion in a unit containing 20 households, for instance. Whether one socially distinctive

FIGURE 8   Gorbals Cross in 1917: the same area as pictured in Figure 3 after the City Improvement Trust had purchased and demolished the decayed buildings, widened the street and encouraged the building of new red-sandstone tenements

household among 4 or 5 was considered more or less indicative of residential intimacy by contemporaries than 5 or 6 amongst 20 cannot now be gauged. It was decided to retain percentage measures as indicators of intra-unit proportions on social class and housing characteristics to be considered in close conjunction. The variables selected for sequential reconstruction were: (1) unit household density, (2) unit house-size and (3) unit social-class composition.

(1) Household density distribution between 'residential units'

Table 5 outlines the basic population dimensions of the district stocks of 'residential units'. Three notable features emerged.

(a) The concentration of the larger-population units in pre-redevelopmnet Gorbals Parish (down to and including 1871) and N Hutchesontown.

(b) The dominance of the modal size-class (3–10) in the other three districts and in post-redevelopment Gorbals Parish. The two southern divisions saw increases in the proportion of units in this category over the census study-period as a whole.

(c) The overall numerical decline of the small-population units (those housing one or two families).

Table 5   *Residential units; household density distributions, 1851–1891, with percentages of district totals*

District	No. of CRGs	1851 No. of units	Percent	1871 No of units	Percent	1891 No. of units	Percent
Gorbals	1 & 2	33	18.3	33	18.8	8	7.1
Parish	3–10	74	41.1	67	38.3	73	65.2
	11–20	47	26.1	48	27.4	23	20.5
	21–plus	26	14.4	27	15.4	8	7.1
	n	180		175		112	
N Lourieston	1 & 2	42	21.0	44	21.5	26	14.8
	3–10	102	51.0	100	49.0	94	53.4
	11–20	49	24.5	52	25.5	49	27.8
	21–plus	7	3.5	8	3.9	7	3.9
	n	200		204		176	
S Laurieston	1 & 2	47	27.2	30	11.8	29	10.2
	3–10	92	53.5	141	55.6	169	59.7
	11–20	24	13.1	66	26.1	71	25.1
	21–plus	10	5.7	16	6.3	14	4.9
	n	172		253		283	
N Hutchesontown	1 & 2	7	6.9	7	8.0	5	6.1
	3–10	38	37.6	29	33.3	26	31.7
	11–20	46	45.5	38	43.6	38	45.3
	21–plus	10	9.9	13	14.9	13	15.8
	n	101		87		82	
S Hutchesontown	1 & 2	4	5.6	6	4.2	3	1.7
	3–10	42	59.1	84	59.5	101	59.1
	11–20	22	31.0	46	32.6	62	36.2
	21–plus	3	4.2	5	3.5	5	2.9
	n	71		141		171	

The three maps in Sequence 1 demonstrate the smaller-scale variations in space over the two intercensal periods. The 'small-population' category picked out the terraced northern edge of Laurieston (Carlton Place) and isolated villas and cottages further south. These together with some partly inhabited tenement units in central Laurieston in 1851 and a scattering of cottages in Gorbals Parish were gradually reduced in number throughout the study period. Except for a number of street sections, continued building resulted in more modal-class occupation (3–10 households). Additionally, the expected general increase in unit population with internal tenement restructuring and higher densities did not occur. Instead, unit population growth appeared locally. City Improvement Trust activity in Gorbals Parish and the southern extensions to the built-up area combined to produce a standardisation of unit population towards the modal size-class.

MAP SEQUENCE 1 TO 3

Gorbals 'Residential Units'

Sequence	Map	Date	Page
1	A	1851	150
1	B	1871	151
1	C	1891	152
2	A	1871	155
2	B	1891	156
3	A	1851	158
3	B	1871	159
3	C	1891	160

Letters representing exclusively non-residential land use
(individual establishments)

B. Public baths and wash-house
C. Churches and chapels
I. Industrial uses
O. Baronial and police office
R. Railway company property
S. Schools
St. Station
T. Theatres

Sequence 1 Map A Gorbals 1851 Residential Units

GORBALS 1871

RESIDENTIAL UNITS

SEQUENCE 1   MAP B
No. C RGs/UNIT

1, 2
3 —10
11 —20
21+
——— Parish boundary

0 metres   100   200   300   400   500

Sequence 1 Map B Gorbals 1871 Residential Units

Sequence 1 Map C Gorbals 1891 Residential Units

(2) House-size distribution between 'residential units'

This sequence defined the degree of structural heterogeneity within individual units as the number of windowed rooms occupied by each household. The unit percentage of households occupying three or more rooms was taken as the pivotal criterion.

Information on house-size is portrayed on Table 6 and Map Sequence 2. The data on room numbers was first collected in 1861, thus restricting the time scale of analysis.

Table 6 *Unit house-size composition; 1871–1891*
A Exclusive percentages of total units/district
B Exclusive percentages of units comprising 3 or more CRGs

District		1871 Exclusively large-house units		Exclusively small-house units	1891 Exclusively large-house units		Exclusively small-house units
Gorbals Parish	A	6.9		51.1	14.4		26.1
	B	3.4	n 175	37.9	12.6	n 112	20.7
N Laurieston	A	37.9		18.2	38.8		19.4
	B	23.6	n 204	12.3	29.7	n 176	14.3
S Laurieston	A	32.9		28.2	33.3		27.3
	B	30.1	n 253	20.6	29.8	n 283	22.3
N Hutcheson-town	A	12.8		18.6	9.9		27.2
	B	8.1	n 87	15.1	4.9	n 82	25.9
S Hutcheson-town	A	28.6		14.3	27.0		16.5
	B	26.4	n 141	12.1	26.5	n 171	15.9

N.B. Small houses comprised 1 or 2 apartments, large houses comprised 3 or more apartments.

The tabulation makes a distinction between the percentages of all units in each district and those occupied by three or more households, in order that tenement and terrace-cottage elements might be distinguished. It was thought possible that variation in intra-unit structural heterogeneity was related to social variation within tenements, a suspicion pursued in the forthcoming section on unit social composition.

From both Table 6 and Map Sequence 2, the correspondence between distributions of large-population units and exclusively 'small-house' (one- and two-apartment) units is clear. The largest district proportion of exclusively 1 and 2 apartment units lay in pre-redevelopment Gorbals Parish. There was a remarkable convergence on this exclusive 'small-house' measure between Gorbals Parish and N Hutchesontown by 1891. The elimination of much of the pre-industrial 'small-house' stock in the Parish coincided with an increase in that proportion in N Hutchesontown.

In the other districts the exclusive proportions remained relatively stable, with a slight overall increase in the Laurieston percentage of exclusively 'large-house' units.

The map sequence demonstrates the concentration of wholly and largely small-house units in particular *milieux* outwith the major Parish concentration. It appeared that the wholly 'small-house' proportion of units in Laurieston was concentrated in the back-lanes and narrower streets of the centre-west at both dates. In Gorbals Parish in 1871, the thin scatter of exclusively three-plus apartment units followed closely the pattern for the smallest unit population-size class in Sequence 1. This suggested that the larger houses were detached, rather than parts of tenements or single-address building complexes. In Laurieston and S Hutchesontown, exclusive or majority large-house tenements were the rule in 1871. The southern building fringe at both dates, and the reconstructed Parish, were characterised by mixed-structure units. Whereas some units did lose their exclusive large-house status, or became exclusively small-house, in others small-house minorities disappeared.

Taken together, the house-size composition sequence again demonstrated the marginality of change. The outlines of universal large-house and minority small-house aggregates appeared relatively constant, with changes in structural status occurring in local contexts. The spread of wholly small-house units was largely limited to the margins of pre-existing small-house *milieux*. Certain increases in the unit house-size measure suggested that reconstruction, or internal conversion, did not always result in the provision of smaller houses. It was the occupation of new, wholly large-house tenements which was lacking in the period 1871–91.

(3) Aspects of social separation (social groups IV and V composition)

In this sequence, social classifications IV and V are taken together as representative of working-class character on the basis of the manual nature of the declared occupations of household heads. Table 7 demonstrates the general decline in the proportion of units occupied wholly by households of social groups I, II and III. Associated with this decline was a more variable rise in the percentage of units exclusively inhabited by groups IV and V. The main exceptions to this change in emphasis were (a) the interruption in the decline in middle-class occupation in Gorbals Parish 1871–91, (b) levelling out in the rate of increase in working-class units in N Laurieston 1871–91, and (c) the decline in exclusive working-class units in S Hutchesontown 1871–91.

GORBALS 1871

RESIDENTIAL UNITS

N

SEQUENCE 2   MAP A
HOUSE – SIZE; C R Gs WITH 3 OR
MORE ROOMS

100
80–99
21–79
1–20
0
Parish boundary

0 metres   100   200   300   400   500

Sequence 2 Map A Gorbals 1871 Residential Units

Sequence 2 Map B Gorbals 1891 Residential Units

Evidently, reduction in the level of middle-class occupancy was nowhere linked automatically to increases in working-class segregation. The table and maps in Sequence 3 indicate the increasing proportion of units in each district which were socially mixed.

Map A of Sequence 3 is a particularly striking portrayal of a segregated social topography. The Parish district is clearly picked out as a concentration of 80 per cent plus working-class units. The most recently developed western block and the southeastern corner of the Parish emerged as the main exceptional areas, with a thin scatter of small-population exclusive middle-class units elsewhere. Indeed, at this date only 1 unit comprised total middle-class occupation and medium population size within the Parish boundary.

Table 7 *Aspects of change in residential exclusiveness; 1851—1891,*
social groups IV and V

A   Exclusive percentages of total units/district
B   Exclusive percentages of units comprising 3 or more households

District		1851		1871		1891	
		Units with NO group IV, V CRGs	Units ALL CRGs of groups IV, V	Units with NO group IV, V CRGs	Units ALL CRGs of groups IV, V	Units with NO group IV, V CRGs	Units ALL CRGs of groups IV, V
Gorbals Parish	A	5.5	25.5	2.2	37.1	3.5	16.9
	B	0.5	16.6	0.0	22.2	0.0	13.4
		n 180		*n* 175		*n* 112	
N Laurieston	A	32.5	10.5	20.5	16.6	11.4	18.3
	B	15.5	7.0	6.8	11.2	3.4	11.4
		n 200		*n* 204		*n* 176	
S Laurieston	A	36.0	23.2	20.1	18.2	12.7	19.8
	B	26.1	8.7	16.6	11.5	8.1	14.8
		n 172		*n* 253		*n* 283	
N Hutcheson-town	A	2.9	12.8	4.5	19.5	3.6	30.5
	B	1.9	8.9	0.0	17.2	1.2	26.8
		n 101		*n* 87		*n* 82	
S Hutcheson-town	A	18.3	4.2	2.8	9.9	1.7	6.4
	B	12.6	4.2	1.4	7.8	1.2	5.8
		n 71		*n* 141		*n* 171	

Sequence 3 Map A Gorbals 1851 Residential Units

Sequence 3 Map B Gorbals 1871 Residential Units

Sequence 3 Map C Gorbals 1891 Residential Units

Beyond the Parish the pattern of exclusive and large-majority groups IV and V units defined the older blocks of buildings, the areally-smaller building plots and those on back-lanes and minor streets. Reference to maps drawn in the 1820s and subsequently (e.g. Smith,[52,53] and Martin[54]) and the Laurieston Feuing Book showed that feuing and building in Laurieston was not restricted to Carlton Place. Although development of the large main-street steadings was slow, smaller plots were being rapidly developed in the badly-planned tract to the west of the Abbotsford Place–S Portland Street axis. It appeared that such neighbourhoods were built up as working-class quarters *ab initio*, in cottages or small-house tenements as Sequences 1 and 2 indicate.

Exclusive middle-class tenements continued to be built and occupied in Laurieston by 1851 in spite of the high-density infill nearby. The characteristic 'T'-shaped configuration is clear, with Carlton Place at the crosspiece. The building fringe of Laurieston was then partly composed of new, exclusive middle-class 'residential units'.

As Table 7 suggests, the contrast between N and S Hutchesontown was most intense in terms of the distribution of socially exclusive units.

The 1871 pattern of Map 3B shows that the social composition of units in the Parish area became more exclusively occupied by groups IV and V. Unit population reductions evident on Maps 1A and B were linked with emergent working-class segregated units. Peripheral duality rapidly changed into majorities of groups IV and V. The Parish in the years immediately preceding the belated application of the Improvement Trust legislation of 1866, had become a class ghetto with a proliferation of segregated units.

In Laurieston, the pattern for 1871 was much closer to that for 1851, excepting a different compositional character on the fringe of development in the south. From Sequence 2 the social mixture of the southern fringe units coincided with structural duality. In S Laurieston, some street-sectors had lost exclusive middle-class profiles by 1871. The general continuity of unit population size in these units (Maps 1A and B) belied suggestion that house subdivision and higher densities were necessarily associated with partial occupation by working-class families.

New development on some streets in S Laurieston progressively assumed structurally and socially lower-status profiles throughout the half century. This was reflected in the varied plot areas in some streets.

The effects of the City Improvement Trust activity in the latter intercensal interval are strikingly rendered on all the Maps of 1891. In detail, the mismatch between the 'pre-industrial' built-up area of the Parish and the area included within the Trust's remit resulted in the survival of some old building groups. These units had become high-density segregated or majority working-class units by 1891, housing what remained locally of the Parish slum population.

Beyond the Parish, especially in N Hutchesontown, the process of working-class unit segregation continued. The building of the embanked railway link to

St Enoch Station north of the Clyde may have further reduced the amenity of the district. Lamont[45] envisaged the displaced *proletariat* of the demolished slums north and south of the Clyde putting pressure on the next-oldest zone of housing, Laurieston and Hutchesontown included. There, increased densities and the outward migration of the middle-class inhabitants were presumed to have resulted in the spread of slum conditions.

In the study area, there does not seem to have been an acceleration in the growth of exclusively working-class units beyond the Parish from 1871 to 1891 over the rate of change in the previous interval. The Maps demonstrate that increased working-class proportions were not evenly spread across the study area. By 1891, the middle-class residential geography of Gorbals had retained its outline and changed in detail. Middle-class majorities replaced many exclusive middle-class profiles in units of the central 'T'-shaped core of Laurieston. The northern edge, Carlton Place, had suffered institutional and commercial impingement. Resident caretakers consequently lowered the social tone of what had been an exclusively *bourgeois* terrace in 1851.

In general, the character of change between censal patterns has tended to marginal rather than radical transformation. Marginal, in the sense that relatively few units changed between middle class and working-class dominance in either twenty-year interval, and also in that aggregations of similarly-charactised units tended to change at their margins rather than in a more widespread fashion.

The final picture, of 1891, differed from the first most obviously in terms of CIT remodelling and associated social changes, and the character of new development in the south. The majority of originally middle-class exclusive units remained at least dominated by middle class residents.

Throughout the 1851–91 period, the decline in number of socially segregated units was most remarkable. The percentage of unsegregated units throughout the study area rose steadily from 65.8 per cent in 1851, to 69.7 per cent in 1871 and 75.0 per cent in 1891.

CONCLUSIONS

In considering the significance of the evidence surveyed, a distinction was made between features of local importance and findings with more general potential. From the outset it was clear that the area under study was of particular interest to the urban historian and geographer alike. Few people in Britain today can be ignorant of the 'Gorbals image'. The name remains a powerful metaphor for violence and squalor, though the environmental and population characteristics of the district have changed radically with clearance and redevelopment in the last three decades.

After 1900, the processes of social and structural standardisation may have reduced the contrasts between Laurieston, Hutchesontown and the Parish, resulting in a broad, general decline in conditions and social status with the interwar slump. During the nineteenth century, a macro-scale distinction did apply between 'planned gentility', 'unplanned speculation' and 'decayed *faubourg*' respectively.

In Laurieston, socio-spatial relationships appeared influenced by the original conditions of land division and building. The considerable working-class component in the Laurieston population appeared to have been segregated in specific back-street *locales*, which were amongst the earliest to have been occupied. Mid- to late-nineteenth-century developments changed the *contrast* of the picture; its structural demarcations between large- and small-house tenements, main street and back-lane and large and small steading, remained apparent.

During the latter half of the nineteenth century, socio-spatial changes in N Hutchesontown most closely followed those in the Parish, though lagging in terms of the intensification of working-class residential dominance. Gorbals Parish fell within the Improvement Trust limits and underwent considerable structural and social modification; N Hutchesontown continued to include increasing working-class unit proportions.

By and large, middle-class distributions traced through the directory evidence predicted, with southern additions, the main axes of post-1850 *bourgeois* settlement.

The built environment of the study area was more rigid than hypothesised; intra-district structural change occurred in association with new building in the south, rather than with massive 'making-down' (house subdivision) in existing tenements.

It emerged from the combined analyses of directories and census volumes that the local history of nineteenth-century degradation in Gorbals, as commonly articulated, was oversimplified. Neither was there an evacuation of the middle-class residents who had arrived in the early decades, nor the expected structural changes in unit capacity. Continuity of character with peripheral change was the overriding theme.

The widespread influence of the Improvement Trust episode may also have been overstated. The Parish area began to be depopulated before 1871; it seems to have been an early example of 'planning blight' by that date. The statute empowering purchase and clearance of the 'pre-industrial' core of Glasgow and Gorbals had been passed five years previously. Clearance and re-building occurred in piecemeal fashion, slowed by recession throughout almost the entire interval from 1871 to 1891.[50] During this time the corporation built central lodging houses, and working-class house-building continued (albeit fitfully) to the west, in Hutchesontown and further afield. The change in the overall residential balance between the classes in Gorbals was a continuation and enlargement of pre-1871 working-class localities. Though threatened, the middle-class heartland in Laurieston was not overrun.

Rather than a general decline into one-class slumdom, there developed a wider intra-unit social diversity. This micro-scale duality was associated with new development within Gorbals Parish after 1871, and in southern accretions from about 1850, when exclusively large-house middle-class buildings appeared to have ceased.

It was not denied that the overall trend was a gradual lowering of social status, but it appeared that the incorporation of new working-class immigrants to the area followed definite pathways to specific areas of settlement. The middle-class presence in Laurieston was not wholly extinguished until the 1930s and 40s; Abbotsford Place was known as the 'Harley Street of Glasgow' until then, a functional continuity traceable to the directory volumes compiled one hundred years previously.

The evidence suggested that during the 1841–91 interval, there was a long term change in general *bourgeois* perceptions of social segregation in Gorbals. It appeared that early levels of social segregation were later compromised. In the 1840s and 50s, there were more segregated residential units and street-sections than subsequently. This was seen in established tenements where working-class minorities did not trigger rapid middle-class departure over forty years, and in new buildings where social heterogeneity was 'built in' by means of structural variety. Smith[55] has shown the rapidity of contemporary North American neighbourhood change within a similar built environment; the Gorbals evidence indicated an altogether different rate and type of change.

The continued middle-class presence in a district transformed from suburb to inner-city during the course of the nineteenth century may be explained with reference to the favourable location of Laurieston. The Suspension Bridge enabled relatively short journeys-to-work to be made in the transpontine central business district. Kellett[26] has related the comparatively late development of commuter railways in Glasgow, which delayed the availability of a suburban alternative to Laurieston.

Perhaps a Scottish cultural theme was also involved. Gauldie[13] was of the opinion that although inter-class differences in housing quality were histori-cally apparent, the gulf between traditional English socio-residential types was not as pronounced in Scotland. The eighteenth-century Edinburgh model, where a close residential association between diverse social elements prevailed, may have survived or have been revived in later, industrialised contexts. Whilst it is no surprise that small, middle-class communities retained central locations in Western cities (à *la* Beacon Hill), the extent and increase in micro-scale inter-class residential propinquity revealed in this study was at variance with the general theory of social segregation scale increase.

There was no reason to expect that the increased proportion of socially heterogeneous units was either permanent or irreversible after 1891. By 1900 transport improvements, particularly the Cathcart Circle Railway, had created new opportunities for middle-class housing on the South Side. The encirclement and eventual dissection of the Gorbals area by embanked railway tracks, busy with main-line and commuter traffic, provided further impetus to middle-class out-migration.

REFERENCES

1   H J Dyos and D A Reeder, 'Slums and Suburbs', in *The Victorian City* (eds. H J Dyos and H Wolff) (London: Routledge, 1973), vol. I, pp. 359—86.

2   R Smith, 'Multi-dwelling building in Scotland, 1750—1970: A study based on housing in the Clyde valley', in *Multi-storey living; the British working class experience* (ed. A Sutcliffe) (London: Croom Helm, 1974), pp. 207—43.

3   F Worsdall, *The tenement; a way of life* (Edinburgh: Chambers, 1979).

4   A Hamilton, 'The decline and rise of Glasgow's tenements', *The Times* (5 May 1978), p. 30.

5   G Sjoberg, *The pre-industrial city past and present* (Glencoe, Ill. Free Press, 1960).

6   P Burke, 'Some reflections on the pre-industrial city', *Urban History Yearbook*, (1975), 13—21.

7   J R Vance, 'Land assignment in the precapitalist, capitalist and postcapitalist city', *Econ. Geog.* **47** (1971), 101—20.

8   R Chambers, *The traditions of Edinburgh* (Edinburgh: Chambers, 1868) (2nd edn 1980).

9   J E Vance, *This scene of man; the role and structure of the city in the geography of western civilization* (New York: Harper and Row, 1977).

10 R J Dennis, Community and interaction in a Victorian city: Huddersfield 1850—1880. Unpublished PhD thesis (1975), Cambridge University.

11 T Chalmers (1821—6), The Christian and civic economy of large towns', in *The idea of the city in nineteenth-century Britain* (ed. B I Coleman) (London: Routledge, 1973), pp. 42—6.

12 B Disraeli (1845), *Sybil: Or, the two nations* (Penguin, 1954 edn).

13 E Gauldie, 'The middle class and working class housing in the nineteenth century', in *Social class in Scotland; past and present* (ed. A A MacLaren) (Edinburgh: Donald, 1974), pp. 12—35.

14 J D Mitchell, 'Wellfield House', in *Regality Club* (third series) (Glasgow: Maclehose, 1899), pp. 1—10.

15 A A MacLaren (ed.), *Social class in Scotland; past and present* (Edinburgh: Donald, 1974).

16 A M Warnes, 'Residential patterns in an emerging industrial town', in *Social patterns in cities* (eds. B D Clark and M B Gleave (I B G Special Publication 5, 1973), pp. 169—88.

17 J E Tunbridge, 'Spatial change in high-class residence; the case of Bristol', *Area*, **9**, 3 (1977), 171—4.

18 A Briggs, *Victorian Cities* (London: Odhams, 1963).

19 J Robb, 'Another Gorbals', *New Edinburgh Review,* **46** (1979), 16—18.

20 A McDonald, Diagram of 17th and 18th century feus in part of Gorbals village, in R Renwick, 'The Barony of Gorbals', *Regality Club* (fourth series) (Glasgow: Maclehose, 1912), pp. 1—60.

21 J McArthur (1778). *Plan of the City of Glasgow.* Strathclyde Regional Archives.
22 T Kyle (1840). *Plan of Gorbals Barony* c.*1790.* Strathclyde Regional Archives.
23 Town Clerk, Report by the (1871). *The superiority of Gorbals.* Strathclyde Regional Archives.
24 J R Kellett, 'Property Speculators and the building of Glasgow; 1780–1830', *Scottish Journ. of Political Econ.* **8** (1961), 211–32.
25 Laurieston Feuing Book (1801–26). *MS register of sasines for Laurieston, Barony of Gorbals.* Mitchell Library, Glasgow.
26 J R Kellett, *The impact of railways on Victorian cities* (London: Routledge, 1969).
27 J R Kellett, 'Glasgow', in *Historic Towns; maps and plans of . . .* (ed. M D Lobel) (London: Lovell Johns, 1969), 1, D1–D13.
28 S G Checkland, 'The British industrial city as history: The Glasgow case', *Urban Studies,* **1** (1964), 34–54.
29 M A Simpson, 'The west end of Glasgow, 1830–1914', in *Middle class housing in Britain* (eds. M A Simpson and T H Lloyd) (Newton Abbot: David and Charles, 1977), pp. 44–85.
30 D Laurie, *A Project for erecting public markets and a Grand Academy on improved principles in the Gorbals, etc.* (Glasgow: Chapman, 1810).
31 D Laurie (1813). *To the Right Hon. Lord Archibald Hamilton M.P., etc., . . . certain grievances in the Gorbals . . . .* Strathclyde Regional Archives.
32 D Laurie (1826). *To the . . . General Assembly . . . of the Church of Scotland.* Mitchell Library, Glasgow.
33 J Ord, *The Story of the Barony of Gorbals* (Paisley: Gardner, 1919).
34 J R Kellett, *Glasgow; a concise history* (London: Blond, 1967).
35 M Lindsay, *Portrait of Glasgow* (London: Hale, 1972).
36 J C Symons, Handloom-weavers; Reports from assistant commissioners (Parliamentary Papers XLII, 1839), pp. 159, 565–6.
37 Shadow (pseud. A Brown), *Glasgow, 1858; midnight scenes and social photographs* (Glasgow University Press, 1976 edn).
38 Medical Officer of Health (1863) Report, in A Hogg, *Scotland; the rise of cities, 1694–1905* (London: Evans, 1973), p. 44b.
39 J Pagan (ed.), *Glasgow; past and present* (Glasgow: Robertson, 1884).
40 Gorbals Police Establishment (1815–22; 1830–6) *Minute Books.* Strathclyde Regional Archives.
41 D Ward, 'Victorian Cities; how modern?', *Journ. Hist. Geog.* **1**, 2 (1975). 135–51.
42 H Carter and S Wheatley, 'Residential segregation in mid-nineteenth century cities', *Area,* **12**, 1 (1980), 57–62.
43 G Gordon, 'The status areas of early to mid-Victorian Edinburgh', *Trans. Inst. Brit. Geogr.* (new series), **4**, 2 (1979), 168–91.
44 T C Smout, *A History of the Scottish people 1560–1830* (London: Collins, 1972).
45 D W Lamont, Population, migration and social area change in Central Glasgow, 1871–1891; a study in applied factorial ecology. Unpublished PhD thesis (1976), Glasgow University.
46 R C Fox, The morphological, social and functional development of the Royal Burgh of Stirling, 1124–1881. Unpublished PhD thesis (1978), Strathclyde University.
47 J Cleland, *Statistical and population tables relative to the City of Glasgow* (Glasgow: Smith, 1828).

48   S A Royle, 'Social stratification from the early census returns; a new approach',
     Area, **9**, 3 (1977), 215–19.
49   M Anderson, 'Standard tabulation procedures for the Census enumerators' books,
     1851–1891', in *Nineteenth century society; essays on the use of quantitative
     methods for the study of social data* (ed. E A Wrigley) (CUP, 1972) pp.
     134–45.
50   C M Allan, 'The genesis of British urban redevelopment with special reference to
     Glasgow', *Econ. Hist. Rev.* (second series), **18** (1965), 598–613.
51   J N Tarn, 'Housing in Liverpool and Glasgow—the growth of civic responsibility',
     Town Planning Review, **39** (1969), 318–34.
52   D Smith (1821), *Map of the City of Glasgow*. Strathclyde Regional Archives.
53   D Smith (1828), *Map of the City of Glasgow*. Strathclyde Regional Archives.
54   G Martin (1840), *Map of Glasgow*. Strathclyde Regional Archives.
55   W F Smith (1964), 'Filtering and neighbourhood change', in *Readings in social
     geography*) (ed. E Jones) (OUP, 1975), pp. 240–9.

8

THE STATUS AREAS OF EDINBURGH IN 1914

G Gordon

The areas were defined in terms of data referring to house valuation, tenure and householder's occupation which are contained in the Valuation Roll of Edinburgh for 1914–15.[1] That source recorded the annual assessment of each property for the purpose of local government rating. Each entry listed the address, name of occupant and owner and type of tenure. Additionally, in many cases the householder's occupation was given.

The Land Valuation Scotland Act 1854 established the principle of house valuation based upon the notion of the annual market rent which properties might be expected to attract. Robson[2] has questioned the consistency and construction of English valuations but it would appear that the Scottish data was more reliable in definition and compilation.[3] The principal determinants of the valuation were the size of the house, the extent of any grounds and the presence of outbuildings or other additional premises. Attachment reduced the value. Thus flats were assessed at a lower value than detached houses of equivalent size.

Valuation data have been used in a number of British studies[4] of the location of status areas in particular towns and cities. The data have the advantages of frequent production (annual rolls), and comprehensive coverage (virtually every property). As a surrogate of mean monthly rental they also afford a means of comparing the patterns of status areas in British cities with ecological and economic explanations of urban structure.[5] In the economically determined housing market which prevailed in Edinburgh, and other British cities, in 1914, valuation statistics provided the only comprehensive data which related to the primary allocative mechanism of the market, the ability to pay. It is perhaps debatable if burgh assessors set values in complete alignment with actual market rents although the fact that more than two-thirds of all houses were rented meant that these officials had a substantial volume of evidence on which to base their computations. For the valuation roll to be an acceptable source in historical empirical studies it is not necessary for the valuations to equate exactly with contemporary market rents but merely that the properties were ranked in true order and that the statutory procedures for valuation were consistently applied. The presence of a substantial number of entries recording the occupation of householders added a further dimension to the data, facilitating

an examination of the relationships between house valuation, tenure and occupation. A sample of 9049 entries was selected from the Edinburgh Valuation
Roll for 1914–15. Occupations were classified according to the scheme adopted
in the 1921 Census of Employment. Pearson's Product Moment Correlation
yielded a positive relationship between house valuation and occupation of
0.76. Similar correlations have been reported in other studies of British cities.[6]
The tenurial and occupational data provided a basis for comparing the status
areas with ecological explanations of urban structure such as those propounded
in the 1920s by the Chicago School of Sociology, notably Park, Burgess and
McKenzie.[7]

PRE-1914 DEVELOPMENT

'Edinburgh, Scotland's history in her every grey stone, with her grave and
kindly people, and her heritage of lore and learning, looking out for ever
northwards across the Firth of Forth, and southward to the Pentland Hills,
towards which her suburbs like long fingers, stretch out to touch the heather.'[8]
Watson has also commented upon the relationship between nation and capital,
'Scotland rushes in upon Edinburgh at almost every turn.'[9]

The city occupies a strategic location in a narrow gap between the Pentland
Hills and the Firth of Forth, controlling east-west routes within the Central
Lowlands and north-south movements between the northeast and the eastern
Highlands and the Borders and England. The site of the capital affords a varied
and stimulating topography with the general altitudinal descent from the
Pentlands to the Firth punctuated by steep-sided ice-eroded volcanic stumps,
ice-moulded ridges, glacially deepened valleys and pro-glacial basins. From
these strands of site and situation history has woven a unique city.

Created a royal burgh c.1124 by David I, the small market town rapidly
developed in economic and social importance to become the national capital
and leading commercial, legal and administrative centre by the late medieval
period. The medieval town developed astride the eastward sloping tail of the
hog-backed Castle ridge. The initial morphology of the royal burgh would
appear to have consisted of a central market place flanked by narrow burgage
plots. Early urban extensions included West Bow and Grassmarket, whilst the
independent ecclesiastical burgh of Canongate was located at the eastern end of
the Castle or High Street ridge.

Many historical studies of Edinburgh contain references to the location of the
houses of prominent persons[10] in the period between the creation of the royal
burgh in the twelfth century and the construction of the Georgian New Town.
Documentation of the residences of people of lesser rank is very limited, so the
reconstruction of the social topography is hampered by incomplete and biased
information.

One of the earliest fashionable sites was at Castlehill strategically located for access to the guardianship of the Castle and to the commerce and civic activities of the royal burgh. Castlehill may have been an early example of a political quarter, housing noblemen, ambassadors and others engaged in the affairs of state but by the late fifteenth century the Canongate district had acquired that function with the royal residence established at Holyrood.

During this lengthy period Edinburgh remained compact and limited in spatial extent. Physical and economic growth were largely attained and contained within the confines of the medieval site. Particular parts of the burgh acquired distinctive functional characteristics[11] relating to predominance in certain professions or trades but the increasing density of development complicated the structure, leaving the impression of a diffuse pattern of social class and an absence of marked spatial segregation. Urban growth, in the absence of commensurate physical extension, necessitated the infilling of burgage plots and the creation of tall lands of tenemented buildings. With a shortage of building land, new mansions perforce were restricted in choice of site. This situation could explain, at least in part, the apparently diffuse social topography of the post-medieval core. Movement of the foci of particular activities and functions, such as the court, further compounded the impression of a complex, almost patternless, social topography. To some extent that interpretation may be incorrect since we lack reliable continuous plot occupancy records which would afford an accurate yardstick of contemporary social segregation.

By the early eighteenth century the social pattern was a complex mosaic in which small clusters of substantial town mansions were set amidst tenement lands. Vertical segregation had become a distinctive feature in the city. Many leading citizens maintained lodgings in the capital, retreating in summer from the smells and noise of the city to their country estates. Moreover, the offspring and relatives of country lairds and leaders in various walks of life also had town lodgings, large or small, thereby adding to the group which maintained seasonal residences in Edinburgh.

To some extent the demands for new, larger and pleasantly situated houses were met by urban expansion southwards from the earliest suburbs at Cowgate on the crest of the adjoining ridge with the erection of Argyle Square and Brown Square. At the other end of the social scale, the influx of poor migrants in the eighteenth century exacerbated the shortage of cheap housing and overcrowding became commonplace in the Grassmarket and in some closes and wynds adjoining the Lawnmarket and High Street.

A period of rapid change commenced in the 1760s with the decision to erect a New Town to the north of the burgh and with the contemporaneous private speculation on the southern periphery at George Square. Within a few decades there was an exodus of the members of the upper and middle classes from the Old Town to the new terraced and flatted Georgian houses. For a few decades the High Street and Canongate districts did retain some social standing with notable enclaves at John Street and New Street. Both were recent developments of small terraced houses which had attracted a number of advocates and judges amongst the first occupants—the legal profession seeking central residences near the courts. But soon the New Town became the locale of the wealthy, the titled and the professions. By 1810 few large houses remained in the Old Town; the area was abandoned by the elite and the middle class and it rapidly degenerated into a slum.

Based upon a design by Craig, the rectangular New Town consisted of three principal thoroughfares (Princes Street, George Street and Queen Street) and two squares (St Andrew Square and Charlotte Square). There were also lesser and minor streets for minor professions, servants and tradesmen. After a slow start, the eastern portion was not finished until 1780, the project proved popular and successful and was completed, in 1810, with the erection of the elegant terraced mansions of Charlotte Square. Extensions to the New Town were started to the west, north and east of the original area.[12] Predominantly intended as high status districts some streets of lesser standing were carefully integrated into the design but the respective status was re-inforced by the architectural design of the different properties.[13]

There were sharp contrasts between the residential environments of the wealthy and the poor. The elegant terraced Georgian mansions stood in counterpoint to the tenements in the numerous closes and wynds which connected the spine of the High Street to the adjoining Cowgate and North Loch valleys. In one such wynd, Blackfriars Wynd, in the 1840s it was reported that 142 houses with a total of 193 rooms accommodated 1025 people.[14] A similar property in Middle Mealmarket Stair housed 56 families in 59 rooms, a total of 248 persons, with no sinks or toilets.[15]

New working-class industrial districts were developed at Fountainbridge near the terminus of the Union Canal and at St Leonards beside the Edinburgh and Dalkeith railway. However, demand for low rent housing greatly exceeded the supply of new properties, with the consequences of overcrowding and sub-division in the older central districts.

Industry also invaded the lanes and lesser streets of the New Town areas. Various craft workshops, such as printing, became a characteristic feature of these areas, especially in the Victorian era.[16]

Some measures were implemented to control the worst facets of squalid housing environments in the second half of the nineteenth century. Fear that such areas bred disease sponsored action in terms of sanitary regulations, water supply, paving, medical inspection, policing and fire prevention.[17] A number of city improvement schemes, notably in the 1860s, created new streets by clearing a number of blocks of inadequate housing in parts of the Old Town.[18] There was, however, a substantial net loss of housing through improvement schemes because roads and institutions were favoured new developments. Substantial new working-class districts were erected at Gorgie–Dalry and Abbeyhill in the last quarter of the nineteenth century. Contemporaneously, a third major component emerged in the social geography of the city, suburban Edinburgh. In these predominantly middle-class suburbs the houses varied in size and style from substantial villas at Merchiston, Morningside, Newington and Inverleith to large flats in tenements at Marchmont and Comely Bank.

The central business district became established in the southern part of the New Town with incursions of offices, shops and other institutions spreading into other parts of the New Town districts and a substantial part of the south-facing slope of Lauriston ridge.

Physical extension of the city was facilitated by numerous adjustments in the nineteenth century of the city boundary, particularly in the years between 1856 and 1901.[19] Transport developments such as the tramways and the suburban railway supported and encouraged suburban growth.[20]

The seaside resort and small industrial centre of Portobello was incorporated in the 1896 boundary extension and several smaller villages were similarly annexed by other adjustments to the urban frontier. Leith, the ancient seaport of the capital, and for centuries of subject commercial standing, remained primarily an industrial working-class settlement despite release, in 1833, from the administrative bondage of Edinburgh. By 1914 the urban fringes of the two settlements met and merged with a continuous urbanised zone around Leith Walk (the main linking thoroughfare) although a more dispersed pattern of development prevailed in the west at Trinity and in the east at Craigentinny.

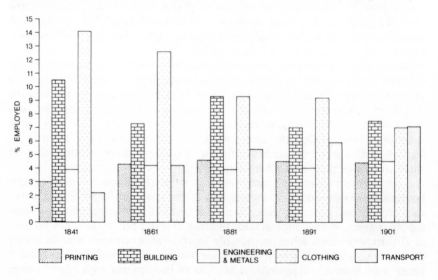

FIGURE 1   Industrial Occupations in Edinburgh 1841–1901

Nor was Edinburgh without industrial growth. The traditional industries, printing, milling and brewing, enjoyed continued prosperity although several firms embarked upon a programme of relocation from central to more peripheral sites. For example, new breweries and maltings were built at Fountainbridge, Roseburn and Craigmillar and new printing works at St Leonards, Abbeyhill and Canonmills. The largest single employer was the rubber factory which occupied the site of old silk mills beside the Union Canal at Fountainbridge. Nonetheless, significant structural changes occurred in the industrial occupational profile of Edinburgh as Figure 1[21] illustrates. Decline was particularly marked in the clothing industries whilst by the end of the century the transport sector had emerged as a leader in terms of numbers employed. The fluctuating fortunes of the building industry with characteristic phases of boom and recession are reflected in the diagram.

Between 1801 and 1911 the combined population of Edinburgh and Leith increased from 82,560 to 320,318. These statistics provide a bald summary of a remarkable phase of physical and economic expansion with an associated transformation, and subsequent evolutionary adjustment, in the topography of status areas in the city.[22]

STATUS AREAS 1914–15

By 1914, a complex mosaic of status areas could be identified in which the principal high-status districts were located in the western and northwestern extensions of the New Town. By contrast, a swath of low-status districts stretched from Gorgie in the west, through the Old Town and St Leonards towards the docks and warehouses at Leith.

Table 1 shows the pyramidal pattern of house valuations in 1914–15, reflecting the pyramidal social structure of the period. The five grades were defined on the basis of the frequency distribution of house valuations and occupational data relating to residents. The antipodal Grade I and Grade V dwellings represented high- and low-status respectively, with Grades II–IV being associated with middle status districts. Warr recognised that, 'the upper and middle classes were divided up into sets and cliques more sharply defined than anywhere else in the country'.[23] Indeed, each valuation category contained some subtle variations but, for the purposes of description and explanation, a three-fold grouping into high-, middle- and low-status districts afforded a manageable and meaningful classification.

In Edinburgh, owner-occupancy was closely related to house valuation, declining from 61 per cent in Grade I to 43 per cent in Grade III and less than 5 per cent in Grade V. The latter Grade contrasted sharply in levels of owner occupancy with Grade IV where the average was 26 per cent, a statistic which re-inforced the allocation of Grade IV districts to the middle-status category. In Figures 2–6[24] houses were mapped individually. Thus pronounced linear patterns on particular maps represented localised dominance of that particular valuation range whereas fragmentary or diffuse patterns reflected deviance or the intricate interdigitation of properties of different valuation ranges.

Table 1   *House valuations 1914–1915*

Grade	Annual valuation	Edinburgh Number of houses	% Total	Leith Number of houses	% Total
I	£115–450	1299	1.8	12	0.1
II	£70–114	2231	3.0	104	0.6
III	£40–69	4629	6.3	682	3.7
IV	£21–39	13,615	18.5	1599	8.8
V	£2–20	51,711	70.4	15,865	86.8
		73,485		18,262	

The residential properties in Edinburgh had a modal value of £10 per annum, a median of £14 and upper and lower quartiles of £22 and £9 respectively. In Leith, the mode was £9 and the median value £11 per annum. The largest house in Edinburgh was assessed at £450 whereas the highest valuation in Leith was only £230, a reflection of the relative status of the two settlements as sites for the houses of the very wealthy. Nonetheless, only 73 residential properties in Edinburgh were assessed at more than £230 per annum, although they were all substantial town or suburban mansions and the homes of some of the most prominent leaders of society.

HIGH STATUS

Grade I residences (Figure 2) represented the high-status households and, in Edinburgh, 59.4 per cent were located in the New Town areas, particularly the enlarged western extension. A further 11.1 per cent were situated across the Dean Bridge on the neighbouring lands of Learmonth. To the west of these areas another small cluster of 70 residences were sited at Coates and on the slopes of the ridge at Murrayfield. Thus, a zone extending from Regent Terrace on the flank of Calton Hill in the east to Murrayfield in the west contained three quarters of the high-status properties in the city.

The southern suburban villa district was the site of 266 Grade I properties, one fifth of the total number of high-status residences. Finally a small cluster of villas was situated at Inverleith and there were a few high-status properties at George Square near the Meadows and at the outlying settlements of Duddingston and Portobello. There was a sharp contrast in house type between the central zone of Georgian and Victorian terraced mansions and the suburbs which consisted of large Victorian villas.

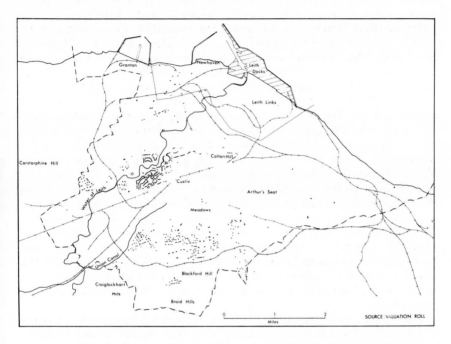

FIGURE 2   The distribution of Grade I houses in Edinburgh and Leith in 1914–15

Invasion by commercial premises had replaced most high-status residential properties in the original New Town although there were 21 Grade I houses in Charlotte Square, the architectural jewel of the plan. Thirteen residents of Charlotte Square were distinguished men of medicine, although the largest houses were the properties of a merchant and the Marquess of Bute. Each of the areas which had been built in the New Town style initially had at least one street of high-status mansions. By 1914 commercial invasion was also in progress in the terraces on the flanks of the Calton Hill but the area remained a small, if somewhat isolated, high-status locality with 20 Grade I residences situated in Regent Terrace. The fine shadings with the upper class which Warr described[25] were illustrated by the fact that the average rental of Grade I properties in Regent Terrace was £123 whereas the corresponding statistic for Charlotte Square was £236. In the northern extension, to the north of Queen Street, Heriot Row and Abercrombie Place were the principal sites of high-status properties. The 35 Grade I houses in Heriot Row had an average assessment

of £160 and the residents included the Lyon King of Arms, the Lord Justice
General, the Solicitor-General, the Registrar-General, the Lord Advocate, a
Sheriff, two judges, eight solicitors, eight advocates, a professor, a paper
manufacturer, a captain, three doctors, a merchant and a knight.

The architect Robert Reid was principally responsible for the northern extension, including Heriot Row and Abercrombie Place, which dated from the
beginning of the nineteenth century.[26] To the west lay an oddly-shaped site on
a bluff above the narrow valley of the Water of Leith. Here James Gillespie
Graham created an elegant scheme on the lands of the Earl of Moray. One
solicitor explained his removal in 1825 to Moray Place from Queen Street as
follows: 'Driven from my former by want of room, approach of building, shops
etc., I am now 500 yards to the northwest of my former house. . . . We are
now on the top of a bank above a ravine—which must exclude building for five
or six hundred yards at least in the rear.'[27] By 1914 the principal streets of the
Moray development remained an important high-status area. The association
with the legal profession remained with more than forty residents recorded in
the Valuation Roll as sheriffs, advocates or solicitors. The prestigious properties
in Moray Place had a mean value of £217, with the largest, No. 28, assessed at
£320 per annum. Along with the houses in Charlotte Square, the properties in
Moray Place were the largest remaining Georgian terraced mansions. Apart
from the size and elegance of the properties they were also within a few
minutes' walk of the offices in the New Town and of the law courts in High
Street and the University and Infirmary at Chambers Street and Lauriston respectively.

The western extension, with its distinctively skewed alignment from the
original New Town, was the principal high-status district. Coates Crescent,
Atholl Crescent, Walker Street and Melville Street dated from the late
Georgian era but some of the largest terraced town houses were erected north
and west of these streets in the late Victorian building booms.[28] Drumsheugh
Gardens, Grosvenor Crescent and Rothesay Terrace were particularly notable
examples with mean assessments in 1914 for Grade I residences of £219, £205
and £238 respectively. Indeed the twenty-three Grade I residences in Rothesay
Terrace had both the highest average value and the largest single property in
the city (No. 3). Commerce and industry were strongly represented in the listed
occupations of householders including merchants, wine merchants, brewers,
and a shipowner, in addition to the customary members of the professions and
titled personages. Several lodging-keepers were situated in Melville Street,
Walker Street and Palmerston Place but these streets remained overwhelmingly
residential in function and of a high-status. No fewer than thirteen of the
occupants of premises in Walker Street were listed as doctors, physicians or
surgeons. In the Victorian era many legal and medical practitioners used their
houses as offices and consulting rooms and this practice may have continued,
particularly for special clients, in the immediate post-Edwardian period.

Institutional invasion had occurred in places, most notably by schools in Atholl Crescent, a street of elegant terraces facing on to the busy and noisy western approach to Princes Street.

Learmonth, an embryonic suburb at the middle of the nineteenth century, had become an important high-status district with 144 Grade I houses. The earliest development, Clarendon Crescent, was slightly overshadowed by later, larger terraced mansions at Belgrave Crescent and Learmonth Terrace. The mean values of houses in these streets were £130, £177, £183 respectively. The largest property, No. 25 Learmonth Terrace, with an assessment of £400, was the residence of a prominent Edinburgh wine merchant.

To the west of Donaldson's Hospital, the small Victorian villa development on the lands of West Coates, erected under very stringent feuing conditions, marked the transition from the terraced mansions of the inner high-status districts to the villa dominated suburbs.

Speculation had commenced at Murrayfield before the district was annexed by Edinburgh and the district was an established high-status suburb by the close of the Edwardian period. The principal suburban zone was located south of the city on the lands between Merchiston and Newington, an area described in the Third Statistical Account as the escape route of radical Victorian Edinburgh.[29] Many of the high-status houses in this zone were large mansions with the pattern involving a dispersion of these properties through the district with only a few areas of concentration. A triangular-shaped cluster of Grade I properties can be identified from Figure 2 at the western periphery of the zone in the area bounded by Polwarth Terrace and Colinton Road. Despite the lack of marked clusters of Grade I properties, in aggregate this was an important location of high-status properties accounting for over one-fifth of the urban total. It was difficult to discern any occupational characteristics of this zone. Several unique occupations did occur such as Archbishop and Rear Admiral but the presence of industrialists and entrepreneurs such as colliery owners may have been indicative of the social profile of this fragmented zone of high-status properties. Equally the proportion of professional men was appreciably lower than that found in the New Town districts.

The northern villa district at Inverleith and Trinity (Leith) was set amidst several playing fields and parks which effectively restricted the scale of the residential development. The small group of villas at Trinity (Leith) were mostly occupied by shipowners illustrating a direct link with the economic function of that settlement.

MIDDLE STATUS

Although the distribution of Grade II residences (Figure 3) had points of similarity with the Grade I pattern (Figure 2), the emphasis differed substantially and significantly. The southern suburban villa zone constituted the dominant

locus (55.1 per cent) whereas the New Town districts had only 18.6 per cent of
the Grade II dwellings. Another cluster (13.1 per cent) was situated at Coates
and Murrayfield and minor enclaves were found at a variety of central
(Learmonth, Lauriston) and suburban (Inverleith, Portobello) locations.

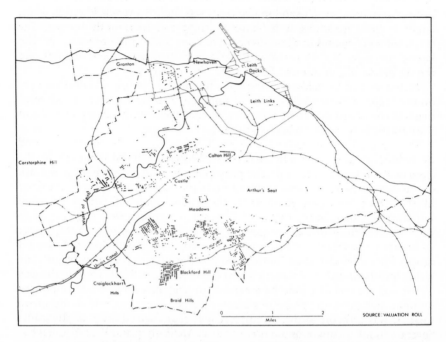

FIGURE 3   The distribution of Grade II houses in Edinburgh and Leith in 1914–15

The pyramidal structure of the assessments was reflected in the fact that the
lowest Grade II value (£70) was also the modal figure and that only 12 per cent
of the properties were rated in excess of £100. Approximately half of the
dwellings were owner-occupied, the figure varying from 48 per cent for
residences assessed at between £70 and £79 to 56 per cent for those valued at
more than £100.

Within the southern suburban zone the largest cluster was sited on the
north-facing slope at Braid. Cluny Gardens and Cluny Drive, the streets with
most Grade II dwellings, had mean assessments for this grade of £77 and £83
respectively. The occupational profiles of these streets were typical of upper
middle status suburban districts. The residents included businessmen (spice
grinder, clothier, bootmaker, leather dresser), industrialists (wire-netting
manufacturer, biscuit manufacturer, manufacturing chemist), merchants (oil,

wine, spirits, coalmaster), traders (wholesale grocer, cattle dealer), public officials (Board of Agriculture, Inland Revenue, Board of Works), doctors, ministers, engineers and various 'white-collar' occupations related to banking, insurance, accountancy and managerial functions.

A similar sizeable cluster of late Victorian and Edwardian villas was located in the Merchiston district at the western extremity of the southern suburban zone. At Braid, most streets contained small and large Grade II dwellings but with a preponderance of properties valued at between £70 and £90. An exception was Corrennie Gardens where the 21 houses had a mean value of £93. In the Merchiston district there were a number of streets in which larger villas, set as elsewhere in the suburbs amidst trees and gardens, were predominant. For example, the mean values of Grade II houses in West Castle Road and Napier Road were £90 and £98 respectively. Their residents included two merchants, a schoolmaster, a bank agent, a solicitor's clerk, an ironfounder, a glass merchant, a minister, a bookmaker, a solicitor, a colonel, a secretary and a druggist.

A more fragmented zone of Grade II properties studded the slopes of Grange and Bruntsfield with another dispersed pattern occupying parts of the lands of Newington. Nonetheless seven streets at Grange and Newington (Mayfield Gardens, Blacket Place, Mayfield Terrace, Craigmillar Park, Mayfield Road, Lauder Road and Fountainhall Road) were the site of more than twenty Grade II properties, although considerable variation occurred in age of development (early nineteenth to early twentieth century) and house style (suburban Georgian to Edwardian). The general pattern of house values and the occupational structure of the Newington area resembled that of other portions of the southern suburban zone.

The cluster of streets of Grade II properties at Murrayfield contained villas and several rows of large late-Victorian and Edwardian terraced dwellings. The homogeneity of design of the terraced buildings was reflected in rateable values with twenty of the twenty-nine Grade II houses in Garscube Terrace assessed at the same rental, £88 per annum. The residents of Garscube Terrace included three merchants, three solicitors, two chemists, a civil engineer, an electrical engineer, a surgeon, a publisher, an actuary, a grocer and a fancy draper.

At Learmonth, Learmonth Gardens, South Learmonth Gardens and Lennox Street contained comparatively large Grade II terraced properties with mean values of £98, £98 and £102 respectively. The residents included nine solicitors, five stockbrokers, two merchants, two secretaries, two military officers, an accountant, a minister and a shipowner. The proximity of the principal high-status district and the occupational and assessment evidence suggested that these streets represented a fine shading bridging high- and middle-status localities.

Within the New Town districts, the northern extension was the principal location of Grade II houses, notably in Northumberland Street, Great King

Street and Drummond Place. For the most part these were comparatively small terraced houses although there were a number of substantial flatted properties in these Georgian buildings. The size of these houses was reflected in the mean value for Northumberland Street of £80. The occupations of the residents suggested the streets enjoyed quite high social standing verging on that of nearby high-status streets such as Heriot Row. The residents of Northumberland Street, for example, included fifteen advocates, five solicitors, four doctors, a sheriff and a sheriff-substitute, in addition to other professional men and businessmen.

Within the western extension clusters of comparatively large Grade II houses occurred at Rosebery Crescent and Coates Gardens; those in the latter had a mean value of £102. There were also substantial Grade II properties in the eastern extension where the mean Grade II values for Royal Terrace and Regent Terrace were £103 and £104 respectively.

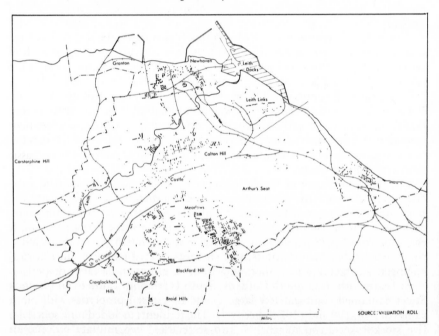

FIGURE 4   The distribution of Grade III houses in Edinburgh and Leith in 1914–15

Thirty Grade II dwellings were situated at George Square, the small speculative scheme which slightly preceded the development of the New Town. These houses were only of average Grade II assessment although the setting remained a pleasant one with terraced buildings facing a private garden. The residents reflected neighbouring functional specialisms with two professors, the director of the Art College, two surgeons, five dentists and four doctors.

Nine Grade II houses were situated at Ramsay Gardens beside the Castle Esplanade where the Town and Gown Association had endeavoured to redress the social decline of the Old Town.

In Leith most Grade II properties were located at Trinity and occupied by businessmen, merchants, professional men and local officials, such as the burgh assessor.

Grade III houses (Figure 4), flats, small terraced and semi-detached residences, had a complex and widely-spread distributional pattern. Despite broad similarities with the pattern shown in Figure 3, the southern suburbs were also the principal Grade III district (56.6 per cent), important differences occurred at both the district and local scales. For example, nearly ten per cent of Grade III dwellings were located in the Duddingston-Portobello district, whilst at the local scale the principal Grade III foci within the southern suburbs and the New Town districts were spatially different from those associated with clusters of Grade II houses. Again the modal and minimum values were co-incident and only ten per cent of Grade III properties had assessed rentals of £65 to £69 per annum. Forty-eight per cent of the houses in the latter group were owner-occupied whereas the Grade III average was 40 per cent.

Gray noted that 'Edinburgh contained an unusually large professional and administrative middle class'.[30] In the mid-Victorian era many middle-class families 'were content to dwell in tenement houses of limited accommodation, generally consisting of only one public room for the family, a small number of bedrooms, and a kitchen with a dark closet, in which the single servant lassie slept'.[31] By 1914 many new middle class properties had been added to the suburban fringe. Living-in servants were becoming less common amongst the families of clerks and members of lesser professions although most would still have the assistance of a daily maid. The new petty-bourgeois suburbs were, according to Gray, 'finely stratified by style and cost of housing, and certainly embracing a wider social range than the highly select New Town'.[32]

The suburban Grade III and IV properties epitomised the varied developments which attracted an outward movement of the lesser bourgeoisie[33] in the late-Victorian and Edwardian eras. Many of the larger Grade III suburban dwellings adjoined, or were within, streets which also contained a number of Grade II properties. Thus Queens Crescent, Newington, which had a mean rental for Grade III residences of £60, was in close proximity to clusters of Grade II houses at Blacket Place, Minto Street and Mayfield Gardens. To some extent the juxtaposition of properties assessed at between £55 and £80 occurred in other portions of the southern suburbs, producing the cumulative impression of a series of good-quality, though finely-shaded, middle-status districts. For example, the occupants of the 31 Grade III properties in Gilmour Road, Newington (mean value £59), included two clerks, an accountant, a minister, a solicitor, a bank teller, a journalist, an agent, a tobacconist, a traveller, a spirit dealer and four merchants (grain, eggs, tea and shoe). Almost a quarter of the Grade III residences were located at Newington. Many of these properties were villas, detached or semi-detached, but there were also terraced dwellings and large flats in middle-status tenements. The latter were mostly assessed at between £40 and £50 and were normally the largest flats in predominantly Grade IV buildings. A typical middle-status tenement would consist of four storeys with two flats on each level. The principal concentration of these properties in the southern suburbs was at Marchmont although minor stands of a few blocks had been constructed at Merchiston, Morningside and Grange.

The largest concentration of Grade III terraced houses in the southern suburbs was situated on the north-facing slope near Morningside Cemetery in streets such as Craiglea Drive, Comiston Drive and St Ninian's Terrace. The Valuation Roll provided the following occupational information for sixteen of the twenty-three houses (mean value £41) in St Ninian's Terrace; four clerks, two travellers, two clothiers, a decorator, coal merchant, professor, accountant, actuary, Inland Revenue officer, unholsterer and surveyor. Elsewhere a few streets of terraced houses formed minor components of villa or tenement districts suggesting that some builders had introduced small speculative ventures in this design on remaining pockets of undeveloped land. Of course, the terraced house never became totally unfashionable with the early and mid-Victorian middle class but the resurgence of that style in the late Victorian and Edwardian period was probably fostered by spiralling feu prices[34] rather than a rejection of the semi-detached villa as a desirable home.

A distinctive minor component of the pattern depicted in Figure 4 involved a number of flatted properties in parts of the New Town districts. The predominant high-status environs were reflected in the occupations of residents of these flats. For example, residents in Grade III dwellings in Great King Street included three advocates, two solicitors' clerks, an engineer, a stockbroker, minister, secretary, music teacher, accountant and stationer. A penumbra of small middle-class speculations flanked the fringe of the northern and eastern extensions to the New Town whilst isolated streets of Grade III terraced or flatted houses occurred at a variety of sites. In some cases they were early suburban developments in districts later dominated by industry and working-class housing. Thus at Gilmour Place the Grade III properties marked the boundary between the canal based industrial zone and the western edge of the middle-status southern suburbs. Unfortunately the Valuation Roll did not list any occupations for that street but the residents of a nearby street of small terraces, Hartington Place, which lay on the 'right side of the tracks', included four solicitors, four ministers, two Professors, a tea merchant, builder, clerk, bank teller, publisher, glass merchant, jeweller, cashier and teacher. It would appear, therefore, that a few streets were deemed to provide an adequate buffer between a middle-status property and industrial low-status districts. Significantly the principal thoroughfares and transport arteries in these situations were faceted either by Grade IV tenements or admixtures of various shadings of middle-status flatted and terraced properties.

The spatially independent cluster of Grade III properties at Portobello provided attractive terraces and villas for commuters and local middle-class businessmen, shopkeepers and white-collar workers. Evidence of a direct occupational link between the residents and Portobello was provided by the presence of two stoneware manufacturers and two bottle manufacturers in the data for Brighton Place and Durham Road. The attractiveness of the area for commuters can be deduced from the existence of a speedy train service to Waverley Station and adduced from the scale of the middle-status developments. Similarly, the Grade III properties at North Leith and Trinity probably served as suburbs for the seaport and the capital. At Trinity a cluster of terraced houses adjoined the suburban railway station whilst all of these suburbs were linked to both settlements by the tramway system.

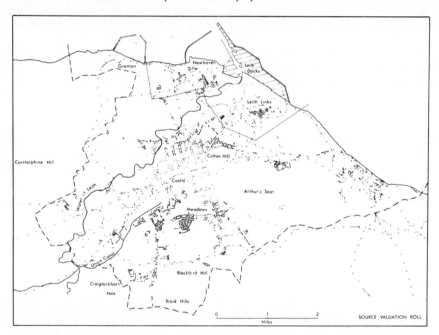

FIGURE 5   The distribution of Grade IV houses in Edinburgh and Leith in 1914–15

The distribution of Grade IV houses (Figure 5), mostly flats and small terraced dwellings with a modal value of £22, revealed marked localisation in particular inner and outer suburbs and distinctive linear patterns in the lesser streets in the New Town districts. The majority, 58.3 per cent, were located south of the Old Town. Within an extensive series of inner and outer suburbs major concentrations occurred at Marchmont, Bruntsfield and Viewforth whilst tentacles spread outwards along major thoroughfares. In some cases, these linear extensions connected the principal inner foci to smaller outer nodes such as those at Ashley and Comiston.

The streets of flatted properties at Marchmont contained over two thousand Grade IV dwellings, the largest cluster in the city. Designed by strict feuing regulations as a good-quality tenement district, these properties had attracted white-collar workers, shopkeepers and a number of skilled craftsmen. The latter group may have represented Gray's aristocracy of labour,[35] although some may have been small employers rather than skilled employees. The vagaries of decision-making by landowners contrived to produce a situation whereby the Marchmont district, conveniently situated to the Meadows and within walking distance of the High Street, was not developed until the later decades of the nineteenth century. Then the higher density of the tenemented scheme reduced the cost of feu charges whilst the locational convenience meant lower transport costs than those incurred by residents of comparable properties at more peripheral developments. Substantial numbers of Grade IV houses were located at Bruntsfield and Newington whilst smaller stands were situated on the southern periphery of the Old Town at Lauriston and in the vicinity of the main thoroughfare leading southwards to Newington.

A comparable, if smaller, zone of Grade IV dwellings lay to the north of the New Town districts at Comely Bank, Broughton, Pilrig and in the vicinity of Leith Walk. Although there were very few Grade IV houses in the original New Town or the Moray Place district, nearly five per cent of the properties in this assessment grade were contained within the northern extension of the New Town. The principal foci were either peripheral streets of flatted properties such as London Street and Scotland Street or similar dwellings in buildings flanking the major thoroughfares such as Dundas Street and Pitt Street. Some professions, e.g. solicitor and minister, were listed amongst the occupations of the residents of Grade IV properties in these streets indicating the possibility that these properties were of higher social status than their valuation implied. By contrast the occupants of correspondingly valued dwellings in Brandon Terrace, north of the New Town districts, included two clerks, two teachers, four butchers, a spirit dealer, modeller, bank messenger, dairyman, lithographic writer, lithographer, printers' reader, fish merchant, publisher, dressmaker, evangelist, post office superintendent, missionary, grocer, gardener, tailor, gunmaker, brassfinisher and a post office overseer. The printing trade was a major employer in the city but the presence of a major printing company in Brandon Terrace and the number of residents occupied in that activity suggested that a degree of localisation between workplace and residence was still a feature of the post-Edwardian city.[36] Most streets in the northern fringe adjoined industrial areas and streets of low status whereas the flats in the New Town districts were principally small properties in preponderantly high- or middle-status localities.

Isolated stands of small terraced properties can be identified from Figure 5 on the western edge of the city at Saughtonhall and northeast of Arthur's Seat in the Willowbrae area. The former district was conveniently situated on the suburban railway network whilst the latter adjoined the tramway route from Portobello to Edinburgh.

At Portobello most of the 832 Grade IV properties were located in two broad zones. First, several streets sited between the coast and the main railway line included a number of Grade IV dwellings. Second, a cluster of terraced and small semi-detached dwellings were situated westwards of Duddingston Park. Finally there were nearly sixteen hundred Grade IV houses in Leith. The principal focus was situated on the slopes overlooking Leith Links where small terraces were the dominant house-type. Many of these houses had comparatively low values. The mean value for the properties in Cornhill Terrace, for example, was £23 per annum. A similar cluster of Grade IV properties occurred in a number of streets to the west of Leith Town Hall.

In summary the Grade IV properties in 1914 could be classified into three types of areas. First, stands, of varying size, of flats or terraces in which Grade IV houses were dominant. Second, areas where these properties were the smaller dwellings in districts dominated by larger properties. Third, a further variant on the minority situation occurred in some predominantly low status districts where some of the largest flats were assessed at more than £20 per annum. Although the data were incomplete, the occupational information appeared to confirm these social shadings with typical Grade IV occupations including teaching, clerical and supervisory work, shopkeeping and skilled trades; occupations which Crossick has associated with the emergence of the lower middle class in Britain.[37] 'On the one hand was the classic petty bourgeoisie of shopkeepers and small businessmen, on the other the new white-collar salaried occupations, most notably clerks but also managers, commercial travellers, schoolteachers and certain shop assistants.'[38] Crossick also argued that minor professional people, such as lesser solicitors were members of the lower middle class.[39] Thus the professional occupants of Grade IV dwellings in Edinburgh may have represented this category, operating on the margins of their respective professions with lesser prestige than their occupations might imply and below-average incomes. Similarly, the occupants of larger flats in predominantly low-status districts may have equated to the aristocracy of labour.

LOW STATUS

All of the low-status houses were small but fine shadings existed within this group as in other rental classes. The modal value of Grade V houses (Figure 6) in Edinburgh was £10 per annum and 53 per cent of the low-status properties were assessed at between £10 and £20. Less than one hundred dwellings in Edinburgh valued at less than £10 were owner-occupied. By comparison 1745 houses (12.7 per cent) assessed at between £15 and £20 per annum were owner-occupied. Most of the larger properties were associated with residents whose occupations correlated with the 'aristocracy of labour'.[40] They were also concentrated in particular locations which were spatially and, doubtless, socially, separate from the cheaper smallest low-status dwellings. Age also separated the low-status properties into two broad groups. The older houses which had been built before the adoption of building and sanitary legislation provided the worst residential environments where squalor and overcrowding were still commonplace. Philanthropic gestures and legislative measures had ensured that from the middle of the nineteenth century new standards were set for low-status housing incorporating at least a minimal provision of ventilation, living space and sanitation. The rows of tenements at Gorgie-Dalry and Easter Road may have resembled stone canyons but the gas-lit passages mostly led to properties with two rooms, a kitchen with a cold water supply and a water closet. Indeed some streets with relatively large flats clearly verged on lower-middle status. For example, the occupants of the houses in Murieston Crescent, Dalry, which were mainly assessed at between £17 and £20, included clerks, insurance agents, travellers and shopmen in addition to several railway servants (engine-drivers, porters, etc.) and numerous craftsmen and employees of public services (policemen, gas company servants, castle guides). Proximity to workplace emerged in the data, notably in the case of railway employees for Murieston Crescent was only a few minutes' walk from a major railway yard at Haymarket. The 186 Grade V flats in Blackfriars Street in the Old Town provided an illustration of the social profile of the cheaper (mostly £5 to £7) properties. The residents included labourers (57), charwomen (7), miners (6) in addition to other characteristic low-status occupations such as hawkers and carters. There was a notable absence of white-collar occupations and skilled tradesmen except those related to building trades (painter, slater, mason). The preponderance of labourers reflected the continued concentration in the Old Town of unskilled men of Irish descent.

A crude index of the improvement in housing conditions was the fall in the death rate from 27.8 in 1871 to 15.4 by 1914, although that reduction stemmed at least in part from various advances in medical treatment.

There was a pronounced correlation between the principal industrial areas and the main foci of Grade V houses at Gorgie-Dalry, Fountainbridge, the Old Town, St Leonards, Abbeyhill, Meadowbank, Stockbridge and Leith. In most districts the tenement flat was the ubiquitous Grade V dwelling but one divergent and distinctive component had been created in the second half of the nineteenth century by the activities of the Edinburgh Co-operative Building

Company. Their schemes at Stockbridge, Abbeyhill, Haymarket and Slateford consisted of two storey narrow blocks in which the lower flat was entered from one side and the upper storey from an external stair on the opposite frontage of the block. The tiny gardens added a further semblance of seclusion and privacy and the properties were sold by instalments. Since manual workers lacked security of employment and constancy of wages, these developments were effectively the domain of the aristocracy of labour, the artisans with regular wages and comparatively secure employment. The occupants of one of the earliest examples, Kemp Place, Stockbridge, mean value £15, included three grocers, two painters, two cabinetmakers, two gardeners, a joiner, warehouseman, plumber, jeweller, glass stainer, marine engineer, police constable, provision dealer, bellhanger, waiter, shoemaker, compositor and a shopman. Thus, these properties resembled the social profile of comparatively large-flatted tenements in the newer working-class districts.

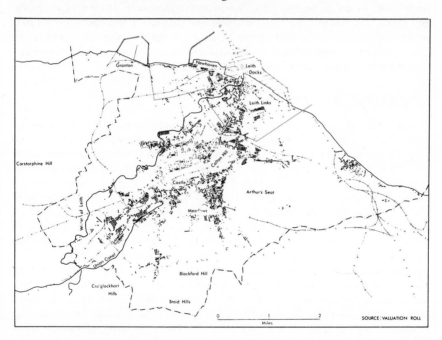

FIGURE 6   The distribution of Grade V and Local Authority houses in Edinburgh and Leith in 1914–15

Two final components in the pattern shown in Figure 6 were the artisan streets which featured in the planning of the New Town districts and the facading of tenements along parts of the major thoroughfares and the small industrial zones in the middle status suburbs. Rose Street, the oldest site of flats for tradesmen and servants in the original New Town, still contained a number of low-status houses. In addition to tradesmen, the residents of these flats included cleaners, charwomen and caretakers engaged in servicing the offices in the adjoining central business district.

Figure 6 shows that Portobello was separate from any other district in Edinburgh. The pattern consisted of three elements. First, there were a number of streets of cottages and tenements near the industrial district astride the Figgate Burn. Second, the High Street was flanked by a series of blocks of working-class tenements. Finally, a small eastern portion was situated at Joppa.

In Leith major clusters of Grade V dwellings occurred near the harbour, Leith Walk, Leith Links and Newhaven. The small terraced cottages at Hermitage on the slope facing on to Leith Links had attracted tradesmen and white-collar workers whilst the tenements between Leith Walk and Easter Road closely resembled, in design and social profile, contemporaneous properties at Gorgie and Dalry. Most of the cheapest, smallest and substandard houses were located in the old core of Leith, east of the harbour. Newhaven also contained many tiny substandard fisher cottages with marked intermarriage patterns suggested by the preponderance of a small number of surnames.[41]

GENERALISED PATTERN

The generalised pattern of status areas in 1914, on the basis of dominant assessment types, is shown in Figure 7. Dominance was defined in terms of the proportion of residential space consumed in addition to simpler factors such as the number of houses. Both the high- and middle-status distributions contained New Town and suburban components but with a reversal of the respective major and minor roles. The Victorian terraces to west of the New Town and the remnants of the Georgian districts at Charlotte Square, Heriot Row and Moray Place, formed the most select high-status areas. The arc of working-class districts between Gorgie and Leith completed a simple tripartite social stratigraphy which Daiches described as 'a sort of three distinct cities'.[42] Equally the antipodal social relationship between the Old Town and New Town districts sustained Stevenson's notion of two distinct cities. 'From their smoky beehives, ten stories, high, the unwashed look down upon the open squares and gardens of the wealthy; and gay people sunning themselves along Princes Street, with its mile of commercial palaces all beflagged upon some great occasion, see, across a gardened valley set with statues, where the washings of the old town flutter in the breeze at its high windows.'[43] Perhaps a fourth component had emerged which transgressed the boundaries of the lower middle and respectable working-classes. In an attempt to identify this category areas dominated by properties valued at between £15 and £25 per annum were shown separately in Figure 7 (mixed lower medium and low). The locational pattern was complex but two trends could be identified. First, these areas frequently occupied intermediate or buffer situations between middle and low status districts. Second, they constituted the high density elements beside major thoroughfares within predominantly middle-status districts. A further source of complexity was the incorporation of previously independent towns

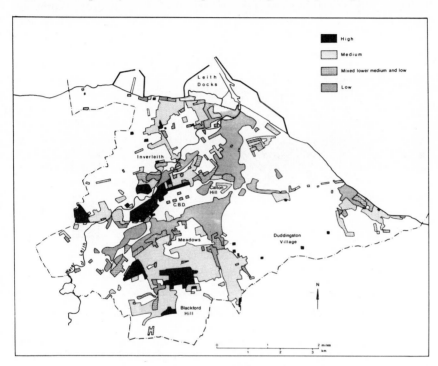

FIGURE 7   Status areas of Edinburgh in 1914

and villages such as Portobello and Newhaven. In 1914 many of these settlements retained an identifiable pattern of nucleation within the broader spatial structure of status areas in Edinburgh. The overall pattern consisted of three or four major structural components, or types of status areas, but the detailed complexity produced a finely-shaded interdigitation of districts of varied size, age, house type and social prestige. In 1914, as at any 'one moment in time the pattern of status areas consists of a myriad of areas, . . . at various stages of development, alteration or ossification and subject to the interplay of numerous factors and processes which are, in turn, at various stages of development and influence'.[44] The persistence of a centrally-situated high-status quarter echoed an important dimension of the pre-industrial city,[45] a centrally located urban elite, the leaders of society and holders of political power. When the spatial base was transformed from individual houses to city wards elements of concentric[46] and sectoral patterns could be identified. In both Figures 8 and 9 Leith was omitted in order to reduce the interference from other urban nuclei. In Figure 8, the low status core of the Old Town and St Leonards formed a peak on a surface which sloped downwards to the periphery, although

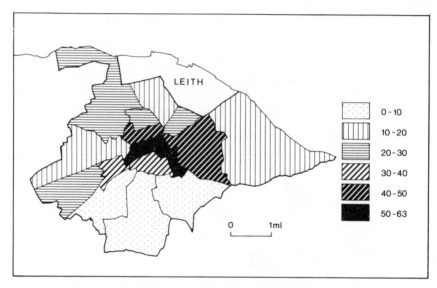

FIGURE 8   Percentage houses valued at less than £10—Edinburgh 1914

the angle of slope varied with a marked decline southwards and gentler descents to the southwest (Gorgie), northwest (Stockbridge) and northeast (Broughton). Arcuate and sectoral features also occurred in the distribution at ward level of houses valued at more than £49 (Figure 9). The pyramidal structure of the house market inevitably influenced these patterns. For example, in the New Town there was a comparatively large number of low-value flats in relation to the total number of houses in that ward. Yet the area was not accorded a commensurately low prestige although invasion by offices and other commercial premises had effectively adumbrated what had been the leading high-status district in Georgian and early Victorian times.

When Leith was also mapped and the emphasis was placed upon middle-and high-value properties a marked sectorial pattern emerged (Figure 10). The extensive array of various shadings of middle-value houses at Morningside, Merchiston, Newington and Murrayfield can be readily identified on this map. Equally pronounced was the comparative homogeneity of newer working-class districts of Gorgie, Dalry, Abbeyhill and Leith, reflecting the influence of building regulations and the adoption of standardised designs.[48]

The pattern of status areas bore little resemblance to the five concentric rings visualised by the Burgess model[49] of urban structure. In the model, the business core was surrounded by a transition zone and successive circles of

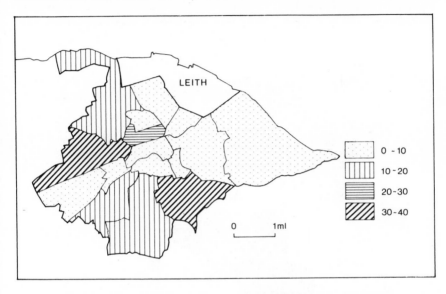

FIGURE 9   Percentage houses valued at £50 or more—Edinburgh 1914

different housing environments with social status increasing outwards from the centre. Edinburgh was not a burgeoning industrial city experiencing successive waves of immigration which were important conditions of the model. Nonetheless, some features did correlate. The expansion of the business district had displaced adjoining residential areas through the processes of invasion and succession, the fundamental dynamics of ecological explanations. Southwards of the Old Town there was a general tendency for an inner low status zone to be succeeded by a middle-status ring. Residential invasion had penetrated the rural-urban fringe with commuter villages at Barnton, Colinton and Corstorphine. In aggregate, however, the concentric model provided an inadequate statement and explanation of the pattern of status areas in Edwardian Edinburgh.

Although the sector model[50] was not propounded until 1939, it offered a more persuasive representation of the pattern. As envisaged in the model high- and low-status districts occupied spatially dichotomous situations. The latter were associated with industrial districts and the former was juxtaposed to the leading edge of the central business districts. Hoyt suggested that the high-status areas would avoid 'dead-end' sectors such as the obstacle of Arthur's Seat. He also deduced that the high-status pole would maintain a particular directional alignment for as long as possible, a trend illustrated in Edinburgh by the centrally-located high-status districts. The location of that district did

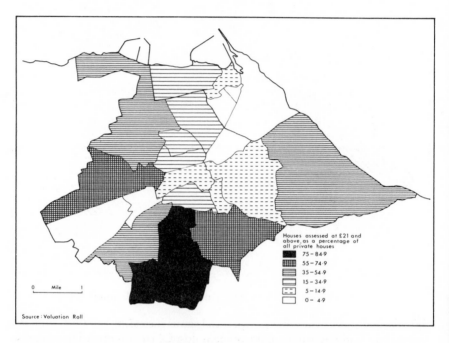

FIGURE 10   Middle and high value houses—1914

not conflict with the predicted structure of the model although the implicit strong centrifugal tendencies of the high-status poles were only in the early stages of development in Edwardian Edinburgh. As Gray noted 'Edinburgh contained an unusually large professional and administrative middle class'.[51] It was that group which initiated the major phase of suburban growth in the Victorian and Edwardian periods. Nonetheless the growth of the central business district was progressively encroaching upon the centrally-sited high-status districts and clusters of suburban mansions had been built, particularly on the southern periphery of the capital.

The persistence of small-scale differentiation[52] at the intra-district level introduced greater complexity than the models anticipated. In part, the models concealed complexity by adopting a relatively large spatial base. Hoyt used the street block[53] as a base unit whilst Burgess applied the vague concept of natural areas.[54] By comparison an interpretation founded upon individual properties must inevitably reveal a more complex mosaic unless the morphology consisted of remarkably homogeneous segments. The grid-iron plan of most American cities probably provided a predisposition towards that situation but the role of landowners[55] and the sequence of developments in Edinburgh, and many British cities, favoured a more fragmented distribution of status areas. A satisfactory account of the pattern in Edinburgh required the inclusion of factors related to the supply of housing. Population growth, economic growth and changing tastes and aspirations combined to create a substantial demand for new housing at a wide range of prices but the satisfaction of these demands was dependent upon a number of factors, many of them having strong sectoral characteristics. Landowners influenced the timing and character of develop-ments, thereby shaping the direction of growth and the evolution of the pattern. Many mid-nineteenth-century projects aimed at providing improved working-class housing faced a struggle to obtain a site because landowners were not disposed towards that sector of the market. In effect the correlation between working-class and industrial districts resulted from an inability to obtain sites in other parts of the city where values had not been blighted by industrial and railway developments. In many instances, landowners also dictated the nature of development through the medium of the feu-charter.[56] This legal document often stated the type of house to be built on the property including details about design and building materials. Thus, any landowner with a potentially prestigious site could seek to ensure that potential was materialised through careful drafting of the conditions of the feu charter.

The development of the tramways and the suburban railways are frequently cited as major factors enabling and promoting suburbanisation in the Victorian and Edwardian city.[57] In the case of Edinburgh, the statement must be treated with some caution. An ambitious plan for villas at Barnton[58] attracted a limited response. Edinburgh could still provide many attractive sites, obviating the need to escape to more distant retreats. Moreover, the city was comparatively compact with travelling distances between suburban home and workplace rarely exceeding three kilometres. The white-collar middle and lower-middle classes were the principal beneficiaries of the developments in transport which allowed a suburban residential location which would have been impossible without the existence of public transport. The presence of tramway routes connecting Gorgie with Easter Road and Leith suggested that there was also a substantial volume of commuting between the working-class industrial and residential districts.

At any point in time, the pattern of status areas will contain fading echoes of an earlier period and heralds of future developments. The former was represented by the remnants of the Georgian housing in the original New Town whilst the latter was illustrated by the suburban growth and by the few hundred houses built by the local authority, under the aegis of the Housing the Working Classes Acts,[59] in the vicinity of the High Street. This account of the pattern of status areas in Edinburgh in 1914 is, therefore, an exposition of a dynamic phenomenon, an evolving structure. However, that particular period marked a social watershed because after the First World War local authorities were vested with the task of the provision of working-class housing. In that sense, the pattern in 1914 marked the culmination of a particular set of processes which subsequently were affected by the entry of a major new sector in the housing market. Edwardian society was visibly stratified on dimensions such as clothing, education, housing and servant-keeping. Thompson noted that 'Edwardians were socially stratified into those who wore tailor-made clothes, those who wore new ready-mades, and those who wore other people's cast-offs'.[60] In addition the upper and middle classes still kept servants and anyone subscribing to middle class ideals sought an aura of respectability of which clothes, speech and housing were observable symbols. Whilst servant-keeping decreased rapidly after 1918 many traits remained important for a further two or three decades, e.g. private education.

The evolution of status areas involved a subtle interplay between social stability, the persistence of earlier patterns, the processes of social and economic change, adjustments in the spatial pattern and new residential developments. At any moment, the upper and middle classes had a choice of established and new residential districts. In 1914 the advantages appeared to favour the established districts for high-status properties but the newer suburbs for the middle classes.

The aggregate pattern summarises a multiplicity of individual decisions, each confronted by choices and constraints. Additionally, the pattern was affected by the spatial and temporal complexities of the supply of housing. The weighting of components may vary but the spatial structure remains the product of thousands of separate individual decisions, taken in response to perceived local opportunities and guided by local and national factors such as the attitudes of landowners and developers, economic policy and climate, housing legislation, social attitudes and changes in social aspirations.[61] The pattern of status areas in Edinburgh in 1914 was a particular resolution in time and space of these relationships and processes.

REFERENCES

1   G Gordon, 'The status areas of Edinburgh: a historical analysis', PhD thesis (1971), Univ. of Edinburgh.
2   B T Robson, *Urban Analysis* (Cambridge, 1979), p. 106.
3   G Gordon, 'Rateable Assessment as a Data Source for Status Area Analysis: the Example of Edinburgh 1855–1962', *Urban History Yearbook* (Leicester, 1979), pp. 92–3.

4   For example: R Jones, 'Segregation in urban residential districts. Examples and
    research problems', Proceedings *I.G.U. Symposium in Urban Geography*
    (Lund, 1960); E Jones, *A Social Geography of Belfast* (Oxford, 1960); B T
    Robson, op. cit. (1969); B S Morgan, 'The Residential Structure of Exeter', in
    K J Gregory and W Ravenhill (eds.), *Exeter Essays in Geography* (1971), pp.
    219–35; R J Johnston, 'The location of high status residential areas',
    Geografiska Annaler xlviiB (1966), 23–35; D W G Timms, 'Measures of social
    defectiveness in two British cities' PhD thesis (1962), Univ. of Cambridge;
    D T Herbert and W M Williams (1962), 'Some new techniques for studying
    urban sub-division', *Geogr. Polonica* **2** (1962), 93–117; R M Pritchard,
    Housing and the Spatial Structure of the City (Cambridge, 1976).
5   E W Burgess, 'The growth of the city: an introduction to a research project', *Pap.
    and Proc. Amer. Sociol Soc.* **18** (1924), 85–97; H Hoyt, *The structure and
    growth of residential neighbourhoods in American cities* (Washington, 1939);
    W Alonso, *Location and land use* (Camb., Mass., 1964).
6   R Jones, op. cit. (1960), p. 434; B T Robson, op. cit. p. 105.
7   R E Park and E W Burgess, *The City* (Chicago, 1925).
8   E Sillar, *Edinburgh's Child* (Edinburgh, 1979), pp. 1–2.
9   J W Watson, 'The Face of the City', p. 15 in D Keir (ed.), *The City of Edinburgh*,
    The Third Statistical Account of Scotland, vol. 15 (Glasgow, 1966).
10 J Grant, *Old and New Edinburgh* (Edinburgh, 1880), vols. I & II; C B Boog
    Watson (1923), 'Notes on the Names of the Closes and Wynds of Old
    Edinburgh', Book of Old Edinburgh Club, vol. 12, pp. 1–156.
11 G Gordon, op. cit. (1971), p. 4.
12 A J Youngson, *The Making of Classical Edinburgh* (Edinburgh, 1966).
13 Ibid. pp. 81–2.
14 D Robertson, *Edinburgh 1329–1929* (Edinburgh, 1929), pp. 21–3.
15 H D Littlejohn, *Report on the Sanitary Conditions of Edinburgh* (Edinburgh,
    1865), p. 31.
16 R Q Gray, *The Labour Aristocracy in Victorian Edinburgh* (Oxford, 1976), p. 16.
17 See earlier chapter by R Rodger.
18 Ethos was outlined in W Chambers (1866), Address to Architectural Institute of
    Scotland (on theme of City Improvement). Changes summarised in G
    Gordon, 'The status areas of early to mid-Victorian Edinburgh', *Trans. Inst.
    Brit. Geog.* (new series) (1979a), vol. 4 no. 2, p. 187.
19 G Gordon, op. cit. (1979a), p. 187.
20 I H Adams, *The Making of Urban Scotland* (London, 1978), pp. 119, 122.
21 Based upon R Q Gray, op. cit. (1976), Table 2.4; pp. 22–3.
22 G Gordon, op. cit. (1979a), G Gordon, 'Working Class Housing in Edinburgh
    1837–1974' in Festschrift K A Sinnhuber, vol. II (Vienna, 1979b), pp. 72–8.
23 C L Warr, *The Glimmering Landscape* (London, 1960).
24 The author is grateful to Leicester University Press for permission to use Figures 2, 3
    and 6 which appeared in his article in *Urban History Yearbook* (1979).
25 Warr, op. cit.
26 Youngson, op. cit. p. 208.
27 Letter from James Hope, solicitor, quoted in A R B Haldane, *New Ways through
    the Glens* (Edinburgh, 1962), p. 202.

28   H W Richardson, J Vipond and R Furbey, *Housing and urban spatial structure: a case study* (Farnborough, 1975), pp. 58–9.
29   D Keir, op. cit. p. 81.
30   Gray, op. cit. p. 19.
31   JBS, *Random Recollections and Impressions* (Edinburgh, 1903), p. 23.
32   Gray, op. cit. p. 17.
33   For discussion of the composition of this group see G Crossick, *The Lower Middle Class in Britain* (London, 1977).
34   Widely cited cause in evidence in *Report of the Royal Commission on the Housing of the Industrial Population of Scotland Rural and Urban* (Edinburgh), 1917.
35   Gray, op. cit.
36   It is impossible to estimate from Valuation Roll data the significance of localisation as against commuting but it does appear probable that a multiplicity of spatial linkages existed between the location of workplace and residence rather than a simple centre-suburb dichotomy.
37   Crossick, op. cit.
38   Ibid. p. 12.
39   Ibid.
40   Gray, op. cit.
41   *Valuation Roll for Leith 1914–1915.*
42   D Daiches, *Edinburgh* (London, 1978), pp. 210–25.
43   R L Stevenson, *Edinburgh: Picturesque Notes* (Edinburgh, 1879).
44   G Gordon, op. cit. (1979a), p. 169.
45   G Sjoberg, *The pre-industrial city* (Glencoe, Ill., 1960).
46   Burgess, op. cit.
47   Hoyt, op. cit.
48   P J Smith, 'Site selection in the Forth Basin', PhD thesis, Univ. of Edinburgh (1964).
49   Burgess, op. cit.
50   Hoyt, op. cit.
51   Gray, op. cit. p. 19.
52   G Gordon and J G Robb, 'Small-Scale Residential Differentiation in Nineteenth Century Scottish Cities', *Scot. Geog. Mag.*, **97**, no. 2 (1981), 77–84.
53   Hoyt, op. cit.
54   Burgess, op. cit.
55   G Gordon, 'The Historico-Geographic Explanation of Urban Morphology: A Discussion of Some Scottish Evidence' *Scot. Geog. Mag.*, **97**, no. 1 (1981), 16–26.
56   Gordon op. cit. (1981); Gordon, op. cit. (1979a); Youngson op. cit. (1966).
57   J H Johnson, *Urban Geography* (Oxford, 1972), pp. 40–1; R Jones, 'Twentieth Century City', pp. 66–7, in J B Barclay (ed.), *Looking at Lothian* (Edinburgh, (1979).
58   I H Adams, op. cit. (1978), p. 119.
59   Ibid. p. 163.
60   P Thompson, *The Edwardians* (London, 1975), p. 312.
61   Pritchard, op. cit. pp. 3–5.

9

TRANSPORT AND TOWNS IN VICTORIAN SCOTLAND

John R Hume

INTRODUCTION

It is indeed surprising, in view of the vital role played by transport in the creation of the Victorian town in Scotland that relatively little has been written on the subject. The major works in the field, Alexander Ochojna's study of tramways and urban development in Glasgow and Edinburgh,[1] and the Glasgow chapter in John Kellett's *Railways and the Victorian City*[2] deal with very specific aspects, as does Michael Simpson in his articles on Glasgow's West End.[3] Studies of individual transport enterprises, such as D L G Hunter's *Edinburgh's Transport,*[4] and the admirable accounts of individual tramways by Ian Cormack, Alan Brotchie and others[5] concentrate on the business side of the undertakings, on routes and rolling stock. Textbooks on Scottish Economic History make only passing mention of the subject.[6] The only serious attempt to come to grips with the general theme is in fact Ian Adams's *The Making of Urban Scotland,*[7] but he concentrates on a limited range of topics, and eschews quantification. This article is not intended to be a definitive analysis of the role of transport in Victorian towns in Scotland, but does attempt to give an overview of some aspects of its influence, to quantify where practicable, and, it is hoped, to stimulate further research in this eternally fascinating area.

The Victorian period saw the functions of transport in urban living change markedly. New modes of communication were introduced, while older systems were developed to serve ever more complex communities. Owing among others, to the complex interactions between the transporting media and the transported, to the operation of economic and political factors, and to geographical considerations, it is difficult to make positive correlations between changes in the use of transport and specific aspects of urban growth, stagnation or decay. It is however contended that despite the problems involved it is worth exploring the nature of the relationships between Scottish urban communities and their transport facilities over a period of particularly dramatic change.

At the dawn of the Victorian era, transport in Scotland, as elsewhere in Britain, was in a transitional stage. The spectacular reconstruction and expansion of the road network throughout the country since the 1780s had made regular postal communication possible, and allowed goods and passengers to travel short distances quite cheaply, and longer distances effectively.[8] This is demonstrated by the dispersal of both water-powered cotton mills and of iron smelting works over a wide area. Canals, as developed from the 1760s, were making significant contributions to the economies of Glasgow, Paisley, Falkirk and Coatbridge, and to a lesser extent to those of Edinburgh and Aberdeen.[9] In addition to their function of transporting goods and minerals, the canals were also competing with coach services with varying degrees of success. Horse-hauled railways, which had proliferated in Central Scotland since the 1750s, were serving Kilmarnock, Troon, Dunfermline, Edinburgh and Dalkeith,[10] and the first locomotive-worked lines, the Monkland & Kirkintilloch, Garnkirk & Glasgow, Dundee & Newtyle and Arbroath & Forfar railways were in operation.[11] Most of these were conceived primarily as mineral carriers, but the public lines were developing passenger traffic. In 1834, according to the *New Statistical Account*, passengers using public transport in the Glasgow district were distributed as in Table 1.[12] The figure for stagecoach passengers was estimated. The predominance of waterways is striking. No less than 64 per cent of all passengers travelled by steamboat or canal. Steamboat and canal services were at that time expanding. The introduction of light iron fly boats on the Paisley canal had resulted in an increase in the number of passengers from 79,455 in 1830–1 to 307,275 in 1833–4.[13] By 1836 the numbers carried by canal and railway had grown substantially (see Table 1).

Table 1   *Passengers using public transport in the Glasgow District in 1834 and 1836.*

Stagecoaches	458,232	—
Steamboats	579,050	—
Forth & Clyde Canal	91,975	198,461
Paisley Canal	307,275	473,186
Monkland Canal	31,784	33,400
Garnkirk & Glasgow Railway	118,882	146,296
Totals	1,587,198	

Sources: For 1834   *New Statistical Account for Scotland*
For 1836   James Cleland, *Statistical Facts descriptive of the Former and Present State of Glasgow* (Glasgow 1837).

Information about goods and mineral traffic in the 1830s is somewhat scanty. Owing to the high cost of transport, heavy or bulky raw materials seem to have been drawn from the immediate vicinity of towns. Building stone came from quarries close to the city centres of Glasgow, Edinburgh and Aberdeen, while Glasgow had brickworks to the south and east.[14] Coal was still being mined on the outskirts of Glasgow, Paisley and Johnstone, but canals and railways were being used to exploit the coalfields of the Monklands and the Lothians, and Aberdeen and Dundee relied on sea-borne coal. Wherever possible pig-iron was moved by water, though land transport was a necessity for some works, and held back their development as large-scale units. The movement of lighter raw materials and manufactured goods seems not to have posed serious problems, but the location of large distilleries, textile mills, foundries and engineering works was obviously being determined by the availability of suitable transport, particularly water-based.[15] The rise of Port Dundas, Tradeston and Anderston in Glasgow of the Saucel and Seedhill districts in Paisley, of the Port of Leith, of Falkirk and of Kirkintilloch as industrial centres was already being stimulated by the existence of canals and navigable rivers. Jean Lindsay[16] quotes the Forth & Clyde Canal as carrying 5080 tons of timber from Grangemouth to Port Dundas in 1823, and in 1837 12,799 tons of stones, and 68,730 tons of coal were carried. By 1841 these figures had risen to 28,456 tons of stones and 82,410 tons of coal. Another bulk cargo was manure, presumably mainly horse and human dung from Glasgow. In 1837 no less than 31,506 tons of this substance were carried. Though tonnage figures do not seem to have survived, the revenue from grain shipments in the 1820s was high enough at over £10,000 in each of the years 1882, 1824, 1826 and 1828 to suggest that this was a major article of trade. Though a proportion of these tonnages was presumably through traffic it is highly probable that most originated from or was destined to towns on the canal or on the linked Monkland and Union canals.

The improved river Clyde navigation[17] was also bringing raw materials in growing quantities into the heart of Glasgow. To quote one positive instance, Pollok, Gilmour & Co, the leading Glasgow firm of timber importers in the early 1830s, brought in six million cubic feet of timber in one year from North America employing twenty-one large ships with a total tonnage of 12,005.[18]

The next fifteen or sixteen years saw dramatic changes in the transport facilities available in Scotland. Railways, at first point-to-point enterprises such as the lines from Glasgow to Greenock, Ayr and Edinburgh, from Dundee to Arbroath, and from Edinburgh to Berwick, became networks with divided ownership but the possibility of through working.[19] Gauges were standardised in anticipation of the creation of a system serving all the developed parts of the country.[20] At the same time, steamboat services expanded.[21] Road and canal passenger services were, however hard-hit by the new railways, which naturally tended to be built where there was an established traffic. Passenger services ceased on the Forth & Clyde, Union, Paisley and Monkland canals, and the Aberdeenshire Canal was drained and converted for most of its length into a railway.[22] Stage-coach services ceased on the long-distance routes, that on the Glasgow-Carlisle road being cut back in stages as the Caledonian Railway was opened.[23] Competition also developed between steamer and railway on the Clyde.[24]

The effect of these changes on the towns does not appear to be well documented. The canal terminals lost their positions as foci for trade with surrounding districts, but although passenger traffic was immediately affected, goods and mineral movement changed more slowly, and some traffics, such as pig iron from the Monklands continued to grow for some time after railway communication was established.[25] The creation of railway terminals resulted in the construction of workshops for the maintenance of locomotives and rolling stock, notably those at Cook Street and Cowlairs in Glasgow, Greenock, Burntisland, Perth and St Margaret's, Edinburgh.[26] Round these began to develop industrial suburbs. The building of disconnected sections of railway, too, began to give significance to ferry terminals, such as Bowling (briefly), Granton, Burntisland, Tayport and Broughty Ferry.[27] The new railway stations in established towns and cities also encouraged commercial activity in their immediate vicinity. The range of transport facilities in the cities at least, remained large. Railways in the 1840s mania were still conceived of primarily as inter-urban routes, and only to a very limited extent catered for intra-urban traffic.

A 'snapshot' of the transport available in Glasgow in 1847–8, taken from the Post-Office Directory for that year,[28] is illuminating, describing as it does the most active period in the railway mania. The Ayr railway timetable was not included, but the Greenock, Edinburgh, Wishaw & Coltness and Garnkirk and Coatbridge lines all were explicitly part of an integrated road-rail-steamer network. The Greenock line, for instance, operated in connection with steamers to Helensburgh, Rhu, Garelochhead, Dunoon, Rothesay, Largs, Millport and Arran, while the Edinburgh & Glasgow Railway ran in connection with coaches for Aberdeen, Dundee, Stirling, Perth, Crieff, Alloa, Dunfermline and Kincardine. The Wishaw & Coltness itself operating in connection with the Garnkirk & Coatbridge, had linked coach services to Lanark from Carluke and omnibus services to Hamilton from Motherwell.

The purely coach services consisted of mail coaches to Carlisle, shortly to be withdrawn on the opening of the Caledonian Railway, and routes to twenty-two Scottish destinations, the further afield being Dundee. Most of the other destinations were local, such as Baillieston, Bothwell, Maryhill, and Neilston. There were three omnibus services, to Partick, Port Dundas and Rutherglen. All the vehicles started from the Trongate, the coaches from the Tontine Hotel at Glasgow Cross (Walker's), from Key's (74 Trongate) or from Mein's (84 Trongate), and the omnibuses from Walker's or 91 Trongate. There were two classes of hackney carriages, operated under a Police Act of 1845. The first class (Noddy, Clarence or Harrington) charged about half as much again as the second class (Minibus or Cab). Fares were expensive, the minimum daytime fare being 5s 6d for 4–5 miles. Official stands for a total of 112 carriages were provided at twenty sites. As far as public haulage of goods was concerned, a set of regulations existed for 'carters plying for hire' (1808) and there were also regulations for 'general' porters (1834), for coal porters (1807), and for porters at the Broomielaw (1825). A directory of carriers included covered the whole of Scotland and most of England. Apart from Northern England, Pickford & Co had a monopoly of carting to points south of the Border. Many Scottish destinations were served by a number of carters. Elgin, for example, was served by six companies, and Galashiels by five. Three concerns, Cameron's Howey & Co and Anderson, Biggs & Co were based at the Queen Street Station of the Edinburgh & Glasgow Railway and presumably made use of its services. Most destinations were served by daily departures, some more frequently. Road and rail services from Glasgow were complemented by direct steamer services to all the major ports in the Irish Sea, and points on the west coast of Scotland as far north as Stornoway. The best served destination was Rothesay, with five sailings a day. Most other destinations were served by at least one sailing a week.[29] It is clear therefore that on the eve of the creation of a full-scale railway network Glasgow at least was the focus for an extensive system for the movement of both goods and passengers throughout Britain.

The Scottish cities and towns experienced between 1850 and 1914 substantial growth in population,[30] accompanied by physical expansion, with consequent effects on both internal and external transport requirements. The functions of the larger communities also changed. They developed stronger links with surrounding areas, offering a wide range of central services, and encouraging industrial specialisation. The concentration of brewing in Edinburgh and Alloa, of light ironfounding in the Falkirk district, of papermaking in the Edinburgh area and round Aberdeen had earlier parallels in skill-based specialisation, such as Paisley thread and shawls, or in resourced-based grouping of textile finishing factories, coal mines and iron smelting works, but tended to be more dependent on medium and long-distance land transport. New or developing centralist roles for the cities in the second half of the nineteenth century included education, hospitals, provision of public utilities, wholesale and retail trade administration. Municipal 'socialism' took in many of these functions, giving new meaning to the term 'city', and through the wholehearted adoption of utilitarian principles giving new value to the mass of the people, a value endorsed by extension of the franchise, by the reform of municipal government, and by the rise of trade unions and of working-class representation in Parliament.[31] The perception of the new role of the city appears to have dawned in Scotland in the 1840s, when the confidence of the merchant and textile princes of Glasgow was shaken by the arrival of the railway, and by the rapid rise to fame and power of the iron, coal, engineering and shipbuilding men of West Central Scotland. The new men, with their new financial institutions—banks,[32] trusts, insurance companies and stock exchanges—were not only in a position to realise dreams of transport improvement but also had a vested interest in their execution. Their influence is most clearly demonstrated in Glasgow. Significantly, James Beaumont Neilson, pioneer of the hot-blast process, was one of the partners in the speculative purchase and development for middle-class housing of the Kelvinside Estate,[33] and Robert Napier played a similar role in the Stobcross Estate,[34] both in Glasgow, and both in the 1840s. These attempts to encourage the upper middle classes, at once more numerous and more wealthy than their predecessors, to move to elegant new suburbs, were not without precedent, but were more ambitious than earlier schemes.[35] Terrace and tenement development in these, and in the Park Estate[36] was followed by villadom, with the creation of Pollokshields, the largest single scheme,[37] and smaller projects in, for example, Dowanhill, Partickhill and Dennistoun.[38] The middle-class fugitives from the old city centre left gaps in the older inner city villa areas to the North East of George Square, and in Sauchiehall Street and the West end of St Vincent Street, which were quickly filled by lower middle class tenements and by commercial and industrial users.[39]

At this stage in the suburban development of Glasgow, reached in the 1850s and early 1860s, there was no sophisticated transport system to back up the geographical expansion. Some of the residents in the new suburbs must have walked to work, though the wealthier kept their own carriages,[40] and there were both hackney carriages and horse-omnibuses for the less well-to-do.[41] A limited number of railway stations catered for 'suburban' passenger traffic, including Shields, Pollokshaws, and on the North Bishopbriggs, Lenzie, Cowlairs and Stepps.[42]

TRAMWAYS

The horse tramway became a practical proposition for town transport at the end of the 1860s. George Train's pioneering lines in Birkenhead and London had failed owing to the use of rails projecting above the road surface.[43] The development of the grooved rail and the initiative of the Liverpool Tramways Co created conditions for the rapid adoption of horse tramways throughout Britain. The basic advantage of the tram as opposed to the omnibus was the greater load which could be pulled by a two-horse team; fifty passengers as opposed to the twenty-five or so of the two horse omnibus.[44] This allowed fares to be reduced, and the greater smoothness and commodiousness of the tram made it instantly popular. Glasgow secured the act for its first routes in 1870,[45] before the general Tramways Act of that year, and Edinburgh followed in 1871.[46] Aberdeen's first two routes were opened in 1874,[47] and Dundee's first tramway started in 1877.[48] Glasgow's tramways became and remained trend setters for Scottish tram systems generally. Because the city was the largest in Scotland, its need for public transport was greatest, and by the time traffic figures were returned to the Board of Trade[49] it had become firmly dependent on tramways. It may be coincidental, but it hardly seems likely, that the 1870s saw house-building in the city on an unprecedented scale,[50] and that the later 1870s saw the Caledonian and Glasgow & South Western railways move into new city centre termini, conveniently sited for horse-tramway communication, but also possible foci for an attack on the horse-tram revenues.[51]

The repulsion of attempts to build railways overground on the east-west axis of Glasgow from the 1850s,[52] however, forced suburban railway development underground, or at best into shallow cutting. Though the Stobcross Branch of the North British Railway gave indirect access to the periphery of the West End, it was the Glasgow City & District Railway, opened in 1886 that was the first true suburban route, driving straight through the city centre from High Street in the east to Partick in the west, linking with the Stobcross Branch, and providing a convenient link with existing routes along the north bank of the Clyde and east to Coatbridge and Hamilton.[54] The success of this north bank line was immediate, and encouraged both the Caledonian Railway to sponsor the parallel Glasgow Central Railway,[55] and the Glasgow District Subway Co to obtain an act for a circular cable-worked underground railway serving the western parts of the conurbation on both banks of the river.[56] The successful promotion of these schemes, and of the first section of the Cathcart District Railway on the 'South Side', in fact reveals the limitations of horse-haulage on the Glasgow streets. Serious traffic congestion was reducing the effectiveness of the horse tramways, and also of horse-haulage of goods.[57] The changeover from dry closets to water closets in working-class districts, implemented after an act of 1890 may also indicate that the disposal of night soil by road was becoming a problem.[58]

The low efficiency of the horse tramway in Glasgow, however was not reflected in declining revenues, and route extensions continued in parallel with railway building.[59] The Glasgow Tramway & Omnibus Co Ltd, lessees of the system since its construction were, however, somewhat ineffective, and as the term of their twenty-one year lease drew to a close, proved reluctant to spend any but the minimum on maintaining the system. The Corporation of Glasgow, flushed with the success of numerous municipal enterprises, finally in 1891 terminated the lease, and took on the responsibility of running the system directly.[60] Despite competition from the former lessees' horse buses, the new Corporation horse tramways were highly successful and major extensions were made to the system during the next seven years.[61] The new regime even made dents in the traffic figures of the Cathcart District Railway, completed as a circular route in 1894,[62] but the relatively limited range of horse-haulage prevented serious competition on longer-haul routes, and did not discourage promotion of such lines as the Lanarkshire & Dunbartonshire and Lanarkshire and Ayrshire, built to link with the Glasgow Central and Cathcart District Railways, and of an ambitious group of railways serving Barrhead, Paisley and Renfrew.[63]

Tramway technology had not, however, been standing still. The main deterrents to the adoption of mechanical traction on Glasgow Corporation routes had been uncertainty about the lease and then the pressing need for the Corporation itself to provide a reliable service.[64] With the success of direct operation assured, electric traction was tried in 1898, and found successful. The forthcoming International Exhibition of 1901 provided a good reason for going ahead with full-scale electrification which was completed in that year.[65] The effects were dramatic. Not only did traffic figures soar, but despite low fares revenue rose.[66] The reduced costs of operation in relation to the horse trams allowed long-distance fares to be kept down, and the higher speeds, cleanliness and greater operating flexibility of the electric cars increased their attractiveness. Existing suburban rail services were hard hit,[67] and the Paisley, Barrhead and District Railway, virtually complete, never opened to passengers.[68] The 'Clutha' water bus service on the Clyde was another casualty (see below). The success of the Glasgow tramway electrification had important repercussions not only for other Scottish tramways, but for systems throughout the world. Until the outbreak of war, the Glasgow system steadily expanded, providing a physical, as well as a technical, stimulus to the creation of a major tramway running from Wishaw to Balloch and from Barrhead and Kilbarchan to Bishopbriggs and Baillieston.[69]

The effect of Glasgow's tramway electrification was not confined to the tapping of existing traffic. As with the horse system thirty years earlier, the electric tramway stimulated house-building. The Shawlands, Cathcart, Langside and Hyndland complexes of red sandstone tenements were all built in the years immediately after electrification, and close to tram routes.[70] The success of electrification was to some extent made possible by a reduction in horse-hauled goods and mineral traffic in the inner city area owing to removal of factories and other industrial premises to outlying areas, often served by both rail and tramway,[71] and to the massive increase in the number of rail-linked premises (see below). Motor and steam lorries with carrying capacities greater than those of horse-hauled vehicles were also beginning to speed up inner city goods transport, though the impact of such mechanised road transport was small before 1914.[72]

The pattern of development in the other Scottish cities was rather different. Glasgow's position as centre of a conurbation housing well over a million inhabitants, by the end of the nineteenth century, and as a major manufacturing centre, was unique. In addition its topography, both natural and man-made, was quite well suited to tramway development. Only Edinburgh offered a setting for tramway building on anything like the scale of Glasgow, and there the steep fall from the New Town ridge towards Leith posed problems for horse tram operation. Though Edinburgh's social structure and settlement pattern were better suited to a prosperous horse tramway system than those of Glasgow, the problems of the northern part of the city held back development until the early 1890s, when the Edinburgh Northern Tramways Co built its cable-worked line.[73] The success of this venture led the Corporation as owners of the track to lease the bulk of the existing horse-hauled system to the Edinburgh Tramways Co, who converted it to cable haulage. Though cumbersome in concept, the cable-hauled system was cost-effective at the time, and provided an integrated, on the whole reliable mechanical transport system at a time when electric traction had not convincingly proved its value.[74]

The Dundee system faced similar problems, as the rise to the northern suburbs from the narrow coastal strip was steep. Here the solution adopted was to use steam traction for the hillier routes and horses for the more level ones, until electrification was undertaken in 1899–1901.[75] Aberdeen's more level layout, however, was well suited to horse traction and the whole system remained horse-hauled until electrification. The impact of tramway construction on Aberdeen's street plan requires further research, but the construction of the Denburn and Rosemount viaducts in 1886 was conditioned by the requirements of the tramways.[76]

Though the cities were by far the most significant users of pre-electric tramways, a number of other communities were large enough or rich enough to develop smaller systems. Of these the most important were the two sections of the Vale of Clyde Tramways, both near-level linear routes. One linked Greenock and Gourock, and joined the Greenock & Port Glasgow line; the other was an extension of the Glasgow system from Glasgow to Govan. The latter was worked primarily by steam, and was the first urban steam tramway in Britain,[77] though originally through horse cars also worked into the city centre.[78] The Glasgow and Ibrox, originally designed for compressed air working, was close to the limit of successful operation.[79] The small Paisley system, opened in 1885–86, was not a success either, owing in part to its small route mileage,[80] but Perth's rather larger tramway opened in 1895 and horse-worked until 1906, was quite prosperous.[81] The other towns with horse systems, Rothesay[82] and Stirling–Bridge of Allan (opened 1874) both combined regular passenger workings with holiday traffic, and both were unusual in operating horse-buses. Stirling's traffic did not develop to any great extent, and the system was never electrified, despite a number of proposals, though experiments were made with steam traction in 1878 and a petrol car was put into service in 1913.[83] Rothesay's tramway, opened in 1882, which catered for ever-growing numbers of Glasgow, Lanarkshire and Renfrewshire holiday-makers, was electrified in 1902 and extended in 1905.[84]

Once it had been demonstrated that electric tramways had lower operating costs and greater speed than horse or steam trams, both municipalities and private companies began to build new systems. Four of these were similar in character to the original horse tram systems, either nuclear or linear, but in either case serving densely urbanised districts. Ayr (1901),[85] Kilmarnock (1904)[86] and Kirkcaldy[87] were municipal systems, and Airdrie & Coatbridge

(1903) was built by the British Electric Traction Company.[88] The flexibility of the electric tram, however, was most in evidence in the new-style tramways linking scattered urban communities (Lanarkshire, (1903 and later),[89] Paisley and District (1904 and later),[90] Dumbarton Burgh & County (1907),[91] Wemyss (1907)[92] and Dunfermline & District (1909)[93] or extending existing or planned urban systems (Aberdeen Suburban (1904),[94] Portobello & Musselburgh (1904)[95] and Dundee & Broughty Ferry (1905).[96] All these systems had long stretches of track through countryside or sparsely populated areas. Some of the pre-1914 extensions of the major city systems, especially Glasgow, were also of this character. They combined the functions of small-scale urban tramways with those formerly performed by railways. Owing to greater frequency, convenience and cleanliness, they challenged existing rail routes, and helped to confine post 1900 railway construction to rural areas too sparsely populated to justify electric tramway building. Apart from those tramways actually built there were serious proposals for a large number of extensions and new systems, which acted as a further deterrent to rail construction.[97] The effects of these tramways on new settlement is difficult to detect, as the period between their construction and 1914 was brief, and coincided with a building slump.

These general comments provide a framework within which both railways and tramways can be analysed for their value as urban transport. The Board of Trade returns for tramways are fairly full from 1877–8[98] and though there are some problems in making detailed comparisons between systems owing to some returns being estimates, and owing to different financial years being quoted for different systems, nonetheless the degree of error is probably insignificant, particularly from the early 1890s. Looking first at the aggregate statistics, some unexpected trends emerge. Analysis of the Scottish figures derived from the Annual Returns produces some interesting results. (Figure 1) The initially high rates of usage measured by the number of passengers/mile of system of the tramways at the end of the 1870s declined during the 1880s, reaching a low point in 1886–7. There was slight recovery in the early 1890s, but the 1877–8 figure was not surpassed until 1895–6. The peak figure for the whole period was reached in 1901–2, a boom year for the economy, and a year when the electrification of the Glasgow system was effected. The figures then show a downward trend, reflecting the more marginal nature of much of the new mileage built in the period to 1914. Looking at the ratio of passengers to capital expended, this peaked in 1896–7, in the heyday of the horse cable tram, and the average of the 1895–1900 period was significantly higher than that of 1900–14. The horse cable tram system was therefore comparatively capital effective. Its operating costs were, however, relatively high (Figure 2). Though they dropped in the period after 1894 they were on average nearly a third greater than those of the electric tram in its early period. There was, however, a tendency for the average operating costs of electric trams to drift up as more marginal systems came into operation. It was on the operating ratio,

(Figures 3, 4), however that the advent of electric traction had the most immediate and obvious effect. The average operating ratio of horse trams was in the region of 0.7–0.8. This dropped to 0.5–0.6 on the introduction of electric traction, though it is interesting to note that the operating ratios of the

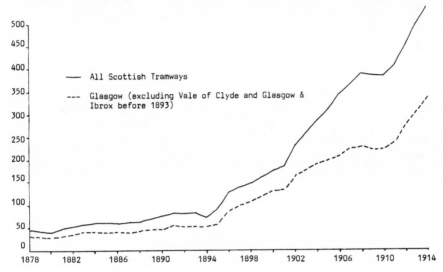

FIGURE 1   Passengers carried by Scottish Tramways 1878–1914 in millions

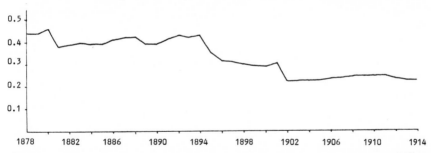

FIGURE 2   Operating cost per passenger on Scottish Tramways 1878–1914 in new pence

cable-worked Edinburgh and Northern and Edinburgh Corporation systems were in the same band as the electric tramways, and only marginally higher. One firm conclusion that one can draw is that electric and cable tramways were the products of a capital-rich community, but that the returns were reliably high. In this sense perhaps they can be considered as among the first 'modern' investments.

These global figures, do in fact conceal a wide variety of experience. As regards intensity of use, Glasgow was much the most significant. As early as 1881 more than one and a half million passengers per mile were being carried, and this had doubled by 1901.

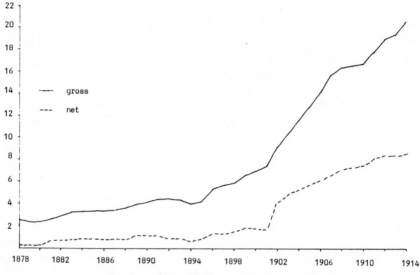

FIGURE 3   Receipts of Scottish Tramways 1878–1914 in £00,000

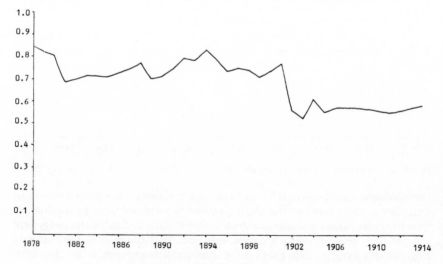

FIGURE 4   Operating ratio of Scottish Tramways 1878–1914

The Edinburgh system in 1901 carried about half that load, and Dundee about a fifth. The disparity between the major cities shrank between 1901 and 1911, when the Glasgow total had dropped to 2.3 million, while the Edinburgh and Dundee figures had risen to 2.0 million and 1.2 million respectively. The gap between the leaders and the 'minor league' was marked. Bottom of the scale in the 1880s was the Stirling system, with a mere 50,000 passengers/mile in 1881, but by 1911 this had risen to a respectable 163,000, more than the electrified Wemyss system, and within striking distance of the Dunfermline & District's 222,000. Of the long-distance interurban systems, the most intensively used was the Lanarkshire tramways, with 619,000 passengers/mile in 1911.

As regards labour productivity, the census figures from 1891[100] allow calculations to be made which show that between 1891 and 1901 the number of passengers per employee in Scotland rose from 55,769 to 60,583, and 8.6 per cent increase. The electrification of existing tramways and the building of new electric systems did not, however, markedly increase productivity which rose only by 3.2 per cent to 62,504 passengers/employee, between 1901 and 1911. Making the assumption that all tramway employees lived within the respective Parliamentary or Municipal Burghs, however, the major urban areas had wide variations in performance. In 1891 Glasgow had 89,273 passengers/employee, but Dundee had only 44,210. By 1901, though the Glasgow figure had dropped to 86,076, Dundee had 97,683, the lowest figure being Aberdeen's, with only 62,870. In 1911 a measure of uniformity had been reached, with all four cities in the range 82,915 (Glasgow) to 86,198 (Aberdeen). Electrification (or cable-operation) then, seems not to have increased labour productivity specifically though it did help a uniformly high standard to be achieved.

To analyse the impact of tramway transport on towns the 'commuter term'[101] has been used to calculate the number of people capable of using the system for travel to work. The total number of journeys has been divided by 1200, being the number of journeys made in a fifty week year by a person working a six day week, and using the tramway four times a day. This takes into account the common custom of returning home for lunch and the comparative rarity of half-day working on a Saturday, and of long summer vacations. This factor therefore in one sense, gives a minimum number of regular uses, though users transferring from one car to another could inflate the figure. As absolute figures, commuter terms are not particularly helpful, but calculated in terms of percentage of total population they give some guide to the relative importance of individual tramways at different times. In 1881, the average percentage in six systems, including those in the cities was 2.1, with Glasgow highest at 4.6 per cent and Edinburgh not far behind at 3 per cent. In 1891 the average had risen to 2.6 per cent, with Glasgow still in the lead with 6.1 per cent and Edinburgh 5 per cent. Glasgow's percentage in 1901 was 12.0, with Edinburgh 8.1 per cent, as against an average for nine systems of 4.6 per cent. In this

instance the Glasgow traffic figure for 1900–1 has been used, with the
population of 1901, to give an approximate figure for the apogee of horse and
cable working. The error will be small. By 1911 the average for 17 systems was
up to 7.4 per cent, with Glasgow top at 17.2 per cent and Edinburgh close
behind at 15.6 per cent. Eight systems, however, had less than 6 per cent,
including those such as Wemyss, Lanarkshire and Falkirk where there was
definitely extensive working-class use. This suggests that Ochojna's contention
that horse tram systems were not much used by the working classes is at best
doubtful. [102] The figures also quantify the much greater significance of trams in
dense conurbations than in the more sprawling systems. Only Paisley, of the
'interurban' tramways approached the nuclear systems of the major cities, with
8.2 per cent tram-dependent in comparison with Dundee's 8.6 per cent. Both
the Glasgow and Edinburgh systems, apart from serving larger geographical
areas gave network coverage, with few inhabitants of the central area and few
industrial premises more than walking distance from the trams.

RAILWAYS

The contribution of railways to urban transport is exceedingly difficult to
define (though see J R Kellett, *The Impact of Railways on Victorian Cities*, pp.
240–3 for Glasgow terminal figures for isolated years). The global statistics of
passengers carried in the Board of Trade returns [103] are not reliable, as the
number of season tickets issued is not consistently recorded until 1902. After
that date the number of seasons is given on the basis of yearly equivalents. On
the grounds that the ratio of receipts from passengers in 1901 and 1902 is
within 0.7 per cent of the ratio of numbers of non-season passenger journeys for
those years, however, it seems reasonable to deflate the pre 1902 figures by the
ratio of the 1902 seasons to the 1901 seasons, though the accuracy of this
deflation obviously is likely to diminish for earlier years.

More significantly, it is impossible to determine the proportion of railway
passengers who were using the railways for travel-to-work in urban
communities. By using the commuter term on the total number of rail
passengers, however, a maximum figure is obtained which can be used for
rough comparison with that for tramways. Given that occasional use of the
railway would not affect statistics much, and that the average level of fare paid
was low, the degree of error should not make comparison meaningless. Cal-
culating the commuter term for railways by dividing the number of 'ordinary'
passengers by 1200, then adding the number of seasons in annual equivalents,
one can plot a graph (Figure 5) showing that there was fairly steady growth
from 1876 to 1884, a slump in 1885, then a rapid rise to 1888 of nearly 70 per
cent, reflecting the opening of the Cathcart District, Paisley Canal and Glasgow
City & District lines. The boom was short-lived, however, as by 1890 the
growth rate was back on the pre-1888 trend. There was no dramatic rise in the

commuter term after the opening of the Glasgow Central line in 1896, but the rate of growth for the years 1895–99, at 8.3 per cent, per annum was more than double that of the years 1890–95 (3.8 per cent). After 1899 there was no sustained growth in passenger dependence on railways, the commuter term varying from a minimum of 178,000 in 1904 to a maximum of 192,000 in 1907 in the years before the First World War.

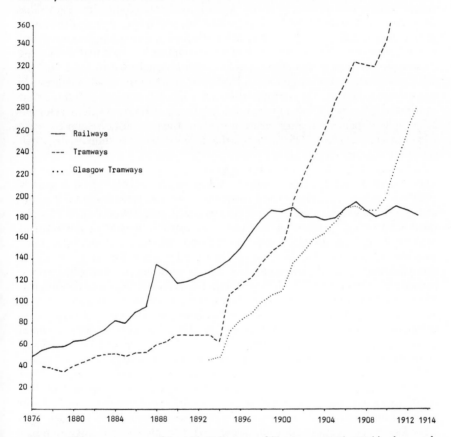

FIGURE 5   Commuter terms of Scottish Railways and Tramways 1876–1914 in thousands

The levelling off of dependence on rail for the journey-to-work, crudely measured by the commuter term, was a recognised consequence of the competition from electric tramways, both new and conversions from horse systems. The failure of rail traffic figures to rise sharply in the 1890s was in large part a consequence of the phenomenal success of the revitalised Glasgow horse-tram system, whose commuter term rose by 130 per cent between 1894 and 1900. Electrification of the tramways was however, almost literally the *coup de grace* to growth.[104] The Glasgow's tramways' commuter term rose by 75 per cent between 1900 and 1907 and after the 1908–9 depression again rose dramatically, by more than 50 per cent between 1909 and 1913. The phenomenon was by no means confined to Glasgow, whose commuter term was consistently some 70 per cent of the Scottish total throughout the 1890s. This proportion had dropped by the mid 1900s to around 60 per cent and remained at that level until 1914. The cumulative effect of tramway improvement was indeed dramatic. The commuter term of the tramways, which had been some 75 per cent of that of the railways in the 1890s, equalled it in 1901, and by 1907 was nearly 70 per cent above it. In the aftermath of the 1908–9 depression not only did the tramway commuter term rise in 1913 to nearly 2.5 times that of the whole Scottish railway system, but the Glasgow tramways alone achieved a figure of 55 per cent higher. Bearing in mind the long distance and country-wide services provided by the railways, the dominance of the tramway in urban transport was indeed complete.

To what extent the overwhelming success of the tramways in the period between 1901 and 1913 represents a failure of the railways must remain a matter of opinion. Certainly the electric tram, with its function limited to the carriage of passengers, and with no effective rival in the streets could respond quickly to changing levels of demand. The low tare weight of the tram in relation to its load was also a significant factor. Most importantly, the tram, without demolishing that which it was intended to serve, and at a low cost in wayleave could provide a door-to-door service well-tailored to the pattern of concentrated nuclear or linear settlement characteristic of lowland Scotland. Much may be made of cheaper fares, but it was convenience that sold tramways to those above the poverty line. The railways in pre-nationalisation days were ill-suited to mount an effective challenge. Glasgow with its four terminal stations owned by three companies,[105] two east-west independently-owned and competing through routes[106] and one very limited cross-river link within the city[107] could not without fabulous expense have developed an integrated rail network. Edinburgh's suburban railway service was in the hands of two competing companies, and its only explicitly suburban route was forced into an indirect link with the city centre by tramway pressure.[108] Dundee and Aberdeen had only minimal suburban services.[109] Only if street congestion had reduced the effectiveness of tramways, as happened with horse trams in the Glasgow of the 1880s, would the railways have been able to recover some of the lost ground.

The railways did, however, continue to perform functions vital to the effective operation of the sophisticated cities of the late nineteenth and early twentieth centuries. They provided central goods stations, which were extended to keep pace with the growth of general merchandise traffic, and which served city centre commercial, wholesale and retail outlets by regular cart and van services.[110] In suburban areas, mineral depots were built at most stations from which coal could be distributed both to houses and to industrial consumers. These depots also served as distribution points for stone, brick and other building materials.[111] The passenger stations also functioned as parcels stations, and to encourage the use of railways by shoppers at least one company, the Glasgow & South Western, provided a service at its St Enoch station, for the reception of purchases made during a day's shopping and delivered by the shop.[112] Not the least important function of the railways was the transport of foodstuffs. Cattle travelled on the hoof in special cattle vans, often attached to passenger trains, though a dead-meat trade also developed.[113] Regular trains ran from the Merklands Lairage, the main point of importation for Irish Cattle, to the Glasgow market. Grain imports of wheat for flour and maize for distilling too travelled very largely by rail. Oats, hay and straw for the maintenance of city horses also came in on the railway—as did potatoes.[114] Milk traffic was a feature of both the Caledonian and Glasgow & South Western lines in Ayrshire and Lanarkshire, particularly after about 1900.[115] Not all foodstuffs flowed into the cities. Manufactured products, especially bread, biscuits and confectionery were distributed widely, the bread trade with the Western Highlands and Islands being particularly distinctive.[116]

Aberdeen, Fraserburgh, Peterhead and Buckie also acted as landing points for fish destined for urban markets both north and south of the border, with facilities being provided at Aberdeen for loading straight from the fish market into vans. Similar transfer took place at Granton, on the Forth, and on the Clyde. Ayr Harbour was a more modest rail-served fish port.[117]

Railways were also vital to the drink trades. The concentration of brewing in Alloa, Edinburgh and Glasgow was only possible because of the extensive use of rail services, and a whole new 'brewery suburb' was created at Craigmillar, Edinburgh with direct rail links.[118] In Alloa, although the principal breweries were not directly rail served, the maltings and bottling plants were.[119] Glasgow alone of the larger brewing centres failed to link its breweries to the rail system, but only one Glasgow brewery was of any real significance, and it was close to the High Street goods station. The establishment of depots in the cities by English brewers such as Vaux, Bass and Whitbread[120] was also made possible by rail transport, though the level of competition with Scottish brewers appears to have been low. The whisky trade came to be heavily reliant on rail transport, though canals also played an important role in the mid nineteenth century, particularly as they could supply water as well as transport. The 'distillery mania' of the 1880s and 1890s was integrally linked with the building of new railways and the extension of old, allowing coal and barley to be moved into distilleries, particularly on Speyside, and permitting whisky to be moved directly by rail to bonded warehouses, mainly in Leith and Glasgow, for blending, bottling and shipment.[121] In Glasgow the railway companies themselves built warehouses for the storage of whisky, and encouraged the use of the arches under their lines for that purpose. [122] In Leith, though few of the bonded warehouses were directly rail-linked, the whisky traffic must have been a potent stimulus to the competitive construction of railways that was a feature of the port. [123]

The influence of railways on urban industrial location was profound. Both producers of heavy goods and minerals and consumers of large quantities of raw materials were virtually forced either to develop rail links with their existing premises, or to build on new sites capable of being rail-served. Extreme examples in the urban setting were shipbuilding and locomotive building, where rail connection was vital for all but the smallest enterprises. [124] Gasworks, too, in the cities and major towns were generally rail served [125] as were most of the larger power stations built from the late 1890s. [126] Examples of companies that moved premises to gain rail access are numerous: for instance Neilson & Co. who moved to Springburn in 1860, the Saracen Foundry, moved to Possil in 1869, P & W MacLellan, moved to Kinning Park in 1872 and Singer, who transferred to Kilbowie in 1882. [127] Singer also chose the Clydebank site for its proximity to the Forth & Clyde Canal. Unlike the other firms quoted Singer used the railway to transport workers in large numbers from the East End of Glasgow where their earlier factory had been sited. [128] A particularly good example of the influence of railways on industrial location was the construction of two lines serving the north bank of the Clyde west of Partick. The Whiteinch Tramway [129] and the Lanarkshire and Dunbartonshire Railway [130] were essential to the building and operation of a chain of shipyards, marine engine works and related premises from the 1880s onwards, culminating in the construction of a new dock, Rothesay Dock, in the early 1900s, and in the building of Yarrows and Beardmores shipyards at the same time, creating a pattern of industrial development unique in Scotland. [131] Cheap workmen's fares allowed the new concerns to draw a part of their labour force from the older industrial areas, though by the time the later works were completed the electric tram was also playing a part.

A rough measure of the relative importance of rail transport to industry and trade in the major Scottish cities may be derived from the lists of facilities in the *Railway Clearing House Hand-book of Stations*. [132] In the 1904 edition Aberdeen had three private sidings and nine public goods stations. Dundee had eighteen sidings and fourteen goods stations. Edinburgh and Leith, on the other hand had no fewer than 83 private sidings though only 19 public goods stations and sidings. Glasgow's total were 718 and 99 respectively. The concentration of rail services was not, as can be seen, related directly to population, and was indeed closely linked with industrial structure. The relatively small burgh of Bo'ness, with one passenger station and three goods stations, had 25 private sidings, mostly to woodyards, as the town was a point of timber importation. Falkirk's private sidings, and several of its 7 goods stations, were mainly linked with the town's numerous light-castings foundries, and Coat-bridge, with 14 goods stations and an amazing 83 private sidings owed its con-centration of facilities to the iron smeltings, wrought iron, coal and heavy engineering trades. Such extensive direct rail services were, however, compara-tively modern in 1904. In 1877 there were only 4 private sidings in Glasgow. This number had risen by 1890 to 54, but declined after 1904, until by 1912 there were only 183.[133]

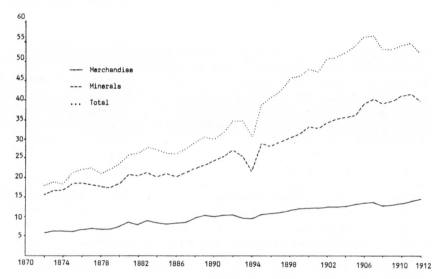

FIGURE 6   Merchandise and minerals carried by Scottish Railways 1870–1912 in millions of tons

The volume of goods and mineral traffic on the railways (Figure 6) was not affected by road competition to the same extent as passenger numbers.[134] Indeed, the mineral traffic showed a sustained growth from 1886 to 1907, rising from just over 27.3m tons to 56.6m, an increase of 107 per cent though after 1907 it fell off, never rising above 55m tons, and dropping to 52.5m in 1914. Merchandise traffic moved more sluggishly. During the same period it increased by 54 per cent, and even during the boom years 1898–1902 it rose by less than 7 per cent. The marked rise in the number of private sidings, then, seems to have been mainly intended to expedite coal and other mineral traffic, rather than to facilitate shipment of finished and semi-finished goods. Given, however, that the Scottish economy was under pressure from competitors else-where in Britain, and from Europe, shipment from private sidings may well have helped to maintain the competitive position of local concerns. In tonnage terms coal accounted for a minimum of about 70 per cent of minerals carried, using the quantity mined as a proportion of minerals carried. As some coal was carried by more than one railway company the proportion was probably higher. The proportion tended to decrease over time, falling from 86 per cent in 1872 to around 77 per cent in the late 1880s and further declining to about 70 per cent in the mid 1900s. At the minimum Scottish coal output represented about 55 per cent of all minerals and merchandise carried by the Scottish railways (in 1905).

STEAMER SERVICES

Though of limited significance to the growth of the cities and larger towns, passenger steamer services were vital to the expansion, and indeed in some instances the creation of a number of towns on the western seaboard of Scotland. From Stranraer in the south to Stornoway, Kirkwall and Lerwick in the north the much greater reliability and safety of steamers made ports of call foci for growth, some of it substantial. Within this overall experience, however, important differences may be noted. Some towns grew primarily as destinations. Rothesay, Millport, Dunoon are the prime examples, with limited hinterlands and a commitment to the provision of facilities for holidaymakers, including both day trippers and longer-term residents. These were extensions of Glasgow in a sense, and were without real parallel elsewhere in Scotland. A second category combined the function of destination with that of transit point. This included Oban[135] and Kyle of Lochalsh. A third group were ports of entry for island or remote mainland communities. In some instances, such as Kirkwall, Lerwick and Campbeltown these entrepots were old-established and developed rural communities. Others like Tobermory, Stornoway, Portree, Tarbert, Loch Fyne, and Port Ellen existed in embryo, but rose to prominence with the advent of steamers.[136] Owing to the operating pattern of nineteenth-century steamships the majority of these settlements served not only as points through which goods and passengers from a distance were funnelled. Commonly they became commercial and administrative centres for other satellite settlements. Thus in the Outer Isles Stornoway assumed minor metropolitan status, and the roles of Kirkwall and Lerwick as focal points for their island groups were strongly reinforced with interisland steamship services developing.[137] Steamboat services also allowed the herring and white fishing industries to develop on a large scale. The fresh herring fishing in Loch Fyne, linked by steamship with the Glasgow market was a stimulus to the growth of Tarbert and Campbeltown.[138] The salt herring trade, which was a larger-scale enterprise, was in part responsible for the rise of Stornoway, Wick, Buckie and a number of smaller ports on both sides of the country.[139] Aberdeen's prosperity in the two decades before the First World War was closely linked with the proliferation of steam trawlers, the fresh fish being transported by fast rail services to the south.[140]

One aspect of the influence of steamer services on urban growth may be singled out. This was the linear development of suburbs of the Clyde coast resorts, served by a fringe of piers. The 'marine villas' so beloved of the middle-class Glaswegian could thus be built along the narrow coastal strips at the foot of the Argyll, Bute or Dumbarton hills, with more complex plans in the immediate vicinity of the piers. Settlements like those from Innellan to Kilmun on the Cowal Peninsula, and the Gareloch-Loch Long fringe from Helensburgh to Cove, though not strictly 'urban', can be conceived of as having a unique kind of suburban character. [141]

These remarkable communities took the form they did because steamboat services were so much more convenient than pre-motor road services. The deficiencies of road transport also encouraged the establishment of Scotland's only river water bus service, the 'Cluthas' of the Clyde Navigation Trust, [142] which plied between Whiteinch and Victoria Bridge in Glasgow's city centre, a distance of about 3 miles. The service started in 1884, with six small twin-screw steamers calling at 11 landing-stages and taking 45 minutes on the journey. By 1897 there were twelve steamers, which carried 2,795,691 passengers in the year to 30 June 1897 at a fare of 1d each. Numbers carried continued to rise until 1900. 'But the introduction by Glasgow Corporation of a system of electric cars on the main roads of the city and its vicinity north and south of the Clyde superseded the necessity for maintaining the 'Clutha' service, and towards the end of 1903 these steamers were withdrawn.' [143] The Clyde Navigation Trust also provided both passenger and vehicular ferries to cater for traffic downstream of Jamaica Bridge, the lowest bridge on the Clyde until 1927. By 1908 there were three combined vehicular and passenger crossings within Glasgow Harbour and seven passenger only ferry routes. Over eight million passengers and half a million vehicles, mainly horse-drawn carts, then used the ferries each year. [144] These short links were thus of great local importance. They were particularly vital to shipyard workers, whose employment depended on frequent moves from yard to yard. [145]

HACKNEY CARRIAGES

Hackney carriages played a limited and largely unquantifiable role in urban transport before 1914, but hackney carriage licences, issued by the Police Commissioners in Glasgow give some measure of the use of the Victorian and Edwardian equivalent of the taxicab. [146] Between 1884 and 1892 the number of licences, with the exception of 1889, fluctuated between 467 and 549, drifting upwards. There was then a marked increase in 1893 to 659, and the number of carriages remained above 600 until 1906, when there began a sharp decline to a level of 400–500. On the eve of the First World War, however, numbers slumped dramatically, from 400 in 1912 to 325 in 1914. A tentative explanation for this pattern would be that the trade cycle exercised a dominating influence on the number of licences up to about 1902. The numbers then dropped initially as a consequence of the vastly improved service offered by the electric tram, and then owing to the introduction of motor-driven taxicabs, which were not included in these figures. It is certainly clear, however, that the numbers using hackney carriages in Glasgow was small in relation to those using other modes of transport.

Having considered the significance of individual ways of travelling in or to Victorian towns and cities, some of the practical implications of their development will now be discussed.

BUILDING MATERIALS

Apart from moving people, their food and fuel, raw materials and manufac-tured goods, urban transport had to supply building materials for urban expansion and renewal. As already stated, in the early Victorian period stone and brick were produced close to city centres, but the exhaustion of accessible reserves and the rising value of land forced builders to seek supplies from further afield. Brickworks and stone quarries were opened further and further away as urban expansion proceeded.[147] Good quality freestone became increasingly difficult to get in Glasgow, and by the 1890s the local white sandstones, quarried for instance at Bishopbriggs and Giffnock were being supplanted by red sandstones from Ayrshire and Dumfriesshire. Quarries at Corncockle and Locharbriggs, Dumfriesshire and at Mauchline in Ayrshire, all rail-served, became increasingly important, and most of the houses built during the Glasgow building boom of 1897–1902 were faced with stone from these quarries. In Aberdeenshire the Aberdeen city quarries, of which the most notable was Rubislaw, were supplemented by quarries in the Kemnay area.[148] Edinburgh abandoned Craigleith and drew most of its stone from the edge of the Pentlands to the West of Edinburgh. Bricks were throughout the period little used for frontages, except in cheap miners' housing, but internal walls, the inner skins of outer walls, and commonly rear walls were brick built. The Scottish clay-brick industry was organised on as large a scale as that in England, but small and medium-sized brickworks were numerous throughout central Scotland. They were often closely associated with collieries, and like them were commonly rail-linked.[149] The low value of bricks in relation to their volume encouraged the dispersal of the industry, which was in any case tied to patchy deposits of suitable clay. By 1914 'composition' bricks made of shales from the coal measures were being made in increasing numbers. Urban expansion also created demands for sanitary fireclay products. Salt-glazed sewage pipes became local specialities, as did white-glazed fireclay lavatories, water closets and sinks.[150] In both instances demand developed most rapidly from the late 1860s, with the increasing availability of piped water and growing realisation of the need for personal hygiene to avoid disease. By that time rail transport was developed sufficiently to allow the companies involved in white ware production, such as Shanks of Barrhead and Howie of Kilmarnock to develop national and indeed international markets, while the salt-glazed ware producers catered for regional demand. The functionally, though not technically related industry of bathfounding had a similar pattern of development.[151]

Throughout the period timber used in house and other building came primarily from overseas, especially from North America and the Baltic, though eastern hardwoods such as teak and mahogany also came into Glasgow. The softwoods were imported through most Scottish ports, but those in the east with their access to the Baltic assumed a growing significance in the late nineteenth century. Though much timber traffic from the Forth ports went by rail, the Forth & Clyde Canal was extensively used by firms such as Brownlee & Co., and Robinson Dunn & Co. and by the early 1900s the main traffic on the canal was imported timber consigned to Glasgow.[152]

The massive quantities of materials required for housebuilding on the Victorian scale were distributed largely by rail, and the suburban goods and mineral depots characteristic of railways constructed after 1880 often acted as distribution points for the materials required to build the houses of the customers for the new passenger stations. This was explicitly true of the Cathcart Circle in Glasgow[153] and there is every reason to generalise from this experience, given the timing of housing construction in suburban areas. Distribution of materials from the depots was by horse and cart, and the limited economic range of this mode of transport justified the provision of depots and sidings at what today seem remarkably frequent intervals.[154] The continuing use of mineral depots for fuel supply was of course an important factor in determining the location of such facilities.

The major exceptions to the use of rail transport for building materials were the supply of sand and gravel, slates and granite setts. Sand was quarried on the eastern outskirts of Glasgow, and distributed by horse and cart. Supplies dredged from sandbanks on the Clyde were also brought in by sailing barge or steam puffers. The slates for roofing Victorian buildings in Scotland were mostly quarried in the Western Highlands.[155] The nearest quarries to Glasgow were at Luss on Loch Lomond, and were served by vessels which could navigate the river Leven, but the most important sources of slate were the islands of Luing, Seil, Easdale and Belnahua, south of Oban, and the mainland of Argyll at Ballachulish. Small sailing vessels or the steam-propelled 'puffers' capable of navigating the Crinan Canal allowed the produce of these quarries to reach the centre of Glasgow, at Kingston Dock or Custom House Quay,[156] the centre of Paisley, where one slating contractor had a private wharf,[157] Greenock, Port Glasgow, and the smaller harbours on the Clyde coast. Argyllshire slate could also be transported by water, via the Caledonian and Forth & Clyde canals, to ports on the east coast of Scotland, though there was also slate quarries in Banffshire and Perthshire, both road and rail served.[158] In Caithness, Orkney and Angus stone split thin was used as a substitute for slate, and in the Forth basin pantiles were very commonly used instead of slate, being made locally.[159] The location of slate deposits and the ease with which their produce could be transported significantly determined the choice of roofing materials throughout Scotland. Though in many respects inferior to Welsh slate from Caernarvonshire or Merioneth, Scottish products held their own until after 1914.

The market for stone setts for street paving was not unlike that for slates, though the sources of supply were rather more dispersed. Glasgow and the West depended on Argyllshire and to a lesser extent on Galloway for granite setts, quarries on Loch Fyne at Crarae and Furnace, on Loch Etive at Bonawe, and at Creetown and Dalbeattie in Galloway being particularly important. Whinstone setts and kerbstones were made in quantity in Renfrewshire, mainly in the Johnstone area and at Gourock.[160] In the east, Aberdeenshire dominated, but whinstone was also worked in the Edinburgh area. The paved roads of urban areas were, however, long lasting, and the market for setts thus fluctuated with the rate of paving. Water transport was preferred, and the quays used for unloading were commonly the same as those used for other building materials.[161] Sand, gravel and lime were also moved where possible by water, lime commonly coming to the west of Scotland from Northern Ireland, while the Earl of Elgin's great Charlestown kilns on the Forth were designed to distribute their produce by coastal vessels, though a branch railway was built c. 1894.[162] The Edinburgh area drew much of its lime from large works in the Lothians which were without parallel elsewhere in Scotland.[163]

COMMERCIAL ACTIVITY

Levels of commercial service and centralised administration became increasingly sophisticated during the second half of the century. Financial institutions grew to maturity, with Scottish banks and insurance companies leading the world in administrative procedures.[164] The facilities offered by the railways for rapid and safe transmission of information and cash must have encouraged the continuing development of branch banking on a large scale, while the concentration of the increasingly central administration of the banks and leading insurance companies in city centres was only possible given adequate transportation for employees to both inner and outer suburban areas. In Glasgow and Edinburgh particularly the central banking and insurance facilities were well developed. The warehousing and distribution of goods also became increasingly centralised. The period after 1870 in particular was characterised by a growing number of large-scale manufacturing processing plants, for example flour milling,[165] bread baking,[166] confectionery manufacture, aerated water production,[167] the making of ready-made clothing,[168] and sewing thread manufacture.[169] These relied on sophisticated transport facilities, both road and rail,[170] as did centralised laundering, a feature of the post 1885 period.[171] It was in the 1880s and 1890s that the fast laundry van and the bread van became familiar features of the urban scene,[172] alongside the more familiar coal cart, milk cart and brewer's dray. The timing of the introduction of these centralised plants is difficult to tie directly to transport improvement, but the extensive provision of paved streets for tramway operation, together with realignment and adjustment of gradients for the same purpose must undoubtedly have facilitated road transport of goods of all kinds. A feature of such road improvement was quite commonly the laying of long paving stones to ease the task of horses, especially on inclines.[173] Certainly the construction of haulage contractors depots in Glasgow at least can be dated in the main to the period after 1870.[174]

One enterprise in particular may be singled out for mention as exemplifying these trends is the Scottish Cooperative Wholesale Society.[175] The SCWS was founded in 1868 as an alternative source of supply for the retail cooperative movement throughout Scotland. Its success was immediate, and up till the First World War its business expanded. Not only did it deal as a wholesaler with bulk commodities like wheat and provisions, it became to an increasing extent a processing and manufacturing organisation. Its purpose-built Chancelot Flour Mills in Leith, the Regent Flour Mills at Partick and the Oatmeal Mill at Leith acquired from private owners, were among the largest in Scotland, and in the immediate vicinity of the Society's central warehousing in Morrison Street, Tradeston, limited manufacturing capacity was developed from 1881. The mills were all directly rail linked, but the industrial premises were not, though they were within easy carting distance of rail parcels, goods, and mineral depots. In 1887 the Society decided to create a new manufacturing complex at Shieldhall, down river from their existing facilities. This was intended to be directly rail-served by a branch from the Glasgow & Paisley Joint Railway, and to incorporate a model housing estate for the employees. In the event, though, the electrified extension of the old Vale of Clyde tram route from Glasgow to Govan to serve the new site made the housing development unnecessary. The large scale of the Society's operations in Glasgow was not equalled elsewhere, but it had its own jute works at Dundee, woollen mill at Selkirk and its own creamery at Bladnoch, near Whithorn, linked into the integrated provision of cooperatively-produced goods for the retail societies.

The rise of the SCWS was paralleled by that of the United Cooperative Bakery Society,[176] which from 1887 developed a very large-scale central bakery in Hutchestontown, Glasgow, with branches in Clydebank and Belfast, supplying retail societies, principally by road. The UCBS's provision for van and horse-stabling was correspondingly extensive. The timing of the Society's expansion relates closely to urban growth in the Clyde Valley and in the Belfast area stimulated by the expansion of shipbuilding, steelmaking and coalmining, and to the development of the roller milling of hard wheat for flour that made white bread of consistent quality both easy to produce on a large scale and an attractive product. The UCBS was only the largest of the many centralised bread and biscuit bakeries founded from the late 1870s onwards. J & B Stevenson, the pioneers, in 1891 had '50 or 60 large vans and about 70 horses for deliveries'.[177]

CIVIC ADMINISTRATION

The centralisation of administration was a notable feature of mid and late Victorian Britain, and was certainly linked closely to improvements in transport and communications. The reform of local government in Scotland in 1833[178] created conditions in which socially conscious local politicians could develop schemes for municipal improvement, but not until transport and communications improved did large-scale projects materialise, stimulated to some extent by a growing awareness of the experiences of other local authorities.

Better postal services led to more efficient local as well as national administration, better transport allowed urban areas to expand, and funnelled more commerce into town and city centres. The increase in rateable value thus created allowed the burden of existing services, such as the maintenance of a police force and the administration of the Poor Law to be spread more thinly, leaving scope for the imposition of rates to support borrowing for major capital projects. The success of the first such schemes, including Glasgow's Loch Katrine water works,[179] encouraged city administrations, led in many instances by prominent businessmen and industrialists, to expand their ideas, taking in gas supply[180] and tramway construction, between 1860 and 1880, as well as hospital building and slum clearance. In the 1890s tramway operation, electricity supply and telephones (briefly) were assumed as municipal responsibilities. The efficient operation of these centrally-provided services had a multiplier effect, increasing the attractiveness of Glasgow in particular as a place in which to live. Most of these services relied on developing transport facilities. Large central hospitals, for instance, could only be operated where internal transport allowed staff, patients and visitors to be moved relatively easily, and where fuel and other essentials could be effectively and cheaply supplied. The massive municipal gas works and electricity generating stations were mostly sited on rail-linked sites to allow cheap supplies of coal to be tapped. Glasgow's and Edinburgh's series of international exhibitions, symbols of civic pride and achievement were also *de facto* celebrations of transport improvement, and it is significant that the electrification of Glasgow's tramways was timed to coincide with the 1901 exhibition and that Edinburgh's Scottish National Exhibition of 1908 had its own rail service with a specially built station.[181]

EMPLOYMENT

The censuses of 1891, 1901 and 1911[182] allow the employment generated directly by transport to be analysed. The full extent of the numbers employed in transport and communications cannot, however, be judged, owing to the grouping of unrelated trades, as in the category 'Messengers, Porters, Watchmen', and to the problem of assessing the proportion of those in the hotel and inn trades who served travellers, and of those who worked in mechanical engineering who were engaged in the manufacture and maintenance of locomotives and electric tramcars. With these reservations, however, approximate calculations can be made which show that the numbers of men directly employed (including private coachmen, chauffeurs, etc.) rose from about 94,000 in 1891 to 121,000 in 1901 and 132,000 in 1911. These totals relate to those returned as engaged in railway and road operation and vehicle (other than locomotive and electric tram) construction. The percentage increases of 29 between 1891 and 1901 and 9 between 1901 and 1911 conceal wide variations in the numbers employed in individual sectors. In the railway service the increase between 1891 and 1901 was 18.6 per cent and between 1901 and 1911 15.5 per cent. Road service operatives increased between 1891 and 1901 by 27.5 per cent, but by only 5.7 per cent between 1901 and 1911, while those involved in road vehicle building increased by 29.4 per cent between 1891 and 1901 and by 27.7 per cent between 1901 and 1911. Geographical subdivision exposes more extreme differences. Though the number of railway service employees increased in all the cities by proportions varying from 21.5 per cent (Glasgow) to 28.1 per cent (Aberdeen) between 1891 and 1901 and from 10.4 per cent (Aberdeen) to 29.3 per cent (Edinburgh) between 1901 and 1911, the numbers of road service employees fluctuated much more dramatically. Increases in the period 1891 to 1901 ranged between 40.8 per cent (Edinburgh) to 70.2 per cent (Aberdeen) for those directly employed in road transport. In contrast, between 1901 and 1911 numbers dropped in all the cities, by proportions ranging from 3.5 per cent (Edinburgh) to 10.2 per cent (Dundee). In vehicle building, despite a substantial overall increase between 1901 and 1911, only Dundee of the cities recorded an increase (7.9 per cent), the others losing numbers by proportions between 0.6 per cent (Edinburgh) to 6.8 per cent (Glasgow). Glasgow's loss was more apparent than real, as three of its major vehicle producers moved outside the boundary during the period, two of them (Albion and Halley) to areas immediately adjacent to the city.

The increasing number of land transport workers employed in urban communities is even more strikingly demonstrated by the Census figures for the 'burghal group', which incorporated the cities. Between 1891 and 1901 the increase for that group was 68 per cent, compared with 37 per cent for the cities and only 23 per cent for the country as a whole. Taking the non-city burghs as a group the increase was nearly 120 per cent. 21 per cent of transport employees were in non-city burghs, 36 per cent in cities and 43 per cent in 'rural' areas. In 1901, however, the 'rural' proportion had declined to 22 per cent, while that of the non-city burghs had risen to 37 per cent and of the cities to 41 per cent. Unfortunately the omission of the 'burghal group' aggregation from the 1911 census makes later comparison impossible, for that category, though the proportion living in the cities had dropped by that year to 37 per cent.

CONCLUSION

Of the few positive conclusions that can be drawn from a study such as this, the most striking is certainly the extent to which public use of passenger transport increased during the period from 1830 to 1914. Assuming that the figures quoted for Glasgow in the New Statistical Account were reasonably accurate, about 1.6m passengers a year used public transport in or into Glasgow. In 1913–14 nearly 337m passengers used Glasgow Corporation Tramways alone, and it seems not unreasonable to suggest that the total number of people using public transport in or into the city was at least 400m. This represents an increase of something like 25,000 per cent. During this period the population of Glasgow rose from about 212,000 to about 953,000, or 450 per cent. The use of public transport per head of population thus increased by a factor of about 55. No more impressive demonstration of the developing significance of transport to the city during the Victorian period can be made.

In some ways use of transport had, however, declined. The development of the telegraph and the telephone reduced the need for the physical communication of messages by letter or by personal contact, though the explosion of communication by all means obscured this phenomenon. The extension of water carriage of sewage reduced the volume of night-soil traffic handled and had all but eliminated this unpleasant custom from the major cities by 1914. Distribution of gas and electricity by pipe and wire also reduced traffic within urban areas, at the expense of volume movement of fuel for gasworks and generating stations. The reduction of these traffics undoubtedly eased the congestion that was a feature of major thoroughfares in all cities by the 1880s, and in conjunction with the facilities offered by the railways for goods and mineral traffic allowed passenger road transport to develop dramatically after 1890.

The author is acutely conscious that this type of paper raises more issues than it can conclusively explore. It is however, contended that the absence of any substantial comparative work in this field, other than Ochojna's pioneering study of Glasgow and Edinburgh, justifies the exploratory approach adopted. Quantitative material does exist in readily accessible sources, and no doubt intensive exploration of the increasingly-well-organised civic and regional archives, and of the British Transport collection in the Scottish Record Office will reveal more. It is hoped that some of the themes introduced in this paper will stimulate both historians and geographers to become involved in this fascinating if difficult area, particularly in comparative studies.

ACKNOWLEDGEMENTS

The author would like to thank his colleagues Tom Devine and Jim Treble for their help in the preparation of this article. He is also most grateful to Miss Karen Sinclair, Miss Dorothy Marshall, Mr R W Brash, and Mr William Hume for information, and to Miss Janet Telfer for typing the manuscript.

REFERENCES

1   Alexander Ochojna, 'Lines of Class Distinction', unpublished PhD Thesis, Edinburgh University, 1974.
2   J R Kellett, *The Impact of Railways on Victorian Cities* (London, 1969).
3   Michael Simpson, 'Urban Transport and the Development of Glasgow's West End', *Journal of Transport History* (2nd series), vol. I, no. 3; see also M A Simpson and T H Lloyd (eds.), *Middle Class Housing in Britain* (Newton Abbot, 1977).
4   D L G Hunter, *Edinburgh's Transport* (Huddersfield, 1964).
5   Ian L Cormack, *Tramways of the Monklands* (1964), *Lanarkshire Tramways* (1970), *Tramways of Greenock, Gourock & Port Glasgow* (1975), all published in Glasgow; Alan W. Brotchie, *Tramways of the Tay Valley* (1965), *The Tramways of Falkirk* (1975), *The Tramways of Stirling* (1976), *The Wemyss and District Tramways Co Ltd* (1976), *The Tramways of Kirkcaldy* (1978), all published in Dundee; also Ian M Coonie and R R Clark, *The Tramways of Paisley and District, 1885–1954* (Glasgow, 1954) and M J Mitchell and I A Souter, *The Aberdeen Suburban Tramways* (Dundee, 1980).
6   R H Campbell, *Scotland since 1707* (Oxford, 1965), pp. 90–6, all on railways, mostly pre 1850. Bruce Lenman, *An Economic History of Modern Scotland,* pp. 166–73, mainly on railways; S G E Lythe and J Butt, *An Economic History of Scotland,* pp.193–200, mainly on railways, and dealing only with the period up to 1870; Anthony Slaven, *The Development of the West of Scotland 1750–1860,* (London, 1975), pp. 41–8, all on railways up to 1870.
7   Ian H Adams, *The Making of Urban Scotland* (London, 1978), pp. 105–25.
8   See the *Statistical Account of Scotland* (OSA) and the *New Statistical Account of Scotland* (NSA), passim.
9   Jean Lindsay, *The Canals of Scotland* (Newton Abbot, 1968).
10 Bertram Baxter, *Stone Blocks & Iron Rails* (Newton Abbot, 1966); George Dott, *Early Scottish Colliery Wagonways* (1947); John Thomas, *A Regional History of the Railways of Great Britain, Vol. 6, Scotland: the Lowlands and the Borders* (Newton Abbot, 1971).

11 Thomas, op. cit.; S G E Lythe, and Charles E Lee, 'The Dundee & Newtyle Railway', *The Railway Magazine 1951*, vol. 97, pp. 546–50, 689–94, 847–51; Don Martin, *The Monkland & Kirkintilloch Railway* and *The Garnkirk & Glasgow Railway* (both Bishopbriggs, 1976 and 1981).

12 *NSA, vol. VI, Lanarkshire*, (Edinburgh, 1845), p. 206.

13 Lindsay, op. cit.

14 Maps of the period, such as George Martin's Map of the City of Glasgow, 1842. See John Gunn and Marion I Newbigin, *The City of Glasgow, its origin, growth and development* (Edinburgh 1921) for an article by John Arthur Brown on the Cartography of the City.

15 Maps of the period; Post Office Directories; see John R Hume, *The Industrial Archaeology of Glasgow* (Glasgow 1974), passim.

16 Lindsay, op. cit. p. 218.

17 J D Marwick, *The River Clyde* (Glasgow, 1909); also John F Riddell, *Clyde Navigation* (Edinburgh, 1980).

18 *NSA*, vol. VI, p. 169.

19 Thomas, op. cit.

20 Scottish Record Office, BTC EGR 1/6 First Minute Book of the Edinburgh & Glasgow Railway, p. 407: 'The gauge was fixed on 4 May 1840 at 4'8½" rather than 5'6", the gauge of the Dundee & Arbroath and Arbroath & Forfar. Conversion of the 4'6" Lanarkshire lines and of the Arbroath railway took place in the mid-late 1840s.'

21 T R Gourvish, 'The Railways and Steamboat Competition in Early Victorian Britain', *Transport History*, vol. 4 (1971), pp. 1–22.

22 Lindsay, op. cit. pp. 99–112; H A Vallance, *The Great North of Scotland Railway* (2nd ed.) (Newton Abbot, 1963).

23 *Glasgow Herald.*

24 Gourvish, loc. cit.

25 Lindsay, op. cit. pp. 62–3.

26 James W Lowe, *British Steam Locomotive Builders* (Cambridge, 1975). See also John Thomas, *The North British Railway*, vol. 1 (Newton Abbot, 1969), ch. 3, and the same author's *The Springburn Story* (Newton Abbot, 1964).

27 Thomas, *Regional History*, pp. 166–8, 239–44.

28 *Glasgow Post Office Directory 1847–1848* (Glasgow, 1847).

29 C L D Duckworth and G E Langmuir, see *Clyde River and Other Steamers* (3rd ed.) (Glasgow, 1972), and Captain James Williamson, *The Clyde Passenger Steamer* (Glasgow, 1904).

30 Censuses. Figures for cities quoted by B R Mitchell and P Deane, *Abstract of British Historical Statistics* (London, 1972), pp. 24–7.

31 See for instance W Ferguson, *Scotland 1689 to the Present* (Edinburgh and London, 1968).

32 S G Checkland, *Scottish Banking, a History, 1695–1973* (Glasgow and London, 1975).

33 [J B M Fleming], *Kelvinside* (Glasgow, 1894), pp. 17–20.

34 G J Kennison, 'Robert Napier: Entrepreneur and Contractor to the Admiralty', unpublished MLitt thesis, Strathclyde University, 1978.

35 As for instance the creation of George Square in 1782, and of Blythswood Square in the 1830s.

36 Designed by Charles Wilson, and built from the early 1850s round the Kelvingrove Park.

37 West Pollokshields, the villa area, was constituted a Police Burgh in 1876.

38 Ordnance Survey maps, Post Office Directories. Dowanhill was developed from the 1850s, Partickhill from the 1840s and Dennistoun from the 1850s.

39 John R Hume, 'The Prehistory of the University', *University of Strathclyde Gazette* (Third Term 1981), pp. 17–21.

40 See the mews lanes in the Park and Kelvinside developments.

41 Post Office Directories, Scottish Development Department *List of Buildings of Architectural and Historic Interest.*

42 *Bradshaw's Railway Guides,* passim.

43 T C Barker and C I Savage, *An Economic History of Transport in Britain* (3rd ed.) (London, 1974), pp. 129–30.

44 Ibid. p. 130.

45 The Glasgow Street Tramways Act, 33 and 34 Victoria, c.175, 1870. For later acts see J D Marwick, *Glasgow: the Water Supply of the City* (Glasgow, 1901).

46 Edinburgh Tramways Act, 34 & 35 Vict c.189, 1971; see also D L G Hunter, op. cit. pp. 17–19.

47 H R MacKenzie and A W Brotchie, *Aberdeen's Trams 1874–1958* (Glasgow, 1974). The first section was built under 35 & 36 Vict c. 194.

48 Alan Brotchie, *Tramways of the Tay Valley,* pp. 21, 23. This first tramway was constructed under 35 & 36 Vict c. 191, 1872.

49 For the year 1877–8 House of Commons Paper 1878, 344.

50 John Butt, 'Working Class Housing in Glasgow, 1851–1914', in S D Chapman (ed.), *The History of Working Class Housing* (Newton Abbot, 1971), p. 71.

51 Colin Johnston and John R Hume, *Glasgow Stations* (Newton Abbot, 1979).

52 Ibid. pp. 56–7.

53 Thomas, *Regional History,* pp. 203–4.

54 John Thomas, *The North British Railway,* vol. 2 (Newton Abbot, 1975), pp. 140–5.

55 Ibid. pp. 216–21.

56 Anon., *Glasgow District Subway: Its Construction and Equipment* (reprinted London, 1970); David L Thomson and David E Sinclair, *The Glasgow Subway* (Glasgow, 1964).

57 Exemplified by the construction of the Glasgow Harbour Tunnel in 1890–1896 to relieve pressure on the bridges, and the rebuilding of the Jamaica Bridge in 1894–9.

58 Glasgow Police (Amendment) Act, 53 & 54 Vict c. 221, 1890, clause 30. *Not* the 1892 Act as stated by F W Worsdall, *The Tenement* (Edinburgh, 1979). I am indebted to Miss Alison Gray, Education Officer, Strathclyde Regional Archives for this reference.

59 Board of Trade Returns show that route mileage increased from 16 miles 64 chains in 1879–80 to 30 miles 17 chains in 1887–8.

60 J M Lamb, 'Glasgow—The Pioneer of Municipal Tramway Enterprise', unpublished BA dissertation, Department of History, University of Strathclyde; Ian Cormack, *1894 and all that* (Glasgow, 1968).

61 Board of Trade Returns show that route mileage increased from 30 miles 17 chains in 1893–4 to 40 miles 36 chains in 1900–1.

62 Jack Kernahan, *The Cathcart Circle* (Falkirk, 1980), pp. 40–1.

63 G H Robin, 'The Lanarkshire & Dunbartonshire Railway', *The Railway Magazine*, (1959), pp. 19–26; 'The Lanarkshire & Ayrshire Railway', Ibid., 1961, pp. 89–96; Thomas, *Regional History*, pp. 224–5.

64 Ochojna, op. cit.; also Lamb, op. cit.

65 For details see James Mitchell, 'The Electrification of the Glasgow Tramways', unpublished BA dissertation, Department of History, University of Strathclyde, 1973.

66 Board of Trade Returns: Receipts role from £489,469 in 1900–1 to £614,413 in 1901–2, and to £899,352 in 1906–7 and to £1,148,837 in 1913–14.

67 Kernahan, op. cit. p. 46; Thomas, *Regional History*, pp. 221–2.

68 Thomas, *Regional History*, pp. 224–5.

69 W H Bett and J C Gillham, *Great British Tramway Networks* (4th ed.) (London, 1962), pp. 132–5.

70 Dean of Guild records of Glasgow and suburban burghs held in Strathclyde Regional Archives.

71 See below COMMERCIAL ACTIVITY pp. 220–222; also John Hume, op. cit. passim.

72 Glasgow companies specialising in goods vehicle building, included Albion, Hally and Alley and MacLellan (Sentinel).

73 D L G Hunter, op. cit. pp. 67–73; also D L G Hunter, 'The Edinburgh Cable Tramways', *Journal of Transport History*, 1953–4, vol. 1, p. 171.

74 Hunter, op. cit. pp. 73–113.

75 Brotchie, *Tramways of the Tay Valley*, pp. 29–34, 41–50.

76 So far the only publication dealing in detail with Aberdeen Corporation's system is the pamphlet, H R MacKenzie and A W Brotchie, *Aberdeen's Trams 1874–1958* (Glasgow, 1974).

77 H A Whitcombe, *History of the Steam Tram* (Lingfield, Surrey, 1961), p. 4 of introduction by Charles E Lee.

78 M Morton Hunter, 'The Govan Burgh Tramways', *Scottish Transport*, 1975, no. 27, p. 3. Ibid. pp. 7, 8.

79 Board of Trade Returns show that from its opening in 1879 to its takeover by The Glasgow Tramway & Omnibus Co. in 1891, there were only four years when a profit was recorded.

80 Coonie and Clark, op. cit. pp. 5–7, see also Board of Trade Returns.

81 Brotchie, *Tramways of the Tay Valley*, pp. 7–11.

82 Alan Leach, 'Rothesay Tramways: a brief history 1882–1936', *Transactions of the Buteshire Natural History Society* (1969), vol. 17, pp. 6–30.

83 Brotchie, *The Tramways of Stirling*.

84 Leach, loc. cit.

85 R W Brash, 'Ayr Corporation Tramways 1901–1931', *Scottish Tramlines* (1963), no. 2.

86 Brian T Deans, 'Kilmarnock's Trams', *Scottish Tramlines* (1969), no. 17, pp. 4–15.

87 Brotchie, *The Tramways of Kirkcaldy*.

88 Cormack, *Tramways of the Monklands*.

89 Cormack, *Lanarkshire Tramways.*
90 Coonie and Clark, op. cit. pp. 11–13.
91 James Campbell, 'A Tram Ride to Loch Lomond', *Scottish Transport* (1973), no. 23, pp. 2–8.
92 Brotchie, *The Wemyss and District Tramways Co. Ltd.*
93 A W Brotchie, 'The Dunfermline and District Tramways Company', *Scottish Transport* (1973), no. 24, pp. 2–8.
94 MacKenzie and Brotchie, op. cit.
95 Hunter, op. cit., pp. 135–40.
96 Brotchie, *Tramways of the Tay Valley,* pp. 82–7.
97 Bett and Gilham, op. cit., pp. 132–46, see also histories of individual systems.
98 Published as House of Commons Papers. The following paragraphs are based on these returns, unless otherwise specified.
99 The operating ratio between operating costs and receipts, expressed as a fraction.
100 *Census Reports for 1891, 1901, 1911,* passim.
101 Used by Ochojna, loc. cit. p. 205.
102 Ibid. p. 228, endorsing Michael Simpson's view in loc. cit.
103 Railway Returns, published as House of Commons Command Papers.
104 See n. 67.
105 Johnston and Hume, op. cit. passim.
106 The City of Glasgow District and Glasgow Central railways.
107 The City of Glasgow Union Railway, see G H Robin, 'The City of Glasgow Union Railway', *The Railway Magazine* (1959), pp. 19–26; Thomas, *Regional History,* pp. 199–202.
108 Hunter, op. cit. p. 152. The Edinburgh Suburban & South Side Junction Railway.
109 There were services to Tayport, on the Arbroath line, local services to Perth and on the Dundee & Newtyle. The Aberdeen suburban services ran to Dyce and Peterculter, H A Vallance, *A History of the Great North of Scotland Railway* (2nd ed.) (Newton Abbot, 1963), pp. 99–100.
110 Johnston and Hume, op. cit. pp. 132–49.
111 Kernahan, op. cit. p. 47.
112 Oral evidence from William Hume, Glasgow, referring to the years immediately before the First World War.
113 Especially imported chilled meat from Glasgow docks.
114 The Caledonian Railway built a large potato shed at Buchanan Street Goods Depot in 1908–9, for the use of six wholesalers. Johnston and Hume, op. cit. pp. 148–9.
115 *Stratten's Glasgow and its Environs* (London, 1891), pp. 222–3, referring to the United Creameries Ltd. whose Dunragit Creamery, near Stranraer, daily sent milk and milk products to Glasgow and Edinburgh.
116 Bread vans were fitted out by the Caledonian Railway, and ran from Buchanan Street Station.
117 The Ayr Harbour Branch was built in 1899; see The Stephenson Locomotive Society, *The Glasgow and South Western Railway* (London, 1950), facing p. 9.
118 There were three large breweries (Deuchar's, Dryborough's and Raeburn) and two extensive maltings (Craigmillar and Tennent's) in this area. See John R

Hume, *The Industrial Archaeology of Scotland: The Lowlands and Borders* (London, 1976), pp. 185, 189–90.

119 Alfred Barnard, *Noted Breweries of Great Britain and Ireland*, vol. II (London, 1889), pp. 431–2, 449, new Export Bulk Cellar 'specially erected for the purpose, by the side of the railway'.

120 Hume, *I A of Glasgow*, Vaux built a store in 1911, (p. 165), Bass and the Annfield Bottling stores (p. 187) and Whitbread built a bottling works in 1907–10 (p. 166).

121 Michael S Moss and John R Hume, *The Making of Scotch Whisky* (Edinburgh, 1981).

122 Hume, *I A of Glasgow*, p. 212, The Glasgow & South Western's whisky warehouse in Bell Street cost £100,000. The arches under St Enoch, Central and High Street Goods stations were all used by blenders.

123 Thomas, *Regional History*, pp. 244–5, 248–9.

124 Neilson & Co, the largest locomotive builders in Scotland moved in 1850 to Springburn to gain rail access. The Stephen and Fairfield yards in Govan laid in rail connections to the Govan Tramways, M Morton Hunter, loc. cit. pp. 3, 4. The Fairfield connection was opened on 27 June 1873.

125 The trend towards municipal ownership encouraged construction of new works on rail-linked sites, e.g. Dawsholm & Provan (Glasgow) and Granton (Edinburgh). The Dalmarnock and Aberdeen works developed rail connections to allow output to expand.

126 Only Port Dundas of the large city stations built from the 1890s was not rail-linked. Partick had its own street tramway.

127 Hume, *I A of Glasgow*, passim.

128 Thomas, *Regional History*, pp. 179–80.

129 Ibid. pp. 204–5.

130 Robin, *Lanarkshire & Dunbartonshire Railway*.

131 This transport-based complex has parallels in England, for instance Trafford Park, Manchester.

132 *Handbook of Stations on the Railways in the United Kingdom* (London, 1904).

133 Quoted in Johnston and Hume, op. cit. p. 134.

134 *Returns of Capital, Traffic &c.*

135 F Groome, *Ordnance Gazetteer of Scotland* (1891 ed.), vol. V, pp. 123–6.

136 C L D Duckworth and G E Langmuir, *West Highland Steamers* (3rd ed.), 1967, gives details of the development of services.

137 Gordon Donaldson, *Northwards by Steam: a History of the North of Scotland Steam Packet Co.* (Edinburgh, 1966).

138 Angus Martin, *The Ring-Net Fishermen* (Edinburgh, 1981).

139 Malcolm Gray, *The Fishing Industries of Scotland, 1790–1914* (Aberdeen, 1978).

140 *Third Statistical Account of Scotland: The City of Aberdeen* (Edinburgh and London, 1953), pp. 161–5.

141 See Ian H Adams, *The Making of Urban Scotland*, pp. 117–18. Iain Hope, *The Campbells of Kilmun* (Johnstone, 1981), has a brief but good introduction on early steamer services to the Holy Loch and the Gareloch.

142 Marwick, *River Clyde*, pp. 228–9.

143 Ibid.

144 Ibid. p. 229.
145 Sylvia Price, 'Riveters' Earnings in Clyde Shipbuilding 1889–1913', *Scottish Economic & Social History*, vol. 1, no. 1 (1981), pp. 42–65.
146 Abstracted from the *Reports of the Chief Constable of the City of Glasgow*, passim, by Dr J H Treble, to whom the author is most grateful.
147 Judith A Lawson, *The Building Stones of Glasgow* (Glasgow, 1981).
148 T M Donnelly, 'The Development of the Aberdeen Granite Industry, 1750–1939', unpublished PhD thesis, Aberdeen University, 1975; also the same author's 'Structural and Technical Change in the Aberdeen Granite Quarrying Industry, 1830–1880', *Industrial Archaeology Review*, 3 (1979), 228–37.
149 Ordnance Survey Maps. Forthcoming report by Scottish Industrial Archaeology Survey on the Brick and Tile Industry in Scotland.
150 Ibid. Kilmarnock, Paisley and Barrhead were noted for white-glazed products, while pipes were made in Lanarkshire, at Dunfermline, at Prestonpans and in the Kilmarnock area.
151 See R L Hunter, Cockburn's 1864–1977, The Rise & Fall of a Falkirk Foundry, privately published 1980; also R H Campbell, *Carron Company* (Edinburgh, 1961).
152 Lindsay, op. cit. p. 218; John L Carvel, *One Hundred Years in Timber* (Glasgow, 1949).
153 Kernahan, op. cit. p. 47.
154 Ordnance Survey Maps; *Railway Clearing House Handbook of Stations*.
155 David Bremner, *The Industries of Scotland* (Edinburgh, 1869), pp. 424–32; Barbara Fairweather, *A Short History of Ballachulish Slate Quarry*, (Glencoe, n.d.) Margaret Macdonald, 'The Economic and Social Development of the Easdale Slate Quarries, 1745–1914', unpublished MLitt thesis, Strathclyde University, 1978.
156 Dan McDonald, *The Clyde Puffer* (Newton Abbot, 1977), p. 47; I L Donnachie, J Hume and M Moss, *Historic Industrial Scenes, Scotland* (Buxton), p. 51.
157 Gillespie (Slaters) Ltd, New Sneddon Street, Paisley.
158 In Perthshire near Aberfoyle, at Craiglea, and Dunkeld. Bremner, op. cit. p. 432. The Aberfoyle quarry was linked by narrow gauge railway to the village.
159 Alexander Fenton and Bruce Walker, *The Rural Architecture of Scotland* (Edinburgh, 1981), pp. 69–70. Pantiles were certainly used earlier and more.
160 Bremner, op. cit. p. 410.
161 See C A Oakley, op. cit. p. 72, illustration showing setts being loaded into works tram at Clyde Street.
162 Thomas, *The North British Railway*, vol. II, p. 206.
163 Basil Skinner, *The Lime Industry of the Lothians* (Edinburgh, 1969).
164 S G Checkland, op. cit.
165 The introduction of roller milling in the 1880s led to the building of large new mills, such as Regent Mills, Glasgow and Chancelot Mills, Edinburgh (see below).
166 Pioneers included R & B Stevenson and the United Co-operative Baking Society. Hume, *I A of Glasgow*, pp. 10–13.
167 Ibid. pp. 8–9, 22–3.

168 For instance Campbells, Stewart & MacDonalds factory in Montrose Street, Glasgow, Strattens Glasgow, pp. 47–9 and Arthur & Co's shirt factory in William Street, Glasgow. John Barclay, *The Story of Arthur & Co Ltd.* (Glasgow, 1953), p. 103.

169 Matthew Blair, *The Paisley Thread Industry* (Paisley, 1907).

170 For example J & P Coats Anchor (formerly Clarks) and Ferguslie Mills in Paisley had rail connections, and the company built a distribution warehouse in Kinning Park in 1907–8. Hume, *I A of Glasgow,* p. 246.

171 Ibid. pp. 44–5.

172 See for instance Donnachie, Hume and Moss, op. cit. p. 123.

173 Notably in Glasgow on West Nile Street from St Vincent Street to Buchanan Street, used intensively for drays, but also in 'dock areas', including Port Dundas.

174 Hume, *I A of Glasgow,* pp. 111–14.

175 Jas A Flanagan, *Wholesale Co-operation in Scotland* (Glasgow, 1919). James Kinloch and John Butt, *History of the SCWS Ltd.* (Manchester, 1981).

176 W Reid, *History of the United Co-operative Baking Society* (Glasgow, 1920).

177 *Stratten's Glasgow,* pp. 57–9.

178 3 & 4 William 1V, c. 76, 28 Aug. 1833; Marwick, *Water Supply,* p. 96.

179 Ibid. pp. 128–44.

180 Glasgow Corporation Gas Department, *The Gas Supply of Glasgow* (Glasgow, 1935).

181 Hunter, op. cit. pp. 159–60.

182 Censuses: women have been excluded, as the numbers employed in transport were tiny.

10

WORKING CLASS HOUSING IN THE SCOTTISH CITIES 1900–1950

J Butt

Since the pioneering volume[1] edited by Dr Stanley Chapman in 1971 the history of working-class housing in Britain has become a major area of study for urban historians and other social scientists concerned with the development of social policy.[2] Books, papers and conference discussions have enlivened what some regard as a dreary subject, and a growing body of theoretical concepts drawn from a range of disciplines has emerged as a tool kit. The nature of the building cycle, social control and working class incorporation, the role of women in agitation for better housing and reform, the position of the 'aristocracy of labour' in housing politics, and the significance of world war as a catalyst for change in national policy have all been examined from new angles, although often on the basis of limited evidence. In particular, comparative experience has been neglected—either in favour of case-studies or, when the desire for safe but limited generalisation has palled, authors have produced wide-ranging books in which aggregate information and exciting hypotheses have warred with one another, with only ideological preconceptions maybe remaining triumphant.

In this essay the comparative experiences of the four cities of Aberdeen, Dundee, Edinburgh and Glasgow are examined in the Scottish context mainly, partly to elucidate what differences existed between them and partly to explain how national policy evolved as it did and with what results. This is in no way to suggest that smaller burghs are not worth examining—or for that matter that rural and village housing problems were unimportant. Although the treatment of the Scottish context must necessarily be brief, I hope it will be possible to dispel any doubts that concentration on these four cities implies any disregard for the housing problems of the rural, village or small town communities. Nonetheless the main burden of the chapter will be concerned with the problems of overcrowding and inadequate household amenities in the cities and how local and national government responded to these challenges, for what reasons and with what consequences.

I

PROBLEMS OF WORKING CLASS HOUSING IN THE SCOTTISH CONTEXT

As anyone who has examined the history of housing in rural or mining villages or small towns will amply confirm, the provision of housing for the working classes was not only a city problem in the early twentieth century. About half the people in Scotland lived in houses of one or two rooms, according to the census of 1901, and there was little shift in this proportion by 1931, when 44 per cent inhabited such dwellings. A major change occurred between 1931 and 1951: at the latter date only 25.8 per cent still occupied these small houses. [3]

One apartment dwellings were an important component of the total housing stock in the early decades of the century but already by 1901 had been roundly condemned for more than twenty years by professional men of influence such as Dr J B Russell (1837–1904) who, apart from his commitment to the problems of Glasgow, was Medical Member of the Local Government Board for Scotland for some years before his death. [4] Yet at the Census of 1901 11.02 per cent of the population of Scotland lived in houses of one apartment; for the burghs of Paisley, Greenock and Kilmarnock the figures were respectively 13.5 per cent, 11.29 per cent and 18.93 per cent. In 1910 most of the miners in Lanarkshire, an expanding coalfield, lived in houses of two apartments—over 52 per cent, in fact—but there were 2,358 'single-ends' or about 10 per cent of the county's housing stock. [5] Of itself, the existence of more rooms than one in a house is not sufficient evidence of improving housing conditions; it is necessary to examine occupancy rates and to investigate the general question of overcrowding which in most mining districts and especially in Lanarkshire was certainly a major problem.

Generally, the poorest sections of the community lived in the most overcrowded conditions, and mortality rates under these circumstances were naturally high. In 1911 56 per cent of all one-roomed dwellings were occupied by more than two persons; this occupancy rate per room was true also of 47 per cent of two apartment houses and of 24 per cent of three-roomed dwellings. [6] The extent of overcrowding was determined partly by income and family size but also by the practice of keeping lodgers. Over 20 per cent of the 'single-ends' of 1911 were occupied by five or more persons, often including at least one lodger. [7] County medical officers as well as urban doctors revealed that Scotland was an overcrowded community as far as its housing stock was concerned: rural communities on Lewis, in Shetland or in Nairn were shown to be as badly accommodated as any city dweller, although, no doubt, their environment and amenity made their housing conditions less obvious to the occasional visitor. [8]

Temporary or seasonal migration also placed additional strains on an overextended housing stock. Local authorities in various parts of Scotland had been long concerned about the public health aspects of this problem. Herring curers and gutters migrated seasonally and in places like Barra trebled the local population for the season, living in poor wooden shacks. Potato-picking, the berry harvest and the building of public utilities posed different facets of the same problem which vigilant local authority sanitary inspectors found embarrassing.[9]

'Farmed-out' houses which were let or rented furnished added another problem for local authorities. Tenants were often poor or improvident; the furnishing was commonly meagre and unclean. Profitable to the house-farmer, these dwellings were a danger to the local community's health and therefore, commonly attracted the attention of the local sanitary inspector.[10] Much property was being 'made down', i.e. subdivided, in already densely populated parts of towns and cities, and there was extensive use of boxrooms as bedrooms, often with the only access to the kitchen.[11]

Insanitary conditions clearly arose from many causes, but the result in housing terms was the development of more and more slum property, some of it old but some of it purpose-built for the working classes in the late nineteenth century. Small burghs such as Port Glasgow encountered this problem in the first decade of the twentieth century just as the cities had met it earlier.[12] They relied on local authority demolition orders, but this accentuated problems since there was little or no building specifically designed to rehouse the dispossessed tenants. Between 1890 and 1913 only 3484 families were rehoused by local authorities, an average of just over 151 each year.[13] Thus the effects of early slum clearance schemes were to push the dispossessed into the next cheapest accommodation and to force up rents and occupancy levels in adjacent districts.

Common lodging houses were generally cheaper than 'farmed' houses, but the inhabitants of both types of property were essentially the same type, unskilled and mobile workers with low incomes earned in insecure and irregular employment. Regulations for controlling lodging houses were often made by the local authority under the terms of the Public Health Act of 1875. Some such as Glasgow provided model lodging houses and were accused of encouraging the break-up of marriages, since they housed the man who deserted his wife along with the single man looking for temporary accommodation. The 'modeller' was certainly regarded as a social problem—the lowest stratum in Scottish society inhabited lodging houses and the most rootless.[14]

Inevitably, the inability of most Scottish workers to live in better conditions rested mainly upon the fact that their incomes were inadequate to pay the rents which would have been demanded for improved accommodation. Although there were some improvident individuals who effectively penalised their families by their addiction to alcohol or gambling or both, the poverty line has to be drawn partly in housing terms. Primary poverty was most obviously represented by the 'single-end'. The unskilled were huddled with their dependents in the poorest housing in the poorest areas, and the more casual their pattern of employment the more likely that they would live in overcrowded conditions and in poorly furnished rooms. [15]

Housing supply, if one ignores the quality of provision, seemed to respond relatively well to this poor market. Between 1875 and 1915 the average annual output of houses was 10,727, but there is evidence that private enterprise by the first decade of the twentieth century had saturated that market and indeed created a glut of one or two apartment dwellings. [16] This was essentially a speculative response by small building firms to the rise in rents which was general in Scottish towns, especially in the 1890s. [17] However, costs were also rising as a result of local authority building regulations and increases in wages paid in the building trade. After 1904 higher interest rates caused a marked decline in authorisations for cheaper housing everywhere in Scotland, and output in 1911–12 and 1912–13 fell to 2757 and 2990 houses respectively. [18]

Local authority officals had come to realise before 1914 that there was a housing question which could only be solved by building more homes for the working classes. However, they had not converted a majority of their elected representatives. The Royal Commission on Housing in Scotland appointed in 1912 symbolised the end of at least a decade of local debates. Four distinct divisions within the housing problem had been established: slum clearance; improvement of defective houses; closure and demolition of uninhabitable houses; the provision of new houses. The latter was essentially the task the twentieth century discovered for itself. In that process of education the Report of the Royal Commission published in 1917 was very significant:

> These are the broad results of our survey: unsatisfactory sites of houses and villages, insufficient supplies of water, unsatisfactory provision for drainage, grossly inadequate provision for the removal of refuse, widespread absence of decent sanitary conveniences, the persistence of the unspeakably filthy privy-midden in many of the mining areas, badly constructed, incurably damp labourers' cottages on farms, whole townships unfit for human occupation in the crofting counties and islands, primitive and casual provision for many of the seasonal workers, gross over-crowding and huddling of the sexes together in the congested industrial villages and towns, occupation of one-room houses by large families, groups of lightless and unventilated houses in the older burghs, clotted masses of slums in the great cities. [19]

II

PUBLIC POLICY AND ITS MOTIVATION

Most of the clues relating to the evolution of public policy on housing in the twentieth century can be found in the private practice of the Scottish cities earlier. Under Police Acts and more particularly, the Nuisances Removal and Contagious Diseases Act of 1846 local authorities acquired powers to compel owners to remove any conditions prejudicial to public health and often the right to demolish dangerous or insanitary property. [20] Even at the beginning of the twentieth century local officials were prepared to accept that the prime motivation of, or at least the first step in, housing reform should be sanitary. For instance, James Henry, Surveyor of Police and Municipal Assessments of Glasgow, remarked to the Municipal Commission on Housing in 1903:

> I would say that with cleanliness and good ventilation, a one apartment house may be healthy and comfortable, and in many cases, quite sufficient for the humble occupants. . . . Cleanliness, in my opinion, is the first step in the right direction, and whatever further steps or efforts are made on behalf of the poor, cleanliness, it seems to me, must be one of the first things aimed at.

Moreover, solidarity between the social groups might thereby be forged because he believed that 'the great barrier between the wealthy and the poor is not the poverty of the poor but their dirty houses. Many philanthropic people would seek to help the poor in their homes were these homes not dirty.' [21]

However crude the connection some made between cleanliness and housing reform, more subtle observers had recognised that mortality and poor housing conditions were closely linked. Dr Henry Littlejohn, Medicine Officer of Health in Edinburgh, had established by the 1870s that the districts of Canongate, Tron, St Giles and Grassmarket had death rates much above the average for the city, [22] and the experience in the central areas of the other cities was much the same. Glagow had acquired its City Improvement Act in 1866 and was given powers to spend £1,250,000 in purchasing congested slum property for demolition; this sum was increased to £1,500,000 by Section 2 of the Glasgow Improvements Amendment Act of 1880. [23] From 1868 Dundee was carefully controlling new building in the city and secured its own Improvement Act in 1871 under which landlords were compelled to improve the sanitary condition of their property. [24] In Aberdeen slum clearance was authorised under a local Act of 1881, and areas such as Gallowgate and Castlehill were attacked first since they were regarded as dangerous to public health. Over the next thirty years 2354 houses were closed; 1799 of these had been demolished by 1913 on account of their poor fabric and insanitary condition. [25]

If concern for public health was one motive for slum clearance and housing control, the early recognition that crime, vice and immorality were inevitable consequences of overcrowding and insecurity of tenure was another. Commonly, the advocates of reform were extremists in their assessment of the causes of poor housing provision. [26] Most ascribed an overwhelming importance to failures or inadequacies of a personal kind; they rarely blamed society or its economic organisation. Poor housing was the individual's fault—or at best, a result of misfortune. Hence the solutions advocated were practically always extensions of self-help or mutual improvement by co-operative action. [27] Occasionally, the 'one-nation' ideas of Disraeli's disciples surfaced locally, and

Tory populism of the kind associated with Lord Randolph Churchill found a responsive chord when housing questions were discussed. [28] Although Scotland remained a Liberal stronghold, there developed a religious consensus that poor housing was a blot upon the public conscience, a sign of man's inhumanity to man, and a challenge to radical good intentions. [29] As Labour became more organised from the 1880s—both industrially and politically—Liberalism countered this potential competitor by moving leftwards on social questions including housing reform and in the process produced defectors. Despite the great electoral victory of 1905–6 'working class votes were lent, not given . . .', and in the wings there were politicians ready with a Labour alternative. [30] Yet the New Liberalism had more than a temporary pre-war effect; its revival after 1918 was central to David Lloyd George's plans for retaining political power. [31]

The growing recognition by articulate members of urban communities that many semi-skilled and unskilled workers fought a continuous battle to stay above the poverty line produced pragmatic housing reform before World War I and paved the way for the government subsidy policy afterwards. Eviction was the penalty for non-payment of rent, and the landlord-tenant relationship was part of a wider class conflict which, from time to time, centred on housing. The landlord's position was not all-powerful: only when demand for housing was buoyant could they evict with impunity; arrears of rent at least recognised a liability to pay and in bad times it might be wiser to practise forbearance; the expense of eviction proceedings was often a deterrent, especially when tenants were prepared to lodge defences. Moreover, eviction did not always weed out undesirable tenants; the persistence of unoccupied houses just before World War I in cities like Glasgow and Dundee reflected not merely the effects of cyclical depression but also the temporary weakness of landlords against which they reacted sharply as economic circumstances changed. [32]

It was the undifferentiating policies of landlords that produced the greatest working-class responses since skilled workers were often pressed into leading a wider cohort of their fellows. For instance, the agitation against legally binding long lets which affected most workers and practically all skilled workers was not led by the slum-dwellers who were most vulnerable to eviction but by the organisations formed by artisans and their wives—Trades Councils, Unions, Co-operative Women's Guilds. [33] The state had to make distinctions to incorporate such groups even if it shelved the reports on letting and rating as long as possible.

Much change was foreshadowed by the Housing, Town Planning etc. Act of 1909. Whereas the Housing of the Working Classes Act of 1890 had given powers to burghs to improve, or to close or to demolish houses and also to build for the working classes if they wished to apply for them, the 1909 Act gave them all these powers. Yet the burghs had no obligation to enforce the Act, and no Exchequer assistance was provided. Subsidies were, however, being discussed, and it is important to realise that when they were introduced under the

1919 Act this reflected existing dissatisfaction with the 1909 Act and was not quite the radical departure so often portrayed.[34]

This concern to establish the continuity of policy should not be regarded as a justification of the view that housing reform is best seen as a case of principled pragmatism.[35] However, it is an argument for suggesting firmly that World War I not only interrupted the course of housing reform but also prevented the post-war revival of the housing market under private enterprise conditions. The 'Garden City' movement had made its nostalgic appeal to radicals of all sorts by 1914, and town planning, as the title of the 1909 Act demonstrates, was officially recognised as the right approach to urban renewal.[36] Yet the incentives to build working-class houses virtually ceased after c. 1904. In most cities there were substantial numbers of vacant houses at the time of the Census of 1911; keen competition for tenants existed, and rents were reduced. Net income from house property was adversely affected by the increased costs of repairs and statutory sanitary improvements, by a rise in owners' rates resulting from the House Letting and Rating Act of 1911 and by augmented rates of interest. The costs of labour and building materials rose by about 25 per cent between 1905 and 1914, and alternative investment in government and foreign stocks was more attractive.

The tenants tended to regard the period after 1904 as the reasonable standard for computing rents whereas the landlord hankered after the high rents of the 1890s. The immediate effect of the war was to increase the demand for housing, a process which was accentuated on Clydeside by the influx of munitions workers. Yet interest rates, labour and raw material costs continued to rise under the pressures of war demand. The recovery of the housing market had taken place, but building had not revived and did not restart.[37] Instead of excess supply a house famine occurred, and upward pressure on rent levels was very marked, especially in the Glasgow area.

The rent strike which followed in 1915 was part of a more widespread conflict arising from the inflationary pressures produced by the war.[38] Skilled, semi-skilled and unskilled workers were all affected, but the 'house famine' was most acute in better working-class districts. The City Labour Party Housing Committee formed in 1913 provided the organisation for resistance, and some of the post-war 'Red Clydesiders' such as John Wheatley, George Buchanan, John McGovern and Neil MacLean were involved in a movement consisting of at least 20,000 rent-strikers.[39] The employers were not unified behind the landlords; their economic interests were different. The cheaper housing and rents, the lower wages could be; yet builders, speculators and landlords gain most when rents are high. The State intervened with the Rent and Mortgage Restriction Act of 1915; in part, this was a response to developing working-class militancy, manifest not only in the rent strike but also associated with industrial battles over wages and conditions. But once price had been controlled by the State, it was inevitable that supply of housing would need to be regulated also.

The Ministry of Munitions controlled building during the war, and activity was severely limited. Rosyth, the new naval base begun in 1909, was intended to be a garden suburb on the Raymond Unwin 'Hampstead' model, but no housing was built until after the outbreak of war, and the munitions centre at Gretna was the other principal beneficiary.[40] Generally, the war effectively distorted the use of resources, and the housing stock in Scotland's cities actually declined as a consequence of closures and demolitions. Aging property was not replaced, and thus further deterioration and lack of proper maintenance stored up problems for the post-war generation.

Meanwhile, these difficulties and the social problems arising from them were being carefully documented by the Royal Commission on Housing, appointed in 1912 but not reporting until 1918, yet another indicator that the war may have delayed housing reform. The evidence given to the Commissioners is instructive not merely in outlining the dimensions of the housing problem but also in conveying the social attitudes of the witnesses.

The *Report* roundly condemned the existing housing provision in Scotland, as we have seen, and emphasised the problems of the cities, especially of Glasgow. Dirt, damp and disease were allies drawing their strength from poor housing conditions. Local authorities had the legislative means at their command to rehouse the affected population; they had development control in their district 'to secure proper sanitary conditions, amenity and convenience'.[41] The major problem was undoubtedly cost: without a subsidy policy the burden on the rates would be excessive, and the *Minority Report* favoured allowing normal market forces to operate in the interests of civic economy and value for money.[42]

Some witnesses recognised that purpose-built tenements depreciated, and expectations changed as time passed. In the Cowcaddens district of Glasgow the ground floor flats of tenements came in for particular criticism:[43]

> Ground floor houses are most unwholesome. The smell here frequently makes visiting ladies ill, and they say it is just a breeding ground of consumption. No matter how clean the houses are kept or how well they are ventilated by open windows, the damp filthy smell is there.

Some tenants managed to rise above their environment; what one witness called 'the eternal heroism of the slums' was beyond the reach of most occupiers:[44]

> there are others whose powers of resistance are not so strong, and who fall to the level of their surroundings. There is a remainder—we are glad to think a small and diminishing remainder—whose habits are so uncleanly, and others whose habits are so destructive, that they require to be specially dealt with.

Councillor John Wheatley concurred with the view that there was a 'destructive class', of tenants requiring extra-ordinary treatment.[45] Others believed that municipal housing should be reserved for the well-behaved who could afford economic rents, i.e. the artisan class. The houses vacated by this group would then be let to those lower down the social scale;[46] this process was widely described as 'filtering up' and became a central tenet of Conservative housing policy between the wars.

Housing allocation served to maintain the divisions within the working classes; sectional and cultural differences were thereby sustained. Mary Laird of the Glasgow Women's Labour League admitted that the body she represented consisted of the better paid and that neither she nor it had direct contact with slum-dwellers. However, she attacked the one-room dwelling as being 'incompatible with family decency', an obstacle to 'a healthy or moral family life' and a cause of a greater incidence of disease, especially of tuberculosis, of a higher general death rate and a higher infantile mortality rate. Newly marrieds took 'single-ends' as did those with large families subject to poverty or sharply fluctuating wages. They formed part of a floating population who moved to better accommodation when income allowed. The one-room dwelling should be outlawed for it 'lies on the extreme margin of industrial civilization'.[47]

Overcrowding provided not only the potential for immorality but also the environment for child neglect. Attempts to control overcrowding by ticketing and inspecting houses at night were practised in Glasgow, and yet this activity may have, on occasion, destroyed human dignity: 'When you put a ticket on a house you have stamped it with a certain character which, in the eyes of the decent working classes, is very sinister.'[48]

The inhabitants of common lodging houses and farmed houses received less sympathy. The population of Glasgow's lodging houses were described by the Medical Officer of Health as 'a permanent sore on civilization', and Dr David Watson thought the people in Glasgow's farmed-out houses were mainly there 'through drink, improvidence and laziness'. Prostitutes lived in some of these premises, and this was one more reason why Glasgow Corporation wished to control the letting of this type of property.[49]

If the local authority was concerned about 'social control' over some groups, there was increasing concern about the causes of industrial unrest at national level. The rent strike, the reception of Syndicalism in Scotland as manifested in the evolution of the shop steward's movement and the activities of the Clyde Workers' Committee, the protest Marxist movement associated with John McLean, the development of the Independent Labour Party's support during the war in the cities—all were indications that there might be a fundamental social and political crisis even before the war ended.[50] The Commission of Enquiry into Industrial Unrest reported in the same session as the Royal Commission on Housing, and both reports echo similar sentiments:

The chief root of industrial unrest is the desire of the workers to establish better conditions of life for themselves and their families . . . bad housing may fairly be regarded as a legitimate cause of social unrest . . . so far as housing is concerned, we cannot but record our satisfaction that, after generations of apathy, the workers all over Scotland give abundant evidence of discontent with conditions that no modern community should be expected to tolerate. Industrial unrest, whatever be its ultimate causes, undoubtedly is stimulated, directly and indirectly, by defective housing.

So ran the Report on Housing.[51] It is important to note that whatever the Cabinet thought, the Commissioners were not alarmed by the workers' responses to poor housing conditions; indeed, they believed discontent to be justified.

According to the Report of the Commission appointed to investigate the industrial unrest, organised labour believed that society had not treated the workers fairly, and this belief had led to more and more critical study of social and economic questions. Although the chief source of unrest was the cost of living, especially the cost of food, housing was an important cause for complaint:

We have had startling revelations of the acute need of houses in industrial centres. The want of housing accommodation is undoubtedly a serious cause of unrest, as well as a danger to public health.

The Government had to take the initiative, according to the Report, 'to grapple with a problem which appears to have grown too great for private enterprise to meet . . .'. This meant providing financial aid in the form of subsidies to local authorities and ensuring that land was available on reasonable terms.[52]

Recent work has tended to place the passing of the 1919 Housing Act too firmly as an 'insurance against revolution', while recognising that the housing problem was well known to the Government. This is too simple an analysis and it ignores the evolutionary character of post-war official thought on housing.[53] The 'Garden City' movement was now part of orthodox architecture; reconstruction had been visualised since 1916 and from the beginning had a housing dimension;[54] deflation caused by high interest rates was considered to be the most likely monetary enemy, and massive unemployment could be checked by a government-sponsored building programme.[55] Politicians and civil servants were temporarily abandoning shibboleths such as private enterprise in building and local authorities' bearing the financial burden of rehousing their local populations.[56] It should be noticed that this mood preceded the Russian Revolution and post-war civil disorder in Britain. The terms of the 1919 Act were partly determined by the fiscal level then prevailing which allowed public expenditure on social policy to occur without increasing tax levels still further and partly fixed by the unwillingness of local authorities to increase local rates to pay for public housing. The City and the Treasury were opposed to increases in public expenditure to subsidise housing but were temporarily overborne.[57]

The mood of reconstruction which involved moving surplus labour from munitions and the armed services into the building industry was set by Christopher Addison, a Radical New Liberal, whom Lloyd George placed in charge of housing policy. But he had influential allies in the Government especially at the Local Government Board. In the debate on the Scottish estimates in August 1917, the Solicitor-General for Scotland promised 'substantial financial assistance from public funds to local authorities who are prepared to provide houses for the working classes'.[58] The Local Government Board of Scotland had already prepared a circular to local authorities, but because of the resistance of the municipalities to the first offer which did not delimit local financial liability, there was a considerable delay in adjusting the extent of the Government's commitment to its subsidy policy.[59] The threat of civil disorder may have determined the chronology and extent of Lloyd George's post-war housing Act, but it could not silence those who favoured building through private enterprise. Moreover, by January 1918 297 out of 311 Scottish local authorities had prepared schemes for house-building, and a partnership between central government and local authorities was in being.[60]

The 'Addison Act' of 1919 set Exchequer subsidies for housing at a level designed to meet any local authority housing deficit in excess of the revenue arising from a rate of 4s.5d. in £1. Virtually removing financial responsibility from local authorities combined with higher costs of building made the revival of monetarism in the Treasury and Cabinet only a matter of time, for although Addison's Act was intended as a temporary measure, it cost £22 million before becoming a victim of dear money policies and the deflation which had been feared. Subsidy policy after 1922 was never again so consistently favourable to the local authorities, and housing results were closely linked to when fresh policies were due for implementation, haste or delay arising from the natural desire to exploit the financial environment prevailing at the time.

The Conservatives during their periods in office, either as a single party or as the chief element in a National government after 1931, placed emphasis on reducing the costs of housing policy by attempting to stimulate market forces. Neville Chamberlain's Act of 1923 failed to produce the houses needed in Scotland: only 73 for rent in November 1924. Chamberlain argued that dwellings vacated by those who bought their own homes or rented on economic terms would gradually become available lower down the social and economic scale; he believed that there was 'a great reservoir of houses of a standard of accommodation very much in advance of what the working man is in possession of today, and these houses will eventually come within his means as their value falls'. His intention was to aid the process of owner occupation for ideological reasons: 'The man who owns his own house is always going to be a good citizen. He is always going to be a friend of law and order. He is not going to support those who want to upset the state of society which has enabled him to become a little capitalist.' This reversion to faith in private enterprise was manifest in the terms of the subsidy of £6 per house per annum for twenty years which was only granted if the local authority could satisfy the Scottish Board of Health that private builders could not or would not build the houses.

After Labour came to office in 1924, John Wheatley and Arthur Greenwood formed a formidable team at the Ministry of Health and set in train, almost immediately, a re-examination of housing policy. The deficiencies of the building industry, especially the shortage of skilled men and essential materials were exposed. A fifteen-year building programme was envisaged, and a planned expansion of the industry, satisfactory to employers and organised labour, was implemented. The Wheatley Act of 1924 increased the subsidy to £9 (£12.50 in rural areas) for forty years, and unlike earlier Acts allowed small subsidies on rents. Houses were not so generously designed, and costs were tightly controlled by the Scottish Office. Local authorities built over 75,000 houses under the terms of this Act and were undoubtedly aided by falling costs between 1925 and 1932. Subsidy policy was, however, not definitely fixed, and political uncertainty aided the concentration of building after 1926 because the expectation was that subsidies would soon disappear, and cuts were actually made in 1928.

The advent of the second Labour Government in 1929 saved Wheatley's Act entirely, and Arthur Greenwood was associated with the first Act (1930) which really attempted to subsidise slum clearance. Cities were given powers to clear slum areas for redevelopment and offered a subsidy of £2.50 per person rehoused for forty years. Linking the subsidy to the people instead of to houses had the desirable effect of discriminating in favour of large families who were generally least able to pay economic or marginally economic rents. Lower building costs and higher subsidies made rehousing the slum-dwellers a definite possibility. The early thirties were inevitably wracked by the consequences of severe depression, but cheap money policies introduced after 1932 made housing progress technically possible since rehousing slum-dwellers could be achieved for rents of 25p per week without increasing the rates beyond the statutory amount for the redevelopment account.

However, after the collapse of the Labour Government, it became a cardinal feature of National Government policy to leave slum clearance to municipal authorities and reserve the rest of the housing market for private enterprise. But this policy did not produce the houses for rent which were needed, and so the idea of filtering up into better accommodation was totally exposed as a sham. As reductions in subsidies operated under the Act of 1933, overcrowding outside the slums became a greater problem, and the Scottish Board of Health documented this gradually over the next two years.[65] The problem was so severe and apparently intransigent that the Housing Act of 1935 relaunched subsidies for all rehousing which attempted to deal with it, although the definition of overcrowding was not particularly generous to tenants so affected. Exchequer support of £6.75 per year for forty years was offered to local authorities for every house built to rehouse slum-dwellers and those overcrowded even in good accommodation.[66] Higher subsidies scaled according to the size of houses built were offered under the Housing Act of 1938 but war intervened before much new building had been undertaken.[67]

In an era of cheaper money local authorities were more prepared to deal with the problem of overcrowding and slum clearance, since paramount concern with the effect on the rates of such a policy was diminished as government subsidies appeared to be more abundant. Surveys of overcrowding had revealed that the problems were acute: 22.6 per cent of all working class houses in Scotland in 1935 were overcrowded compared with 3.8 per cent in England and Wales.[68] However, as local authority building activity increased, a shortage of labour and materials manifested itself in sharply rising costs to coincide with the problems occasioned by rearmament and war.[69]

Only houses already begun were completed during the second world war, except for two special programmes authorised in 1943 and 1944.[70] Yet planning for a post-war attack on overcrowding and slum clearance was well in hand by early 1944, and the Scottish Office produced two important reports that year by the Scottish Housing Advisory Committee which set the tone for later action. *Planning Our New Homes* was concerned with layout and design, standards of construction and fitting and was similar in outlook to the Tudor Walters Report produced after World War I, although no one has yet suggested that fear of post-war revolution was its main stimulus. In particular, the Committee recommended that the overcrowding standard of 1935 should be discarded as being too penal on those requiring rehousing. It found also that over 337,000 houses had been built between 1919 and 1939, less than 61,000 by private enterprise without assistance but more than the Royal Commission had estimated in 1917 as being needed. Yet in 1944 there were accumulated arrears in building estimated at a minimum of half a million houses, double the number of 1917. This estimate was regarded as catering only for basic needs and took no account of the prospective increase in family formation after the war was over nor did it anticipate rebuilding necessary to replace deteriorating housing stock.[71]

Distribution of New Houses, the other report of 1944, reflected the evolution of a commitment post-war to industrial regeneration which in the minds of many planners was inextricably linked with the social objective of providing housing. The programme for building had to be planned to allow migrating workers to find accommodation, and subsidy policy had to be consistent enough to encourage local authorities to build houses for a considerable period after the war ended. Yet the effort was implicitly national and not merely local (albeit aided by the State), since migration of skilled labour was inevitable if industrial development in Scotland was to occur, a fact already generally recognised in the PEP report on the location of industry in Britain, published in March 1939.[72]

The extension of the 1938 level of subsidies to cover general housing needs

Table 1   Houses (including hostels) of all forms of construction completed since 1919 years ended 31 December

| Period | Local authorities | | | Scottish National Housing Co. Ltd | Second Scottish National Housing Co. Ltd | Scottish Special Housing Association | Private enterprise | | | Government departments | Temporary houses | | Total |
	With assistance	Without assistance	Total				With assistance	Without assistance	Total		Local authorities	Government departments	
1919 to 1938	203,793	4,572	208,365	100	2,552	2	40,519	60,106	100,625	—	—	—	311,644
1939	18,714	216	18,930	—	—	188	58	6,353	6,411	—	—	—	25,529
1940	9,586	117	9,703	108	—	663	228	3,504	3,732	—	—	—	14,206
1941	3,982	38	4,020	26	—	668	68	624	692	—	—	—	5,406
1942	2,827	38	2,865	—	—	207	21	203	224	—	—	—	3,296
1943	2,633	—	2,633	—	—	84	28	64	92	—	—	—	2,809
1944	1,575	—	1,575	—	—	808	36	134	170	—	—	—	2,553
1945	1,351	—	1,351	—	—	77	27	114	141	—	437	—	2,006
1946	3,321	—	3,321	—	—	490	52	447	499	—	12,119	—	16,429
1947	8,919	—	8,919	—	—	1,854	86	1,288	1,374	2	11,974	20	24,143
1948	16,615	—	16,615	—	—	2,932	138	1,417	1,555	109	7,550	—	28,761
1949	20,064	—	20,064	—	—	4,116	242	932	1,174	493	76	—	25,923
1950	21,147	—	21,147	—	—	3,167	273	600	873	624	—	—	25,811
1951	18,091	—	18,091	—	—	2,906	328	956	1,284	647	—	—	22,928
1952	22,878	—	22,878	—	—	4,745	529	1,998	2,527	797	—	—	30,947
1919 to 1952	355,496	4,981	360,477	234	2,552	22,907	42,633	78,740	121,373	2,672	32,156	20	542,391

Source: Scottish Home and Health Department Report for 1953, Appendix 22.

rather than simply slum clearance, as a temporary measure for two years, was included in the Housing Act of 1944.[73] Meanwhile prefabricated houses were manufactured under order from the Ministry of Works for erection by local authorities, and eventually Scotland received 32,000 or about 20 per cent of these.[74]

The election of a Labour government, committed to public spending, ultra-cheap money and full employment ensured that the Coalition's plans were implemented. However there was a steep rise in costs, despite attempts to control contracts, partly arising from shortages of materials and labour but also from poor productivity in the building industry. Targets were amended downwards, the Scottish Office's architects began planning lower costing housing, and yet progress was a great deal better after 1945 than it had been after 1918, as Table 1 indicates.

In an Act of 1946 which replaced the 1944 Act, subsidies were increased: to £21.50 for a house of three apartments or less; to £23 for a house of four apartments; and to £25.00 for a house of five apartments or more. These subsidies applied to 'any housing accommodation for the working classes . . . approved by the Secretary of State'.[75] As targets failed to be achieved, the improvement of existing houses became a more significant objective, thereby postponing the demand for new houses; the Housing Act of 1949 aided this process by empowering local authorities to monitor applications for subsidies. Existing legislation was codified in the Housing Act of 1950 which made no new provisions but simplified the prevailing laws.[76]

By that date the Scottish housing market was being almost entirely supplied as a result of public enterprise, a complete reversal of the situation in 1900. Of 25,811 permanent houses completed in 1950, only 873 were built for private ownership; the local authorities had emerged as the principal suppliers of low-rent housing.[77] Private enterprise had apparently atrophied.

III

THE EXPERIENCE OF THE FOUR CITIES

Although there were often major differences of scale between Aberdeen, Dundee, Edinburgh and Glasgow, they shared common housing problems: unfit houses, sometimes cellar dwellings, occupied by the poorest section of the working class, a deteriorating housing stock which generally undersupplied community needs but grossly did so after the two world wars during which each retarded bursts of building activity, overcrowded and insanitary wynds and closes, linking housing, income and mortality in a tightening circle. Reform was a common issue in all four cities well before 1900, and each had a coterie of self-help groups such as Social Unions which investigated the local housing problem and were horrified by it. Yet little had been achieved in terms of municipal housebuilding before 1914; attention had focused principally upon building regulations, demolitions, and the abatement of nuisances using the legal authority conferred by local Acts or by the Acts of 1890 and 1897.

What appeared to be new in the decade before 1914 was the recognition by professional people, notably the clergy and public servants, that private enterprise after c.1904 had ceased to supply new housing for rents that many working-class people could afford. The unskilled were thereby denied the opportunity 'to filter up' into older housing being vacated and as for the unemployed and paupers, The Royal Commissioners investigating the operation of the Poor Laws in 1909 reported a commonplace picture of struggling to keep a home together in the slums from which escape seemed impossible. The Dundee Social Union investigated a sample of 5888 houses in 1904 and found lack of sanitation and gross overcrowding including 'lack of separation of the sexes' prevalent.[78] Glasgow's municipal commission in 1901 had detailed similar problems, and the city administrations in Aberdeen and Edinburgh had become involved in the demolition of slums and a very small amount of building for those able to pay economic rents.

Table 2   *Housing distribution among families (%) in 1901*

Accommodation	Aberdeen families %	Dundee families %	Edinburgh families %	Glasgow families %
1 room	13.1	19.7	17.0	26.1
2 rooms	37.3	52.1	31.4	43.6
3 rooms	26.2	16.5	19.2	16.5
Totals	76.6	88.3	67.6	86.2

Source: Census of Scotland, 1901

When this century began, families living in Glasgow and Dundee occupied fewer rooms on average than those living in Aberdeen and Edinburgh. Table 2 summarises the information provided by the Census of 1901, limiting the survey to families living in up to three rooms. On this count Dundee was marginally worse than Glasgow with 88.3 per cent of its families living in three rooms or less. However, the differences in scale were very marked: in terms of population Glasgow had over 762,000 inhabitants as opposed to Dundee's 161,000; moreover, Dundee had 37,403 families with their lodgers to accommodate and Glasgow 163,258. Further, Glasgow had many more people living in 'single-ends'; Dundee's working-class families mainly resided in two-apartment houses. Aberdeen had fewer families in 'single-ends' than Edinburgh, and if one considers one-and two-room houses together, the differences—apart from the number of families—were marginal, since Edinburgh had 48.4 per cent of its families in these types of houses and Aberdeen 50.4 per cent. The equivalent figures for Dundee and Glasgow were 71.8 per cent and 69.7 per cent respectively. At the extreme of overcrowding Glasgow was much the worst of the four cities. Using the measure of six people or more living in a single room, Glasgow had 1850 families (1.13 per cent of all families in the city), and Dundee and Edinburgh were similar on this scale: 351 families in Edinburgh (0.5 per cent), and 204 families in Dundee (0.5 per cent). Aberdeen had both the lowest proportion of its families living in 'single-ends' and only 70 families of six or more people (0.2 per cent) living in such accommodation. One suspects that these residential patterns reflect the income levels in the various cities, and in this respect, more of Edinburgh's families, it should be noted, lived in houses of more than three rooms.

As the Royal Commission on Housing found, the civic social conscience was most sensitive to the plight of those dwelling in 'single-ends', for overcrowding, poor facilities for sanitation and hygiene and poor building standards were encapsulated most clearly in this kind of accommodation. Accommodation for families in two rooms seemed, in contrast, to be the immediate aim for many reluctant reformers, fearful of the effect of higher rates on the electorate's voting behaviour and anxious to avoid making their particular city an apparent Mecca for the unskilled and/or those earning low wages.[79] The very fact that Dundee had the highest proportion of its families already ensconced in two-apartment houses may well have delayed the city administration's participation in house-building before World War I and ironically, hastened civic activity in the 1920s when expectations about housing had moved beyond the two-apartment dwelling.[80] Equally, Edinburgh's minor activity before 1914 with the building of houses for 601 families may partly reflect an awareness of the paradox between the city's general wealth and the relatively large percentage of its families housed in 'single-ends'.[81] Aberdeen built houses for 131 families before 1914, but a much smaller percentage of its families had two-room houses than was true of Dundee.[82] Everywhere the belief that it was the individual's responsibility to house his own family was paramount. Failure to perform this elemental duty brought with it a social stigma which the workhouse first conferred and later rehousing by the city authorities in slum clearance schemes.[83]

If a social stigma was attached to public authority housing, subsidising rents from rates was a policy guaranteed to drive an administration from office. Hence all city authorities built at first to let at economic rents even in Glasgow where the defeat of Provost Blackie in 1867 over the issue of rate support for city improvement had become part of the mythology of local politics.[84]

Pressure from 'dangerous radicals' such as Councillor John Wheatley and the very burden of the housing problem in Glasgow caused the Corporation to plan for greater action after 1900. Local opinion, however, still included the influential view that undue expenditure on drink was a prime reason why the poor could not afford higher rents and therefore better accommodation, and Glasgow Corporation policy after 1905 was to reduce the number of public houses in working-class districts and to be reluctant to grant licences in 'new districts'.[85] Higher and higher land prices, especially in central districts, also caused the Corporation to proceed with caution as did higher interest charges on local authority debt. The effect of the depression after 1907 made the regular payment of rent more difficult for many families, and there was an increase in the number of unoccupied houses in the city from 7225 in 1901 to 20,903 in 1911 and a tendency for rent levels to stagnate. Landlords viewed the housing market as in the grip of excess capacity at the same time as there was increases in rates, interest charges and costs of repairs to bring buildings up to local authority standards.[86] Thus, the supply of new working class housing for rent had virtually dried up. After 1911 some recovery in demand for houses was associated with the revival of the city economy, associated with the armaments race, but supply did not respond effectively for upward movements in rents were at first slight but then gathered speed, preparing the ground for the wave of rent strikes during the war.[87]

Meanwhile, the Medical Officer of Health had prepared a report in 1910 which detailed the main 'insanitary and obstructive buildings in congested areas in Glasgow' and linked different ward death rates with variations in housing conditions.[88] From 1908 onwards the Corporation had acted on the basis that slum property needed to be cleared piecemeal, and in 1911 the Common Good Fund was being used to buy 'backlands'-which obstructed light and ventilation—over which the City had no statutory control.[89] Because of the earlier activities of the City Improvement Trust and the sanitary inspectorate, the Corporation had at its disposal excellent information about the slum problem. Properties were bought and demolished in Broomielaw, Tradeston and Cowcaddens at a cost of over £25,000, and the Executive Committee on Housing, established in 1913, had closed 1099 houses and demolished 672 by the end of the war.[90]

In 1916 the Corporation appointed a small specialist commission familiar with working-class housing, together with the City Engineer, Medical Officer of Health, the Chief Sanitary Inspector and the Manager of the City Improvements Department. This commission surveyed the whole of the city, and thus the detailed basis for post-war housing programmes was laid.[91] The Housing Committee was established in November 1916 and planned a housing scheme of 92 houses at Garngad Road almost immediately, but permission to proceed was not received from the Ministry of Munitions till December 1917.[92] Thus, Glasgow's reconstruction policy was initiated before the Royal Commission on

Housing reported and before Government intentions about post-war housing finance were known. However, the Government had, during the war, sponsored some house-building with subsidies, and this was well known to local authorities.

Even before the war Glasgow's officials had begun a private discussion within the Corporation with the intention of producing a consistent housing policy. The Town Clerk estimated that 40,000 people lived in 'uninhabitable houses', and that to purchase these and make some of them habitable would cost between £1m and £1.5m. Others were 'in a state of extreme structural disrepair, ruinous and should be demolished'. The Corporation, in his view, should close houses that were clearly beyond repair, apply for compulsory purchase and demolish. Under the terms of the Act of 1909 houses let at under £16 per annum had to be made fit to live in, and thus, any landlords who were remiss could be compelled to keep their property in good order. 'Obstructive' houses which kept the light from others could also be demolished after compulsory purchase had occurred. Demands on the Common Good Fund or upon the ratepayers were to be kept to the minimum; this was the prime obsession of councillors and officials alike, both before and after the war, although clearly other concepts occasionally assaulted their consciousness. Property-owners who gained from the demolition of obstructive property which was otherwise in good repair were to be rated to compensate those landlords who lost.[93]

Peter Fyfe, the Chief Sanitary Inspector, who became the first Director of Housing in 1920, did not favour applying the laws rigorously in 1914 because he thought this would increase the total number of homeless people in the City. His staff just before the war notified proprietors of over 20,000 cases of nuisance in house property. In his view the best results would be achieved by giving 'informal' or 'courtesy' notices to landlords to improve and repair their houses, this work to be undertaken within a month. If this procedure turned out to be ineffectual, legal proceedings could be instituted without offending the proprietors as a group. Fyfe was exceedingly well informed about overcrowding and had lists of slum properties which could be used as a basis for planning a rehousing programme.[94]

The City Assessor had come to the conclusion in 1913 that there were two possible courses of action. Areas of the City could be selected and property acquired. This policy might be 'ideal' but would be very costly. The alternative was to acquire individual properties as they became available. This would be cheaper and had the merit that it would distribute the effects of the Corporation's improvement policy throughout the City. All that was necessary was discreet advertising that the Corporation would acquire property if the price was right.[95] This judgement may have been correct, since the House Factors and House Owners' Associations made no attempt in 1914 to defend slum proprietors or owners of obstructive buildings, although they favoured the payment of compensation to those whose properties were acquired.[96]

Land costs were a significant factor: £9 per square yard was the average cost before rebuilding began in the areas acquired up to 1914 under the terms of the 1897 Act. New central housing schemes were out of the question for rents could not be economic; the City's officials, therefore, concluded accurately, 'the problem of the rehousing of the working classes is wholly an economic one'.[97] By 1916 they also knew that 'the supply of houses in good sanitary condition has practically been exhausted' and feared that unemployment after the war would become a significant problem which the existence of detailed plans for rehousing the working classes might offset. Moreover, they did accept that those fighting for King and country deserved better than a slum dwelling.[98]

In September 1917 the Government issued its first circular to local authorities offering unspecified financial assistance for house-building. However, the terms of the Government's first offer proved unacceptable and was rejected by the local authorities because their financial liabilities—i.e. the likely burden on the rates—were not delimited.[99] The making of the Addison Act of 1919 was clearly the result of negotiation over a considerable period, and the Scottish local authorities were called together by Glasgow on 4 March 1919 to consider the availability of the subsidy and the relative financial burdens to be borne by central Government and local ratepayers. They favoured a seven-year housing programme instead of the two years originally offered and a split of 75 per cent paid by Whitehall and 25 per cent from local rates.[100]

Meanwhile, subject to reservations about the financial details of Government subsidy policy, local authorities had begun to submit schemes to the Scottish Office. Already by the end of November 1917 twenty-eight had responded to the September circular, and the Secretary of State believed that another one hundred had plans in active preparation.[101] Two months later he reported to the House of Commons that 297 out of 311 local authorities had made returns offering to build about 99,000 houses.[102]

Glasgow's Housing Committee had first decided that 47,000 houses were needed immediately; thereafter, 5000 per annum were required for a lengthy period simply for normal replacements. Land already owned by the Corporation would provide room for only about 5000 houses, and there was not enough available ground within the City's boundaries for the number of dwellings needed. The Housing Committee urgently began to seek land on the fringes of the City in order to meet the requirements of its housing plan. The first draft contained three main elements. Apart from the erection of new houses it was proposed to reconstruct slum areas, a project involving over 10,000 houses. The possibilities of temporary accommodation were also explored: large unoccupied houses could not be acquired for there were no legal powers available to the City to compel owners to release them; a small number of wooden houses were to be erected.[103]

Glasgow's revised estimate, submitted to the Scottish Board of Health on 15

October 1919, provided for 57,000 houses, none of less than three apartments: 25,948 three-apartment dwellings, 25,944 four-apartments and 5108 five-apartment houses or more. Apart from these permanent houses, 500 temporary wooden houses were included in the estimate.[104] The provision for various groups within the total figure of 57,000 houses gives some indication of motivation: 21,000 were intended to relieve overcrowding; 3000 to replace 'uninhabitable' houses to be closed and/or demolished; 7000 to provide for those made homeless by improvement and reconstruction schemes carried out under the Act of 1890; 15,500 to deal with population growth; 5000 to house people to be employed in new industries; 5500 for demobilised service-men.[105] The City possessed 5106 acres suitable for housing, including estates on the periphery such as Castlemilk, Cardonald, Giffnock, Thornliebank, Pollokshaws, Millerston and Shettleston.[106]

Dundee was also quick off the mark. James Thomson's *Report*, completed in 1918 but obviously based on earlier investigations, set out plans for corporation housing in well planned estates. Local propaganda fostered the thought that Dundee was most advanced in its house-building activities in the 1920s but in fact, this related more to quality than quantity. By the end of 1922, when the Addison Act expired, only 674 houses had been completely finished, and for the decade 1919–28 about 4000 dwellings were completed, of which about 30 per cent were built by private enterprise and not the City.[107] The following decade 1929–38, despite the trend to lower interest rates, produced an output of less than 6000 houses.[108] The standard of some of the early schemes was very high for the times: Logie estate had centrally heated houses whose economic rents were obviously beyond large numbers of Dundee's families, but it was the quality of building—Craigiebank and Taybank being other similar estates—which won the City its reputation for activity in urban renewal in the 1920s and 1930s.[109]

The housing problems in Dundee remained acute throughout the inter-war years, although there was a tendency for the population to grow only marginally. The City possessed too many small houses: 56 per cent of the population in 1931 lived in 'single-ends' or two-apartment houses.[110] Many houses were overcrowded, in poor structural condition or lacking amenities. After a survey undertaken in 1935, when over 3000 houses were found to be occupied but unfit for human habitation, an emergency programme of slum clearance was begun with a target of 2000 houses per annum for five years. However, progress was initially slow: only just over 700 were under consideration or completed in the summer of 1935.[111] During the second world war some building proceeded but at less than half the rate of the 1930s.[112] By 1951 solid progress had been made with an average of 794 houses per annum between 1946 and 1950, but there was nothing to match the advanced designs of post 1919.[113]

Improvements in the housing stock allowed substantial social advances between 1931 and 1951. By the latter year only 48 per cent of the houses were

'single-ends' or two-apartment dwellings compared with 62 per cent in
1931.[114] Yet 40 per cent of all families were still living in overcrowded conditions in 1951—over 21,000 households. That Census Report lists also five basic
amenities—sink, kitchen stove or range, running water, fixed bath and water
closet. Throughout Dundee and, therefore, including all social classes, only 38
per cent of families had exclusive use of all five. Forty-three per cent were
sharing water closets, and 58 per cent had no fixed bath. The smaller or older
the house, the less well provided it was with these facilities, and in 1951
Dundee was, in percentage terms, the Scottish city with the poorest housing
stock: more houses of one or two rooms than Glasgow, Aberdeen or Edinburgh
relative to total stock.[115]

On the surface Aberdeen's housing problems in 1919 seemed more
amenable to solution than those of any of the other cities. Overcrowding was
apparently under the clear control of the Sanitary Inspector's Department,[116]
and the housing market seemed to have worked reasonably well. But this com-
placency was rapidly shattered in the early 1920s. The cessation of house-
building during the war negated normal market forces, and a shortage rapidly
developed. This would have proved a major embarrassment for the City administration save that Aberdeen was tending to lose population by migration,
and indeed housing conditions, measured in terms of room density, were better
in 1921 than they had been in 1911—1.36 persons per room compared with
1.40.[117] Filtering up by poorer tenants was still happening, but the increase in
the number of marriages after 1918 threatened to stop this largely fortuitous
progress. Sub-letting began to develop on a significant scale as newly-weds
could not get sole tenancies, a phenomenon virtually unknown before 1914.[118]

Although the Town Council had adopted a report from its Finance and
Public Health Committees on working-class housing in 1917 ready for implementation after the war, it gravely under-estimated the likely problem. It
provided for 1500 houses for emergency replacement; this estimate was rapidly
revised after investigation in 1918–19, and under the terms of the Addison
Act, Aberdeen submitted an estimate for 4000 houses to the Board of
Health.[119] These, it was thought, would be needed by 1922, but in fact by early
1923 only 242 had been built or approved. There was a steady improvement in
activity from 1924 onwards, and by 1939 over 11,000 houses— slightly more
than in Dundee with its better reputation—had been built by the Corporation
and private enterprise.[120] The private group of builders concentrated on the
west of the City mainly and built exclusively for middle-class owner occupiers,
releasing much good quality property for other tenants. The Corporation built
about 60 per cent of the dwellings erected between the wars and constructed
large estates in a variety of styles, but mostly of low-rise and good quality for
working class tenants who could pay economic rents.[121]

Clearance from poorer housing conditions was only slow, and following a
survey in the winter of 1935–6 it was found that nearly 24 per cent of the

houses in the City were overcrowded, and 5821 houses were uninhabitable and yet occupied. These twin problems, as in Dundee and the other cities, were largely the consequence of a deteriorating housing stock of one and two room dwellings.[122] Moreover, in 1938 about 26,000 houses lacked proper sanitary facilities; shared water closets were very common, and the number of houses without indoor water and sinks—4905 out of a total housing stock of 45,842— compared badly with Dundee, Edinburgh or Glasgow. The Corporation from 1936 onwards increasingly pressured landlords to provide these basic amenities, but Aberdeen granite buildings were not easily altered. Rent restriction did not assist owners to believe that there was economic benefit in improvement relative to the costs involved.

Undoubtedly the almost complete ending of building during the second world war—only 852 houses were built—badly compounded this group of problems. So short did accommodation become that even 'uninhabitable' houses could not be demolished, and some were actually reoccupied.[123] Thus, Aberdeen emerged after 1945 with a major housing problem, and in early 1951 it was estimated that, although 4216 houses had been built since 1945, a further 10,000 were urgently needed. Population had increased since 1931, and after the second world war the rate of marriages and new family formation sharply moved upwards.[124] Overcrowding was more a problem after 1945 than it had been in 1939. A survey conducted in 1946 showed that 15,000 houses were overcrowded or unfit for human habitation, whereas on the eve of the second world war, 13,000 houses were so designated.[125] However, Aberdeen's problems, arising from this particular question of overcrowding and unfit dwellings, were less than those of either Dundee or Glasgow.

As might be expected, Edinburgh's housing problem attacked the public conscience less stridently after 1919 than in any of the other cities. Undoubtedly, there were many inhabitants poorly housed, but because of the more favourable economic structure of the city and its region the private housing market revived in the 1920s and 1930s more vibrantly than elsewhere. Moreover, as we have already noticed, the legacy presented by the existing housing stock was more conducive to a steady process of reform than in the other cities. The underprivileged tended to be concentrated in small houses in central wards of the city such as St Leonards, St Giles and Holyrood or in central districts of Leith which was absorbed within Edinburgh's boundaries in 1920. However, industrial slums of the type found in Glasgow and Dundee were rare.[126]

Representative of the major difference between Edinburgh and the other cities was the interest in the subsidy to private housing under the 1923 Act: 2000 houses were built with grants of up to £70 each in the early years of this scheme.[127] The major Corporation activity occurred in the 1930s in the suburbs and often at very favourable building densities, usually in the range of 16 to 24 houses per acre. This was the period in which estates such as those at Niddrie,

Prestonfield, Restalrig and Lochend and Craigentinny, and Craigmillar were begun, the basis for much later activity, particularly in the 1950s. About £2 million per year was spent on housing in the first half of the 1930s, but Edinburgh's experience was unusual in that nearly two-thirds of it was accounted for by private building and only slightly more than one-third by the Corporation. In the whole period 1919–39 the City built 14,816 permanent houses for working class tenants, mostly three-apartment dwellings in low-rise developments.[128]

Despite favourable press notices for its activities in the early 1930s,[129] the Corporation had allowed overcrowding to become a serious problem. The survey of 1935 revealed that 18.4 per cent of all the housing stock was overcrowded, and in 1936 it was estimated that 13,594 new houses were needed immediately. Progress was far from satisfactory, although by 1938 ten sites had been cleared for rebuilding to occur; 858 houses were built as slum clearance properties in 1935, 402 in 1936 and 618 in 1937 against a target rising from 750 to 1000.[130] The civic will was clearly far from firm, no doubt rendered so weak in part at least by pressure from rate-payers.

In consequence of pre-war failures, Edinburgh's task after World War II was the more difficult. By 1946 sub-letting had developed significantly: 133,261 families in the city lived in 120,265 houses, i.e. 12,996 were living in sub-letted property. Overcrowding in houses with an annual rental of £45 or less affected 15.71 per cent of this substantial segment of the total stock, judged on the Board of Health's 1935 criteria. Revised and generous standards introduced in 1944 raised overcrowding to 32.7 per cent; the estimated housing requirements in 1946, therefore, were 50,000 new houses and 12,000 reconstructed properties.[131] By 1951 Edinburgh had made no appreciable inroads into this backlog, despite the extensive use of prefabricated houses.

Yet the city's population was better housed in 1951 than it had been in 1931, and infinite improvement had occurred since 1901. Across the whole of the housing stock 93 persons per 100 rooms was the average density. But averages are misleading. Craigmillar and Pilton, two pre-war housing estates, presented particular difficulties for despite the newness of the properties the densities were among the highest in the city. More than 25 per cent of those living in Craigmillar ward were living more than two persons to a room. Overcrowding on a lesser scale—since population had been declining since 1931—was still a problem in St Giles, Holyrood and Central Leith wards. Of the five basic conveniences, earlier listed, over 40 per cent of all the housing stock lacked one or more.[132]

The most intractable problems after 1918 were found in Glasgow, much the largest of the cities in terms of population.[133] A survey conducted in 1915 disclosed that the total housing stock was composed of 212,223 houses. 41,354 or 19.49 per cent were 'single-ends'; of these the overwhelming majority, 92.88 per cent, shared common water closets. The largest category of housing consisted of two room dwellings, 111,451 houses or 52.5 per cent of the whole stock. 42,513, or 38.15 per cent, had a separate toilet; 68,938, or 61.85 per cent shared.[134] Significantly, in its post-war plans, Glasgow Corporation did not intend to build any more houses of less than three rooms. Overcrowding was an even more desperate problem. According to the Census of 1911, the last available census before the war, over 62 per cent of Glasgow's people lived in one or two room dwellings. 55.7 per cent lived in houses with more than two persons to a room; 29.9 per cent more than three to a room and 10.7 per cent more than four to a room. Using the standard of three inhabitants per room, over 200,000 people in the city lived in overcrowded conditions.[135]

After 1921 the proportion of two room dwellings declined, but even as late as 1951 50.6 per cent of families were living in one or two room houses. Inter-war building, as Table 3 reveals, concentrated on three room houses; by 1951 28.2 of the total stock were in this category housing 27 per cent of the total number of families. There was also a significant increase in the number of four apartment dwellings beginning pre-1939, but most clearly occurring after 1945. Occupancy rates certainly improved in the city as a whole, and even though tenements formed the principal category of houses built—especially between 1920 and 1945, they were not so high as those of earlier years, their facilities were better and their population densities were relatively low.[136]

As is apparent from Table 3, the intention of building 57,000 houses relatively quickly was frustrated, and the concentration on three apartment houses was greater than originally planned. The one-apartment dwellings were provided in hostels and intended for migratory or homeless single persons; the two-apartment houses were intended for couples without children and increasingly for pensioners. However, housing policy was not consistently pursued: the peaks in activity tended to occur when changes in government and/or subsidy policy made the future uncertain—in 1922–3, 1929, 1934, 1938 and 1950–1. Local government rating assessment effects were certainly not ignored, whatever the political complexion of Glasgow Corporation. The assessment for housing did not move consistently upward, itself a reflection of the erratic building performance; the fall in the mid-thirties, for example, was very sharp from £272,838 (5p in £1) in 1933–4 to £75,370 (less than 1p in £1) in 1935–6.[137] Despite the cheap money policies of the post 1931 era Glasgow did not much improve its performance in the 1930s, as Table 4 indicates; and 1929 was the best single year of the whole period. The 1940s, as might be expected, witnessed a fall in housing output, but this was largely a consequence of World War II which undoubtedly interrupted a building boom which began in 1938. Considering the poor performance of the early 1940s, the recovery after 1945 was spectacular but lost steam in 1950–1.

'Decrowding' houses was a long-established policy in Glasgow, but costs of land, building materials and labour added to the fear of rising rates; these remained fundamental obstacles and often ironically after a commitment to

Table 3   *Houses completed by the Corporation of Glasgow 1920–1951*

Year	1 apt	2 apts	3 apts	4 apts	5 apts	Total houses	Total apts
1920			250	18		268	822
1921			305	51	48	404	1,359
1922			799	531	240	1,570	5,721
1923		162	1,122	833	244	2,361	8,242
1924		400	232	137	8	777	2,084
1925		324	315	198	86	923	2,815
1926		344	1,048	477	79	1,948	6,135
1927		428	2,329	859	93	3,709	11,744
1928		370	2,372	816	54	3,612	11,390
1929		278	4,659	1,379	51	6,367	20,304
1930		474	2,098	595	61	3,228	9,927
1931		472	1,823	387	3	2,685	7,976
1932		190	1,874	350	2	2,416	7,412
1933	33	288	2,079	433	10	2,843	8,628
1934	33	318	3,310	775	3	4,439	13,714
1935		762	2,386	774	4	3,926	11,798
1936	33	84	1,384	478	6	1,985	6,295
1937		12	1,066	667	96	1,841	6,370
1938			1,154	1,394	240	2,788	10,238
1939			771	1,215	201	2,187	8,178
1940			376	481	123	980	3,667
1941			271	466	54	791	2,947
1942			459	539	126	1,124	4,163
1943			373	446	112	931	3,463
1944			168	238	78	484	1,846
1945	36		176	254	106	572	2,110
1946			859	760	112	1,731	6,177
1947			1,548	1,172	124	2,844	9,952
1948			607	1,989	198	2,794	10,767
1949			667	2,634	332	3,633	14,197
1950	56		708	3,263	108	4,135	15,772
1951	72		1,259	2,280	128	3,739	13,609
Totals	263	4,906	38,847	26,889	3,130	74,035	249,822
Average pa	8.22	153.31	1213.97	840.28	97.81	2313.59	7806.93

Source: Glasgow Corporation Housing Department

end the problem, was made.[138] In 1931 153,503 houses, or 59.9 per cent of the total stock, were overcrowded, if the standard definition of 1944 were applied; in 1951 this figure had fallen to 130,435 houses or 44.2 per cent of the total.[139] In terms of people, the survey of 1935 was a telling indictment of inter-war policy: 82,109 families (over 31 per cent of all families in Glasgow) were over-crowded under the not particularly exacting standards established in the Act of 1935.[140]

Table 4   *Corporation of Glasgow   Housebuilding by decade*

Decade	Houses	%	Apartments	%
1920–9	21,939	29.63	70,616	28.27
1930–9	28,338	38.28	90.536	36.24
1940–9	15,884	21.45	59,289	23.73

Source: Calculated from Table 3
Note: Percentages are calculated of totals built 1920-51

If these comments seem a far cry from the concept that housing policy was designed to be 'reinsurance against revolution', it is fair to point out that I have concentrated upon practical results in 'Red' Glasgow and not intentions. It is very doubtful whether housing policy in the city made a significant contri-bution to any general programme of reducing class identity or solidarity for it was ineffectual in dealing with the social problems which it was apparently designed to solve. When Glasgow Corporation temporarily closed its housing list in 1933, there were 80,000 names on it. There was no way in which these other families could be incorporated within an existing political consensus, for it made no room for them.[141]

Indeed, rehousing under the 1935 Act from slum property was generally associated with disadvantage, for a social stigma attached itself to those cleared, and the house type built, particularly the high tenements of Blackhill and Calton (1933–8), were distinctively different from other corporation types, and, therefore, noticeable.[142] Whatever importance one assigns to qualitative human prejudice, the lot for most Glaswegians was often a lifetime on the Corporation waiting list, and in private housing rent control broke down after 1923 as landlords achieved vacant possession in properties; rack-renting and key money for entry to small houses commonly represented stark reality.[143]

CONCLUSION

The most obvious and yet banal conclusion is that housing policy improved the general position of civic communities, but within average experience massive pockets of deprivation survived throughout the period. Glasgow and Dundee apparently made greater efforts than Edinburgh and Aberdeen but were no more successful in solving their housing problems because the order of magnitude was generally greater. Essentially, overcrowding was most apparent in the burghs of Scotland. As late as 1935 23.8 per cent of all the houses in Scotland (196,984 in total) were found to be overcrowded, according to a fairly relaxed standard, and 25 per cent of the houses in all the burghs (174,641 houses).[144] Despite all efforts occupancy at more than two people per room still affected 15.5 per cent of the people of Scotland in 1951 compared with 2.1 per cent of the English and Welsh.[145]

The ability to pay rent was central to the issue; as one parliamentarian put it, in 1935, 'wages are at the root of the matter'.[146] The banner reputedly carried during one of the 1915 rent strikes carrying the slogan, 'Our husbands are fighting Prussianism in France, and we are fighting the Prussians of Partick' may reveal the feminist militancy of articulate artisans' wives,[147] but it undoubtedly conceals the fact that the civic economy of Glasgow had created a large casual and unskilled labouring class who could only afford to house themselves badly even when times were relatively good.[148] The commitment to poorly paid occupations arose from the civic economic structure, and this applied equally to Dundee. Market forces continued to work best where the civic economy was most diversified, particularly in Edinburgh and to a lesser extent in Aberdeen.

In 1951 173,598 people still lived in one-room houses, and 86,592 or 49.9 per cent of this total lived in Glasgow, and 23,497 in the other three cities. In two-apartment houses Glasgow had 350,739 people or 32.2 per cent of the total whereas the other three cities had 188,272 or 17.3 per cent. In three-room dwellings Glasgow housed 303,332 or 20 per cent of its people, and the other three cities 263,237 or 17.3 per cent. The occupancy density rate of not more than two persons to a room improved from 54.3 per cent of all houses in 1901 to 65 per cent in 1931 and 85.3 per cent in 1951. By 1951, as the Table 5 indicates, experience between the cities still varied markedly. Relatively, the housing 'pecking order' of the four cities had not changed since 1901, although there had been a general improvement in the provision of dwellings which by 1952 had cost £80 million in subsidies since 1919.[149]

Regions surrounding the cities as well as the cities themselves did not seem to be able to provide the skilled men to keep the rest of the building labour force employed at stable labour costs. This was apparent in house costs in 1920, 1938 and post 1945.[150] John Wheatley, that complex but exceedingly able Red Clydesider who became Minister of Health in the 1924 Labour Government,[151] shared with Alfred Mond[152] an acute dissatisfaction with the organisation of the building industry and the organisation of building materials supply. Neither made a permanent impact on the cost structure of the Corporation house market, but both recognised another couple of significant weaknesses on the supply side which only temporarily disappeared between 1924 and 1935 as costs

Table 5   *Housing occupancy rates in the cities 1951*

City	Persons per household	Rooms per household	Persons per room
Aberdeen	3.19	3.12	1.02
Glasgow	3.44	2.71	1.27
Dundee	3.15	2.79	1.13
Edinburgh	3.12	3.33	0.94

Source: Census of 1951

fell in consequence of developing depression and slackening private activity. Housing reform for Wheatley was 'the Red Cross work of the class struggle' but throughout the period there remained victims without recourse to even first aid.[153]

REFERENCES

1   S D Chapman (ed.), *The History of Working-Class Housing* (Newton Abbot, 1971).
2   Cf. John Burnett, *A Social History of Housing 1815–1900* (Newton Abbot, 1978); Enid Gauldie, *Cruel Habitations. A History of Working-Class Housing 1780–1918*, (1974); J N Tarn, *Working-Class Housing in Nineteenth-Century Britain*, (1972): *idem, Five Per Cent Philanthropy* (1973); Anthony Sutcliffe (ed.), *Multi-Storey Living, The British Working-Class Experience* (1974); J Melling (ed.), *Housing, Social Policy and the State* (1980); Mark Swenarton, *Homes Fit for Heroes: The Politics and Architecture of Early State Housing in Britain* (1981).
3   Censuses, 1901–51.
4   Cf. J B Russell, *Public Health Administration in Glasgow*, edited by A K Chalmers (Glasgow, 1905).
5   Census 1901; Report by the County Medical Officer of Lanark on the Housing Conditions of Miners, 1910, p. 16.
6   Census, 1911
7   Ibid.

8 Reports by the County Medical Officers of Lewis, Shetland and Nairn.

9 Thomas Ferguson, *Scottish Social Welfare 1864–1914* (Edinburgh, 1958), pp. 136–8.

10 J Butt, 'Working-class Housing in Glasgow, 1851–1914', in S D Chapman (ed.), op. cit. pp. 76 ff.; T Ferguson, op. cit. pp. 138–9.

11 T Ferguson, op. cit. pp. 139–41; J Butt, op. cit. pp. 68–9.

12 T Ferguson, op. cit. pp. 57 ff.; W T Gairdner, 'Defects of House Construction in Glasgow', *Proceedings of Royal Philosophical Society of Glasgow*, vii (1870–1), pp. 245 ff.; John Honeyman, 'Social and Sanitary Problems', ibid, xx (1888–9), pp. 25–39; B Lenman, C Lythe and E Gauldie, *Dundee and its Textile Industry 1850–1914* (Abertay Historical Society Publication no. 14, 1969), pp. 79 ff.; A Keith, *A Thousand Years of Aberdeen* (Aberdeen, 1972), pp. 490–1; J Anderson, *History of Edinburgh* (Edinburgh, 1856), pp. 508–9.

13 HMSO (Cmd 8731) 1917, *Royal Commission on the Housing of the Industrial Population of Scotland, Rural and Urban*, Minority Report, p. 387.

14 J Butt, op. cit. pp. 78–9; *The Lord Provosts of Glasgow* (Glasgow, 1883), p. 87; T Ferguson, op. cit. pp. 143–8.

15 Cf. J H Treble, 'The Seasonal Demand for Adult Labour in Glasgow 1890–1914', *Social History*, 3, 1 (Jan. 1978); idem, 'The Market for Unskilled Male Labour in Glasgow, 1891–1914, in *Essays in Scottish Labour History* edited by I MacDougall (Edinburgh, 1978), pp. 115–42; J Butt, op. cit. pp. 82 ff.; J B Russell, 'Life in One Room', in A K Chalmers, op. cit. pp. 189–206; B Lenman, C Lythe, E Gauldie, op. cit. p. 77.

16 HMSO (Cmd 6741, 1946), *The Provision of Houses for Owner Occupation*, p. 6; J Butt, op. cit. pp. 74–5.

17 R G Rodger, 'Speculative Builders in Scottish Burghs 1860–1914', Urban History Group Conference Paper, 1978; J Butt, op. cit. p. 72.

18 *The Provision of Houses for Owner Occupation*, table on p. 6; J Butt, 'Working-Class Housing in Glasgow, 1900–1939', in MacDougall, op. cit. pp. 146–7.

19 Report of the Royal Commission . . . 1917, para 2232.

20 T M Cooper and W E Whyte, *The Law of Housing and Town Planning in Scotland* (Edinburgh 1920) gives the best general account of housing legislation from 1846 to 1919.

21 Glasgow City Archives, C 3.2.18 Minutes of Evidence before Glasgow Municipal Commission on the Housing of the Poor, 1903, pp. 1–2.

22 H Littlejohn, *Report on the Sanitary Condition of the City of Edinburgh* (Edinburgh, 1865).

23 Cf. C M Allan, 'The Genesis of British Urban Redevelopment with *special* reference to Glasgow', *Economic History Review*, second series, **XVIII** (1965), pp. 598–613; J Butt (1971), pp. 58 ff.; H W Bull, 'Working-Class Housing in Glasgow, 1866–1902' (unpublished Strathclyde University MLitt thesis, 1974); S Chisholm, 'The history and results of the operation of the Glasgow City Improvement Trust', *Proceedings of Royal Philosophical Society of Glasgow* **XXVII** (1895–6); J B Russell, 'The Operations of the City Improvement Trust', in A K Chalmers, op. cit. pp. 95–132.

24 B Lenman, C Lythe, E Gauldie, op. cit. p. 91.

25   H Mackenzie (ed.), *The City of Aberdeen* (Edinburgh, 1953), p. 117.

26   For example, J B Russell; cf. A K Chalmers, op. cit. pp. 259 ff.

27   W H Marwick, *Economic Developments in Victorian Scotland* (1936), pp. 209–19.

28   For example, George William Fox, 9th Lord Kinnaird (1807–78) who had considerable influence in Dundee. Cf. B Lenman, C Lythe and E Gauldie, op. cit. pp. 81 and n. 22.

29   Clergy such as Revd Dr James Begg, Revd John Smith, Revd Dr Thomas Guthrie, Revd William Mackenzie were all active. Cf. W H Marwick, op. cit. pp. 210 ff.

30   The phrase quoted belongs to H Perkin in 'Land Reform and Class Conflict in Victorian Britain', *The Victorians and Social Protest*, edited by J Butt and I F Clarke, (Newton Abbot, 1973) p. 214; cf. also J R Hay, '*The Origins of the Liberal Welfare Reforms, 1906–1914*', passim.

31   P Rowland, *Lloyd George* (1975), pp. 463, 466 and 508.

32   S Damer, 'State, Class and Housing: Glasgow 1885–1919', in *Housing, Social Policy and the State*, edited by J Melling (1980), pp. 73–112; D Englander, 'Landlord and Tenant in Urban Scotland: the background to the Clyde Rent Strikes, 1915', *Journal of Scottish Labour History Society*, no. 15 (1981), pp. 4–14.

33   BPP Cmd 3792 (1908), Minutes of Departmental Committee on House Letting in Scotland and also the Report in BPP Cmd 3715 (1907).

34   P Wilding, 'Towards Exchequer Subsidies for Housing 1906–1914', *Economic and Social Administration*, 6, 1 (1972), pp. 15–16.

35   Cf. Marion Bowley, *Housing and the State 1919–1944* (1945), p. 10.

36   Glasgow City Archives, Minutes of Evidence taken before Glasgow Municipal Commission on Housing (1902–3), pp. 254 ff.; B Lenman, C Lythe, and E Gauldie, op. cit. pp. 39, 93–8.

37   BPP Cmd 811 (1914–16), Report to the Committee appointed to inquire into the increase of house rents (Scotland), passim.

38   J Butt (1978), pp. 147–8; J Melling, 'Employers, Labour and the Glasgow Housing Market 1880–1920', SSRC Conference Paper (May 1978); idem, 'The Glasgow Rent Strike and Clydeside Labour', *Journal of Scottish Labour History Society* no. **13** (May 1979), pp. 39–44; J McHugh, 'The Clyde Rent Strike', ibid no. 12 (Feb. 1978); D Englander, op. cit. pp. 4–14.

39   B Horne, '1915: The Great Rents Victory', *Scottish Marxist*, no. **2** (Winter 1972); R K Middlemas, *The Clydesiders* (1965), pp. 61–2; D Kirkwood, *My Life of Revolt* (1935), pp. 58, 108–10; J Melling, 'Clydeside Housing and the Evolution of State Rent Control', in Melling (1980), pp. 139–67; *Forward*, 13 Nov. 1915.

40   M Swenarton, *Homes fit for Heroes: The Politics and Architecture of Early State Housing in Britain* (1981), pp. 44 and 58 ff.

41   BPP Cmd 8731 (1917–18), Report of the Royal Commission on Housing . . ., paras. 22–256.

42   Ibid. Minority Report pp. 179 ff.

43   Ibid. Report, para. 414.

44   Ibid. paras. 625–6.

45   Ibid. Minutes, Q 22592.
46   Ibid. QQ 33427–30, 33456 and 33475–86.
47   Ibid. Report, paras. 646–74.
48   Ibid. paras. 794–804.
49   Ibid. paras. 831–57.
50   J Hinton, *The First Shop Stewards' Movement* (1973); H McShane, *No Mean Fighter* (1978), pp. 74 ff.; R Challinor, *The Origins of British Bolshevism* (1978) passim; N. Milton (ed.), *In the Rapids of Revolution* (1978); ibid, *John Maclean* (1973); W Gallacher, *Revolt on the Clyde* (1936); D Kirkwood, *My Life of Revolt* (1935).
51   Report of the Royal Commission on Housing . . . para 2230.
52   BPP 1917–18 (Cmd 8669) Report of the Commission of Enquiry into Industrial Unrest (Scotland), paras 3–8.
53   M Swenarton, 'An Insurance against Revolution': Idealogical Objectives of the Provision and Design of Public Housing in Britain after the First World War', *Bulletin of the Institute of Historical Research*, LIV no. 129, (May 1981), pp. 86–101; B B Gilbert, *British Social Policy 1914–1939* (1970) pp. 137–61.
54   P B Johnson, *Land fit for Heroes: the Planning of British Reconstruction, 1916–19* (Chicago, 1968); Royal Institute of British Architects, Housing of the Working Classes in England and Wales, Cottage Competitions. Conditions (1917); BPP 1918 (Cmd 9191) Report . . . on building construction . . . (Tudor Walters Report).
55   C Addison, *Four and a Half Years: a Personal Diary from June 1914 to January 1919*, (1934), ii, p. 414; *Hansard*, 2 May 1918, Speech of Hayes Fisher, Parliamentary Secretary to Local Government Board; S Howson, 'The Origins of Dear Money, 1919–20, *Economic History Review* (2nd series) 27 (1974), pp. 88–107.
56   S Marriner, 'Sir Alfred Mond's Octopus: a nationalised house-building business', *Business History*, 21 (1979), pp. 26 ff.; P Abrams, 'The failure of social reform 1918–20', *Past and Present*, 24 (1963); P Wilding, 'The Housing and Town Planning Act 1919: a study in the making of social policy', *Journal of Social Policy*, 11 (1973), pp. 317–34; *Hansard*, 31 July 1917, speech of W Hayes Fisher.
57   S Howson, op. cit. pp. 94 ff.
58   *Hansard*, 8 Aug. 1917.
59   Ibid. Glasgow City Archives (GCA), DTC/8/18, Box 1919–20 Notes on Housing; City Chamberlain's Notes, Aug. 1919.
60   *Hansard*, 5 July 1917; 13 Dec. 1917; 31 Jan. 1918; 2 May 1918; 9 May 1918; 14 Nov. 1918.
61   9 & 10 Geo V c. 60; J Butt (1979), pp. 149–50 and 154; Report of Dept. of Health for Scotland 1952 (Cmd 8799), Appendix 23.
62   13 & 14 Geo V c. 24; *Hansard* 16 Dec. 1924; J Butt (1979), pp. 160–1.
63   R W Lyman, *The First Labour Government 1924* (1957), pp. 110–27; R K Middlemas, op. cit. pp. 35–41, 46–54 and 145–52; 14 & 15 Geo V c. 35.
64   R D Cramond, op. cit. pp. 14–19; B B Gilbert, *British Social Policy 1914–39* (1970), pp. 199–200; 20 & 21 Geo V c. 40.
65   Annual Reports of Scottish Board of Health Cd 4469 1934 and 1935.

66   25 & 26 Geo V c. 41; Cramond, pp. 21–2.
67   2 & 3 Geo VI c. 3.
68   Annual Report of Scottish Board of Health 1936 (Cmd 5407), p. 21.
69   Report on Scottish Building Costs 1939 (Cmd 5977).
70   Cramond, p. 25.
71   *Planning Our New Homes*, Department of Health for Scotland (1944), passim.
72   *Distribution of New Houses in Scotland* (Cmd 6552) 1944, passim; PEP, *Report on the Location of Industry in Great Britain* (1939), pp. 145 ff.
73   7 & 8 Geo VI c. 39.
74   Cramond, p. 27.
75   9 & 10 Geo VI c. 54.
76   12 & 13 Geo VI c. 61; *Modernising Our Homes*, Department of Health for Scotland (1947) passim; *Hansard* 13 Apr. 1949; 14 Geo VI ch. 34.
77   Cf. Table 1.
78   *Report on Housing and Industrial Conditions in Dundee*, Dundee Social Union, 1905.
79   W Smart, *The Housing Problem and the Municipality* (Glasgow University Free Lectures, 1902) passim; Glasgow City Archives, GCA C3/2/17, Note of evidence given by the Lord Provost, 1902; John Mann, *Better Houses for the Poor; Will They Pay?* (Glasgow, 1902).
80   Lenman, Lythe and Gauldie (1969), pp. 94 ff.
81   Ferguson (1958), p. 90.
82   Third Statistical Account, *The City of Aberdeen* (ed. H MacKenzie) (Edinburgh, 1953), pp. 117–18; Sanitary Inspectors' Reports 1906 onwards.
83   My views here have been greatly influenced by J J McKee, Glasgow Working Class Housing 1919–39 with particular reference to Polmadie, Strathclyde University MLitt thesis, 1977.
84   For Provost Blackie's career cf. *Biographical Sketches of the Lord Provosts of Glasgow, 1833–1883* (Glasgow, 1883), pp. 220–40.
85   GCA, DTC 8/19/1 Papers on Housing 31 Aug. 1905.
86   Census of Scotland 1901 and 1911; BPP 1914–16 (Cd 8111), Report of the Committee appointed to inquire into the increase of house rents (Scotland), pp. 3–4.
87   In 1912 and 1913 only 661 new houses were built in Glasgow, but there were still 13,178 vacant houses in 1914.
88   CGA, DTC 8/19/1 Report of Medical Officer of Health . . . 1910.
89   CGA, DTC 8/19/1/2 Executive Committee on Housing, Notes.
90   Ibid.
91   Corporation of Glasgow, *Review of Operations 1919–1947* (1948), p. 12.
92   CGA, DTC 8/19/1, 31 Jan. 1917; DTC 8/19/2 Notes on Housing 1917–18.
93   CGA, DTC 8/19/1 Town Clerk to Lord Provost, June 1913.
94   Ibid. Report on the Housing Question by Peter Fyfe, 1914.
95   Ibid. City Assessor to Lord Provost, June 1913.
96   Ibid. Submissions of House Factors and House Owners, 1914.
97   Ibid. Statement from City Improvement Department, 1914.
98   Ibid. Report, 12 Dec. 1916.
99   CGA, DTC 8/19/1/2 Executive Committee on Housing, Notes.

100   Ibid. City Chamberlain's Notes, Aug. 1919.
101   *Hansard*, 31 Dec. 1917.
102   Ibid. 31 Jan. 1918.
103   CGA, DTC 8/19/1/2 Executive Committee on Housing, Notes.
104   Ibid. Estimate to Scottish Board of Health, 15 Oct. 1919.
105   David Stenhouse, *Glasgow*, (1934), pp. 133–4.
106   CGA, DTC 8/19/1/2 Estimate to Scottish Board of Health, 15 Oct. 1919.
107   *Third Statistical Account of Dundee,* ed. J M Jackson (Arbroath, 1979), pp. 46,
        87, Table 14.11 on p. 371.
108   Medical Officer of Health Reports 1929–38.
109   *Third Statistical Account of Dundee*, p. 46.
110   Census of Dundee, 1931.
111   *Hansard*, 31 May and 27 June 1935.
112   The average annual rate was 241 houses between 1939 and 1945, *Third Statistical
        Account of Dundee*, p. 371.
113   Ibid. 794 houses per annum were built between 1945 and 1950 compared with an
        annual rate of 589 dwellings between 1929 and 1938. Cf. also p. 47.
114   Census of Dundee, 1951.
115   Census of Aberdeen, Edinburgh and Glasgow, 1951.
116   Aberdeen Sanitary Inspector's Reports 1916–23.
117   Census of Aberdeen 1921 and 1911.
118   At the Census of 1921 Aberdeen had a total of 1172 houses, i.e. 3.5 per cent of
        the City's housing stock with sub-let sections.
119   *Third Statistical Account of Aberdeen*, ed. H Mackenzie (Edinburgh, 1953),
        pp. 120–1.
120   Ibid. pp. 121–2.
121   Ibid. pp. 123–4.
122   Ibid. p. 125; Report of the Aberdeen Sanitary Inspector, 1938; *Hansard,* 28 June
        1938.
123   *Third Statistical Account of Aberdeen*, pp. 125–7.
124   Ibid. pp. 128–9; Housing Returns for Scotland 1950–1.
125   *Third Statistical Account of Aberdeen*, pp. 128–9.
126   *Third Statistical Account of Edinburgh*, ed. D. Keir (Glasgow, 1966), pp. 370 ff.
127   Ibid. p. 373.
128   Ibid. pp. 373–4.
129   Cf. *The Times*, 5 Mar. 1936.
130   *Hansard,* 28 June 1938; Edinburgh overcrowding survey, 1935.
131   Edinburgh overcrowding survey, 1946.
132   Census of Edinburgh, 1951.
133   Much that follows is based on J Butt, 'Working-Class Housing in Glasgow,
        1900–39', in *Essays in Scottish Labour History*, ed. Ian MacDougall (Edin-
        burgh, 1979), pp. 143–69.
134   Royal Commission on Housing, 1917, paras 572 ff.; Butt, op. cit. p. 151.
135   Census of Glasgow, 1911.
136   Census of Glasgow, 1951; Housing Department returns; Butt, op. cit. pp. 158 ff.
        and Table.

137 *Third Statistical Account of Glasgow*, ed. J Cunnison and J B S Gilfillan (Glasgow, 1958), Table 83.

138 Butt, op. cit. pp. 152 ff.

139 Census of Glasgow 1931; Census 1951.

140 Corporation of Glasgow Overcrowding Survey, 1935.

141 Butt, op. cit. p. 165.

142 My judgments here have benefited from the work of J J McKee who studied Polmadie and took oral evidence and also John Dillon's unpublished work on Springburn.

143 Cf. Report of the Inter-Departmental Committee on the Rent Restriction Acts Cd 5621 (1937–8), para. 16.

144 BPP 1936 Department of Health for Scotland: Housing Overcrowding Survey, Cd 5171; *Hansard* 11 July 1935.

145 Royal Commission on Scottish Affairs 1950–4 Report (Cd 9212).

146 *Hansard* 4 July 1935.

147 *Hansard* 14 Oct. 1915.

148 Dr J H Treble has begun to investigate the origins and extent of this problem. Cf. his 'The Market for Unskilled Male Labour in Glasgow, 1891–1914' in MacDougall, op. cit. pp. 115–42.

149 Census of 1951; Report of the Department of Health for Scotland 1952 (Cd 8799), Appendix 22.

150 Butt, op. cit. pp. 163 ff.; BPP Cd 1411, Report of the Committee of Enquiry into the High Cost of Building Working Class Dwellings in Scotland, passim; H W Richardson and D H Aldcroft, *Building in the British Economy between the Wars* (1968), pp. 123–6 and pp. 174 ff.; *Hansard* 20 July 1938; Cd 5977, 1938–9, Report of the Committee on Scottish Building Costs, passim; Cd 8799, 1952, Report of the Department of Health for Scotland also emphasises shortages of materials as a main problem after 1945.

151 R W Lyman, *The First Labour Government 1924* (1957), pp. 110–27. R K Middlemas, *The Clydesiders* (1965), pp. 35–41, 46–54, 136–9, 145–52.

152 Cf. S Marriner, 'Sir Alfred Mond's Octopus: a nationalised housebuilding business', *Business History*, **21** (1979) pp. 26 ff.

153 *Hansard*, 16 Dec. 1924.

INDEX OF PERSONAL NAMES

INDEX OF PLACE-NAMES

INDEX OF SUBJECTS